Journal of Ancient Egyptian Interconnec

Volume 25

March 2020

Demon Things:

Ancient Egyptian Manifestations of Liminal Entities

Papers inspired by the "Demon Things: Ancient Egyptian Manifestations of Liminal Entities" conference held 21–24 March 2016 at Swansea University

edited by

Kasia Szpakowska

Journal of Ancient Egyptian Interconnections, new series, volume 25

Cover design by Noreen Doyle

Library of Congress Cataloging-in-Publication Data
DEMON THINGS: Ancient Egyptian Manifestations of Liminal Entities
Edited by Kasia Szpakowska
ISBN-13: 979-8636145790

Journal of Ancient Egyptian Interconnections

VOLUME 25
MARCH 2020

TABLE OF CONTENTS

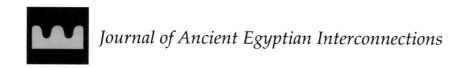

Journal of Ancient Egyptian Interconnections

About This Journal

The *Journal of Ancient Egyptian Interconnections* (*JAEI*) is an online scholarly publication integrating Egyptian archaeology with Mediterranean, Near Eastern, and African studies—providing a dedicated venue for this growing field of interdisciplinary and inter-area research.

The journal has a somewhat wider geographical and temporal range than existing publications (such as the excellent *Ägypten und Levante*) while specializing in all aspects of interaction between ancient Egypt and its neighbors. *JAEI* publishes full-length articles, short research notes, and reviews of published works (as well as reports and announcements of relevant conferences, symposia, etc.), each of which has been peer-reviewed in a blind screening process by an Egyptologist and specialist from the outside area of interaction. As such, the screening of contributions is as rigorous as that employed for printed scholarly journals. The permanent location of the journal at the University of Arizona ensure as stable and tangible a publication base as those enjoyed by print serials.

The Editors are assisted by an Executive Editorial Board composed of distinguished scholars from a number of countries around the world and by Editorial Liaisons who are experts in the cultures of ancient Egypt's neighbors or aspects of their interaction with Egypt (see Editorial Personnel). In this way, *JAEI* is well-equipped to provide a solid publication platform for an area of study with true focus yet wide application within Egyptology and general historical studies.

The wholly online nature of *JAEI* carries a number of advantages. While online periodicals are relatively new in Egyptology and related areas of research, they are not new in many fields of scientific endeavor, where their advantages have become obvious. Not only does *JAEI*'s online format enable very rapid publication of articles, reviews, and reports, it also enables the retrieval of that published material from any part of the world where an Internet-connected computer can be found—and in far less time than printed sources can usually be retrieved.

The *Journal of Ancient Egyptian Interconnections* is published four times a year on a subscription basis, though the option to purchase individual articles is available. Subscriptions may be obtained with secure online payment by following the subscription link on the journal's home page, or by contacting the subscriptions manager at JAEI@egyptianexpedition.org. A Guide for Contributors to *JAEI* is available for download. Submissions and editorial queries should be sent to the Editors at JAEI@egyptianexpedition.org.

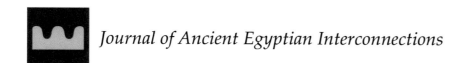

Journal of Ancient Egyptian Interconnections

Journal of Ancient Egyptian Interconnections

Subscription Instructions

The *Journal of Ancient Egyptian Interconnections* is published in digital format at least four times a year on a subscription basis, although the option to purchase individual articles is planned for the future. Login-based individual and IP-based institutional annual subscriptions are available. Both types of subscriptions include electronic access to all current and past issues of the journal throughout the subscription period.

An individual subscription costs $40 per year and provides access for one user. Institutional subscriptions cost $150 per year; there are no limitations to the number of IP addresses that can be assigned to an institutional subscription. Institutional subscriptions can also be configured to use a domain rather than a set of IP addresses or IP ranges, in which case only one domain is permitted per subscription account.

Both types of subscriptions can be purchased using major credit cards through our online system in a secure environment or via Paypal. Subscriptions can also be paid by check or wire transfer by contacting the journal at JAEI@egyptianexpedition.org.

Subscription by check is preferred. Please make check payable to "Journal of Ancient Egyptian Interconnections" and mail to:

Journal of Ancient Egyptian Interconnections
1303 E University Blvd Box 20840
Tucson AZ 85719-0521
USA

Please note that online subscriptions are purchased in a simple two-stage process.

1) Both individual and institutional subscriptions first require registration in our online system, using the "Register" link in the "User" box at the right side of the journal home page.

2) Once a user is registered with the *Journal of Ancient Egyptian Interconnections*, the purchase of either an individual or institutional subscription can then be completed using the "My Subscriptions" link on the right hand side of the home page. Alternatively, payment can be made via Paypal (contact the subscriptions manager).

For further information about subscriptions, use of IP ranges, terms longer than one year or any other questions regarding journal subscription procedure and access, please contact the journal staff at JAEI@egyptianexpedition.org.

Updated March, 2020

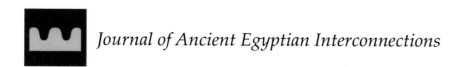

Journal of Ancient Egyptian Interconnections

Guide for Contributors

Topics for Contributions

The *Journal of Ancient Egyptian Interconnections* is a scholarly, peer-reviewed online journal that will consider potential contributions on any aspect of interaction (one- or two-way) between ancient Egypt and other cultures of the ancient world. Normally, these other cultures are ones directly or closely surrounding Egypt in Africa, the Near East, and the Mediterranean world, although demonstrable interactions between Egypt and more distant regions are also acceptable. Posited interactions between Egypt and the New World will not be considered. Topical interconnections will be considered (e.g., application of new or novel scientific methods to Egyptological subjects).

Types and Lengths of Contributions

The *JAEI* publishes three types of studies: full-length articles, short research notes, and reviews. Articles should be of a length commensurate with that of articles in printed journals. Contributors should check with the editor before submitting an unusually long contribution. There is no minimum length for short research notes as long as these clearly make a significant point. Reviews may be of any length, depending on the significance and size of the work reviewed. For more specific guidelines, contributors are advised to consult with the editor.

Spelling and Punctuation

For submissions in English, United States spelling and grammar conventions are preferred. British spellings will be accepted, but either the British or the U.S. convention must be used consistently (exclusive of quotations, which must retain their original spellings). The *UCLA Encyclopedia of Egyptology* should be followed for preferred spellings of transliterated place names and personal names unless the argument of the contribution requires alternatives that are explained in the contribution itself (https://uee.cdh.ucla.edu/spelling/). Only American punctuation conventions will be used (e.g., period or comma inside the closing quotation mark; superscript number for endnote always after punctuation; period after abbreviated titles such as "Dr."). Use of the serial comma (a.k.a. "Oxford comma") is preferred. Do not use superscript for ordinals (e.g., 18th, *not* 18th). For a range of numbers, such as pages or dates, use an en-dash (–), not a hyphen (-).

Dates

The *JAEI* does not publish calendar dates, ranges, or estimates (e.g., for dynasties, reigns, or events) predating 664 BCE (the beginning of the Late Period) unless dates are material to the argument of the contribution. All dates are to be designated "BCE" or "CE." The *UCLA Encyclopedia of Egyptology* "Preferred

Chronology" should be followed for general chronological matters and associated terminology (https://uee.cdh.ucla.edu/chronology/).

Format of Contributions

The preferred language for submissions is English; French and German contributions are also acceptable. All contributions must be submitted in MS Word format (.doc, .docx). Submissions with special fonts must include a note naming the font and a PDF or hardcopy of the text. If a font is not available to the author, they may transliterate Egyptian in the standard Manual de Codage (ASCII) style. The typesetter will then employ an appropriate font.

Normally, texts in ancient languages should be in transliteration. If it is important to show the actual script (hieroglyphic, hieratic, cuneiform, etc.), these texts should be submitted as digital image files noting their intended placement in the text of the manuscript. Such images must be high quality and must remain legible at small size.

The first page of the manuscript should carry the title of the article, with the name and affiliation of the author, followed by a short abstract (not more than 150 words) and then the main text. If the text includes figures or tables, the positions of these should be indicated by captions. Note that the typesetter might need to vary this placement for logistical reasons.

Tables and figures must be submitted as separate documents, not embedded in the manuscript with the main text. Authors may suggest placement within the paper, but the typesetter will make final decisions in this regard. To conform to the style and/or general appearance of the *JAEI*, the typesetter may typeset tables provided by the author.

Submission Procedures, Publication, and Copyright

Contributions should include a cover letter with the 1) author's name, 2) affiliation, 3) email, 4) mailing address, and 5) **a list of three potential referees with email addresses**. Contributions may be sent to the editor at JAEI@egyptianexpedition.org, transmitted via an online file download site, or mailed on a USB drive (other media will not be accepted) to: University of Arizona Egyptian Expedition, 1303 E University Blvd Box 20840, Tucson AZ, 85719-0521, USA.

Because the *JAEI* is a scholarly, peer-reviewed publication, contributions to the journal are not automatically accepted and may be declined if editorial reviewers do not support their publication. The *JAEI* is published quarterly; if accepted by the journal, submissions will normally appear within a few months of receipt. Copyright of submitted material remains with the contributor. Submissions may be freely shared by their authors in other venues six months after their publication in the *JAEI*.

Permissions & Illustrations

Authors must obtain permissions for the reproduction of copyrighted images or material used in their submissions. The *JAEI* cannot research or obtain permissions for its contributors.

Images (photographs [color or black and white], line art, etc.) to illustrate submissions should be sent in separate, individual digital files (not printed on paper). Images may be submitted in compressed format (jpg/jpeg), provided that they are of sufficient size and quality to allow clear screen display and printing. At least 300 dpi is preferred. Large image files should be submitted via an online file-download site rather than as email attachments. Authors wishing to include more than 10 images in an article should clear this with the editor. All figures must be numbered consecutively; maps are considered figures.

References to figures in the main text are to be given as, for example: Fig. 1, Figs. 3–7; Figs. 2, 5, 9. Captions should begin with Figure 1: (note the colon) and include a photo/illustration credit or other citation. (See below for citation style.) Captions may not contain endnotes.

Notes and Citations

A reference list of all cited works must be provided, following the guidelines below. (Given names may be provided in full or as initials.) Online citations must include a full URL and information regarding author, page title, website, and so forth. URLs will be checked for accuracy and updated or removed if necessary. Do not include hotlinks in the manuscript.

References and other notes must be given as endnotes indicated by superscript numbers at relevant places in the text. The *JAEI* does not use footnotes. Standard Egyptological abbreviations (e.g., *JAEI*, PM; K*RI*, *Wb.*, etc.) are not generally used. If the author does choose to employ bibliographic and related abbreviations in the reference list, endnotes, main text, captions, or tables, these must be provided as list placed before the reference list.

Endnotes cannot be placed in the title, byline, abstract, or captions. (An acknowledgments section, between the main text and the reference list, may be used to offer information commonly placed in title or byline foot/endnotes.) Citations in tables must be kept within the table itself, that is, not incorporated among the endnotes of the text. They must be either in-text citations or footnotes given as superscript lower-case letters. Table footnotes will be typeset in a designated footnote row at the bottom of the table. If the author provides a camera-ready table, they must similarly keep any footnotes within the body of the table.

Examples for Reference List:

Journal Article

Koch, Ida, Sabine Kleiman, Manfred Oeming, Yuval Gadot, and Oded Lipschits. 2017. "Amulets in Context: A View from Late Bronze Age Tel Azekahs." *Journal of Ancient Egyptian Interconnections* 16: 9–24.

Article or Chapter in Book

Shinnie, Peter L. 2001. "Meroë." In Donald B. Redford (ed.), *The Oxford Encyclopedia of Ancient Egypt* vol. 2, 283–284. Oxford: Oxford University Press.

Book

Wengrow, David. 2006. *The Archaeology of Early Egypt: Social Transformation in North-East Africa, 10,000–2650 BC.* Cambridge: Cambridge University Press.

Edited Volume

Bietak, Manfred and Ernst Czerny (eds.). 2004. *Scarabs of the Second Millennium BC from Egypt, Nubia, Crete and the Levant: Chronological and Historical Implications.* Vienna: Verlag der Österreichischen Akademic der Wissenschaften.

Online Source (note: do not *make the URL a hyperlink/hotlink in the manuscript)*

Muhlestein, Kerry. 2008. "Execration Ritual." In Jacco Dieleman and Willeke Wendrich (eds.), *UCLA Encyclopedia of Egyptology*. Los Angeles: eScholarship. < https://escholarship.org/uc/item/3f6268zf >, accessed 1 April 2013.

Metropolitan Museum of Art. n.d. "Relief Fragment with a Ship Under Sail, ca. 2465–2458 B.C." *The Met.* < https://www.metmuseum.org/art/collection/search/543894 >, accessed 1 April 2019.

Example Citations to Works in the Reference List *(note: do* not *use "ibid.," "op. cit.," and similar abbreviations)*

Koch et al. 2017, 13 fig. 6; Shinnie 2001; Wengrow 2006, 115–132; Bietak and Czerny 2004; Muhlestein 2008, 3; Metropolitan Museum of Art n.d.

Journal of Ancient Egyptian Interconnections

A Brief Introduction by the Editor

Kasia Szpakowska
Department of Classics, Ancient History and Egyptology, Swansea University

"Darmok and Jalad. At Tanagra."
Star Trek: TNG S05 E02.

This volume brings together papers inspired by the conference Demon Things: Ancient Egyptian Manifestations of Liminal Entities that took place March 21–24, 2016, at Swansea University in Wales.[1] The goal of this international event was to explore the range and variation of liminal entities the ancient Egyptians believed capable of harm and help. The discussions focused on manifestations of demons through iconography, objects, or textual descriptions, moving on from previous demonological conferences that had focused on issues related to the thorny problems of categorization and definitions.[2] Scholars were encouraged to present their findings in the hopes that Wales, a land blanketed with mythology, legends, sacred spaces, megaliths, and castles, would serve as a creative venue for converging different areas of research, through which a fuller picture of these multifaceted entities could emerge. Professor Martin Stringer[3] launched the conference by reminding us to recognize and respect religious diversity (whether that of the past or the present) and the need to understand religious behavior through real-life situations. The beings we try to study so objectively were not just theoretical constructs, nor theological speculations, but were part of everyday experiences. Our demons energetically attacked, defended, and danced. They played drums, rushed like the wind, and bellowed like hippos. Capable of penetrating bodies and minds, bringing both disease and rapture, they evoked both extreme fear and hope. Whether or not these particular supernatural entities fit our own individual preferences and experiences is irrelevant—for the believer, these beings were tangible and real. They were part of the numinous landscape of ancient

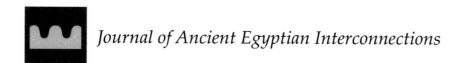

Egypt—they were found in towns and villages, homes and temples, throughout the *duat*, in borderland outposts and even quarries. In the tradition of the late historian of religion Jonathan Z. Smith, we can say that these demons belong to the Here, the There, and the Anywhere.[4]

Some of the best-known liminal entities are those found on objects associated with the funerary and mortuary sphere, with beings who exist over "there." The earliest to appear both in text and image are found in the Middle Kingdom Coffin Texts. In "The Anatomy of a Coffin Text Demon," Zuzanna Bennett applies a systematic forensic technique, dissecting the morphology, attributes, behavior, and functions of over 400 different groups and individuals whose role was to maintain *maat* in the afterlife. Nika Lavrentyeva and Ekaterina Alexandrova approach the need to maintain cosmic balance by examining "Liminal Sources of Dangerous Powers: A Case of the Black Ram." Their approach is to structure the image of the black ram as an icon and mytheme, looking at the concept of the black ram and related solar creatures, particularly in the Pyramid Texts Book of Two Ways. In "A Particular Depiction of Anubis from the Tomb of the Sculptor Nakhtamun (TT335): Is Anubis a Demon?" Arnaud Quertinmont closely examines the iconography of the armed guardian demons who manifest as canines. The distinctive attributes of the Anubis in TT335 are used as a case study to demonstrate the complexity of roles played by Egyptian *nṯr.w*.

Moving forward in time to late Dynasty 26 to early Dynasty 27, Ladislav Bareš introduces us to "Underworld Demons in the Decoration of the Large Late Period Shaft Tombs at Abusir." A number of these inhabitants of the netherworld are known from Book of the Dead 144, but others have rarely been attested. Their function and possible reasons for their selection and inclusion into the iconographical program of this burial chamber are discussed. Renata Landgráfová continues to explore the site by examining in more detail the "The Guardians of Menekhibnekau: Chapter 144 of the Book of the Dead in the Shaft Tomb of Menekhibnekau at Abusir." Their specific configurations as presented in the iconography and accompanying texts are examined in the context of their arrangement within the architectural layout of the burial chamber itself.

In "Fear and Loathing at Amarna: A Case Study of the Development of Sacred Objects in Response to Communal Anxiety," Kasia Szpakowska moves the focus away from the inhabitants of the *duat* to people still living on earth ("here"). She approaches the introduction of clay cobra figurines at Amarna as an example of protective traditions created as a response to profound emotional upheaval, adding to recent studies in the archaeology of anxiety. Moving away from the Egyptian Nile Valley, Erin E. Bornemann and Stuart Tyson Smith present findings from their recent fieldwork at Tombos in "Liminal Deities in the Borderlands: Bes and Pataikos in Ancient Nubia." Through iconographical analysis, materiality studies, and entanglement theory, they demonstrate how these two amuletic forms continued to be valued through time, for aiding the transition from life to death for individuals even beyond the borders of Egypt and into Nubia. In "The Maned Hippopotamus at Lahun: Identifying Homes and Names," Stephen Quirke and Campbell Price interpret a late Middle Kingdom limestone figurine. By combining recent settlement archaeology with close reexamination of its production, morphology, provenance, and excavation history, they reveal the performative power that was part of the creative process itself.

Emphasizing the dual nature of all ancient Egyptian divine beings, Sabrina Ceruti turns to the darker side of the hybrid hippo by considering "The *Bꜣw* of Taweret: Vindictiveness (and Forgiveness) of the Hippopotamus Goddess." Close readings of texts reveal the ambiguous nature of this complex divine being, who, far from being simply a benevolent protectress, is capable of inciting fear alongside piety. Susanne Beck presents a comparative approach in her study of "Disease Demons in Mesopotamia and Egypt: Sāmānu as a Case Study." She first provides an overview of how these demons were conceived of in Mesopotamia as compared with Egypt, before moving on to a study of a specific demon, Sāmānu/Akhu, who appeared in texts of both cultures. In "The Impact of the Manifestation of Demoniacal Winds on Terrestrial Life: The Role of Demon Gangs in Dispersing the *Ꞽꜣdt-rnpt*," El Zahraa Megahed examines the role of pestilential winds as bearers of affliction on an annual basis. Sekhmet makes an appearance here, where the author notes the constant link between these demons and the goddess. Emphasizing again their dual nature, in "The Slaughterers: A Study of the *Ḫꜣ.tyw* as Liminal Beings in Ancient Egyptian Thought" Danielle Sass presents a detailed orthographical and etymological analysis of these hostile hordes known nearly exclusively through texts. Sekhmet again makes an appearance, but the focus is primarily on the role that the *ḫꜣ.tyw* performed whether or not they were under the command of a greater deity. Also focusing on texts is Renata Schiavo, who uses letters to the dead to understand "Ghosts and Ancestors in a Gender Perspective." Intriguingly, this approach highlights the importance of rituals to maintain a positive mutual relationship between female ancestors and the household.

The role of an individual liminal entity is discussed by Rita Lucarelli in "Baba and the Baboon Demons." Tracing his development from the Pyramid Texts to Book of the Dead and on through Ptolemaic temple texts, Lucarelli shows how the ancient Egyptians used their native fauna, in this case the baboon, as models for the form and characteristics of the god Baba, as well as related guardian beings. Amr Gaber also investigates the history of another individual being, in this case the aggressive "*Mnḥ*, 'The Butcher' and Lord of the Butcher Demons." A full presentation of every attestation of the demon is included, from the Middle Kingdom Coffin Texts to Roman Period papyri. That the Egyptians continued to rely on liminal entities for protection "anywhere" is demonstrated in "Symbolae Sacrae: Symbolic Formulae for Protection and Adoration within the Quarries of Gebel el Silsila," presented by Maria Nilsson. Moving to the very peripheries of the Egyptian landscape, she introduces the reader to quarry marks and schematic renditions of sacred symbols inscribed into the very rock of the quarries by worried workers.

Ultimately, this conference and the contributions in this volume allow us to catch only tantalizing glimpses of a veritable swarm of beings whose very existence seems to surf waves of chaos and of order. We call them "liminal beings," for they exist in that threshold, able to cross the boundary area between the world of the mundane and that of the divine. A range of lenses have been brought into play through the systematic collection of textual, representational, and figural examples found on a range of sources: from otherwise ordinary objects to compositions that were perhaps only ever meant for divine consumption. Throughout runs the recognition of the importance of understanding the past history and provenance not only of the objects, but also of the history of our own study of the meaning and interpretations of rituals and beings. We do not have the luxury of talking to ancient Egyptians—all we have is the complex iconography, compositions, and objects that were often symbolic and perhaps could be understood as metaphors or allegories themselves. It is my sincere hope that this volume starts to bring to light some of the lesser-known liminal beings whose very survival in the archaeological record testifies to their importance, and encourages the understanding of both them and the individuals who used them.

Acknowledgements

The conference marked the culmination of the Ancient Egyptian Demonology Project: Second Millennium BCE. The project and the doctoral positions of Sophie Felicitas Weber and Zuzanna Bennett, as well as the development of our database, were funded by a Leverhulme Trust Research Project Grant. Although it is no longer accessible online, hopefully the *Demonbase* will resurrect one day on DemonThings.com. The conference could not have taken place without the generous support of The Egypt Centre Museum of Egyptian Antiquities, my co-organizers Felicitas Weber, Zuzanna Bennett, Carolyn Graves-Brown, and Wendy Goodridge, who ensured that the conference would run smoothly—despite the many gremlins. I am grateful to Ken Griffin, Meg Gundlach, Lauren Wale, Rex Wale, Syd Howells, Beverly Rogers, the volunteers, and all the delegates, speakers and audience alike, who participated with gusto and good humor even in "atmospheric" rain and fog. Supporting parties included the South West Wales Branch of the Classical Association, the Research Institute for Arts and Humanities, and the College of Arts and Humanities, Swansea University.

I am deeply grateful to the editors of the *Journal of Ancient Egyptian Interconnections*, Pearce Paul Creasman and Noreen Doyle, for their help and patient support. To each of the individual authors I extend sincere thanks for agreeing to contribute to this volume and for sharing their time, expertise, and hard work. The volume would not have begun without the help of Felicitas Weber and Aris Legowski, nor been completed without the assistance of John Edward Rogers. Finally, I am grateful to my beloved Jon for lovingly yet relentlessly vanquishing my own inner demons.

References

Kousoulis, P. I. M. (ed.) 2011. *Ancient Egyptian Demonology: Studies on the Boundaries between the Demonic and the Divine in Egyptian Magic.*

Orientalia Lovaniensia Analecta 175. Leuven: Peeters.

Smith, Jonathan Z. 2003. "Here, There, and Anywhere." In Scott B. Noegel, Joel T. Walker, and Brannon M. Wheeler (eds.), *Prayer, Magic, and the Stars in the Ancient and Late Antique World*, 21–38. University Park, PA: Pennsylvania State University Press.

Notes

1 Summaries of the conference can be found starting at < http://www.demonthings.com/conference22march/ >.

2 For the purposes of this volume, we can simply understand "demons" as a blanket term for those beings between human, animal, and major god, who were not worshipped in temples. To reflect the lack of consensus as to definition, scholars use a range of terms to refer to these beings, and we have not attempted to impose any artificial consistency during the conference, nor in this volume. Previous gatherings included the International Specialists' Symposium: Ancient Egyptian Theology and Demonology: Studies on the Boundaries between the Divine and Demonic in Egyptian Magic (Rhodes, Greece, June 27–29, 2003), Ancient Egyptian Demonology: A Comparative Perspective (Rheinische Friedrich-Wilhelms-Universität Bonn Institut für Kunstgeschichte und Archäologie, February 28–March 1, 2011), and Evil Spirits, Monsters and Benevolent Protectors: Demonology in Ancient Egypt and Mesopotamia (Institute for the Study of the Ancient World, New York University, April 23, 2012). Papers from these conferences can be found in Kousoulis 2011 and volume 14(1) (2013) of *Archiv für Religionsgeschichte*, respectively.

3 Anthropologist and Pro Vice Chancellor of Swansea University.

4 Smith (2003, 23) offers a means of understanding religious practices through spatial topography as

> (1) the "here" of domestic religion, located primarily in the home and in burial sites; (2) the "there" of public, civic, and state religions, largely based in temple constructions; and (3) the "anywhere"e of a rich diversity of religious formations that occupy an interstitial space between these other two loci, including a variety of religious entrepreneurs, and ranging from groups we term "associations" to activities we label "magic."

In the context of this volume, "there" can also refer to the *duat* itself—the abode of the dead, damned, demons, and divinities.

Journal of Ancient Egyptian Interconnections

Underworld Demons in the Decoration of the Large Late Period Shaft Tombs at Abusir

Ladislav Bareš
Czech Institute of Egyptology, Charles University in Prague

Abstract
In the decoration of the large shaft tombs at Abusir, dated to the late Twenty-sixth/early Twenty-seventh Dynasty, several series of the underworld demons can be found. They appear in different positions—either separately, as on the inner sarcophagus of Iufaa and on the outer wooden coffin of Nekau (buried in one of the lesser burial chambers in the tomb of Iufaa), or as part of the Book of the Dead chapter 144 on the side of the burial chamber of Menekhibnekau. Another series of demons—for technical reasons mostly inaccessible—seems to exist on the inner sarcophagus of Menekhibnekau. In this paper, each of those series of demons is treated in respect to its position in the decoration of the entire burial chamber. In addition to that, several question connected to their position and use in the tombs are discussed.

A number of definitions can be found for demons as creatures other than deities, deified, or simply dead persons or different from those, be it in Egyptology or in general.[1] To find a greater consensus is a much desirable goal, but I do not discuss the definitions here, but rather present what we, dealing with the large Late Period shaft tombs at Abusir, consider—rightly or wrongly—to be demons.

All the large shaft tombs that have been excavated at Abusir so far (the structures of Udjahorresnet, Iufaa, Menekhibnekau, Padihor, and the anonymous R 3) seem to have been built in the very last years of the Twenty-sixth Dynasty, between perhaps 531 and 525 BCE.[2] Most probably, some of them at least might have served for the burials of their owners and other family members even later, up to the end of the 6th century BCE. While the construction activities in those tombs presumably ended with the Persian conquest, the decoration of their burial chambers, as well as sarcophagi and coffins, might have continued in the first years of the Twenty-seventh Dynasty, although this cannot be proven in any way.

Among the large shaft tombs thus far excavated at Abusir, representations of underworld demons can be found in the structures of the priest Iufaa[3] and the general Menekhibnekau.[4] The decoration in the burial chamber of Udjahorresnet[5] had only been started and was thus left unfinished, the small burial chamber of Padihor[6] has no pictures (except for receptacles containing sacred oils), and in the anonymous tomb R 3,[7] the construction of the burial chamber had not even commenced. Additionally, representations of demons might exist in the burial chambers of the yet unexcavated tombs at Abusir as well.[8] In general, two groups of representations of underworld demons are attested in the large shaft tombs at Abusir:

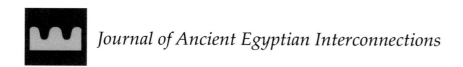

1) a series of about 70 demons arranged on the sides of a sarcophagus or coffin; such a group is for the first time attested on the sarcophagus of Merenptah later usurped by Pasebakhaenniut (Psusennes I);[9]
2) demons guarding the underworld gates in the vignettes of the Book of the Dead chapters 144 through147.[10]

The first group is attested three times altogether at Abusir: on the outer sides of the chest of the inner sarcophagus of both Iufaa[11] and Menekhibnekau,[12] and on the inner side of the chest of the wooden outer coffin (unfortunately badly damaged) of the priest Nekau, who was buried in one of the lesser burial chambers in the tomb of Iufaa.[13]

On the inner sarcophagi of Iufaa and Menekhibnekau, the images of the demons are well preserved.

On the chest of the inner sarcophagus of Iufaa, the usual series appears in its entirety. On the southern (i.e., in this case left-hand) side:

1) *ꞽnp(w)* (FIG. 1)
2) *Ḏwn-ḥr*
3) *Sḫm-nṯrw*
4) *Ḥr* (FIG. 2)
5) *Nḏ-ꞽt.f*
6) *Sbḫt-štꜣt*
7) *ꞽwn-mwt.f*
8) *Nḥmmt* (FIG. 3)
9) *Sḳd-ḥr* (FIG. 4)
10) *ꜥnḫ-m-fnṯw*
11) *Sḫd-ḥr*
12) *ꜣḫ* (or *bnw*?) (FIG. 5)
13) *ꞽr-rn.f-ḏs.f*
14) anonymous (FIG. 6)
15) *Sḫm-ḥr*
16) *Hꜣḳw*
17) a palace-sign (without any name)
18) anonymous[14] (FIG. 7)
19) *Ḏwꜣ-mwt.f*
20) *Ḳbḥ-snw.f*
21) *Ḏḥwty*
22) *Šw* (FIG. 8)
23) *Ḥpwy*
24) *Srḳt*
25) *ꞽfw* (FIG. 9)
26) *Tfnwt*
27) *ꞽsds*
28) *Snḏt*
29) *Ḳbḳb*
30) *Hrn*
31) *Ḫssy* (FIG. 10)
32) *Šꜥ-tb*
33) *Ḫnfꜣ*
34) *Tnḫ*
35) *ꞽnp(w)*

On the northern (i.e., right-hand side):

1) *Sḥr-ḏw* (FIG. 11)
2) *Wr-nrw*
3) *Mꜣꜣ-ꞽt.f*
4) *Rs-ꞽb*[15]
5) *Ḫsf-m-tp-ꜥ* (FIG. 12)
6) *Wnm-ḥwꜣꜣt*
7) *Nfr-ḥr*
8) *Smt*
9) *ꞽf*
10) *Sḫd-ḥr* (FIG. 13)
11) *Db-ḥr.k*
12) *ꞽmy-wt* (FIG. 14)
13) *Dwn-ḥꜣt*
14) *Ḫnfꜣ*
15) *ꞽmst*
16) *Ḥpy* (FIG. 15)
17) *Dwꜣ-mwt.f*
18) *Ḳbḥ-snw.f*
19) *ꞽmst* (FIG. 16)
20) *Ḥpy*
21) *Rwty*
22) *Spd-ḥr*
23) *Nt*
24) *Ḥng-rꜣ*
25) *Ḥwn(t)* (FIG. 17)
26) *ꞽnpw*
27) *Smd*
28) *ꜥnn-ꜥbwy*
29) *Šsry*
30) *Mꜥꜥt* (FIG. 18)
31) *Ḫꜣbs*
32) *Kkw*

In the case of Menekhibnekau, however, only a small part of the decoration of the inner sarcophagus is accessible, since it is still firmly embedded inside the outer sarcophagus. Because of this, the number of demons, as well as their arrangement, can only be presumed. On the southern (i.e., foot) end of the chest, *Sḥr-ḏw* and perhaps also *Wr-nrw* and *Mꜣꜣ-ꞽt.f* can be discerned to the east of the longitudinal axis (i.e., in the direction to the southeast corner of the

FIGURE 1: Chest of the inner sarcophagus of Iufaa, south side, Nos. 1–3; photo Martin Frouz.

FIGURE 2: Chest of the inner sarcophagus of Iufaa, south side, Nos. 4–7; photo Martin Frouz.

FIGURE 3: Chest of the inner sarcophagus of Iufaa, south side, No. 8; photo Martin Frouz.

FIGURE 4: Chest of the inner sarcophagus of Iufaa, south side, Nos. 9–11; photo Martin Frouz.

FIGURE 5: Chest of the inner sarcophagus of Iufaa, south side, Nos. 12–13; photo Martin Frouz.

FIGURE 6: Chest of the inner sarcophagus of Iufaa, south side, Nos. 14–17; photo Martin Frouz.

FIGURE 7: Chest of the inner sarcophagus of Iufaa, south side, Nos. 18–21; photo Martin Frouz.

FIGURE 8: Chest of the inner sarcophagus of Iufaa, south side, Nos. 22–24; photo Martin Frouz.

FIGURE 9: Chest of the inner sarcophagus of Iufaa, south side, Nos. 25–30; photo Martin Frouz.

FIGURE 10: Chest of the inner sarcophagus of Iufaa, south side, Nos. 31–35; photo Martin Frouz.

FIGURE 11: Chest of the inner sarcophagus of Iufaa, north side, Nos. 1–4; photo Martin Frouz.

FIGURE 12: Chest of the inner sarcophagus of Iufaa, north side, Nos. 5–9; photo Martin Frouz.

FIGURE 13: Chest of the inner sarcophagus of Iufaa, north side, Nos. 10–11; photo Martin Frouz.

FIGURE 14: Chest of the inner sarcophagus of Iufaa, north side, Nos. 12–15; photo Martin Frouz.

FIGURE 15: Chest of the inner sarcophagus of Iufaa, north side, Nos. 16–18; photo Martin Frouz.

FIGURE 16: Chest of the inner sarcophagus of Iufaa, north side, Nos. 19–24; photo Martin Frouz.

FIGURE 17: Chest of the inner sarcophagus of Iufaa, north side, Nos. 25–29; photo Martin Frouz.

FIGURE 18: Chest of the inner sarcophagus of Iufaa, north side, Nos. 30–32; photo Martin Frouz.

chest), while *ꞽInpw*, *Dwn-ḥr*, *Sḫm-nṯrw* and *Ḥr* are arranged to the west from the axis. On the eastern (i.e., left-hand) side of the chest, directly around the southeastern corner of it, *Rs-ỉb* and perhaps also *Ḫsf-m-tp-ꜥ* seem to be written.[16] Judging from the small part of this series that is accessible on the sarcophagus of Menekhibnekau, their arrangement—and perhaps their number, as well—seems to correspond to the series of demons that appears on the sarcophagus of Iufaa.

The position of the series of demons differs, however, on the sarcophagi of both dignitaries. On the sarcophagus of Iufaa, they are arranged axially around the head part of it (thus pointing to the east), while in the case of Menekhibnekau, they seem to center on the foot end of it, i.e., in the direction of the entrance to his burial chamber situated in the south and protected by representations of the usual door-guardians (that will be discussed later). Generally speaking, the differences in orientation, inner arrangement, and other features are quite numerous among the large shaft tombs at Abusir, in spite of the fact that they seem to have been constructed during a rather short span of time and, probably, by an identical group of architects and workmen.

In the tomb of Menekhibnekau, the underworld demons seem to strengthen the protection of the deceased against any danger coming through the entrance to the burial chamber. In that way, they follow the usual pattern of the arrangement of a burial chamber already known from the Old Kingdom and repeatedly attested in other Late Period tombs.[17]

On the sarcophagus of Iufaa, however, they are placed just opposite the entrance that, in this case, is situated on the west side of the burial chamber, i.e., in sheer contrast to the habits of the time. I have no explanation for this fact, except perhaps for a (rather improbable) possibility that the entrance to the chamber might have originally been planned on its eastern side.[18] On the other hand, a number of spells dealing with the protective forces in the form of snakes appear on the western side of the chamber of Iufaa, i.e., around the entrance to it. Contrary to the usual spells protecting the deceased against the evil forces of snakes (particularly Pyramid Texts spells 226 through 243) that are arranged around the entrances to the burial chambers in other contemporary Egyptian tombs,[19] such creatures seem to be rather helpful and caring in the structure of Iufaa.[20]

On the box-shaped wooden outer coffin of Nekau, the series of demons has not been carved in relief but only drawn in a greyish color, now badly faded.[21] Once again, it starts behind the head of the deceased, i.e., in the direction of the entrance situated on the eastern side. Due to the limited space, the demons are arranged into two rows situated above each other. On the northern (i.e., right-hand) side, the usual sequence *Rs-ḥr* (or *Rs-ỉb*?), *Ḫsf-m-tp-ꜥ*, *Wnm-ḥwꜣꜣt*, *Nfr-nfrw*, *Smt*, *ꞽIf*, *Sḫd-ḥr*, *Db-ḥr.k*, *ꞽImy-wt*, *Dwn-ḥꜣt*, *Ḫnfꜣ*, *ꞽImst*, *Ḥpy*, *Dwꜣ-mwt.f*, and *Ḳbḥ-snw.f* appears in the upper row. Among the ten deities depicted in the lower row, only *Ḥpy*, *Rwty*, *Ḥng-rꜣ*, *Ḥwn(t)*, *ꞽInpw*, *Smd*, and perhaps also *ꜥnn-ꜥbwy* and *Mꜣꜥt* can be identified. On the southern (i.e., left-hand) side, *Nḏ-ỉt.f* and *ꞽIwn-mwt.f* are depicted as guardians of a high gate decorated with a pair of *udjat*-eyes and described as *sbḫt štꜣt*. Behind them, *Nḥmmt*, *Sḳd-ḥr*,

ʿnḫ-m-fnṯw, *Sḫd-ḥr*, *ꜣḫ*, *Ỉr-rn.f-ḏs.f*, an anonymous creature, *Sḫm-ḥr*, *Ḥꜣḳw*, and another anonymous creature follow. The plank with the lower row of demons has, unfortunately, been completely destroyed by white ants. Judging from the preserved parts of the decoration, however, it seems that the position of demons on the coffin of Nekau more or less corresponds to their arrangement on the sarcophagus of Iufaa.

The second group of the underworld demons, namely the door-guardians, are attested only once at Abusir, on the southern side of the burial chamber of Menekhibnekau. In the upper part of this wall, they accompany the depiction of the seven gates of the netherworld. Below, the remaining part of this side contains the text of Book of the Dead chapter 144. In this arrangement, the decoration of the southern side of Menekhibnekau's burial chamber is paired with the decoration of its northern part, where Book of the Dead chapter 148 appears, accompanied with the usual vignettes of the celestial cows, together with the four sons of Horus and four steering-oars.

The arrangement of door-guardians on the southern side of the burial chamber of Menekhibnekau is rather uniform, as each group of them is situated in a rectangle separated from each other by dividing lines. In the upper part, the number of each of the gates (*ʿryt tpt*, *ʿryt sn.nw*, etc.) is written, accompanied by *rn n* "the name of." Below, the three demons are always depicted, with their usual designation (*ỉry ʿꜣ* "He who belongs to the door/Door-keeper,"[22] *s[ꜣw].s* "He who guards it," *smỉ ỉmy.s* "He who makes report in it") and their name written in one column in front of them. Usually the demons are represented in therianthropic form, with a human body and an animal head, standing, sitting or kneeling, and with either empty hands or holding various artifacts (sticks, knives, etc.) or animals. All depictions are looking right, i.e., to the west.

GATE 1 (FIG. 19)

ỉry ʿꜣ.s	*Sḫd-ḥrw-ʿšꜣw-ỉrw* "Inverted faces (SIC),[23] many-formed";[24] standing with empty hands, ram-headed
s[ꜣw].s	*[S]mt*[25] "Overhearer"; kneeling and holding a small gazelle, human-headed
smỉ ỉmy.s[26]	*hw*[27]*-ḫrw* "Loud?-voiced"; standing, with a long stick ended with an ear of corn, baboon-headed

GATE 2 (FIG. 19)

ỉry ʿꜣ.ss	*Dwn-ḥꜣt* "Fore-stretched";[28] semi-seated (in sitting posture), with one hand raised, ram-headed
s[ꜣw].s	*[S]ḳd-ḥr* "Angle-faced";[29] standing, in a form of a mixed creature with the body of a (female?) hippopotamus, leonine head, and crocodile tail, holding a long knife in one hand
smỉ ỉmy.s	*ꜣsb*[30] "Blazing"; standing, with a long stick ended with an ear of corn, baboon-headed

GATE 3 (FIG. 20)

ỉry ʿꜣ.s	*Wnm-ḥwꜣt* "Eater of detritus";[31] seated with left hand on the chest and the right hand semi-raised and holding a long knife, with the head replaced by a turtle
s[ꜣw].s	*Rs-ỉb*[*sic?*][32] "Alert-hearted"; standing, with left hand raised, lion-headed
smỉ ỉmy.s	*ʿꜣ*[*sic?*][33] "He who curses"; standing, with a long stick ended with an ear of corn, baboon-headed

GATE 4 (FIG. 19)

ỉry ʿꜣ.s	*Ḫsf-ḥr-ʿšꜣ-ḫrw*[34] "Repellent-faced, many voiced"; standing with empty hands, ram-headed
s[ꜣw].s	*Rs-ḥr*[35] "Alert-faced";[36] standing with empty hands, human-headed
smỉ ỉmy.s	*Ḫsf-ỉdw*[37] "Repeller of crocodiles";[38] standing, with a long stick ended with an ear of corn, baboon-headed

GATE 5 (FIG. 19)

ỉry ʿꜣ.s	*ʿnḫ-m-fntt*[39] "One-who-lives-on-worms"; semi-seated (in sitting posture), holding bovine forelegs in folded hands, Bes-like head with face turned frontally
s[ꜣw].s	*ꜣšb(w)*[40] "Fiery"; standing with empty hands, bull-headed
smỉ ỉmy.s	*Nb(ỉt)-ḥr-khb-ỉt*[41] "Face-afire, violent-timed(?)"; standing, with a long stick ended with an ear of corn, baboon-headed

GATE 6 (FIG. 21)

ỉry ʿꜣ.s	*ꜣk[n]-t(ꜣw)-khb-ḫrw*[42] "Bread-scooper, violent-voiced"; standing with empty hands, ram-headed

s[ꜣw].s — *Ỉn-ḥr* "Face-bringer";[43] standing with empty hands, lion-headed

smỉ ỉmy.s — *Mds-ḥr-ỉry-pt*[44] "Sharpened-faced, warden of the sky"; standing, with a long stick ended with an ear of corn, baboon-headed

GATE 7 (FIG. 22)

ỉry ꜥꜣ.s — *Md(s).sn* "Their sharpener";[45] standing with empty hands, ram-headed

s[ꜣw].s — *ꜥꜣ-ḫrw*[46] "Loud-voiced"; standing with empty hands, ram-headed

smỉ ỉmy.s — *Ḫsf-ḫmỉw* "Repeller of attackers";[47] standing, with a long stick ended with an ear of corn, baboon-headed.

Below the gates, the main body of the text of Book of the Dead chapter 144 (i.e., without the end words) is written in 33 columns, with always eleven columns on both sides and the same number above the entrance to the chamber proper. The text roughly corresponds to other known Late Period versions of this chapter,[48] with some minor variations[49] and changes.[50] This is especially the case at the end of the

FIGURE 19: Burial chamber of Menekhibnekau, south wall, BD chapter 144, gates 1–2, 4–5; photo Martin Frouz.

FIGURE 20: Burial chamber of Menekhibnekau, south wall, BD chapter 144, gate 3; photo Martin Frouz.

Figure 21: Burial chamber of Menekhibnekau, south wall, BD chapter 144, gate 6; photo Martin Frouz.

Figure 22: Burial chamber of Menekhibnekau, south wall, BD chapter 144, gate 7; photo Martin Frouz.

text, in the lowermost part of its final column, where the lack of space available for writing can clearly be observed.

Some demons appear in both groups mentioned above, although their existence on the inner sarcophagus of Menekhibnekau can only be assumed:

[S]ḳd-ḥr = No. 9 on the southern (left-hand) side of the inner sarcophagus of Iufaa (identical picture, except for the *sꜣ*-sign in Iufaa contrary to a knife held in Menekhibnekau);

ꜥnḫ-m-fntt = No. 10 on the southern (left-hand) side of the inner sarcophagus of Iufaa (identical picture except for knives held in both hands in Iufaa contrary to bovine forelegs in Menekhibnekau);

Sḫd-ḥrw-ꜥšꜣw-îrw = see No. 11 on the southern (left-hand) side of the inner sarcophagus of Iufaa (the image differs, however: ram-headed male figure on the southern side of Menekhibnekau's chamber contrary to female figure on the sarcophagus of Iufaa where, moreover, only the—shortened?—form of the name *Sḫd-ḥr* appears);

Rs-îb = No. 4 on the northern (right-hand) side of the inner sarcophagus of Iufaa (snake-headed figure holding a piece of linen in Iufaa, contrary to a leonine-headed one in Menekhibnekau);

Wnm-ḥwȝt = No. 6 on the northern (right-hand) side of the inner sarcophagus of Iufaa (identical picture in Iufaa and Menekhibnekau);

[S]mt = No. 8 on the northern (right-hand) side of the inner sarcophagus of Iufaa (identical posture; however, female figure in Iufaa contrary to a male one in Menekhibnekau);

Nb-ḥr-khb-ỉt? = see No. 11 on the northern (right-hand) side of the inner sarcophagus of Iufaa (jackal-headed male figure in both cases; however, sitting in Iufaa and standing in Menekhibnekau; perhaps a shortened written form of the name in Iufaa and erroneously? written in Menekhibnekau);

Dwn-ḥȝt = No. 13 on the northern (right-hand) side of the inner sarcophagus of Iufaa (identical posture; however holding a snake? in Iufaa and empty-handed in Menekhibnekau).

In the row of demons depicted on the inner sarcophagus of Iufaa, two guardsmen always appear who are also attested on each of the gates 1, 2, 3 and 5 on the southern wall of Menekhibnekau. With only one exception, namely *smỉ ỉmy.s* of the fifth gate, all other guardsmen attested in the tombs of both Iufaa and Menekhibnekau belong to the categories of *ỉry ꜥȝ.s* (four attestations) and *s[ȝw].s* (three attestations).

The purpose of both groups of demons in the Late Period tombs at Abusir is the same, namely to protect the deceased. The same apotropaic function might perhaps be ascribed to other images that appear in the contemporary tombs, such as the burial chamber of Panehsi at Heliopolis, where representations of twelve flame-spitting uraei can be found borrowed from the ninth hour of the *Amduat*.[51] Similar representations appear in the burial chamber of Iufaa and Menekhibnekau as well, although their classification as demons is more or less vague and may be disputed.

On the southern wall of the burial chamber of Iufaa, among a number of texts dealing with the nourishment of the deceased and his transformation into a blessed spirit, depictions of several creatures (or just symbols?) appear. Recently, H. Kockelmann has published exact parallels to some of them in his magisterial book about the late mummy wrappings, describing them as "Leinenamulette" (amulets on linen).[52] The same protective forces might have been connected with the frieze of objects that runs along the entire length of the burial chamber of Menekhibnekau, although the individual items of this frieze can hardly be described as "demons."[53]

According to the present knowledge, the number of demons and apotropaic images similar in character that are found in the burial chambers of Iufaa and Menekhibnekau is unique among all the contemporary tombs of the same kind. In many respects, they seem to resemble the situation known from the tombs dating to the Twenty-ninth and Thirtieth Dynasties and the early Ptolemaic period. Certainly, almost no tombs of higher dignitaries are known from the times of the first Persian rule, although the names of several such persons at least are attested in the written evidence.[54] We may ask, therefore, whether the massive use of demons and other apotropaic creatures and pictures in the shaft tombs at Abusir represents just one (although perhaps rather important) step in the long development of the decoration of the burial structures or whether it reflects more the personal choice of their owners. Additionally, the reasons for choosing certain specific motifs and representations in the tomb decoration are only rarely discussed, especially what concerns the Late Period structures.[55] In view of the amount and variety of texts and images that appear especially in the burial chamber of Iufaa, the second option might perhaps be preferable.

Acknowledgments

This study was written within the Programme for the Development of Fields of Study at Charles University, No. P14 *Archaeology of non-European Regions*, sub-programme *Research of ancient Egyptian civilization. Cultural and political adaptation of the North-African civilizations in ancient history (5,000 B.C.E. – A.D. 1,000).* The work was supported by the European Regional Development Fund-Project "Creativity and Adaptability as Conditions of the Success of Europe in an Interrelated World" (No. CZ.02.1.01/0.0/0.0/16_019/0000734).

References:

Abdelrahiem, Mohamed. 2006. "Chapter 144 of the Book of the Dead from the Temple of Ramesses II at Abydos." *Studien zur Altägyptischen Kultur* 34: 1–16.

Allen, Thomas George. 1974. *The Book of the Dead or Going Forth by Day: Ideas of the Ancient Egyptians Concerning the Hereafter as Expressed in Their Own Terms*. Studies in Ancient Oriental Civilization 37. Chicago: The University of Chicago Press.

Altenmüller, Hartwig. 2006. "Aspekte des Grabgedankes in der Dekoration von drei Grabanlagen des Alten Reiches." In Martin Fitzenreiter and Michael Herb (eds.), *Dekorierte Grabanlagen im Alten Reich. Methodik und Interpretation*, 19–36. Internet-Beiträge zur Ägyptologie und Sudanarchäologie 6. Berlin—London: Golden House Publications.

Assmann, Jan. 1977. *Grabung im Asasif 1963–1970 6: Das Grab der Mutirdis*. Archäologische Veröffentlichungen, Deutsches Archäologisches Institut, Abteilung Kairo 13. Mainz: Ph. v. Zabern.

——. 1989. "Death and Initiation in Ancient Egypt." In William K. Simpson (ed.), *Religion and Philosophy in Ancient Egypt*, 135–159. Yale Egyptological Studies 3. New Haven: Yale Egyptological Seminar.

Bareš, Ladislav. 1999. *The Shaft Tomb of Udjahorresnet at Abusir*. Abusir 4. Prague: Universitas Carolina Pragensis; The Karolinum Press.

——. 2007 "Lesser Burial Chambers in the Large Late Period Shaft Tombs and Their Owners." In Zahi Hawass and Janet E. Richards (eds.), *The Archaeology and Art of Ancient Egypt: Essays in Honor of David B. O'Connor* I, 87–97. Annales du Service des antiquités de l'Égypte, Cahier 36. Cairo: Supreme Council of Antiquities Press.

——. 2010. "Procession of Deities and Demons on the Inner Sarcophagus of Iufaa." In H. Győry (ed.), *Aegyptus et Pannonia IV. Acta Symposii Anno 2006*, 1–12. Budapest: MEBT – ÓEB.

——. 2013 "Object Frieze in the Burial Chamber of the Late Period Shaft Tomb of Menekhibnekau at Abusir." *Études et Travaux* 26: 75–85.

——, Jiří Janák, and Renata Landgráfová. In press. "The Iconography of the Late Period Shaft Tombs at Abusir." In Joachim Friedrich Quack and Daniela C. Luft (eds.), *Proceedings of the Workshop "Wand, Rezitationsrolle und Grab. Wechselnder Materialisierungen religiöser Texte im Alten Ägypten: Praktische Verwendung religiöser Artefakte (Text/Bildträger)" (Heidelberg, September 20–22, 2013)*. Heidelberg.

——, and Květa Smoláriková. 2008. *The Shaft Tomb of Iufaa*, vol. I: *Archaeology*. Abusir 17. Prague: Czech Institute of Egyptology, Faculty of Arts, Charles University in Prague.

——, and —— 2011 *The Shaft Tomb of Menekhibnekau*, vol. I: *Archaeology*. Abusir, 25. Prague: Czech Institute of Egyptology, Faculty of Arts, Charles University in Prague.

Coppens, Filip. 2009. "The Tomb of Padihor." In Filip Coppens and Květa Smoláriková, *Lesser Late Period Tombs at Abusir: The Tomb of Padihor and the Anonymous Tomb R3*, 23–84, pls. 2–10. Abusir 20. Prague: Czech Institute of Egyptology, Faculty of Arts, Charles University in Prague.

Daressy, Georges. 1917. "Fragments de deux cercueils de Saqqarah." *Annales du Service des antiquités de l'Égypte* 17: 1–20.

Gestermann, Louise. 2005. *Die Überlieferung ausgewählter Texte altägyptischer Totenliteratur („Sargtexte") in spätzeitlichen Grabanlagen*, vol. I: *Text*. Ägyptologische Abhandlungen 68. Wiesbaden: O. Harrassowitz, 2005.

Herb, Michael. 2006. "Ikonographie – Schreiben mit Bildern: ein Essay zur Historizität der Grabdekoration des Alten Reiches." In Martin Fitzenreiter and Michael Herb (eds.), *Dekorierte Grabanlagen im Alten Reich. Methodik und Interpretation*, 111–213. Internet-Beiträge zur Ägyptologie und Sudanarchäologie 6. Berlin—London: Golden House Publications.

Hornung, Erik. 1963. *Das Amduat. Die Schrift des verborgenen Raumes, herausgegeben nach den Texten des Neuen Reiches*, Vol. I: *Text*, vol. II: *Übersetzung und Kommentar*. Wiesbaden: Harrassowitz.

——. 2000. *Das Totenbuch der Ägypter, eingeleitet, übersetzt und erläutert*. 2nd ed. Zürich: Artemis.

——. 2002. *Die Unterweltsbücher der Ägypter, eingeleitet, übersetzt und erläutert*. Zürich: Patmos.

Huss, Werner. 1997. "Ägyptische Kollaborateure in persischer Zeit." *Tyche* 12: 131–143.

Hussein, Ramadan B. 2013. "Recontextualized—The Pyramid Texts 'Serpent Spells' in the Saite Context." *Études et Travaux* 26: 273–290.

Kanawati, Naguib. 2009. "Specificity in Old Kingdom Tomb Scenes." *Annales du Service des antiquités de l'Égypte* 83: 261–278.

Kockelmann, Holger. 2008. *Untersuchungen zu den späten Totenbuch-Handschriften auf Mumienbinden*. Studien zum Altägyptischen Totenbuch 12. Wiesbaden: Harrassowitz.

Kousoulis, Panagiotis I. 2013. "Egyptian Demonology within the Phylogenetic and Polymorphic Environment of the Late Period and Ptolemaic Egypt:

Searching for Modes of Demonic Conception, Progression and Praxis." *Journal of Ancient Egyptian Interconnections* 5(4): 20–21.

—— (ed.).2011. *Ancient Egyptian Demonology: Studies on the Boundaries Between the Demonic and the Divine in Egyptian Magic*. Orientalia Lovaniensia Analecta 175. Leuven: Peeters.

Landgráfová, Renata, Filip Coppens, Jiří Janák, and Diana Míčková. 2017. "Myth and Ritual in the Burial Chamber of the Shaft Tomb of Iufaa at Abusir: Snakes and Snake-like Beings." In Miroslav Bárta and Filip Coppens (eds.), *Abusir and Saqqara in the Year 2015 (Proceedings of a Conference, Prague 2015)*, 613–626. Prague: Charles University.

Leclant, Jean. 1962. "Les génies-gardiens de Montouemhat." In Nina V. Pigulevskaya, Dmitriy P. Kallistov, and Isidor S. Katznelson (eds.), *Drevniy mir. Sbornik statey. Akademiku Vasiliyu Vasilyevitshu Struve*, 104–129. Moscow: Izdatelstvo vostochnoy literatury.

Leitz, Christian. 1996. "Die Schlangensprüche in den Pyramidentexten." *Orientalia* 65: 381–427.

—— (ed.). 2002. *Lexikon der ägyptischen Götter und Götterbezeichnungen*, vols. 1–7. Orientalia Lovaniensia Analecta 110–116. Leuven: Peeters.

Lloyd, Alan B. 2014. "The Egyptian Attitude to the Persians." In Aidan M. Dodson, John J. Johnston, and Wendy Monkhouse (eds.), *A Good Scribe and an Exceedingly Wise Man: Studies in Honour of W. J. Tait*, 185–198. London: Golden House.

Lopez, Francesco. 2015. *Democede di Crotone e Udjahorresnet di Saïs*. Pisa: Pisa University Press.

Lucarelli, Rita. 2010a. "Demons (Benevolent and Malevolent)." In J. Dieleman and W. Wendrich (eds.), *UCLA Encyclopedia of Egyptology*. Los Angeles: University of California. < https://escholarship.org/uc/item/1r72q9vv >, accessed 4 October 2019.

——. 2010b. "The Guardian-demons of the Book of the Dead." *British Museum Studies in Ancient Egypt and Sudan* 15: 85–102.

——. 2011. "Demonology during the Late Pharaonic and Graeco-Roman Periods in Egypt." *Journal of Near Eastern Religions* 11(2): 109–125.

——. 2013a. "Towards a Comparative Approach to Demonology in Antiquity: The Case of Ancient Egypt and Mesopotamia." *Archiv für Religionsgeschichte* 14: 11–25.

——. 2013b. Review of P. Kousoulis, (ed.), *Ancient Egyptian Demonology: Studies on the Boundaries between the Demonic and the Divine in Egyptian Magic*, Orientalia Lovaniensia Analecta 175 (Leuven: Peeters 2011). *Magic, Ritual and Witchcraft* 8(1): 99–105.

——. 2015. "Ancient Egyptian Demons: The Evidence of the Magical and Funerary Papyri of the New Kingdom and the Third Intermediate Period." In Panagiotis I. Kousoulis and Nikolaos Lazaridis (eds.), *Proceedings of the Tenth International Congress of Egyptologists, University of the Aegean, Rhodes, 22–29 May 2008, I*, 1187–1194. Orientalia Lovaniensia Analecta 241. Leuven: Peeters.

——. 2016. "Les démons dans l'Égypte ancienne." In Arnaud Quertinmont (ed.), *Dieux, génies et demons en Égypte ancienne: à la rencontre d'Osiris, Anubis, Isis, Hathor, Rê et les autres*, 54–59. Paris: Somogy éditions d'art.

Maaßen, Ildikó. 2015. "Schlangen- und Skorpionbeschwörung über die Jahrtausende." In Andrea Jördens (ed.), *Ägyptische Magie und ihre Umwelt*, 171–187. Philippika 80. Wiesbaden: Harrassowitz.

Munro, Irmtraut. 2006. *Der Totenbuch-Papyrus des Hor aus der frühen Ptolemäerzeit (pCologny Bodmer-Stiftung CV + pCincinnati Art Museum 1947.369 + pDenver Art Museum 1954.61)*. Handschriften des Altägyptischen Totenbuches 9. Wiesbaden: Harrassowitz.

Qahéri-Paquette, Sépideh. 2014. *Recherches sur la cour royale égyptienne à l'époque saïte (664–525 av. J.-C.)*. PhD dissertation. Université Lumière–Lyon 2.

Quack, Joachim Friedrich. 2015. "Dämonen und andere höhere Wesen in der Magie als Feinde und Helfer." In Andrea Jördens (ed.), *Ägyptische Magie und ihre Umwelt*, 101–118. Philippika 80. Wiesbaden: Harrassowitz.

Quirke, Stephen. 2013. *Going out in Daylight*—prt m hrw*: The Ancient Egyptian Book of the Dead, Translation, Sources, Meanings*. GHP Egyptology 20. London: Golden House Publications.

Sabek, Yasser. 2003. "Die Schlange und ihre Verehrung in Ägypten in pharaonischer und moderner Zeit." In Martin Fitzenreiter (ed.), Tierkulte im pharaonischen Ägypten und im Kulturvergleich: Beiträge eines Workshops am 7.6. und 8.6.2002, 137–157. Internet-Beiträge zur Ägyptologie und Sudanarchäologie 4. London: Golden House.

Sawi, Ahmad el-, and Farouk Gomaà. 1993. *Das Grab des Panehsi, Gottesvater von Heliopolis in Matariya.*

Wiesbaden: Harrassowitz.
Smoláriková, Květa. 2009. "The Anonymous Tomb R3." In Filip Coppens and Květa Smoláriková, *Lesser Late Period Tombs at Abusir: The Tomb of Padihor and the Anonymous Tomb R3*, 85–110, pls. 11–25. Abusir 20. Prague: Czech Institute of Egyptology, Faculty of Arts, Charles University in Prague.
Stammers, Michael. 2009. *The Elite Late Period Egyptian Tombs at Memphis*. BAR International Series 1903. Oxford: Archaeopress.
Stauder-Porchet, Julie. 2016. "Les actants des autobiographies événementielles de la Ve et de la VIe dynastie." In Philippe Collombert, Dominique Lefèvre, Stéphane Polis, and Jean Winand (eds.), *Aere perennius: mélanges égyptologiques en l'honneur de Pascal Vernus*, 579–591. Orientalia Lovaniensia Analecta 242. Leuven: Peeters.
Szpakowska, Kasia M. 2009. "Demons in Ancient Egypt." *Religion Compass* 3(5): 799–805.
——. 2014 "The Ancient Egyptian Demonology Project." *Journal of Ancient Egyptian Interconnections* 6(4): 58–59.
Theis, Christoffer. 2015. "Defensive Magie im alten Ägypten. Der Schutz der Grabstätte." In Andrea Jördens (ed.), *Ägyptische Magie und ihre Umwelt*, 119–170. Philippika 80. Wiesbaden: Harrassowitz.
Verhoeven, Ursula. 1993. *Das saitische Totenbuch der Iahtesnacht. P. Colon. Aeg. 10207*, 3 vols. Papyrologische Texte und Abhandlungen 41. Bonn: Dr. Rudolf Habelt GmbH.
Vonk, Thomas. 2015. "Von Betrügern und schimpfenden Hirten. Über den Humor einiger 'Reden und Rufe.'" *Göttinger Miszellen* 245: 79–93.
Waitkus, Wolfgang. 1987. "Zur Deutung einiger apotropäischer Götter in den Gräbern im Tal der Königinnen und im Grabe Ramses III." *Göttinger Miszellen* 99: 51–82.
Walsem, René van. 2005. *Iconography of Old Kingdom Elite Tombs: Analysis and Interpretation; Theoretical and Methodological Aspects*. Mémoires de la Société d'études orientales "Ex Oriente Lux" 35. Dudley, MA: Peeters.
——. 2006. "Sense and Sensibility: On the Analysis and Interpretation of the Iconography Programmes in Four Old Kingdom Elite Tombs." In Martin Fitzenreiter and Michael Herb (eds.), *Dekorierte Grabanlagen im Alten Reich. Methodik und Interpretation*, 277–332. Internet-Beiträge zur Ägyptologie und Sudanarchäologie 6. Berlin—London: Golden House Publications.
——. 2013. "Diversification and Variation in Old Kingdom Funerary Iconography as the Expression of the Need for 'Individuality.'" *Jaarbericht van het Vooraziatisch-Egyptisch Genootschap Ex Oriente Lux* 44: 117–139.
——. 2016. "Quantitative Means for Establishing the Qualitative 'Individuality Degree' of Hetepka's Elite Tomb at Saqqara." In Jacobus van Dijk (ed.), *Another Mouthful of Dust: Egyptological Studies in Honour of Geoffrey Thorndike Martin*, 495–542. Leuven: Peeters.
Wessetzky, Vilmós. 1991. "Fragen zum Verhalten der mit den Persern zusammenarbeitenden Ägypter." *Göttinger Miszellen* 124: 83–89.
Willems, Harco. 1997. "The Embalmer Embalmed: Remarks on the Meaning of the Decoration of Some Middle Kingdom Coffins." In Jacobus van Dijk (ed.), *Essays on Ancient Egypt in Honour of Herman Te Velde*, 343–372. Groningen: Styx Publications.

Notes

1 Cf., e.g., Mohamed Abdelrahiem 2006, 13; Lucarelli 2010a, 2010b, 2011, 2013a, 2013b, 2015, 2016; Kousoulis 2013; Kousoulis (ed.) 2011; Szpakowska 2009; see also Assmann 1989, 147–149. On the definition of "demons" in Egyptology, see recently Szpakowska 2014 and Quack 2015, 101–103 and *passim*.

2 Bareš and Smoláriková 2011, 69.

3 Bareš and Smoláriková 2008.

4 Bareš and Smoláriková 2011.

5 Bareš 1999; for a recent discussion, see also Stammers 2009, 27–28, 111–112 and *passim* and Lopez 2015, 90–94 and *passim*.

6 Coppens 2009.

7 Smoláriková 2009.

8 At present, two large shaft tombs (situated to the northeast of the tomb of Udjahorresnet and to the southeast of the tomb of Menekhibnekau, respectively) and perhaps two to four smaller structures of the same kind have only partly been excavated or remain completely unexplored.

9 See Leclant 1962, 106–109, Waitkus 1987, 51–82

(especially 80–82); see also Assmann 1977, 92–94, Willems 1997, 358–359, and Quack 2015, 104 (with footnotes 17 and 18).

10 Lucarelli 2010b; see also Quack 2015, 105.

11 Bareš and Smoláriková 2008, 57–58, see also Bareš 2010.

12 Bareš and Smoláriková 2011, 54–55.

13 Bareš and Smoláriková 2008, 124–127; see also Bareš 2007.

14 Perhaps *Ḫsf-sbỉw*; see Leitz 2002, V, 958.

15 For the fluctuation between the signs *ỉb* and *ḥr* in the name of the deity *Rs-ỉb/ḥr*, see Leitz 2002, IV, 712 and IV, 716–717.

16 Due to the technical problems—the inner sarcophagus is still firmly embedded inside a rather tightly fitting depression in the chest of the outer sarcophagus—no photo or any copy of the depiction of demons is available at the moment.

17 Hussein 2013, 277–290.

18 The position of the entrance to the burial chamber on the eastern side, which appears, e.g., in the nearby tomb of Udjahorresnet, was quite usual during the Late Period.

19 Gestermann 2005, 377–378. On "Schlangensprüche" in general, see recently Theis 2015, 129–142 (referring also to Yaser Sabek 2003). According to Theis (2015, 153), those spells reappear more often during the Twenty-sixth Dynasty.

20 Bareš, Janák and Landgráfová in press, Landgráfová, Coppens, Janák and Míčková 2017. The possible protective function of snakes in the entrances to the burial chambers is reflected by Theis 2015, 132–134 (referring to Leitz 1996, 389), and Maaßen 2015, 172.

21 For similar decoration on wooden coffins, see Bareš and Smoláriková 2008, 126, footnote 30; Daressy 1917, 5–11.

22 More often, the doorkeeper of this gate is called *ỉry ꜥryt*; see Abdelrahiem 2006, 3; Quirke 2013, 324–325, etc.

23 More often, the guardsman of this gate is called *Sḫd-(ḥr)-ꜥšꜣw-ỉrw*, i.e., "He whose face is inverted…"; see Leitz 2002, VI, 592–593: "Der mit gesenktem Gesicht und vielen Gestalten," Abdelrahiem 2006, 3; Hornung 2000, 276: "Der mit umgedrehten Gesicht, der Vielgestaltige." Might the plural form *ḥrw* be adapted to the following plural form *ỉrw*?

24 For variant translations, see Abdelrahiem 2006, 5–10.

25 Leitz 2002, VI, 358: "Der Hörende."

26 The second sign *s* seems to be superfluous; either as a scribal error or perhaps to fill the empty space?

27 Cf. Abdelrahiem 2006, 6 (d); Quirke 2013, 324. Verhoeven 1993, 273 (with her footnote 9) translates *ꜣhꜣ-ḫrw* "Jammerer" (literally "der mit klagender Stimme"). See also Leitz 2002, IV, 789–790: *Hꜣ-ḫrw* "Der mit jubelnder Stimme."

28 Leitz 2002, VII, 526–527: "Der mit ausgestreckter Stirn." See also Quirke 2013, 324.

29 Leitz 2002, VI, 660: "Der mit wachsamem Gesicht." See also Hornung 2000, 276: "Dessen Gesicht losfährt."

30 Cf. Leitz 2002, I, 79; Abdelrahiem 2006, 6 (c); Verhoeven 1993, 274 (with footnote 3).

31 Cf. Leitz 2002, II, 408–409; Hornung 2000, 276: "Der das verfaulte aus seinem Hinterteil frißt."

32 Leitz 2002, IV, 712: "Der mit wachsamem Herzen." The sequence of the guardsmen of the third and fourth gate seems to be reversed here, perhaps due to a scribal error? In most cases, *Rs-ḥr* belongs to the third gate, while *Rs-ỉb* to the fourth one. See Mohamed Abdelrahiem 2006, 7; Munro 2006, Photo-Taf. 19 + Taf. 20; Hornung 2000, 276; Verhoeven 1993, I, 274 and II, 106*; Quirke 2013, 325.

33 Certainly an error instead of *Wꜥꜣ*. See Leitz 2002, II, 290: "Der Schmähende"; see also Abdelrahiem 2006, 7 (and note [c]); Quirke 2013, 325; Munro 2006, Photo-Taf. 19 + Taf. 20. Cf. also Verhoeven 1993, I, 274, footnote 5: literally "der mit Schmähreden," II, 105* clearly written *wꜥꜣw*; Hornung 2000, 277: "Der mit Schmähreden." For the deity *ꜥꜣ*, see Leitz 2002, II, 9–10: "Der Große."

34 Leitz 2002, V, 957: "Der mit abweisendem Gesicht, der Geschwätzige."

35 Leitz 2002, IV, 716–717: "Der mit wachsamem Gesicht".

36 See above, our footnote 32.

37 Perhaps an abbreviated form of *ꜥ3-ḥr-ḫsf-ỉdw*. Cf. Abdelrahiem 2006, 7 (with footnote [c] on page 8): "Grim of visage who repels the aggressor"; Leitz 2002, II, 35–36: "Der mit großem Gesicht, der die Wütenden abwehrt"; see, however, Leitz 2002, V, 954: *Ḫsf-3d* "Der den Wütenden abwehrt."

38 Cf. Hornung 2000, 277: "Der mit großem Gesicht, der den Gierigen abwehrt."

39 Leitz 2002, II, 142–143: "Der von den Maden lebt."

40 Cf. Leitz 2002, I, 81–82. The name of this guardsman fluctuates between *wšbw* (e.g., Quirke 2013, 325) and *3šbw* that is clearly written here. See also Munro 2006, Photo-Taf.19 + Taf. 20; Verhoeven 1993, II, 106*, I, 274 with footnote 8. Hornung 2000, 277 translates "Feuriger" as well. See also Abdelrahiem 2006, 8: *Š[3bw]* "Fiery," with note (b) on p. 9.

41 The name of this guardsman fluctuates between *Db-ḥr-kh3-3t* "Hippopotamus(?)-faced, violent-timed" (e.g., Quirke 2013, 325) and *Nb(ỉt)-ḥr-kh(3)b-ỉt* "Face-afire, violent-of-strength" (Abdelrahiem 2006, 9, note [c] referring to T. G. Allen; Verhoeven 1993, II, 106*, and I, 274 with the translation: "Flammengesicht mit rasender Wut"); see also Leitz 2002, vol. IV, 196: "Das Flammengesicht mit rasendem Augenblick," mentioned as an alternative of *Db-ḥr-kh3-3t* "Der Nilpferdgesichtige mit rasendem Augenblick."

42 Leitz 2002, I, 569–570: "Der Brote ergreift, der mit brüllender Stimme(?)." The iconography mentioned by Leitz is different, however.

43 Leitz 2002, I, 377–378: "Der das Gesicht herbeibringt(?)," mentioning, however, Hornung 2000, 277 "Der auf die Flamme fortholt."

44 Cf. Leitz 2002, III, 472, s.v. *Mds*. An exact parallel *Mds-ḥr-ỉry-pt* "Der mit schneidendem Gesicht, der zum Himmel gehört" is dated here to the Graeco-Roman times.

45 Leitz 2002, III, 473: "Der sie zerschneidet." See also Quirke 2013, 325 and, for a variant meaning, Mohamed Abdelrahiem 2006, 10 (with note a): "He who cuts them down." Verhoeven 1993, I, 274 translates "Der Hüter des siebten Tores ist der Schärfste von ihnen" (not as a personal name); cf. Hornung 2000, 278 "Schärfster von ihnen."

46 Leitz 2002, II, 41: "Der mit lauter Stimme" (not attested in the Saite Period?).

47 Leitz 2002, V, 957: "Der die Umstürzenden abwehrt." See also Abdelrahiem 2006, 10 (with note [c] on page 11).

48 See, e.g., the Book of the Dead of Iahtesnakht, Verhoeven 1993, I, 275–277 and II, 106*–107*.

49 See, e.g., the writing of *wsrt* in the final column—with the sign F 12 added to the Horus falcon on the standard.

50 See, e.g., the mention of Apophis (as in most of the BD 144 texts) instead of Seth, who is named in the papyrus of Iahtesnakht. Verhoeven 1993, I, 275 and II, 107*.

51 El-Sawi and Gomaà 1993, 41–42. See also Hussein 2013, 284 with footnote 31.

52 Kockelmann 2008, II, 329–330.

53 See Bareš 2013.

54 See, e.g., Wessetzky 1991; Huss 1997; Lloyd 2014; Qahéri-Paquette 2014. A dissertation dealing with the high dignitaries of Egypt in the times of transition between the Twenty-sixth and Twenty-seventh Dynasties (from Ahmose III/Amasis to Darius I) is currently being prepared by Nenad Marković at the Charles University in Prague.

55 See, e.g., Altenmüller 2006; Herb 2006; Walsem 2005, 2006, 2013, 2016; Kanawati 2009 (with a critical remark by Stauder-Porchet 2016, 590, footnote 38); Vonk 2015, 88–89. All these publications deal mostly with the Old Kingdom tombs.

Journal of Ancient Egyptian Interconnections

Disease Demons in Mesopotamia and Egypt: Sāmānu as a Case Study

Susanne Beck
Institute for Ancient Near Eastern Studies, University of Tuebingen

Abstract
This article gives a brief overview about previous approaches whether the use of the term "demon" is constructive in Egyptology and Ancient Near Eastern Studies. Additionally, the similarities and differences between Egyptian and Mesopotamian representations of disease demons are compared in general, and then the demon Sāmānu/Akhu (*ʿḫ.w*) is analyzed as a case study.

What Is a Demon?

The term "demon" is derived from the ancient Greek word δαίμων, which has several meanings. Primarily, it means "god/goddess" or "the divine power." Additionally, it can describe "the power controlling the destiny of individuals" or a "spiritual" or "semidivine being."[1] Obviously, δαίμονες had a wide range of actions and could positively as well as negatively affect persons. While the term had a neutral connotation in antiquity, over the following centuries, as Christianity spread throughout Europe and the Mediterranean world, it acquired a more negative connotation. Δαίμονες began to be associated with the devil and both their actions and their nature classified as evil. The modern term "demon" is typically used in this latter (Christian) sense.[2] In this paper the term "disease demon" is used to specify only these kinds of beings that cause different ailments.

The Mesopotamian Concept

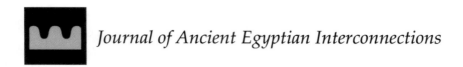

There are many different ways to classify Mesopotamian beings who are not human or divine by scholars of the ancient Near Eastern studies. Karen Sonik has developed a model in which supernatural creatures are classified as *Zwischenwesen* ("in-between" beings).[3] She argues that every entity that does not belong to the human or the divine sphere is a *Zwischenwesen*. These beings can then be subdivided into different groups: viziers, monsters, *daimons*, sages, heroes, witches, and ghosts. Viziers (Sumerian: s u k k a l/Akkadian: *sukkallu*) are the emissaries of the Mesopotamian major deities.[4] Monsters—also known as creatures of chaos—and *daimons* are *Mischwesen* (hybrid creatures)[5] whose bodies consisted of both zoomorphic and anthropomorphic elements. *Daimons* are differentiated into genii that were benevolent guardian spirits and "real" demons that were malevolent beings who afflicted humans with diseases and could potentially cause death.[6] Furthermore, there are sages (abgal/*apkallu*) known from Mesopotamian myths, heroes (ursaĝ/*qarrādu*) who were part of legends, witches who were usually involved in evil interactions, and ghosts (gidim/*eṭemmu*) of those who had died an unnatural and premature death.[7]

In this context monsters and *daimons* are of special interest because they shared a key feature: both entities were hybrid creatures whose natural habitats were desolate regions such as deserts and mountains. The difference between the beings was their sphere of interaction. Monsters only interacted with gods or occasionally with heroes (as *Zwischenwesen*; see above) and thus were limited to the divine sphere. In contrast, *daimons* were restricted to the human world with the exception of two creatures: Ašu and Sāmānu.[8] As mentioned above, *daimons* are classified in two subcategories: genii and "real" demons.[9]

Frans Wiggerman has suggested another approach to differentiate the Mesopotamian entities that are neither human nor divine.[10] He divides hybrid creatures into monsters and demons. According to his definition, the former originated from the primeval ocean, always appeared in pairs, and had apotropaic features. In contrast, he sees demons as asexual, lacking families, and without a place in the cosmic order.[11] In contrast to Sonik's model, Wiggerman consolidates monsters and genii into the term *monsters*. Demons stay demons (malevolent beings).[12]

In the illustrated dictionary *Gods, Demons and Symbols of Ancient Mesopotamia* by Jeremy Black and Anthony Green, another very popular approach is presented: In modern studies of Mesopotamian iconography and art, scholars have applied the term "demon" to hybrid creatures who have a bipedal human body, whereas hybrid creatures on four legs are considered "monsters."[13] This definition unfortunately cannot be applied to the entire range of demonic beings because only two (disease) demons, Lamaštu and Pazuzu, are ever depicted in Mesopotamian reliefs and statuary.[14]

According to Manfred Hutter, "demons" can be classified as *lesser gods* or *anti-gods* who are not as powerful as major deities but are still different from human beings. They belong to the divine sphere and can interact with mankind either benevolently or malevolently. They are differentiated from gods in ancient Near Eastern texts by their otherness, i.e., their non-human elements.[15] So Hutter categorizes all types of supportive and destructive hybrid creatures as "demons"—basically as the term δαίμων was used in Greek in the classical period.

The Egyptian Concept

Clear distinctions between the various Egyptian beings are also problematic. As Herman te Velde stated:

> A satisfactory definition of the term demons and a consistent delimitation of what it meant in Egypt can hardly be given, since our idea of demons is not without ambiguity, and the word does not correspond to one specific Egyptian name.[16]

Egyptologists often call the creatures of the underworld mentioned in funerary texts[17] "demons," even though they typically played a more protective role or acted as guardians. It was their task to keep out *trespassers* who were not allowed in the netherworld. Again serving in a protective role, these *guardians* of the underworld are found on Late Period temple walls.[18]

According to Rita Lucarelli, there are two kinds of "demons": *guardians* and *wanderers*. The distinction derives from the context in which they appear. The former were bound to the places they inhabited, places such as passages and sacred sites in the mortal world and the netherworld. Usually, they were depicted or described as anthropomorphic hybrid creatures with animal heads. Their primary function was protective. *Wanderers* roamed between heaven and earth, throughout the human world and even beyond. These creatures, typically appearing in groups (e.g., *wpw.tjw*, *ḫ3.tjw*), could afflict humanity with diseases and often acted as "emissaries" for certain gods (e.g., Sakhmet, Osiris) who used them to punish mankind.[19] But Lucarelli argues that a definitive typology of these entities still needs to be developed.[20]

Dieter Kurth has suggested another way to interpret the divine and the demonic in Egypt.[21] According to him, magic and religion, which belonged to opposite poles of the same scale, could be understood respectively as *acting and examining* (*Handeln und Betrachten*).[22] Further, while the power of both demonic and divine beings was beyond that of humans, the power of "demons" was restricted to a specific purpose, but divine power was a mysterious force that ran through everything. Demons were merely components of a broader divine source of power. Thus demonic beings could produce concrete effects that originated from concrete thoughts while abstract thoughts would lead to searching, examining, worshiping and praying and this would allow people to perceive an almighty power underlying everything and thus the existence of the gods. He therefore concludes: "Dämonen bzw. Götter entspringen entgegengesetzten Ausrichtungen des menschlichen Denkens."[23] "Demons" as components were derived from gods and acted as their emissaries even when they disturbed the cosmic order. Moreover, even if a deity was worshiped in a temple, that same deity could also function as a "demon" component, i.e., as a specific aspect, subordinate to another deity who was the major god of another temple. The actions of these "demon" components could thus be either benevolent or malevolent depending on the context.[24] Yet Kurth, like Lucarelli, admits that a conclusive definition of "demons" is still wanting.[25]

These different approaches clearly show that it is not easy to categorize Egyptian entities. These entities are able to act in many ways—positively and negatively—depending on one's perspective. For example, underworld creatures who guard doorways and gates are benevolent towards individuals who are supposed to pass through such areas, but they are dangerous adversaries to those who trespass. Thus we should be careful of broadly classifying them as "demons" because, for many modern readers, this term implies an evil nature due to the modern-day usual (Christian) connotation (as previously discussed). Therefore, it would be suitable to use another term and not the word "demon" if one is referring to them in a more general way. Perhaps the word *daimons* or "in-between" creatures should generally be applied, as suggested by Sonik for Mesopotamian entities.[26] Nevertheless the term "demon" for an evil being can easily be used for one category of entities in Egypt: disease demons.

Disease Demons in Egypt and Mesopotamia

Disease demons generally have a lot in common in Egypt and Mesopotamia (Table 1). However, neither Sumerian/Akkadian nor Egyptian has a generic term for demonic beings. Specific names for gangs of demons and individual types do exist in both cultures, such as Lamaštu, Pazuzu, *Utukkū lemnūtu* or *ḫꜣ.tjw*, *shꜣḳḳ*, and *ꜥḫ.w*, etc.[27]

Mesopotamian as well as Egyptian evil entities originated and lived in mountains, deserts, waters, and marshes—usually territories where no one lives and people only pass by.[28] Remote places and the unknown were perceived as uncanny. The foreign was often demonized.[29] Thus the Spells for Mother and Child, spell D, from Berlin P. 3027 referring to the demoness Iššiu, daughter of Ittiu, states:

> *šp ꜥꜣm.t tn jy.t ḥr ḫꜣs.t nḥs.yt [tn jy.t] ḥr mr.w*
>
> Discharge, O you Asiatic woman who has come from the foreign country! Discharge, O [you] Nubian woman who [has come] from the desert![30]

Similar statements—that evil beings have a foreign origin—can be found in incantations against the evil *Utukkū* who wandered through the cities at night but originate from the steppe or mountains:

> udug ḫul a-la$_2$ ḫul kitim ḫul gal$_5$-la ḫul kur-ta im-ta-e$_3$ du$_6$-ku$_3$ kur-idim-ta ša$_3$-ba im-ta-e$_3$
>
> Evil *utukku*, evil *alû*, evil ghost (and) evil *gallû* have emerged from the netherworld, and they came out from the midst of the distant mountain, the holy mound.[31]
>
> udug ḫul an-edin-na du-a a-la$_2$ ḫul an-edin-na dul-la a$_2$-sag$_3$ nig$_2$-ge$_{17}$ an-edin-na lal$_2$-a // *[u$_3$]-tuk-ku lem-nu ša$_2$ ina ṣe-e-ri il-la-ku [a-lu-u le]m-nu ša$_2$ ina ṣe-e-ri i-kat-ta-mu [a-sak-ku mar-ṣu ša$_2$ ina] ṣe-e-ri it-te-ne$_2$-'i-lu-u$_2$*
>
> As for the evil *utukku* who walks in the steppe, (and) the evil *alû* who envelops (one) in the steppe, the dangerous *asakku* who always roams around in the steppe.[32]

Furthermore, knowledge of the demonic being's name is essential for expelling them in both cultures because knowledge of the name grants power over these creatures.[33] Demons can have more than one name, and when they do, all have to be named to exorcize the creature. Lamaštu, for example, must be addressed with her seven names:

> ^{d}DIM$_3$.ME DUMU AN-*a šumša ištēn šanû aḫat ilī ša sūqāti šal su patru ša qaqqada ilattû rebû ša išāta inappaḫu ḫanšu iltu š panūša šakṣū šeššu paqid qāti leqât Irnina sebû nīš ilī rabûti lū tamâti*
>
> "Dimme, child of An" is her first name, the second is "sister of the gods of the streets," the third is "sword that splits the head," the fourth is "she who lights the fire," the fifth is "goddess whose face is *wild*," the sixth is "*entrusted one, adopted daughter of* Irnina," the seventh is "by the spell of the great gods may you be bound."[34]

Frequently a list of creatures is recited, if the conjurer does not know the specific demonic being:

> *ḥꜣ=k ḫft.y pf.t(j) m(w)t m(w)t.t ḥm.wt-rᶜ* (...)
>
> Back off, you, enemy, yonder, male dead, female dead etc.[35]

A difference can be found in the description of the shape of disease demons. The (outward) appearance of Mesopotamian entities is exactly described:[36]

> *šinni imēri šinnāša pan nēši dapini panūša šaknū kīma nimri tukkupā kalâtūša kīma kalê lēssa arqat*
>
> (Lamaštu ... with) teeth (like) donkey's teeth, a face (like) the face of a mighty lion. The small of her back is speckled like a leopard, her cheek is yellowish pale like ochre.[37]

In Egypt, demonic beings were typically not described.[38] There are only a few exceptions. For example, the demon *Shꜣḳḳ* who was not originally Egyptian is described:

> *shꜣḳḳ (...) jr.tj=fy m tbn=f ns.t=f m ᶜr.t=f*
>
> *shꜣḳḳ* (...) whose both eyes are in his head, whose tongue is in his hinter parts[39]

Another demonic being whose name is not mentioned is depicted in the Spells for Mother and Child, spell C:

> *fnd=f ḥꜣ=f ḥr=f ᶜn.w*
>
> His nose is (at the) back of his head (and) his face is turned."[40]

In both cases it seems more important to outline their otherness in contrast to *mꜣᶜ.t*, rather than to describe their shape. Additionally, Mesopotamian demonic and divine entities are easier to distinguish —the major deities always have an anthropomorphic body whereas demons always appear as hybrid creatures.[41] Such a distinction does not exist for Egyptian entities.[42]

However, the form of the Mesopotamian and Egyptian disease demons are similar. These beings are described in both cultures as a kind of *breeze* that can enter the human body through the body orifices.[43] In P. Edwin Smith, different kinds of demonic beings are described as a breeze coming from the outside:

> *ky n(.j) ḫsf tꜣw n(.j) dḥr.t ḫꜣ(y).tjw nḏs.tjw wpw.tjw sḫm.t (...)*
>
> Another of repelling the breeze of sickness, disease demons, *nḏs.tjw*-beings (and) the messengers of Sakhmet. (...)[44]

In Mesopotamia it is not uncommon to classify demons as wind or storm figures, as, for example, the evil *Utukkū*:

> u$_4$-šu$_2$-uš im-ḫul dim$_2$-ma-a-meš u$_4$ ḫul im-ḫul igi-tuḫ-a-meš u$_4$ ḫul im ḫul igi-du-a-meš // *u$_4$-mu up-pu-tu$_4$ ša$_2$-a-ri lem-nu-tu$_4$ šu$_2$-nu u$_4$-mu ša$_2$* ḪUL-*ti$_3$ im-ḫul-lu a-me-ru-ti$_3$ šu$_2$-nu u$_4$-mu ša$_2$* ḪUL-*ti$_3$ im-ḫul-lu a-lik maḫ-ri šu$_2$-nu*
>
> they are clouded-over days and evil winds, they are seen to be storms which are evil, an ill-wind, they are storms which are evil, an ill wind at the forefront.[45]

Demons are able to seize victims of their own accord due to their evil nature but they may also act on divine orders.[46] In Mesopotamia, a god is, in fact, always directly or indirectly involved because every Sumerian and Akkadian had a personal deity for his or her protection. This god can be viewed as a kind of divine *immune system*. When someone angered his personal god, willingly or unwillingly, this deity

Table 1: Comparison between Mesopotamian and Egyptian disease demons.

	Mesopotamia	**Egypt**
Generic Term	no	
Distribution	desert, mountains, waters	foreign countries/desert, waters, marshes
	uninhabited territories	
Names	necessary to know in order to exorcise them	
Shape	hybrid creatures	unknown
Form	wind, storm ("breeze")	"breeze"
	entering body as "breeze"	
Instigation of Action	of their own accord or by divine orders	

could send a disease demon to punish the delinquent or could turn a blind eye when a demonic being was approaching.[47]

Sāmānu as a Mesopotamian and an Egyptian Disease Demon

The ancient Near Eastern disease demon Sāmānu is attested in numerous texts in Mesopotamia and Egypt. In Mesopotamia, Sāmānu is attested from the Ur III period to the Hellenistic Period (approx. 330–63 BCE) in incantations, medical texts/recipes, lexical lists, omens and astronomical diaries. As a Mesopotamian demonic being, he is able to afflict gods, mankind, animals (cattle, sheep and donkey), plants (as rust and as pest), and as an occurrence in rivers.[48] In Egypt, the demon, who is also known as Akhu (*ʿḫ.w*), only occurs as an affliction of men in magical-medical texts which date almost exclusively to the New Kingdom.[49]

The demon's shape is precisely described in the Near Eastern sources:

> sa-ma-na ka piriĝ-ĝa zu$_2$ muš ušum-gal umbin [ḫu-ri$_2$]-in-na kuĝ$_2$ a[l]-lu$_5$
>
> Sāmānu, (with) a lion's mouth, teeth of a dragon's snake, claws of an eagle (and) a crab's tail[50]

Additionally, the idea of *red evil* is significant because the name Sāmānu is a nominal derivation from the Akkadian word *sāmu* "red" and literally means "the red one."[51] Mesopotamian texts play with this association; so, for example:

> [s]a-ma-na šu ḫuš [ĝ]iri$_3$ ḫuš ^{d}en-lil$_2$-la$_2$
>
> Sāmānu, reddish claw, reddish paw of Enlil[52]

Another important aspect of the demon is his representation as dog. In the ancient Near East, he is usually described as the evil dog of the different deities, especially of the healing goddess Gula:[53]

> ur ḫuš ^{d}en-lil$_2$-la$_2$ gu$_2$ sur ^{d}en-ki-ka ka uš$_2$ tuḫ-tuḫ ^{d}nin-^{si}isin$_2$-na-ka ur ka tuḫ-a diĝir-re-ne
>
> red dog of Enlil, neck-breaker of Enki, the frequently opening bloody mouth of Ninisina, dog with opened mouth of the gods[54]

As is typical, the bodily form is usually not described in Egypt. Neither the redness nor the canine form occurs. In Egyptian, however, the demon can also be called Akhu (*ʿḫ.w*). The word *ʿḫ.w* is derived from the root *ꜥḫj*[55] and means "the burning/burned one." However, it is unclear if the term Akhu is a reference in any way to the Mesopotamian tradition regarding the demon's redness.[56] The only statement alluding to Sāmānu/Akhu as dog, can be found in P. Leiden I 343 + 345, which is the major source for this disease demon in Egypt:

> *[p]ꜣ jwjw wšꜥ[{.t}] ḳs.w*
>
> O dog who chews bones[57]

Furthermore, the origin of the entity is mentioned in the Mesopotamian sources. As is typical for such beings, he comes from the mountains:

> kur-ta ĝen-na kur-ta <e$_{4}$>-da sa-ma-na kur-ta ĝen-na kur-ta e$_{4}$-da [ḫur-sa]ĝ ki sikil-ta du [kur-t]a e$_{4}$-da
>
> coming from the mountains, <coming down> from the mountains, Sāmānu, coming from the mountains, coming down from the mountains, coming from the [foothil]ls, the pure place, coming from the [moun]tains[58]

A similar statement is made in the Egyptian sources:

> *jw=k n nꜣ n(.j) ꜥꜣ.w šmꜣ{m}.w n.ty ḥr ḫꜣs.t*
>
> You belong to the wandering donkeys which are in the desert.[59]

The wandering donkeys, which can only refer to undomesticated animals, particularly stress the foreign origin of Sāmānu/Akhu in Egypt.

Sāmānu's actions are a major theme in ancient Near Eastern texts. He is capable of afflicting gods in Mesopotamia which is extremely uncommon:[60]

> diĝir an-na an-na im-mi-keše$_{2}$ diĝir ki ki-a im-mi-ib$_{2}$-keše$_{2}$ ^{d}utu an-ur$_{3}$-ra i[m-mi]-ib$_{2}$-k[eše$_{2}$] ^{d}nanna su$_{4}$-an-n[a im]-mi-i[b$_{2}$-keš]e$_{2}$
>
> He has bound the god of heaven in heaven, he has bound the god of earth in earth, he has bound Utu in the horizon, he has bound Nanna in the red evening sky[61]

But the most common victims of Sāmānu are mankind:

> ⸢guruš⸣ ḫaš$_{2}$-a-na-⸢ta⸣ ba-⸢ni⸣-i[n ...] //
> *eṭ-lu [ina] šap⸣-ri-šu$_{2}$ i[ṣ-bat]*
> ki-sikil GIŠ.GABA-na-⸢ke$_{4}$⸣ // [...] ⸢ar$_{2}$⸣-[...]
> *ina ši-ti-iq ⸢ir⸣-ti-ša$_{2}$ i[ṣ-bat]*
> lu$_{2}$-tur ga-naĝ-e sa gu$_{2}$-bi ba-[...] //
> *šer$_{2}$-ru e-niq ši-iz-bi ina la[-ba-nu iṣ-bat]*
>
> the man's thigh is seized (by him), the woman's breastbone (?) is seized (by him), the suckling child's neck-tendons are seized (by him).[62]

Usually, humans are affected on the skin of their heads, necks, shoulders, breasts (especially those of women), and thighs.[63] Furthermore, this entity can afflict different animals—cattle, donkey, and sheep:

> gud-e a-ub-<ba> ba-ni-ba udu umbin-si-ba ba-ni-ba anše ĝeštu-ba ba-ni-ba
>
> The bull caught him by <his> horn's edge. The sheep caught him by his hoof. The donkey caught him by his ear.[64]

Additionally, the demon is attested as an occurrence in rivers as well as a plant disease in the ancient Near East. In the case of the latter, Sāmānu can afflict plants either as a fungus (rust) or as a pest. In an incantation, one of the Mesopotamian rivers is afflicted by Sāmānu:

> idigna pu$_{2}$ (LAGAB)-ba ba-ni-ba
>
> The Tigris caught him by his side (?).[65]

As a plant disease—mostly attested in omens—Sāmānu usually afflicts barley:

> DIŠ *i-na qu$_{2}$-tu-un qer-bi* MI.IB.ḪI *⸢sa⸣-mu na-di nu-uḫ-ḫu-ul-lu i-te-eb-ba-am-ma še-a-am sa-ma-nu* DAB-*at*
>
> If a red sign lies in the constrictions of the entrails: *Nuḫḫullu* (= a destructive storm) springs up and Sāmānu affects the barley.[66]

If he is addressed as pest, Sāmānu is able to destroy any field crops:

KA.INIM.MA ⸢BURU$_5$ *mu*⸣*-na* ⸢*a-ki-la mu*⸣*-bat-*⸢*ti-ra ṣa-ṣi-ri*⸣ *sa-ma-*⸢*na*⸣ *kal-mat* A.ŠA$_3$ *ina* ŠA$_3$ A.ŠA$_3$ *šu-li-i*

Incantation to remove locust, caterpillar, "devourer"-pest, *mub-battiru'*-pest, cricket, Sāmānu, (and) the vermin of the field from within the field.[67]

In Mesopotamia, this demonic being acts as a kind of universal evil from whom nobody and nothing is safe.[68] In contrast, Sāmānu/Akhu is limited to humans in Egypt, but there he can occur on and in the entire body, not just the skin:

m pꜣ rd 2 n.ty ḥr šm.t° m tꜣ mn.t(w) 2 n.ty ḥr sḫsḫ° m pꜣ pḥ.wj n.ty ḥr kz.t=f° m {nꜣ}<tꜣ> jꜣ.t pꜣ zꜣy(w) <n.j> ʿ.t° m pꜣy=f rmn 2 m nḥb.t=f m t[ꜣ]y=f ḏr.ty 2° n.ty [...] n=f n.ty m-ʿ=f° m jw-ḏꜣ-mʿy-nꜣ° n.ty m mẖt(.w)=f n.ty mꜣʿ(.w)° [m] gg.t 2° ḥnʿ pꜣ ḥꜣ.ty m wfꜣ(w)=f° ḥnʿ ḏrw.w=f m pꜣy=f [...]° m tꜣy=f sp.t 2 n.ty ḥr md(w){w}.t° m {rš}<šr>.t=f tꜣ ʿbʿb(y) [m tꜣj]j=f jr.tj 2.t n.ty ḥr ptr(j)° m tꜣ ṯ(ꜣ) z.w<t> 7 n.t ḏꜣḏꜣ=f°

in the two lower legs that walk, in the two thighs that run, in the back that bows, in the spine, the beam <of> the body, in his two shoulders, in his neck, in both h[i]s hands that [...] for him, which is with him in the *Jḏmn* (?) which is in his entrails which are in good condition, [in] the two kidneys (?) and in the heart, in his lung and his sides, in his [two ears that hear (?)], in his two lips that speak, in his nose, the bubbling one (?), [in his] both eyes that see, in the seven orifices of his head.[69]

Furthermore, he can have an impact on the cosmic order:

jn-jw jy.n=k r [wjꜣ ...] j[n]-j[w ... wjꜣ] n(.j) ḥḥ° r nḥm s:ḳd m wjꜣ° jn-[j]w [j]y.n=k r ḥr(.t) jtn° r jšf šw.t

Did you come to [the barque ... Did you come ... to the barque] of the Millions to prevent travel in the barque? [Did] you come to keep away [the sun disk], to enlarge (?) the emptiness?[70]

In the Egyptian incantations, it is far more important to enumerate the actions that are undertaken against Sāmānu/Akhu. So it is described that the demon does not act alone but commands an entire gang that has to be expelled, too:

jr nꜣ n.w zmꜣ.yt jn.n=k ḥnʿ<=k> r ʿḥꜣ dd.tw ḥmt ʿšꜣ m ḏꜣḏꜣ.w=sn jr pꜣ stp(.w) n.j r(m)ṯ jn.n=k ḥnʿ=k r ʿḥꜣ ḫꜣʿ=sn nꜣy=sn nꜣkꜣw st wʿrt(.w)

As to the band whom you have brought with you to fight: In their heads, much copper shall be given. As to the choicest of people whom you have brought with you to fight: They abandoned their trulls (?). They have fled.[71]

The most important opponent of Sāmānu/Akhu is the weather god Seth/Baal. He usually defeats him in the Egyptian sources:

pꜣ kh(ꜣ)b(w) n(.j) 4tẖ r pꜣ [ʿḫ.]w/p[ꜣ s-m-n]° pꜣ ḥḏnḏn n(.j) Bʿyr r=k° pꜣ kh(ꜣ)b n(.j) pꜣ ẖꜣ[ẖꜣ.tj] jw=f ḥr jb ḥ(w)<.t> r tꜣ p.t r=k° kꜣ ʿḏn=f tꜣ pḥ.ty pꜣy=f ḫpš 2 ḥr=k° kꜣ dp{.t}=k nꜣ dp(w) pꜣ [...]n-mʿ m ḏr.t=f

The rage of Seth is against [Ak]hu/[Sāmānu]. The uproar of Baal is against you. The rage of the storm while it is thirsting for rain from the sky is against you. It shall exhaust its (bodily) strength [...] (lit. to put an end to), his two arms above you. You shall taste that which the [S]ea has tasted by his hand![72]

Thus the Egyptian attestations focus on the actions against the demon rather than the demon's own actions.

Comparison between the Mesopotamian and Egyptian Sāmānu

The Mesopotamian concept and the Egyptian concept of the disease demon Sāmānu/Akhu diverge considerably (Table 2). In the ancient Near East, the entity's shape was precisely described as was common in Mesopotamian incantations. Other Mesopotamian demons, such as Pazuzu, Lamaštu, and the evil *Utukkū*, were likewise described in their spells, too.[73] In contrast, descriptions of the outward appearance of Egyptian (disease) demons usually did not play a role in the Egyptian texts. The

Mesopotamian Sāmānu was also a kind of dog. He was the dog of the gods, especially the *evil* dog of the healing goddess Gula, and this theme was of major importance in the ancient Near Eastern sources. But in Egyptian incantations, the canine aspect is only mentioned once. Both cultures agree that Sāmānu had a foreign origin and came from uninhabited territories. However, this is to be expected because—as mentioned before—every demon came from such areas.[74] In Mesopotamia, the people and things that are afflicted are of major interest. Therefore, Sāmānu played an *active* part. He was a "universal evil" who could affect a broad range of victims, both animate and inanimate. In Egypt, it was more significant to describe the actions that had to be taken against the demon. So Sāmānu played a *passive* role in the textual sources, although this does not mean that he was any less dangerous. Furthermore, this entity acted alone in Mesopotamia, while in Egypt, he was the commander of an entire group that had to be expelled, too. Additionally, the address used in the incantations differed: Mesopotamian spells tended to use the third person singular with a few exceptions,[75] but Sāmānu was always addressed in the third person singular with no exceptions. However, the Egyptian spells usually used the second person singular[76]—so do the incantations against Sāmānu/Akhu.[77]

In conclusion it can be stated that the disease demon Sāmānu, also known as Akhu in Egyptian, was attested in Mesopotamia and Egypt. Nevertheless, their conception of Sāmānu was completely different. Both cultures tended to utilize specific mechanics particular to their civilizations in exorcising this evil creature.

References

Ahn, Gregor. 2006. "Demon/Demonology." In Kocku von Stuckrad (ed.), *The Brill Dictionary of Religion* 1: *A–D*, 501–502. Leiden: Brill.

Beck, Susanne. 2015a. "Sāmānu. Konzepte der Dämonendarstellung" In Gregor Neunert and Henrike Simon and Alexandra Verbovsek and Kathrin Gabler (eds.), *Text: Wissen—Wirkung—Wahrnehmung, Beiträge des vierten Münchner Arbeitskreises Junge Aegyptologie (MAJA 4), 29.11. bis 1.12.2013*, 89–103. Gottinger Orientforschungen IV.59. Wiesbaden: Harrasowitz Verlag.

——. 2015b. *Sāmānu. Ein vorderasiatischer Dämon in Ägypten*. Ägypten und Altes Testament 83.

Table 2: Comparison between Mesopotamian and Egyptian Sāmānu.

	Mesopotamia	**Egypt**
Shape	lion's mouth, teeth of a dragon's snake, "red appearance," etc.	unspecified
"Dog"	dog of gods, especially the healing goddess Gula	(yes)
Origin	mountains	earth, mound
	"uninhabited territories"	
Actions	Sāmānu's campaigns against everybody/ everything → "active"	campaigns against Sāmānu → "passive"
Address	3rd person singular	2nd person singular masculine

Münster: Ugarit Verlag.
——. 2015c. "Sāmānu as a Human Disease" *Le journal des médicines cunéiformes* 26: 33–46.
Black, Jeremy, and Anthony Green. 2011. *Gods, Demons and Symbols of Ancient Mesopotamia: An Illustrated Dictionary*. Austin: University of Texas Press.
Borger, Rykle. 1987. "Pazuzu." In F. Rochberg-Halton (ed.), *Language, Literature, and History: Philological and Historical Studies Presented to Erica Reiner*, 15–32. American Oriental Series 67. New Haven, London: American Oriental Society.
Borghouts, Joris F. 1971. *The Magical Text of Papyrus Leiden I 348*. Oudheidkundige mededelingen uit het Rijksmuseum van Oudheden te Leiden 51. Leiden: Brill.
Breasted, James H. 1930. *The Edwin Smith Surgical Papyrus: Published in Facsimile and Hieroglyphic Transliteration with Translation and Commentary*, I–II. Chicago: The University of Chicago Press.
Capomacchia, Anna M. G., and Verdame, Lorenzo. 2011. "Some Considerations about Demons in Mesopotamia." *Studi e Materali de Storia delle Religioni* 77(2): 291–297.
Černý Jaroslav, and Alan H. Gardiner. 1957. *Hieratic Ostraca* I. Oxford: University Press.
Edwards, Iorwerth E. S. 1968. "Ḳenḥikhopeshef's Prophylactic Charm." *Journal of Egyptian Archaeology* 54: 155–160.
Erman, Adolf. 1901. *Zaubersprüche für Mutter und Kind aus dem Papyrus Berlin 3027 des Berliner Museums*. Berlin: Verlag der königlichen Akademie der Wissenschaften.
——, and Hermann Grapow (eds.). 1926. *Wörterbuch der Aegyptischen Sprache* I. Berlin: Hinrichs.
Farber, Walter, 2014. *Lamaštu: An Edition of the Canonical Series of Lamaštu Incantations and Rituals and Related Texts from the Second to the First Millennia B.C.* Mesopotamian Civilizations 17. Winona Lake (Indiana): Eisenbrauns.
Fischer, Henry G. 1987. "The Ancient Egyptian Attitude towards the Monstrous." In Ann E. Farkas and Prudence O. Harper and Evelyn B. Harrison (eds.), *Monsters and Demons in the Ancient and Mediaeval Worlds: Papers Presented in Honor of Edith Porada*, 13–26. Mainz: Philipp von Zabern.
Fischer-Elfer, Hans-Werner 2015. *Magika Hieratika in Berlin, Hannover, Heidelberg und München*. Ägyptische und Orientalische Papyri und Handschriften des Ägyptischen Museums und Papyrussammlung Berlin 2. Berlin: de Gruyter.
Geller, Markham J. 2007. *Evil Demons. Canonical* Utukkū lemnūtu *Incantations*. State Archives of Assyria Cuneiform Texts 5. Helsinki: Neo-Assyrian Text Corpus Project.
Grapow, Hermann. 1956. *Kranker, Krankheiten und Arzt*. Grundriss der Medizin der alten Ägypter 3. Berlin: Akademie-Verlag.
Green, Anthony. 1994. "Mischwesen.B." In Dietz O. Edzard (ed.), *Reallexikon der Assyriologie und Vorderasiatischen Archäologie* 8, 246–264. Berlin; New York: de Gruyter.
Haas, Volkert. 1986. *Magie und Mythen in Babylonien. Von Dämonen, Hexen und Beschwörungspriestern*. Merlins Bibliothek der geheimen Wissenschaften und magischen Künste 8. Gifkendorf: Merlin Verlag.
Heeßel, Nils P. 2000a. *Pazuzu. Archäologische und philologische Studien zu einem altorientalischen Dämon*. Ancient Magic and Divination 4. Leiden, Boston, Cologne: Brill, Styx.
——. 2000b. *Babylonisch-assyrische Diagnostik*. Alter Orient und Altes Testament 43. Münster: Ugarit Verlag.
——. 2007. "The Hand of Gods: Disease Names, and Divine Anger." In Ivring L. Finkel and Markham J. Geller (eds.), *Disease in Babylonia*, 120–130. Cuneiform Monographs 36. Groningen; Leiden: Styx.
——. 2011. "Evil Against Evil: The Demon Pazuzu." *Studi e Materali de Storia delle Religioni* 77(2): 357–368.
Hutter, Manfred. 1988. "Dämonen und Zauberzungen. Aspekte der Magie im Alten Vorderasien." *Grenzgebiete der Wissenschaften. Sonderdruck* 37(3): 215–130.
——. 2007. "Demons and Benevolent Spirits in the Ancient Near East." *Deuterocanonical and Cognate Literature Yearbook:* 21–34.
Jacobsen, Thorkild. 1976. *The Treasures of Darkness: A History of Mesopotamian Religion*. New Haven, London: Yale University Press.
Jansen-Winkel, Karl. 1999. "Dämonen: II. Ägypten." In Hubert Cancik (ed.), *Der neue Pauly* 3, 259. Stuttgart; Weimar: Metzler.
Kákosy, László. 1989. *Zauberei im alten Ägypten*. Leipzig: Koehler und Amelang.
Kaper, Olaf E. 2003. *The Egyptian Tutu: A Study of the Sphinx-god and Master of Demons with a Corpus of Monuments*, Orientalia Lovaniensia Analecta 119. Leuven; Paris; Dudley (MA): Peeters.

Kousoulis, Panagiotis. 2011. "Introduction: The Demonic Lore of Ancient Egypt: Questions on Definition." In Panagiotis Kousoulis (ed.), *Ancient Egyptian Demonology: Studies on the Boundaries between the Demonic and the Divine in Egyptian Magic*, IX–XXI. Orientalia Lovaniensia Analecta 175. Leuven; Paris; Walpole (MA): Peeters.

Krebernik, Manfred. 2012. *Götter und Mythen des Alten Orients*. Munich: C. H. Beck.

Kurth, Dieter. 2003. "Suum Cuique. Zum Verhältnis von Dämonen und Göttern im Alten Ägypten." In Armin Lange, Hermann Lichtenberger, and Diethard Römfeld (eds.), *Die Dämonen: die Dämonologie der israelitisch-jüdischen und frühchristlichen Literatur im Kontext ihrer Umwelt = Demons: The Demonology of Israelite-Jewish and Early Christian Literature in Context of Their Environment*, 45–60. Tübingen: Mohr Siebeck.

Leibovici, Marcel. 1971. "Génies et demons en Babylonie." *Sources orientales* 8: 85–112.

Legge, Francis. 1901. "The Names of the Demons in the Magic Papyri." *Proceedings of the Society of Biblical Archaeology* 23: 41–49.

Leitz, Christian. 1994. *Tagewählerei. Da Buch* ḥ3t nḥḥ pḥ.wy ḏt *und verwandte Texte*. Ägyptologische Abhandlungen 55.1–2. Wiesbaden: Harrassowitz Verlag.

——. 2004. "Deities and Demons: Egypt." In Sarah I. Johnston (ed.), *Religions of the Ancient Word: A Guide*, 393–396. Cambridge (MA); London: Harvard University Press.

Liddell, Henry G., Robert Scott, and Henry S. Jones. 1996. *A Greek-English Lexicon*. Oxford—New York: Clarendon Press, Oxford University Press.

Lucarelli, Rita. 2006. "Demons in the Book of the Dead." In Burkhard Backes, Irmtraut Munro, and Simone Stöhr (eds.), *Totenbuch-Forschungen. Gesammelte Beiträge des 2. Internationalen Totenbuchsymposiums*, 203–211. Studien zum altägyptischen Totenbuch 11. Wiesbaden: Harrassowitz Verlag.

——. 2010a. "Demons (Benevolent and Malevolent)." In Jacco Dieleman and Willeke Wendrich (eds.), *UCLA Encyclopedia of Egyptology*, 1–10. Los Angeles. < http://escholarship.org/uc/item/1r72q9vv >, accessed 4 October 2019.

——. 2010b. "The Guardian-Demons of the Book of the Dead." *British Museum Studies in Ancient Egypt and Sudan* 15: 85–102.

——. 2011. "Demonology During the Late Pharaonic and Greco-Roman Period in Egypt." *Journal of Ancient Near Eastern Religions* 11: 109–125.

——. 2013. "Towards a Comparative Approach to Demonology in Antiquity: The Case of Ancient Egypt and Mesopotamia." *Archiv für Religionsgeschichte* 14(1): 11–25.

Maul, Stefan. 1999. "Dämonen: I. Mesopotamien." In Hubert Cancik (ed.), *Der neue Pauly* 3, 258–259. Stuttgart, Weimar: Metzler.

Meeks, Dimitri. 1971. "Génies, anges, demons en Égypte." *Sources orientales* 8: 17–84.

Nunn, Joris F. 1996. *Ancient Egyptian Medicine*. London: British Museum Press.

Pinch, Geraldine. 1994. *Magic in Ancient Egypt*. London: British Museum Press.

Quack, Joachim F. 2015. "Dämonen und andere höhere Wesen in der Magie als Feinde und Helfer." In Andrea Jördens (ed.), *Ägyptische Magie und ihre Umwelt*, 101–118. Philippika. Altertumswissenschaftliche Abhandlungen 80. Wiesbaden: Harrassowitz Verlag.

Rendu Loisel, Anne-Caroline. 2011. "Gods, Demons and Anger in the Akkadian Literature." *Studi e Materali de Storia delle Religioni* 77(2): 323–332.

Riley, Greg J. 1999. "Demon, Δαίμων, Δαιμόνιον." In Karel van der Toorn, Bob Becking, and Pieter W. van der Horst (eds.), *Dictionary of Deities and Demons in the Bible*, 235–236. Leiden—Boston—Cologne: Brill.

Scurlock, JoAnn. 2006. *Magico-medical Means of Treating Ghost-induced Illnesses in Ancient Mesopotamia*. Ancient Magic and Divination 3. Leiden—Boston: Brill, Styx.

Sonik, Karen. 2013. "Mesopotamian Conception of Supernatural: A Taxonomy of *Zwischenwesen*." *Archiv für Religionsgeschichte* 14(1):103–116.

Szpakowska, Kasia. 2001. "Demons in the Dark: Nightmares and Other Nocturnal Enemies in Ancient Egypt." In Panagiotis Kousoulis (ed.), *Ancient Egyptian Demonology: Studies on the Boundaries between the Demonic and the Divine in Egyptian Magic*, 63–76. Orientalia Lovaniensia analecta 175. Leuven: Peeters.

Thompson, Reginald C. 1903. *Devils and Evil Spirits of Babylonia: Being Babylonian and Assyrian Incantations against the Demons, Ghouls, Vampires, Hobgoblins, Ghosts, and Kindred Evil Spirits, which Attack Mankind*. Luzac's Texts and Translation Series 14. New York: Luzac.

Toorn, Karel van der. 2003. "The Theology of Demons

in Mesopotamia and Israel. Popular Belief and Scholarly Speculation." In Armin Lange, Hermann Lichtenberger, and Diethard Römfeld (eds.), *Die Dämonen: die Dümonologie der israelitisch-jüdischen und frühchristlichen Literatur im Kontext ihrer Umwelt = Demons: The Demonology of Israelite-Jewish and Early Christian Literature in Context of Their Environment*, 61–83. Tübingen: Mohr Siebeck.

Velde, Herman te. 1975. "Dämonen." In Wolfgang Helck (ed.), *Lexikon der Ägyptologie* 1, 980–984. Wiesbaden: Harrassowitz Verlag.

Weber, Otto. 1906. *Dämonenbeschwörungen bei den Babyloniern und Assyrern*. Der alter Orient 7/4. Leipzig: Hinrichs.

Westendorf, Wolfgang. 1970. "Beiträge aus den medizinischen Texten III. Incubus-Vorstellungen." *Zeitschrift für ägyptische Sprache und Altertumskunde* 96: 145–151.

——. 1992. *Erwachen der Heilkunst: die Medizin im Alten Ägypten*. Zurich: Artemis & Winkler.

——. 1999. *Handbuch der altägyptischen Medizin*. Handbuch der Orientalistik I.36.1. Leiden, London, Cologne: Brill.

Wiggerman, Frans A. M. 1994. "Mischwesen.A." In Dietz O. Edzard (ed.), *Reallexikon der Assyriologie und Vorderasiatischen Archäologie* 8, 222–246. Berlin, New York: de Gruyter.

——. 2000. "Lamaštu: Daughter of Anu: A Profile" In Marten Stol (ed.), *Birth in Babylonia and the Bible: Its Mediterrean Setting*, 217–249. Cuneiform Monographs 14. Gronigen, Leiden: Styx.

——. 2011. "The Mesopotamian Pandemonium." *Studi e Materali de Storia delle Religioni* 77(2): 298–322.

Zandee, Jan. 1960. *Death as an Enemy According to the Ancient Egyptian Conceptions*. Leiden: Brill.

Yamazaki, Naoko. 2003. *Zaubersprüche für Mutter und Kind. Papyrus Berlin 3027*. Achet, Schriften zur Ägyptologie B2. Berlin: Achet Verlag, 2003.

Notes

1 Liddell et al. 1996, 365–366.

2 Riley 1999. See also Ahn 2006; Kousoulis 2011; Hutter 2007; Lucarelli 2010a; Lucarelli 2013, 14; Heeßel 2000a, 4–6; and Sonik 2013, 109–110.

3 Sonik 2013, 103–115, fig. 1.

4 Sonik 2013, 104.

5 For *Mischwesen* see Wiggerman 1994; Green 1994.

6 Sonik 2013, 110–113.

7 Sonik 2013, 107–114.

8 See Sonik 2013, 115 footnote 37. For Sāmānu see below and Beck 2015a; Beck 2015b.

9 Sonik 2013, 107, 109–110, 112–115. For general information on "demons" see van der Toorn 2003; Maul 1999; Haas 1986, 109–119; Leibovici 1971; and Thompson 1903, XXI–LXV (the reading of some of the Sumerian and Akkadian words are different from today's reading).

10 Wiggerman 2011), 302–311.

11 Wiggerman 2011, 302–311.

12 "Demons" are worshiped neither in Egypt nor in Mesopotamia; see Haas 1986, 155; Maul 1999, 258, Wiggerman 2000, 226; van der Toorn 2003, 75, 77; Wiggerman 2001, 308 for Mesopotamia; for Egypt see Jansen-Winkel 1999; Lucarelli 2010a, 2; Lucarelli 2013, 16. Lucarelli 2010a, 7, states that from the Late Period onward, "demons" start to have private cults in certain places.

13 Black and Green 2011, 63.

14 This is mentioned by Black and Green (2011, 63), too. Most information on "demons" comes from the Sumerian and Akkadian incantations. Compare this to Wiggerman 2011, 309. For Lamaštu and Pazuzu see Wiggerman 2000, 217–249 (Lamaštu); Heeßel 2000a; Borger 1987. See especially Heeßel 2011.

15 Hutter 2007, 21, 23–24, 25–26, 28–32.

16 te Velde 1975, 980. For general information on "demons," see Pinch 1994, 33–46; Kákosy 1989, 66–89; Jansen-Winkel 1999, 259.

17 See Zandee 1960, especially 1–44, 192–226.

18 Lucarelli 2010b, 87–88; Lucarelli 2006, 207; Lucarelli 2011, 110, 115, 119–121; Szpakowska 2001, 75; Leitz 2004, 395. See also the PhD dissertation by Carolina Teotino, *Die apotropäischen Gottheiten des Osiris. Eine Studie zu den Schutzgöttern nach Quellen der Spät- und griechisch-römischen Zeit* (working title, in preparation).

19 Lucarelli 2013, 17, Lucarelli 2010a, 2–5. Compare also her statements in Lucarelli 2006, 203–212. For general information on the *wpw.tjw* and *ḫ3.tjw* and the gods they obey, see, among others,

Kaper 2003, especially 60–63; Leitz 1994, 224–246.

20 Lucarelli 2013, 16–17.

21 See Kurth 2003.

22 Kurth 2003, 45–46.

23 Kurth 2003, 49, 54–55.

24 Kurth 2003, 50–55. But even Kurth admits that there were few beings who had only one reason for their existence and this did not include any elements of a vision of god (Kurth 2003, 53).

25 Kurth 2003, 58. Kurth states that some Egyptian creatures were pure demons whereby others were pure gods–even if this occurred very rarely.

26 Sonik 2013, 110–111. Cf. Lucarelli 2006, 203, who argues against the use of the word *daimones*. See also Kousoulis 2011, XIV, who argues against the use of the word "demon" for any Egyptian entity.

27 For Mesopotamia see Sonik 2013, 104; Capomacchia and Verdame 2011, 293; Heeßel 2000a, 4; Maul 1999, 258; and for Egypt see Lucarelli 2013, 12; Kurth 2003, 54; Jansen-Winkeln 1999, 259; te Velde 1975, 980. Compare also the discussion by Quack 2015, 105–106.

28 Mesopotamia: Sonik 2013, 107, 112–113; Capomacchia and Verdame 2011, 295; Maul 1999, 258; Hutter 2007, 30; Hutter 1988, 220; Haas 1986, 125–127; Leibovici 1971, 88; Weber 1906, 11; Thompson 1903, XXXVI, XXIX–XLI; Egypt: Jansen-Winkeln 1999, 259; Pinch 1994, 35, 41; te Velde 1975, 981.

29 For demonization of the foreign see, e.g., Hutter 2007, 30; Haas 1986, 112–114; Hutter, 1988, 220–221; Lucarelli 2011, 119.

30 R:II7–8, Erman 2003, 16, pl. 3.

31 Tablet VII 69–70: Geller 2007, 138, 222.

32 Tablet VII 98–100: Geller 2007, 139, 223.

33 Mesopotamia: Rendu Loisel 2011, 330; Heeßel 2000b, 78. Cf. Haas 1986, 120–122; Egypt: Beck 2015a, 93, 94 (table 1); Nunn 1996, 104; Westendorf 1992, 29, 33; Kákosy 1989, 118; Legge 1901, 42–43.

34 LAM I 1–7: Farber 2014, 144–145.

35 R:VI4 (spell 13), see Borghouts 1971, 21, pl. VI–VIa, 23.

36 Compare, for example, the incantations against the *Utukkū lemnūtu* (Geller 2007), Pazuzu (Heeßel 2000a) and Lamaštu (Farber 2014, Wiggerman 2000), as well as the explanations in the following text on Sāmānu.

37 LAM II 36–38: Farber 2014, 168–169.

38 Beck 2015a, 93, Lucarelli 2010a, 4, 5.

39 Composite text of O. Leipzig 42 R:1–2 (Černý and Gardiner 1957, pl. III), O. Gardiner 300 R:1 (Černý and Gardiner 1957, pl. XCI), and P. BM EA 10731 V:1 (Edwards 1968, pl. XXIV). For *shꜣḳḳ* in general, see Fischer-Elfer 2015, 230–248.

40 R:I9–10: Erman 1901, 12; Yamazaki 2003, 14, pl. II. The spell begins with *k.t* "another," but it is rather unlikely that it was directed against *tmy.t* as the former spell because the disease demon is addressed as male and not as female.

41 Wiggerman 2011, 299; Hutter 2007, 25–26; van der Toorn 2003, 77–78; Wiggerman 2000, 232; Maul 1999, 258.

42 For hybrid creatures and their perception in general, see Fischer 1987, especially 13–21, 26, pls. I–VI.

43 Mesopotamia: Hutter 2007, 28; Hutter 1988, 221; Haas 1986, 118; Leibovici 1971, 87, 97. Some of the Mesopotamian demons, such as Lamaštu or Sāmānu, only seized their victims. Egypt: Lucarelli 2010a, 3; Westendorf 1992, 28; Westendorf 1970, 145; Grapow 1956, 32.

44 V:XVII11–12, See Breasted 1930, I, 502, II, pls. XVIII–XVIIIa. For other examples, see Westendorf 1999, 373–374.

45 Tablet V 76–78 : Geller 2007, 121, 210.

46 Mesopotamia: Sonik 2013, 109–110; Wiggerman 2011, 310–311 ; Hutter 2007, 21, 31 ; van der Toorn 2003, 72–73; Egypt: Meeks 1971, 21; Grapow 1956, 27, 33.

47 Heeßel 2007; Scurlock 2006, 73; Jacobsen 1976, 147–164.

48 For a general overview of the Mesopotamian Sāmānu, see Beck 2015b, 171–174, for the attestations, Beck 2015b, 3–91, in each case with further references.

49 See Beck 2015b, 174–176, for general information and Beck 2015b, 93–169, for the sources in Egypt (with further references). The most recent attestation dates to the Ptolemaic Period.

50 AO 11276 R:1–5: see Beck 2015b, 10–14 (with further references).

51 Beck 2015b, 172.

52 HS 1555 + 1587 R:1–2, see Beck 2015b, 6–10 (with further references). For the god Enlil see, e.g., Black and Green 2011, 76 ("Enlil"); see also Krebernik 2012, 76, who convincingly speaks against the interpretation of Enlil as a kind of storm god.

53 Beck 2015b, 176–179.

54 AO 11276 R:6–9: see Beck 2015b, 10–14 (with further references). See also cuneiform tablet HS 1555 + 1587 R:3–4 (Beck 2015b, 6–10), VAT 6819 R:1–7 (Beck 2015b, 18–19), S.U. 51/128 + 129 + 233 (= STT 178) and duplicates (R:2–7; Beck 2015b, 22–31). For the gods, see, among others, the particular keyword in Black and Green 2011.

55 Erman and Grapow 1926, 223.13–20, 224.13.

56 See Beck 2015b, 174, 246.

57 P. Leiden I 343 + 345 V:IV9 (incantation 12 line 1–2), see Beck 2015b, 155–158 (with further references). It could be that this topic is missing due to the partially fragmentary condition of the manuscript.

58 6 NT 145 R:I1–7 (e_4 = e_{11}.d): see Beck 2015b, 3–6; compare also S.U. 51/128 + 129 + 233 (=STT 178) and duplicates (R:8–9; Beck 2015b, 22–31) with a similar statement.

59 P. Leiden I 343 + 345 R:III7–8/V:VI2–3 (incantation 3 line 7): see Beck 2015b, 111–119 (with further references).

60 According to Sonik's taxonomy, *daimons* were usually restricted to the human sphere but she mentions Sāmānu as an exception to this "rule," see above. For Sāmānu as dangerous to gods, see Beck 2015b, 181–182.

61 A 7885 R:5–8: see Beck 2015b, 15–17 (with further references). Compare also HS 1555 + 1587 R:5–8 (Beck 2015b, 6–10).

62 S.U. 51/128 + 129 + 233 and duplicates (Beck 2015b, 22–31). Similar statements are given in 6 NT 145 R:I8–I9 (Beck 2015b, 3–6), HS 1555 + 1587 R:10–12, V:13 (Beck 2015b, 6–10), AO 11276 R:11–15 (Beck 2015b, 10–14).

63 For an analysis of Sāmānu as a disease of humankind from a current day perspective, see Beck 2015b, 182–193, and Beck 2015c.

64 HS 1555 + 1587 V:14–16 (ba = b-a_5 (AK)): see Beck 2015b, 6–10 (with further references). For a discussion of Sāmānu as a disease of sheep, cattle and donkey, see Beck 2015b, 193–199.

65 HS 1555 + 1587 V:17: see Beck 2015b, 6–10 (with further references). See also Beck 2015b, 207–208.

66 AO 7539 V:72′: see Beck 2015b, 72 (with further references). Compare BM 22696 V:22′–23′ (Beck 2015b, 72), K 2162+ R:19 (Beck 2015b, 74–75), K 229 R:18′ + (Beck 2015b, 73–74), BM 46229 V:32–33 (Beck 2015b, 76), Farmer's instructions line 71 (Beck 2015b, 70–71). For an analysis of Sāmānu as a plant disease, see Beck 2015b, 199–203.

67 S.U. 52/214 V:1–2: see Beck 2015b, 77–78 (with further references). Compare also BM 45686 R:II29–31 (Beck 2015b, 81–82), tablet 81-2-4,319 R:6′–7′ (Beck 2015b, 80), BM 123370 II6′ (Beck 2015b, 80–81). For a discussion of the demon as pest, see Beck 2015b, 204–207.

68 Beck 2015b, 174, 241–242.

69 P. Leiden I 343 + 345 R:VII11–VIII4, O. Strasbourg H 115 R:5–11 (incantation 5 line 22–29), see Beck 2015b, 126–140 (with further references).

70 P. Leiden I 343 + 345 V:IX9–10 (incantation 13 line 9–11), see Beck 2015b, 158–160 (with further references).

71 P. Leiden I 343 + 345 R: II4–6/V:III10–IV:2 (incantation 2 line 12–14), see Beck 2015b, 103–111 (with further references).

72 P. Leiden I 343 + 345 R:IV9–13/V:VII5–7 (incantation 4 line 1–5), see Beck 2015b, 119–126 (with further references).

73 For these demons, see note 36, as well as above in the text.

74 See table 1.

75 For example, LAM II 137: *sūtâku* "I (= Lamaštu) am a Sutean woman!" (Farber 2014, 176–177).

76 The first person singular is also used, usually by

the conjuror (e.g.: "It is not I saying this. It is the deity X saying this.").

77 For this comparison see also Beck 2015a and Beck 2015b, 237–249.

Journal of Ancient Egyptian Interconnections

The Anatomy of a Coffin Text Demon

Zuzanna Bennett
Swansea University

Abstract
At first glance, the vastly varying forms of the more than 400 different demonic entities described and illustrated in the Middle Kingdom Coffin Texts appear strange and "monstrous," but a more detailed analysis demonstrates that their appearances have greater symbolic and practical use than previously believed. The most frequent forms of these demons are figuratively dissected here, and each component is examined to identify which animal species are utilised. The anatomy of demons can also be linked to their other attributes, assisting, enabling, or inspiring them to perform particular functions or behaviours. The variety and complexity of the physical appearances of Coffin Text demons not only demonstrate their importance as manifestations of ancient Egyptian hopes and fears but could also be key to understanding the functions of funerary demons.

Introduction

The Middle Kingdom Coffin Texts make reference to over 400 different demonic individuals and collectives. Together, these entities have the primary role of maintaining the *mꜣʿt* (order) in the afterlife, which they achieve by forming a complex defence system for this realm and its inhabitants.[1] Any being attempting to access the afterlife, such as the newly deceased ancient Egyptian, must overcome a series of challenges presented by these demonic obstacles. The correct password-like spell should be announced to the right gatekeeper, knowledge of the afterlife must be demonstrated, and labyrinthine pathways must be navigated. Failure to pass any single part of this test has dire consequences, resulting in absolute bodily and spiritual destruction.

Coffin Text demons are vividly described and sometimes intricately illustrated, but the meaning of their appearances remains largely elusive and uncertain. The artistic customs and use of symbolism and metaphor in ancient Egyptian art are still being deciphered in modern scholarship. Evans has previously demonstrated that two-dimensional representations of ancient Egyptian animals are actually encoded with symbolic meaning that is closely linked with particular behaviours and characteristics, as well as representing physical attributes.[2] Perhaps, then, by understanding the appearances of the somewhat similar demonic entities that to the Egyptians were tangible and animate, scholars may gain a clearer insight into their behaviours and other dynamic attributes. Coffin Text demons, specifically, are an excellent source for such an analysis because of the wealth of background information on these beings: appearance is both described and depicted. This information is enhanced and explained by text detailing their context and other attributes. This contrasts with other sources on demons, which have a narrower range of evidence provided: for example, the parades of entities on ivory wands only exist in pictographic form with little textual evidence to describe their individual and collective natures and roles.[3]

Through the examination of structural characteristics, the identity of Coffin Text beings can be further discerned. Although discussions of demon appearances typically focus on the strange and "monstrous,"[4] Coffin Text evidence demonstrates that morphology can be far wider ranging and has greater symbolic and practical use than previously believed. Significance is encountered in minor details such as their pose or the objects that they hold as equally as in anomalous hybrid anatomy. This paper focuses on a single appearance variable: anatomy.

The term "anatomy" is used to describe the details of entity morphology in this paper. Here, the most frequent forms of Coffin Text demons are figuratively dissected and each component is examined to identify which animal species are utilised and why. The data used derives from 110 coffins dated to around the Middle Kingdom, all of which were used by de Buck in his transcriptions of the Coffin Text spells.[5] Both textual and pictorial data is examined, combining evidence from appellations, descriptions, and visual representations. Ancient Egyptian depictions of demonic entities are rare, and evidence from this source is no different.[6] Only four of the 110 coffins contain demon depictions: coffin B5C, B1C, B1P, and G1T.

Demon Anatomy Types

At least 18 different types of anatomy are present in the data. The graph in Figure 1 shows that serpentine, reversed, and humanoid anatomy types are mentioned most frequently. Half of the remaining anatomy types are commonly occurring, whilst the other half are indicated infrequently (fewer than ten times).

Serpentine

Serpentine anatomy is the most common in the dataset, which is unsurprising given the popularity of similarly shaped beings on ancient Egyptian artefacts and texts, both religious and literary.[7] Most of these are entirely serpentine, but there are also a wide variety of snake-hybrid forms. Serpent anatomy can be the head and upper torso component with the head of another animal in place of a tail. Alternatively, demons can have serpentine lower torsos joined with human upper torsos, or ram, hare, or scarab heads (Fig. 2).

The use of serpentine anatomy here may assist guarding and attacking demons in the performance of their functions, or even inspire the fiery associations of individuals such as the giant snake

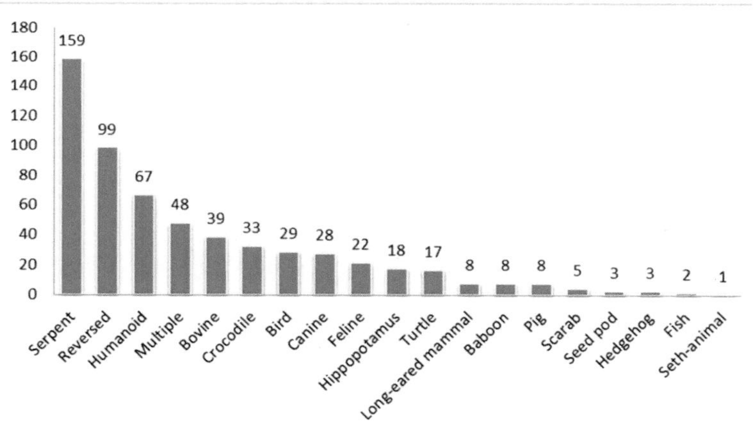

Figure 1: Graph showing the frequency of each anatomy type in Coffin Text demons in each occasion that anatomy is specified. Texts from each coffin are considered separately to account for individual variations that may reflect subtle differences in personal or local beliefs.

Figure 2: Two examples of hybrid demons with serpentine torsos from CT 1071 in the Book of Two Ways on the bottom of coffin B1C (sketch by author). The scarab hybrids shown here are two entities from a collective of nine, all depicted with the same anatomy.

"He who is in his burning" (*jmy whm.f*). The venomous bites of the reptiles were evidently greatly feared by ancient Egyptians, since several daily life spells are designed to protect against them and treat unfortunate attacks.[8] The venom's effects were likened to fiery burning to the degree that in the Book of Caverns a cauldron is heated by the venom of spitting cobras.[9] The dangerous bite and powerful venom of the snake is elsewhere harnessed as a symbol of protection; for example, uraei adorn the brows of royalty and deities, as well as being depicted on temple walls. Whereas these uraei were normally avatars of female goddesses,[10] the Coffin Text serpents either have an unspecified gender (in 67 occasions) or are textually described using masculine noun and pronoun forms (91 times).[11]

Figure 3: Image of "Protector of the god," who is "Keeper" of a bend in the land path in the Book of Two Ways, from the bottom of coffin B1C (sketch by author).

Reversed Anatomy

Faces may appear backward to facilitate a demon's function. The ferrymen "He who sees backwards" (*mꜣ ḥꜣ.f*) and "He whose face is behind him" (*ḥr.f ḥꜣ.f*) have their faces reversed either permanently or momentarily so that they can navigate their course, as the rower must sit with their back to the direction of travel.[12] Similarly, a guardian along the Book of Two Ways paths is depicted with his head turned towards his back (Fig. 3). This may be a representation of the demon's vigilance and multi-directional guarding function, since he is situated within a bend of the land path. His appearance enables him both to be watchful for approaching entities and to maintain vigilance on those that continue along the path behind him.

Other manifestations of reversed anatomy are being upside down and having body parts exchange their normal places, emphasising their distance from normality.[13] For example, the "Seven spirits" of CT 205 are not only said to walk upside down but also have reversed digestion in that they consume faeces and urine. Conversely, just the tongue and phallus of "Archer of Shu" (CT 698) have exchanged places so that his tongue is in his crotch and his phallus is in his mouth.

Humanoid

Humanoid anatomy most frequently occurs as the torso component combined with the head or face of an animal. This homosomatic form is also frequently used in depictions of deities and personifications, where it is used as an attempt to render their supernatural nature, characteristics, and attributes.[14] It is likely that similar techniques were used to express demonic behaviours in a visual manner. However, humanoid anatomy can also have a practical purpose. For example, the use of human mouths, lips, and tongues may indicate the type of vocal behaviours attributed to "Sad-voiced one" (CT 1038) and "Loud-voiced one" (CT 653): speaking and shouting are denoted, rather than animal-like growls, barks, or hissing. In other examples, fingers and arms (as opposed to animal paws or claws) enable slaughterers, knife-wielders, and fishers to manipulate their equipment and perform their functions. In particular, the use of nets and traps is a human method of fishing, whereas animals and birds do not require such equipment, instead utilising their natural forms (claws and beaks).

Multiple Forms

The use of multiple anatomical components (more parts of the body than would naturally appear) could be indicative of hybridity in demons or it could suggest a repetition of features. Multiplicity can be specified by number or indicated through the adjectives *ꜥšꜣ* "many," *wḥm* "repeating," *jdn* "imitation," *ḫpr* "changing" and *šbn* "various."

Demons with "changing," "imitation," or "various" anatomies may use these forms to disguise their identities, making it more difficult for the deceased to overcome them. In fact, seven of eighteen demons with this form are from the same panel of tribunal judges described in CT 627. Such versatile and indiscernible physical appearance is reminiscent of the forms of deities, whose nature may be encapsulated by more than one manifestation.[15]

The use of multiple heads or faces is particularly associated with the guardians stationed in particular segments of the Book of Two Ways landscape, such as "One whose two faces are in dung (?)" *ḥrwy m ꜣrwt* (CT 1066) and "Many-faced one" *ꜥšꜣ ḥr.w* (CT 1077). Their forms may assist their guarding function through heightening their awareness and allowing them to better detect approaching beings. The number of faces does not appear to be connected to a particular attribute, perhaps indicating that the important factors are simply the presence of multiple faces and the emphasis on vigilance. Elsewhere, different parts of the body can be similarly multiplied in order to emphasise their associated qualities. Thus, the form of "He who has two phalli" *ḥnnwy.f* (CT 627) accentuates his masculinity. Equally, "Many-mouthed snake" *ꜥšꜣ rꜣ ḏꜣḏt* (CT 1077) has a form that is made even deadlier than that of other serpentine demons through increasing his ability to bite and inject venom.

Bovine

The majority of bovine demons have homogenous forms, but there are also some bovine-headed beings that have humanoid, crocodile, and seed-pod torsos. This anatomy is generally used for demons that employ a powerful opposing force. Individuals such as "He who drives off those who would demolish" *ḫsf ḫmw* (CT 1037) specifically have appellations that indicate a repelling function that is described using the term *ḫsf*. Perhaps these entities *ḫsf* "drive off, oppose" enemies through the use of a bovine charge, with head and horns down, thus using their anatomy in a practical manner.[16]

Crocodiles

Crocodiles are connected with rapacious aggression, which is no doubt why these forms are used for demons with thieving behaviour, assisting them in the snatching of magic.[17] However, several of the "Keepers" along the Book of Two Ways paths are depicted with crocodilian torsos.[18] Here, the traits that are being highlighted are more likely to be the stealthy watchfulness, and hiddenness of the animal, characteristics that are certainly fitting for such guardians.

Avian

It is the species of the bird (rather than belonging to the general bird class) that is connected to particular demonic attributes.

Goose-like anatomy occurs only in the form of "One who lives beside the Fledgling Lake" (CT 1045). His ability to successfully patrol both land and water is enhanced by his avian anatomy, since geese are both able to fly and are found close to water. Additionally, his avian form may be connected to the name of the lake he guards ("Fledgling Lake" *ṯꜣ š*).

Falcon anatomy is conversely associated with thieving and vigilant behaviour in demons. For example, the "Falcons" (*bjkw*) of CT 75 use the talons of a raptor to snatch the souls of unsuspecting intruders. Another reason for the choice of avian species may be to create a parallel to the deity Horus: "Falcons" are listed alongside "Pigs" (*šꜣw*), "Earth-gods" (*ꜣkrw*), and "magic" (*ḥkꜣ*) as entities that attempt to attack the deceased. Since falcons and pigs are animals that are associated with the deities Horus and Seth respectively, the use of both animal species for the forms of the demonic animals alludes to a similar divine pairing.[19]

Avian anatomy may also inspire perceivably reversed digestion or unpleasant behaviour. For example, spells CT 667 and 688 state of "Vulture" *gbgꜣ* that "his dues are faeces." This could be a reflection of the bird's eating habits, since they scavenge the rotting carcases of animals that have already died. Similarly, "One who lives on maggots (*fnṯw*)" (CT 1109) is depicted with an avian torso.[20] This demon's diet could have been seen as a reversal of normal behaviour from the perspective of a human, but the consumption of maggots and similarly shaped insects is natural behaviour among some species of birds. Thus, the appellation is here an indicator of avian form rather than abnormal behaviour.

Canine

The dog, jackal, or fox components in demon anatomy can vary from the whole form to just the head. Almost half of these individuals have textually described guarding functions, and the rest are specifically stationed within particular sections of the landscape (such as along pathways or within mapped segments of the Book of Two Ways). Canine anatomy may be used as an expression of this guarding function, likening them to similarly functioning jackal divinities such as Anubis and Wepwawet. This has the secondary result of emphasising an association to the realm of the dead. Fennec anatomy in particular may have a practical purpose as well: the alert senses of "Sharp of vision" (CT 1057 and 1168) are enhanced by the nocturnal vision attributed to the animals.[21]

Feline

Feline anatomy occurs fairly equally in homogenous forms as it does in multianimal and homosomatic hybrids. Corporeal fusions include feline-headed beings with human, bird, or seed-pod torsos, and feline torsos are only found with sphinx-like human-headed beings. Felines generally represent a dual nature; cats symbolise a placid character and lions represent the aggressive and destructive nature.[22] This resonates with the protective-aggressive role of demons, particularly since both cat and lion anatomy is used here.

Hippopotamus

The majority of demons with this anatomy have hippopotamus-like faces, but three individuals are depicted as Taweret-like multi-animal hybrids, two with snakes as dorsal appendages.[23] Here is another example where anatomy inspires particular noises, since "Hippopotamus-face" (CT 1062 and 1170) has the raging bellow of this animal.

Turtle

Turtle-shaped individuals can have homogenous forms or be textually described as turtle-faced. Perhaps the animal's ability to retract and cover its head, as well as submerge into murky waters, is the reason for its use in demon anatomy. These qualities are particularly highlighted for one of the two entities under the name "The two whose faces are covered" (CT 1155).[24]

Long-eared Mammals

Demons can be depicted with similarly shaped heads and ears of some length. They share no additional common attributes. It is difficult to interpret their exact species as they are often simplistically drawn, perhaps depicting hares, gazelles (or other ungulates), fennecs, Seth-animals, or donkeys. Ear and muzzle shape even varies slightly within apparently same-species collectives (see Figure 4).

Baboon

Baboon anatomy is likely used to convey the type of aggressive behaviour attributed, as suggested by the pose of such demons when depicted.[25] One demon with such anatomy is stationed along the Book of Two Ways map and is depicted clearly as a male, standing upright in an active pose with knife in hand.

Scarab

The scarab, usually associated with regeneration, is only found as the head component of snake or humanoid torsos. Thus, the scarab-headed form of "One who spits out the Nile" (CT 1076) enhances

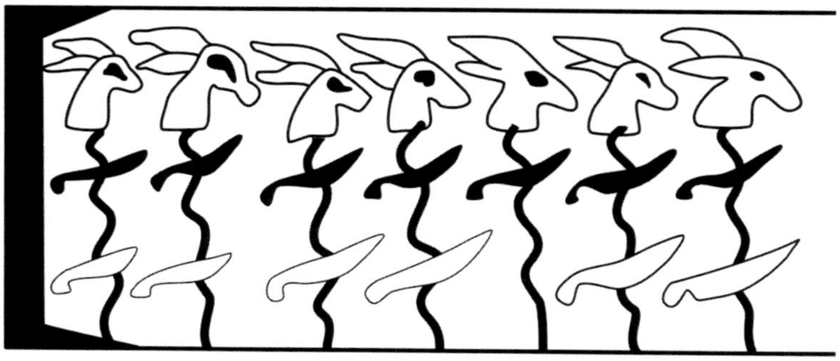

Figure 4: A collective of demons with snake torsos and the heads of long-eared mammals, from the vignette of CT 1181 on coffin B5C (sketch by author).

and reflects his regenerative connection with the life-giving water and fertile Nile floods.

Seed Pod

Three entities are depicted with upper torsos outlined in undulating lines that taper to a curved point at the bottom. These most likely represent a seed pod (such as a carob or moringa pod) rather than an insect cocoon, as shown in Figure 5.[26] The dots along the entities' torsos could represent the seeds within, inspiring connotations of regeneration and fertility.

Others

Other less frequently occurring species may still have significance in their forms, although conclusions are more difficult to draw from such limited use. For example, hedgehog representations are elsewhere used to avert dangers, so a similar function may be alluded to in the forms of three entities depicted on coffin B5C.[27] Equally, the only two individuals with fish anatomy ("*Abaa*-fish" *ʿbꜣꜣ* and "*Saiu*-fish" *sꜣjw*) both sit on the same tribunal panel in CT 627, perhaps linking this form to their function or context.

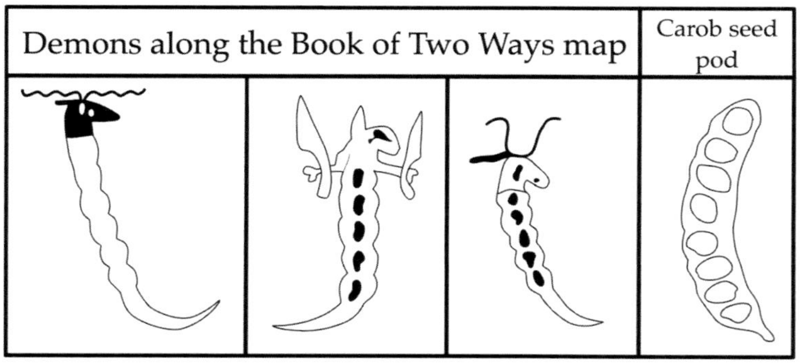

Figure 5: Images of demons depicted on the bottom of coffin B1C (sketch by author). Compare the shape of their torsos with the shape of a carob seed pod (right).

Demon Anatomy in Other Sources

Although a comprehensive study of demonic forms is yet to be undertaken, scholars occasionally summarise the most common zoomorphic appearances. For example, Lucarelli summarises demon anatomy as consisting of "reptiles (especially snakes), felines, and canids; other mammals (donkeys, baboons, hippos, goats, bulls), insects, scorpions, and birds (falcons, vultures)."[28] A large proportion of these species are encountered in the Coffin Texts dataset, but goat and scorpion forms are absent; either these two forms are limited to later time periods or these appearances are not as statistically common as previously estimated. Table 1 shows a comparison of Coffin Text demon anatomies with those on contemporary sources (ivory wands and a faience cup) and later objects of daily life (headrests).[29] Entities from the Coffin Texts have a wider range of anatomy than those of the other sources, emphasising how the afterlife defenders are more greatly distinguished from one another. This is the opposite of headrests, where a select few entity types perform the role of protecting the sleeper. Conversely, the entities on ivory wands and the faience cup may have a more fluid identity (particularly since they are never individually named). These differences may be influenced by the fact that the deceased human must correctly identify Coffin Text beings in the journey to the afterlife, whereas entities from sources such as wands have already been harnessed by a magical practitioner.

The presence or absence of particular anatomy in entities on each source material could be caused by the purpose of the object that they decorate. For example, Bes-type and frog morphology are absent from coffins but are present on apotropaic items. The direction of the face could also be linked with the function and context of entities. Similar reversed faces can be encountered in the Book of the Dead as in the Coffin Texts, but they are absent from ivory wands and headrests, suggesting that this type of vigilance is reserved for funerary demons.[30] At the same time, frontally facing demons are absent from coffins, but appear in the Book of the Dead, ivory wands, headrests, and cup.[31] This position is identified by Volokhine as indicative of increased watchfulness in guardians and movement in Bes-images, perhaps indicating that Coffin Text demons have a slightly different type of awareness and vigilant behaviour compared to other beings.[32] Thus, anatomy can be used to distinguish demons associated with apotropaic objects, which are used to create a shield-like barrier to protect a vulnerable person, from demons that act as a filtration system to defend a sacred space and its inhabitants.

Conclusion

Anatomy can have a practical use, wherein it can physically assist and enable demonic beings to perform their defensive role. Entities performing destructive actions are able to hold and manipulate weapons and equipment in humanoid hands, whereas sharp claws, talons, and teeth are better for seizing and maiming intruders. Attacking power can be increased by multiplying the number of mouths with which to bite. Vigilance and awareness (for guarding and ferrying) can be amplified using the anatomy of both diurnal and nocturnal species. Additionally, the direction (reversed anatomy), scope of vision (long distance, such as falcons), or ability (multiple anatomy) of awareness can be improved.

However, it is also clear that the forms of supernatural entities can be visual manifestations of intangible attributes such as behaviour. This demonstrates that demons may have been perceived in a similar manner to deities, whose forms (and true names) were mysterious and unknown to the ancient Egyptians.[33] This is particularly highlighted by demons with homosomatic forms or multiple anatomies that suggest a changeable nature. It is unclear whether particular behaviours are manifested visually, or whether appearance inspires particular behaviours. Impurity and chaotic behaviour can manifest through the reversion of demon anatomy, or can be normalised (birds consuming maggots). The type of noises created could be influenced by anatomy, with humanoid vocal chords creating shouts or words and hippopotami creating aggressive bellows. Different types of aggression are expressed through the associated animal species. The aggression of a baboon (accompanied by loud cries and the baring of teeth) is distinct from that of a bovine (charging towards enemies with head and horns down). Varying types of specific characteristics can be attributed to the demons based on the animals selected, such as stealth (crocodiles and turtles), rapaciousness (falcons, pigs and crocodiles), and dual qualities of protective nurturing (felines, hippopotami, and cows). Thus, the exact species used in demon anatomy can indicate a particular behavioural trait with specific nuances.

TABLE 1: Table showing a comparison of demon anatomy from four types of sources. Where examples occur less frequently, an object is specifically referenced.

ANATOMY	CTs	IVORY WANDS	FAIENCE CUP (MMA 44.4.4)	HEADRESTS
Snakes	Yes	Yes	Yes	Yes (Petrie Museum UC16065)
Turtles	Yes	Yes (MFA 20.1780)	Yes	No
Crocodiles	Yes	Yes	Yes (on hippo)	Yes (Hiedelberg, Seminar für Ägyptologie 209)
Felines	Yes	Yes	Yes	No
Canines	Yes	Yes	No	Yes (Louvre E 3443)
Baboons	Yes	Yes	No	No
Hippopotami	Yes	Yes	Yes	Yes (Egyptian Museum JE 6269)
Goats	No	No	No	No
Bulls	Yes	Yes (British Museum EA 24426)	No	No
Other Bovines	Yes	Yes (Egyptian Museum CG 9434)	No	No
Insects	Yes	Yes (scarab: British Museum EA 18175)	No	No
Scorpions	No	No	No	No
Falcons	Yes	Yes (MMA 32.8.3)	No	No
Vulture	Yes	Yes	No	No
Goose	Yes	No	No	No
Long-eared Mammal	Yes	Yes (MMA 22.7.1288)	No	No
Hedgehog	Yes	No	No	No
Fish	Yes	No	No	No
Pig	Yes	No	No	No
Seed Pod	Yes	No	No	No
Reversed	Yes	No	No	No
Multiple	Yes	Yes (British Museum EA 24426)	No	No
Bes-like	No	Yes	Yes	Yes
Frog	No	Yes (MFA 03.1703)	No	No
Seth-animal	Yes	Yes (Musée royaux de Bruxelles E 2673)	No	No

This suggests that the structural characteristics of demons are not primarily intended to assist the deceased in the visual identification of these beings. Instead, the depictions and descriptions may have assisted the deceased in determining the behaviours or functions most central to their characters, thus facilitating identification through other means. This theory is further supported by the fact that 61% of demons in the Coffin Texts have no part of their anatomy described or depicted on any of the coffins in the dataset (although they may have another appearance variable detailed, such as their gender or pose). Even in cases where anatomy is described, the demons may still be difficult to visually identify, particularly in cases where forms are concealed (multiple or turtle anatomy).

Additional evidence to substantiate this is found when comparing textual and pictorial data. Of the 168 demons that have at least one part of their anatomy detailed, only 12 have this variable both depicted and described (combining data from all coffins). The data correlates for only three of these individuals. In the remainder, the demon's size can be described differently, the number of faces can differ and the animal species mentioned do not correlate. For example, the appellations of "Hippopotamus-face, bellowing of strength" (CT 1062 and 1170) suggest the form and vocalisation of a hippopotamus,[34] but he is depicted as bovine-headed on coffin B1C. Both animals can have connotations of strength, nurturing and fertility, so their use together emphasises these qualities.[35] Similarly, "Great-face, one whose shape is big" is not only depicted using the anatomy of a naturally small animal (fennec on coffin B1C), but the depiction could even be proportionally smaller than those of other demons on the coffin.[36] However, a variation of spell CT 1064 instead names *ṯsm ḥr* "Dog-face." This suggests that there is a canine nature to the path-guardian in this particular location that is expressed textually on some coffins and visually on others.

Evidently, there are some clear distinctions and general trends of specific species being used in the anatomy of demons with particular behaviours and functions. Since the appearance of these entities is meaningful rather than arbitrary, it can be used to elucidate their role in these funerary texts. These findings also have a wider application. Coffin Text demons may be key to interpreting images of other supernatural entities that are encoded with visual metaphor and symbolism but have no corresponding textual descriptions, such as those carved into headrests and ivory wands. The anatomy used for each individual on such objects could identify how each unnamed entity behaves and how these different characteristics interlink to perform their collective roles of protecting a vulnerable sleeper or mother and infant. Furthermore, since particular qualities of animals are used to highlight specific demonic behaviours, these attributes may be used to enhance our knowledge of how ancient Egyptians perceived the animals in their world.

Overall, a wide variety of identifiable species are used to depict and describe the morphology of Coffin Text demons. The distinctiveness of each individual suggests that a great level of imagination was used to create and manifest these entities. This demonstrates that there was a great deal of human time involved in the discussion and detailing of demonic appearances, functions, and behaviours. However, these attributes are not just idiosyncratic, inconsequential aspects designed to frighten and intrigue uninitiated ancient Egyptians. Instead, they are a vital factor in the defensive role performed by each being. Anatomy can inspire and enable the functions and behaviours that they use to perform their role of maintaining *mꜣꜥt* in the afterlife. The combination of these distinct characteristics creates a complex and effective demon network that is designed to act as an essential filtration system for the afterlife, ensuring that only those beings judged favourably are allowed to exist in this realm. In this way, demons are not simply dangerous obstacles to overcome, but form a continued trial and varied assessment of any being undergoing the journey to the afterlife.

References

Altenmüller, Hartwig. 2012. "Die Schildkröte in Ritual und Magie des alten ägypten." *Studien zu den Ritualszenen altägyptischer Tempel* 12 (= *Festschrift für Horst Beinlich*): 15–30.

Baum, N. 1998. *Arbres et arbustes de l'Egypte ancienne: la liste de la tombe thébaine d'Ineni.* Leuven: Peeters.

Bennett, Zuzanna. 2016. *An Interpretive Analysis of the Role of the Demons in the Ancient Egyptian Coffin Texts.* PhD dissertation, Swansea University.

Borghouts, Joris F. 1978. *Ancient Egyptian Magical*

Texts. Leiden: E. J. Brill.

Bresciani, Edda 2005. "Sobek, Lord of the Land of the Lake." In Salima Ikram (ed.), *Divine Creatures: Animal Mummies in Ancient Egypt*, 199–206. Cairo: American University in Cairo Press.

de Buck, Adriaan. 1935–1961. *The Egyptian Coffin Texts*. Chicago: University of Chicago Press.

Depuydt, Leo. 1992. "Der Fall des 'Hintersichschauers.'" *Göttinger Miszellen* 126: 33–38.

Evans, Linda. 2008. *Animal Behaviour in Egyptian Art: Representations of the Natural World in Memphite Tomb Scenes*. Oxford: Oxbow.

Favard-Meeks, Christine. 1992. "Face et profil dans l'iconographie égyptienne." *Orientalia Lovaniensia Periodica* 23: 15–36.

Fischer, Henry G. 1968. *Ancient Egyptian Representations of Turtles*. New York: Metropolitan Museum of Art.

——. 1987. "The Ancient Egyptian Attitude Towards the Monstrous." In Ann Farkas, Prudence Harper, and Evelyn Harrison (ed.), *Monsters and Demons in the Ancient and Medieval Worlds: Papers Presented in Honor of Edith Porada*, 13–26. Mainz: Philipp von Zabern, 1987.

Frandsen, Paul J. 2011. "Faeces of the Creator or the Temptations of the Dead." In Panagiotis Kousoulis (ed.), *Ancient Egyptian Demonology: Studies on the Boundaries between the Demonic and the Divine in Egyptian Magic*, 25–62. Leuven: Peeters.

Guilhou, Nadine. 1999. "Génies funéraires, croquemitaines ou anges gardiens? Étude sur les fouets, balais, palmes et épis en guise de couteaux." In Sydney Aufrère (ed.), *Encyclopédie religieuse de l'univers vegetal*, 365–417. Montpellier: Presses Universitaires de la Méditerranée PULM.

Hornung, Erik. 1968. *Altägyptische Höllenvorstellungen*. Berlin: Akademie-Verlag.

——. 1996. *Conceptions of God in Ancient Egypt: The One and the Many*. Trans. by John Baines. Ithaca: Cornell University Press.

——. 2000. "Komposite Gottheiten in der ägyptischen Ikonographie." In Christoph Uehlinger (ed.), *Images as Media: Sources for the Cultural History of the Near East and the Eastern Mediterranean: 1st Millennium BCE*. Göttingen: Vandenhoeck and Ruprecht.

Johnson, Sally. 1990. *The Cobra Goddess of Ancient Egypt: Predynastic, Early Dynastic, and Old Kingdom Periods*. London: Kegan Paul International.

Leitz, Christian . 1996. "Die Schlangensprüche in den Pyramidentexten." *Orientalia* 65 (1996): 381–427.

—— (ed.). 2002. *Lexikon der ägyptischen Götter und Götterbezeichnungen*, vol. 5. Leuven: Peeters.

Lichtheim, Miriam. 2006. *Ancient Egyptian Literature, Vol. 1: The Old and Middle Kingdoms*. Berkeley: University of California Press.

Lucarelli, Rita. 2010. "Demons (Benevolent and Malevolent)." In Jacco Dieleman and Willeke Wendrich (eds.), *UCLA Encyclopedia of Egyptology*. < http://escholarship.org/uc/item/1r72q9vv >.

Meeks, Dimitri. 2010. "De quelques 'insectes' égyptiens: entre lexique et paléographie." In Zahi Hawass, Peter Der Manuelian, and Ramadan Hussein (eds.), *Perspectives on Ancient Egypt: Studies in Honor of Edward Brovarski*, 273–304. Cairo: Supreme Council of Antiquities Press.

Osborn, Dale J. and Jana Osbornová. 1998. *The Mammals of Ancient Egypt*. Warminster: Aris and Phillips.

Quirke, Stephen. 2016. *Birth Tusks: The Armoury of Health in Context—Egypt 1800 BC*. London: Golden House Publications.

Ritner, Robert K. 1993. *The Mechanics of Ancient Egyptian Magical Practice*. Chicago: The Oriental Institute of the University of Chicago.

Schweizer, Andreas. 2010. *The Sungod's Journey through the Netherworld: Reading the Ancient Egyptian Amduat*. Ed. by David Lorton. Ithaca: Cornell University Press.

Shalomi-Hen, Racheli. 1998. "Gluttony and the Desert Fathers." In Irene Shirun-Grumach (ed.), *Jerusalem Studies in Egyptology*, 345–351. Wiesbaden: Harrassowitz.

Simandiraki-Grimshaw, Anna. 2010. "Minoan Animal-Human Hybridity." In Derek Counts and Bettina Arnold (eds.), *The Master of Animals in Old World Iconography*. Budapest: Archaeolingua.

Szpakowska, Kasia. 2013. "Striking Cobra Spitting Fire." *Archiv für Religionsgeschichte* 14(1): 27–46.

te Velde, Herman. 1992. "Some Egyptian Deities and Their Piggishness." In Ulrich Luft (ed.), *The Intellectual Heritage of Egypt: Studies Presented to László Kákosy by Friends and Colleagues on the Occasion of His 60th Birthday*, 571–578. Budapest: Chaire d'égyptologie.

Vernus, Pascal and Jean Yoyotte. 2005. *Le bestiaire des pharaons*. Paris: Perrin.

Vinson, Steve. 1998. *The Nile Boatman at Work*. Mainz: Von Zabern.

Volokhine, Youri. 2000. *La frontalité dans l'iconographie de l'Égypte ancienne*. Geneva: Société d'égyptologie.

Volokhine, Youri. 2014. *Le porc en Égypte ancienne*. Liège: Presses Universitaires de Liège.

Wengrow, David. 2014. *The Origins of Monsters: Image and Cognition in the First Age of Mechanical Reproduction*. Princeton: Princeton University Press.

Werning, Daniel A. 2011. *Das Höhlenbuch: Textkritische Edition Und Textgrammatik, Teil II: Textkritische Edition Und Übersetzung*. Wiesbaden: Harrassowitz Verlag.

Zandee, Jan. 1960. *Death as an Enemy: According to Ancient Egyptian Conceptions*. Leiden: Brill.

Zivie, Alain and Roger Lichtenberg. 2005. "The Cats of the Goddess Bastet." In Salima Ikram (ed.), *Divine Creatures: Animal Mummies in Ancient Egypt*, 106–119. Cairo: American University in Cairo Press.

Notes

1 This article is based on the findings of my PhD thesis, which was generously funded by the Leverhulme Trust as part of the Ancient Egyptian Demonology Project: Second Millennium BC at Swansea University. The same definition that was used for "demon" in this thesis is also used in this paper.

2 Evans 2008.

3 On ivory wands, see Quirke 2016.

4 For example, see Wengrow 2014 and Fischer 1987.

5 De Buck 1935–1961.

6 See Lucarelli 2010. A notable exception occurs when demons are enlisted for personal protection, such as on ivory wands.

7 Supernatural snake entities appear in funerary literature such as the Pyramid Texts or *Amduat:* see Leitz 1996 and Schweizer 2010. They also appear in Middle Kingdom literature such as "The Shipwrecked Sailor" (Lichtheim, 2006, 211–215) and objects such as ivory wands (EA 65439 in the British Museum).

8 Borghouts 1978, 91–94 (spells 136–143).

9 Werning 2011, 262. See also Szpakowska 2013 and spells 84, 85 and 103 in Borghouts 1978, 52, 55, and 75. Within the cauldron are depicted bound and decapitated anthropomorphic beings, most likely representing the damned (Book of Caverns, fifth division, scene nine).

10 Johnson 1990.

11 This is not an unusual division of genders in serpents. For example, the serpents in the Pyramid Texts or in magical spells to prevent dangerous bites are generally male.

12 Depuydt 1992, 34 and Vinson 1998 suggest that the ferryboat was coxless and so the ferryman had to keep referring to both the back and the front of the boat.

13 Ritner 1993, 168–169; Zandee 1960, 73–78; Hornung 1968, 15–16 and 29; Frandsen 2011. To be upside down is to be in a state of reversal from normality, non-existence or chaos.

14 Hornung 1996, 110–104; Hornung 2000. "Homosomatic" is a term used to describe the anatomical fusion of human and animal components as outlined by Simandiraki-Grimshaw 2010.

15 Hornung 1996, 126.

16 See Evans 2008, 131 on bovine aggressive behaviour.

17 Vernus and Yoyotte 2005, 249; Bresciani 2005, 199; Shalomi-Hen 1998, 348. For examples, see the groups of magic-stealing crocodiles from CT 342 and 424.

18 On its identification as crocodilian, see Bennett 2016.

19 Leitz 2002, vol. 5, 230; te Velde 1992; Volokhine 2014.

20 An earlier manuscript, known as the Cairo leather roll, provides further information about the appearance and function of this demon and his fellow gatekeepers and is currently being studied by Wael Sherbini.

21 See Bennett 2016, 128 on their identification as fennecs.

22 Zivie and Lichtenberg 2005.

23 See CT 652, 1069, 1142 and 1178.

24 Fischer 1968; Altenmüller 2012.

[25] Osborn and Osbornová 1998, 34; Evans 2008, 138.

[26] See Baum 1989, 129–135 on the moringa tree and 162–168 for the carob. Compare this with the form of insect cocoons as discussed in Meeks 2010.

[27] Osborn and Osbornová 1998, 19; Evans 2008, 124–125.

[28] Lucarelli 2010, 5. See also Guilhou 1999 on demons from BD 144.

[29] This data is collected from the Demonology Project database, < http://www.demonthings.com/demonbase/ >.

[30] See the Papyrus of Ani (BM EA 10470) in the British Museum (< https://research.britishmuseum.org/research/collection_online/search.aspx?searchText=papyrus+of+ani&museumno=10470 >, accessed 7 February 2020) and the Papyrus of Pai-Nefer-Nefer (Ägyptische Sammlung, INV 3860) in the Kunsthistorisches Museum Wien (< http://www.khm.at/de/object/b32eed9a93/ > accessed 7 February 2020).

[31] For example, see the Papyrus of Pai-Nefer-Nefer in the Kunsthistorisches Museum Wien and headrest UC16065 in the Petrie Museum.

[32] Volokhine 2000, 76–77. On frontality, see also Favard-Meeks 1992.

[33] Hornung 1996, 110–114.

[34] Evans 2008, 135–137 on hippopotamus aggression.

[35] Osborn and Osbornová 1998, 147; Vernus and Yoyotte 2005, 248.

[36] Osborn and Osbornová 1998, 74 indicate that the average shoulder height for fennecs is 19–21 cm.

Journal of Ancient Egyptian Interconnections

Liminal Deities in the Borderlands: Bes and Pataikos in Ancient Nubia

Erin E. Bornemann
Department of Anthropology, University of California, Santa Barbara

Stuart Tyson Smith
Department of Anthropology, University of California, Santa Barbara

Abstract

This paper examines amulets in the forms of the apotropaic liminal gods Bes and Pataikos, as represented in the archaeological assemblage from the site of Tombos in Upper Nubia. Through examination of these amulets under anthropological and archaeological conceptions of materiality, they can be linked to the individuals that would have come in contact with and used them; likewise, both object and individual can be connected back into the larger contemporary social sphere of which they would have been an active part. Tombos provides the primary case study for examining these amuletic forms in the Eighteenth and Twenty-fifth Dynasties, and examples from this site will be compared to others from sites in both Egypt and Nubia. This paper exemplifies the utility of materiality studies as applied to archaeological investigations of the daily lives and deaths of individuals in ancient Egyptian and Nubian society and hopes to foster further discussion of amuletic forms that made the transition from life into death.

Small, grotesque, ugly. Despite their many differences, the lesser Egyptian deities Bes and Pataikos share these basic iconographic traits. These two ancient Egyptian dwarf deities were not the primary subjects of state-level worship in grand Egyptian temples, but they were extremely popular among the common people, functioning primarily as protective personal and household deities. Their popularity skyrocketed during the New Kingdom continuing into the Nubian Napatan Period and even extending all the way through the Graeco-Roman Period. Bes and Pataikos are commonly represented in the form of apotropaic amulets, which would have been worn by anyone seeking extra protection, and are most commonly associated in archaeological contexts with women and children. This paper examines the liminal gods Bes and Pataikos in terms of their iconographic form, their place in personal and household religion, and the qualities associated with their protective natures. We then apply anthropological theories of entanglement and materiality to the case study of the Egyptian colony of Tombos—at the third cataract in Sudanese Nubia—in order to investigate their social and archaeological context. It is our hope that this paper will foster further discussion about these liminal deities in terms of their adoption into household and eventually state worship in the Egyptian-Nubian borderlands during the New Kingdom and Napatan Periods.

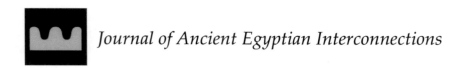

FIGURE 1: Amulets of Bes (left) and Pataikos (right) found at Tombos.

DWARFS AS LIMINAL DEITIES

Bes and Pataikos are two of the most popular and well-known dwarf gods in ancient Egypt (FIG. 1). They are most commonly referred to, albeit generally, as *nmw* in ancient Egyptian religious and magical texts.[1] Although certainly present in somewhat murkier forms earlier in Egyptian history, it is in the New Kingdom—especially from the Eighteenth Dynasty onwards—that a number of dwarf gods entered the Egyptian pantheon.[2] These gods are usually depicted in the form of achondroplastic dwarfs, with overly large heads, long torsos, and disproportionally short, thick limbs that are often bowed in shape.[3] Although the name Bes is consistently used throughout this paper, it is worth noting James F. Romano's conception of the "Bes-image," which refers to the body of dwarf deities resembling Bes while also acknowledging the Egyptian's conception of the multiple forms in which a deity could manifest.[4] Over time, a divergence developed in the worship of these dwarf deities, which eventually resulted in the differing iconographic forms of Bes and Pataikos.[5] Despite the fact that some may consider these dwarf deities to be physically malformed, disproportionate, and grotesque, the ancient Egyptians had positive associations with both humans and gods who exhibited dwarfish physiques. In regard to this positive relationship with dwarfs and dwarfish forms, Dasen comments that, "their liminality was made symbolically acceptable by association with positive religious concepts."[6] As we can see in the textual, artistic, and archaeological record, dwarf gods are primarily associated with apotropaic and benevolent magic; they were commonly made into everyday amulets, in addition to playing a prominent role in other types of personal and household magic.[7]

The final resting place of the amulets within our

Figure 2: Map of ancient Egyptian-Nubian Border with sites indicated.

study establishes a relationship with both ancient Egyptian and Nubian cultures, providing a further layer of liminality for these two deities. Our case study focuses on the site of Tombos, which lay at the third cataract within an ancient borderland, a crosscutting zone of intercultural exchange between Egyptians and Nubians (Fig. 2). This fortuitous location affords us the right set of circumstances to examine the larger context of interactions between ancient Egypt and Nubia. Within anthropological theory, studies of culture contact have integrated bottom-up approaches into their analyses, allowing the voices of the "colonized" to finally be heard and pushing back against the traditionally accepted colonizer-dominant, colonized-submissive narratives.[8] When combined with analysis of a rich material record, such a theoretical framework can illuminate the agency of the indigenous/colonized in the integration of new beliefs like the veneration of Bes and Pataikos in Nubia.

The concept of *entanglement* developed out of these theoretical frameworks, being used to examine how different cultural groups have interacted over time. *Entanglement* as a concept emphasizes the many ways that ideas, traditions, and material culture are part of a dynamic back-and-forth exchange between different cultural groups.[9] Michael Dietler has developed the idea of *entanglement* further in an archaeological setting and used the concept to examine the material evidence of interactions between Etruscan, Greek, and Roman colonists and the indigenous peoples of Mediterranean France over six centuries.[10] In order to do this, he analyzes these interactions at a multi-scalar level, which draws attention to the effects of the interconnectedness among all groups involved and further exemplifies why the bounded notions of acculturation and domination are inappropriate explanations for colonial contexts.[11] This analytical framework has already been adapted to incorporate both biological and cultural interactions at Tombos.[12] Even though the majority of individuals buried at Tombos during the New Kingdom present an outward Egyptian cultural identity in terms of their grave style, grave goods, and burial position, we see increasing examples of the coexistence and interweaving of both Nubian and Egyptian traditions in the later history of the cemetery, from the late Ramesside period to the Third Intermediate Period.

In order to more fully understand the long-term cultural dynamics in place at Tombos, we must rely heavily on the archaeological record in our interpretations, which are best understood through archaeological conceptions of materiality. We define materiality to include the symmetric (but not necessarily *equal*), relational, and recursive relationship that exists between human beings and material objects.[13] Part of this relationship includes the final context of the object: in our case, an amulet's association with the individual with whom it is buried. As a result, we are able to say much more than if we had the amulet without any contextual information. The application of materiality and entanglement theories allows us to tease out some of the complexity of the longstanding relationship between Egypt and Nubia, providing for a more realistic picture of how these relationships would have played out in the past for the individuals within our study.

Case Study: Amuletic Forms of Bes and Pataikos at Tombos, Upper Nubia

Both Bes and Pataikos became very popular in Nubia, the former arriving during the period of New Kingdom colonization, the latter at some point during the Third Intermediate Period. A total of twelve Bes and Pataikos amulets have been recovered during our excavations at Tombos, and the site provides an interesting locus for examining the kinds of long-term entanglements that resulted in the prominence of these liminal deities south of Egypt (Fig. 3). The Egyptian colony at Tombos was established around the reign of Amenhotep II, although a date in the later reign of Thutmose III is possible. Located just 10 km north of Kerma, the former capital of Kush, Tombos lay at the headwaters of the third cataract of the Nile. Inscriptions left by Thutmose I and later Viceroys of Kush marked the site as a symbolic as well as geographic boundary within the empire. Tombos is notable in that it was the southernmost Egyptian colony within the empire, part of a string of colonies founded below the third cataract during the New Kingdom, including Amara, Sai, Sedinga, Soleb, and Sesebi.[14]

Four Bes amulets made of faience were found in a large chamber tomb dating to the mid-Eighteenth Dynasty (Fig. 4). One was found loose on the floor of the back chamber, dating around the reign of Amenhotep II, but three were still around the neck of a woman who was buried in flexed, Nubian position around the reign of Amenhotep III. Two of these Bes amulets were rather crudely modeled, but two of the examples found *in situ* provide a detailed but simple example of Bes's typical iconography. Aspects of Bes's liminality can be plainly observed in his grotesque appearance defying normal categories, as he is both "comic and frightening, young and old, human and animal at the same time."[15] In addition to his dwarfish form, Bes is most notable for his leonine appearance, complete with scraggly mane of hair, which may include facial hair. His grotesque appearance is further completed with lion's ears and tail.[16] One theory on the leonine appearance of Bes, put forth by Wilkinson, suggests that perhaps Bes initially was depicted as a dwarf wearing a lion-skin cape that eventually morphed into being a physical part of his iconographic form.[17] Adding further to his grotesque and unnerving appearance, depictions of Bes usually convey his overt nakedness,[18] which sometimes includes a prominent belly and protruding breasts.[19] His grotesque and unrefined facial features[20] are often highlighted by his tongue menacingly protruding towards any onlookers, reinforcing his leonine aspect.[21]

The second example of Bes from this group of amulets, although broken in antiquity, reflects a different iconography popular at Amarna, where the deity was shown in profile, actively dancing while

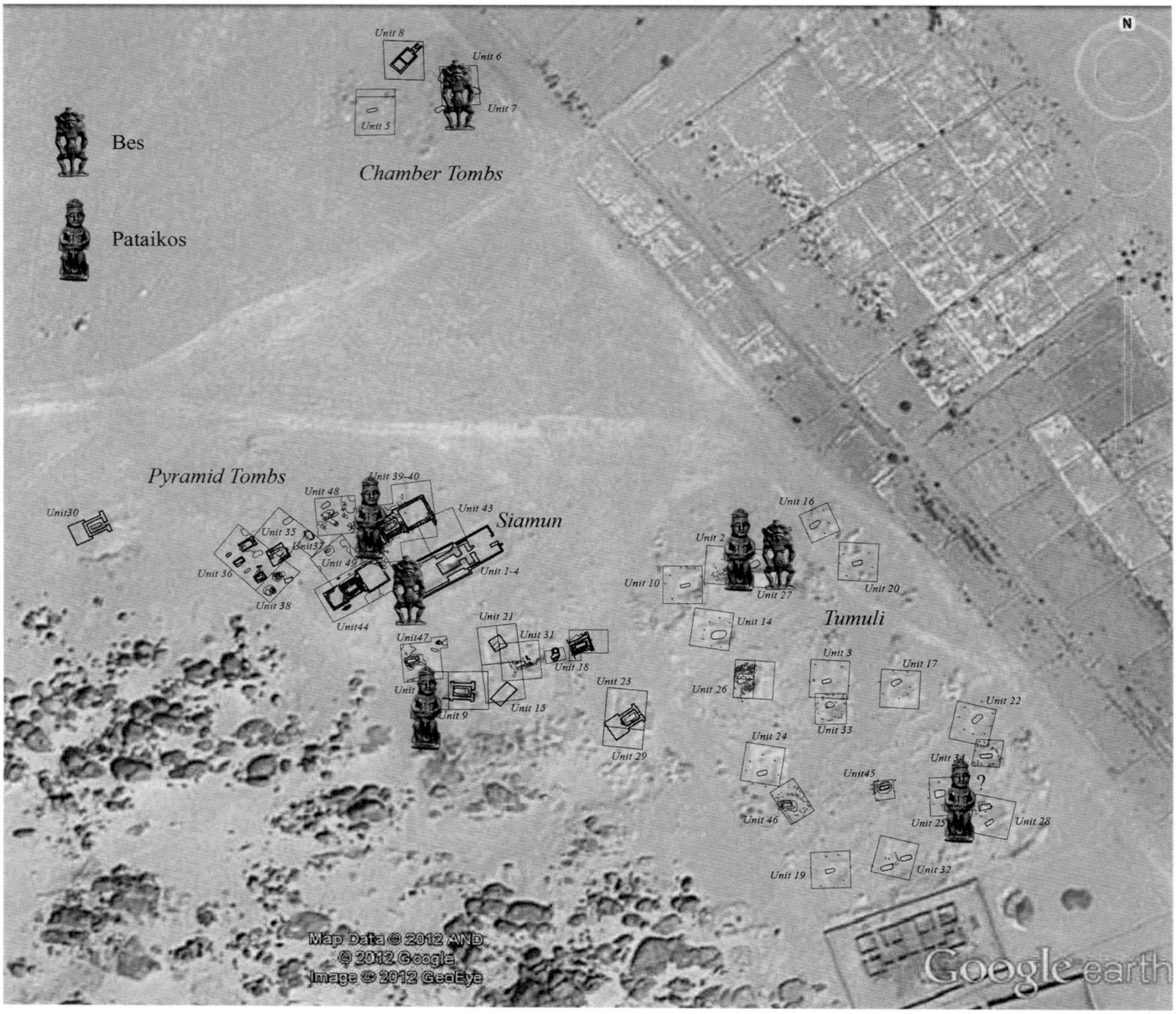

FIGURE 3: Aerial view of the cemetery at Tombos with locations of Bes and Pataikos amulets indicated.

looking over one shoulder and holding a tambour (FIG. 5).[22] Depictions of Bes such as this one can be attributed to his popularity within the household as a deity commonly associated with the goddesses Hathor and Taweret.[23] Thus, Bes has ties to health and beauty, making him a popular deity among women and on items incorporated into toilet kits, and his earthly attributes extend to celebrations of music, dancing, wine, and general merrymaking.[24] Broken in antiquity, our amulet was so valued by the Nubian woman who wore it (and/or the relatives who buried it with her) that it was strung through the raised arms rather than discarded when the head broke off.

Two additional examples of Bes (one of these likely representing Beset) date slightly earlier within the Eighteenth Dynasty, likely during the reign of Amenhotep II. These examples were found as part of a larger string of simply rendered apotropaic amulets that were placed around the neck of a child

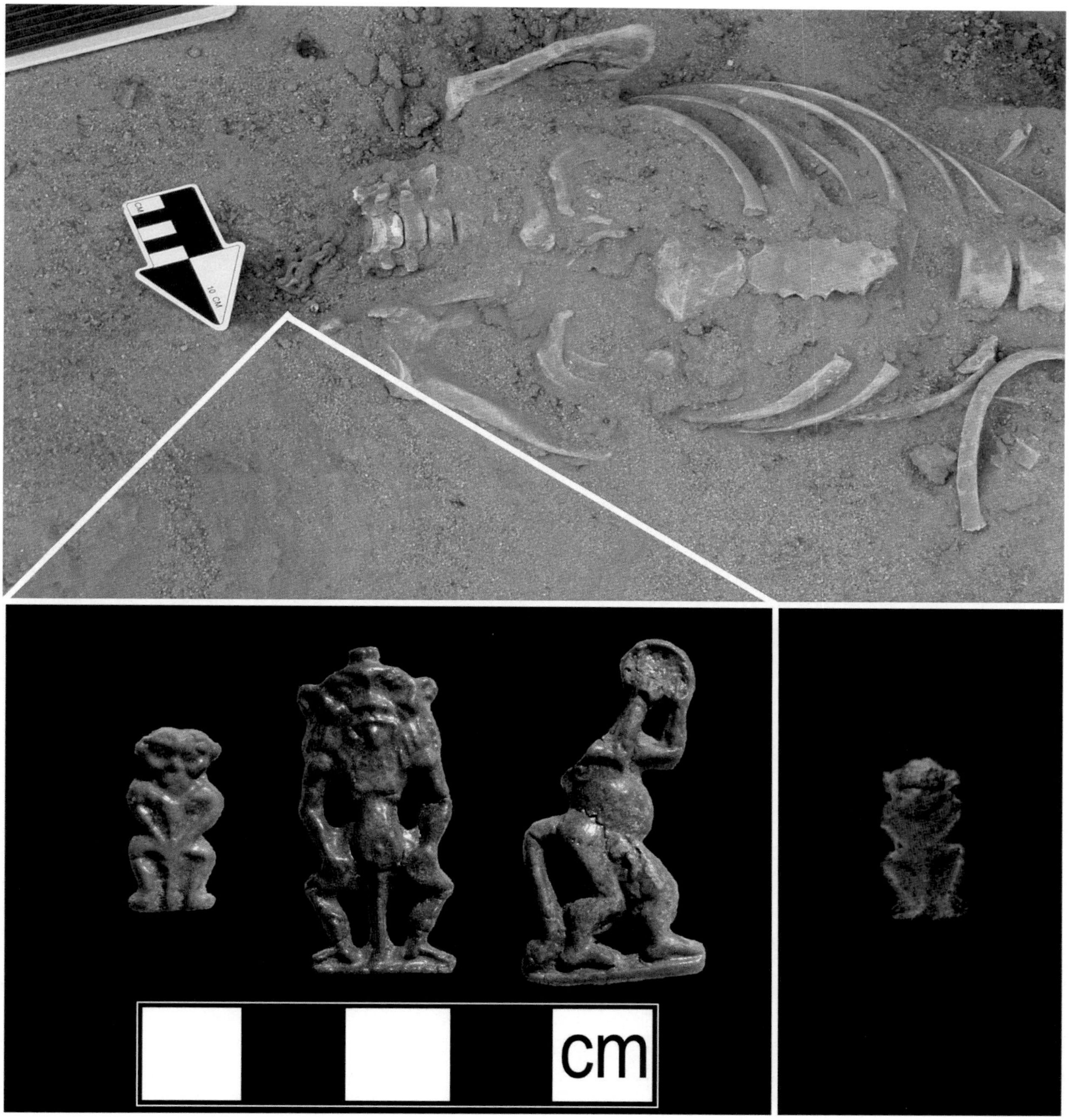

Figure 4: Four Bes amulets from an Eighteenth Dynasty tomb at Tombos. The Bes amulet to the far right was found nearby the burial but not in situ with the other three amulets.

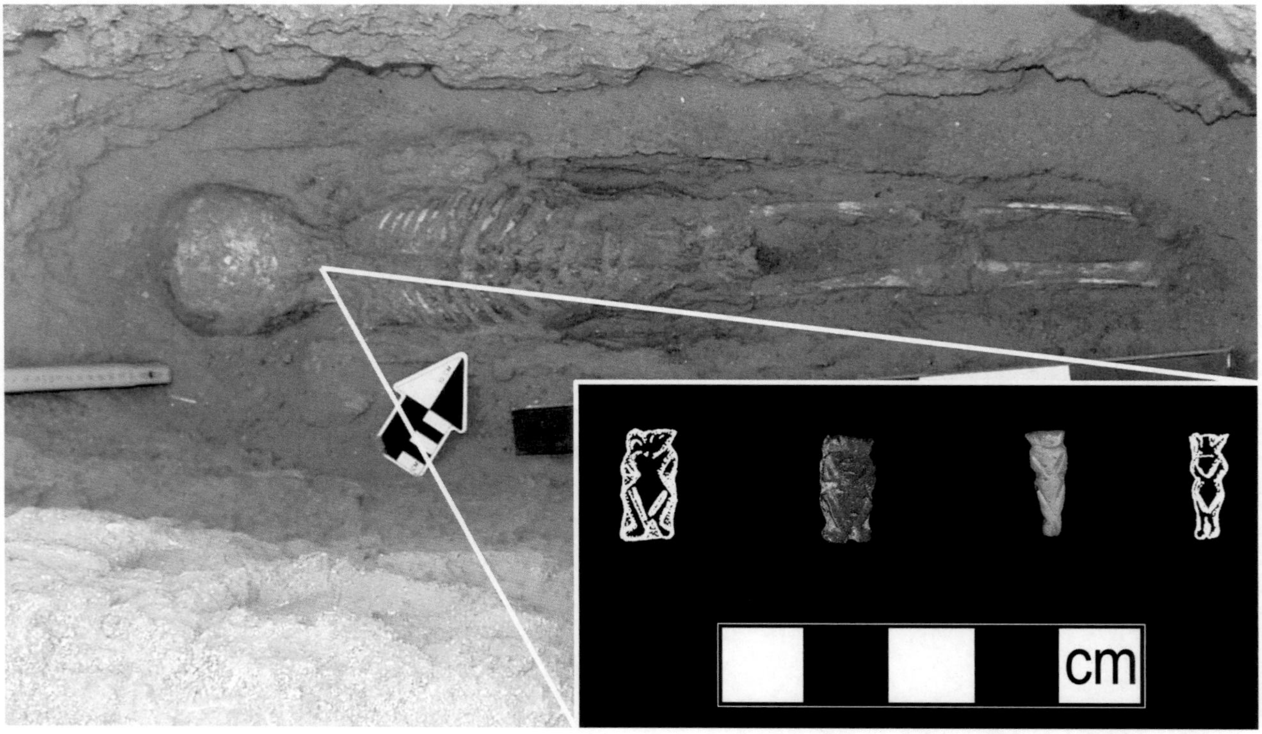

Figure 5: Amulets of Bes and Beset from an Eighteenth Dynasty child burial. Line drawings are provided on either side of the amulet to show detail.

buried in Egyptian style. The fact that Bes/et amulets were found in the burial of a child harkens to the deities' qualities as a protector of children, especially in childbirth.[25] Although far more crudely manufactured than the previous examples, the iconographic traits of Bes are apparent. It is tempting to consider the second example as representing Bes's female counterpart Beset, given the similarly rendered head and posture, but distinctly female form with legs firmly together, contrasting with that of Bes's open bent legs.[26] Bes and Beset share many iconographic elements and qualities as deities including their benevolent nature towards humans and focus on music, dancing, and childbirth.[27] Representations of Beset emerge on apotropaic wands as early as the Middle Kingdom, so it is not out of the realm of possibility that this amulet could represent Beset.[28]

An amulet found within an adjacent, more Nubian component of the cemetery provides another simply rendered example, which could represent either Bes or Pataikos (Fig. 6). This tomb provides an excellent case of entanglement, since it combines a Nubian-style tumulus superstructure with an Egyptian-oriented east-west shaft. Moreover, the burial was in a coffin, head to the west, wrapped and probably mummified Egyptian style, but placed upon a bed in a longstanding Nubian tradition. The amulet was found among a variety of objects placed in a basket at the foot of the deceased's bed. It is tempting to suggest that it may in fact be a representation of Pataikos rather than Bes, which is plausible since the context dates to the Third Intermediate Period with a calibrated radiocarbon date taken from cordage associated with the bed of 831–792 BCE (100% at 2 sigma). Pataikos is typically represented in the form of a youthful achondroplastic dwarf with an over-

Figure 6: Bes/Pataikos amulet from a Third Intermediate Period Nubian tumulus.

large flat-topped head, prominent ears, and sturdy bowed legs. Additionally, he is often nude or semi-nude, with hands near his hips, making it easy to make out his large, round belly, which usually has a distinctly rendered belly button.[29] Given its simple design, it is likely to date earlier rather than later during this time range, as representations of Pataikos during the Third Intermediate Period become increasingly more elaborate.[30] This is consistent with the eclectic character of the other objects found in the basket, which included broken amulets and beads that appear to have been collected from the surface of the cemetery for personal or perhaps magical reasons. This particular amulet thus likely dates to an earlier period than the interment, which a radiocarbon date establishes was made during the Third Intermediate Period (831–792 BCE, calibrated to 2 sigma). It could have been an heirloom, but was more likely either taken from an older tomb or simply collected from the debris of ancient looting in the older part of the cemetery.

Another example of a Pataikos amulet was found within the chapel of a large pyramid complex dating to the Ramesside or Third Intermediate Period. This Pataikos amulet is made of blue-green faience and is pierced through the neck for suspension (Fig. 7). It has the recognizably human features of Pataikos rather than the beastly features of Bes, and it wears a tight-fitting cap above his large prominent ears and has a distinctly rendered belly button. Although the context of this amulet is not its original one, we can surmise that ancient looters discarded the amulet on their way out of the tomb chamber in favor of more valuable pieces of jewelry.

Dating to the late Ramesside or early Third Intermediate Period with a calibrated radiocarbon date of 1130–980 BCE (taken from scraps of linen, 98.9% at 2 sigma) is another interesting example of Nubian-Egyptian cultural entanglements, the burial of a woman in a Nubian-style tumulus, as in the previous example with an east-west oriented shaft, head to the west in Egyptian fashion to face the rejuvenating power of the rising sun, but situated upon a bed in Nubian style (Fig. 8). While placed in a supine position and likely mummified Egyptian style, she lacked a coffin. She was interred with many Egyptian amulets, including one Bes amulet and one Pataikos amulet. A second, larger Pataikos was associated with a later burial that was badly disturbed but with lower legs

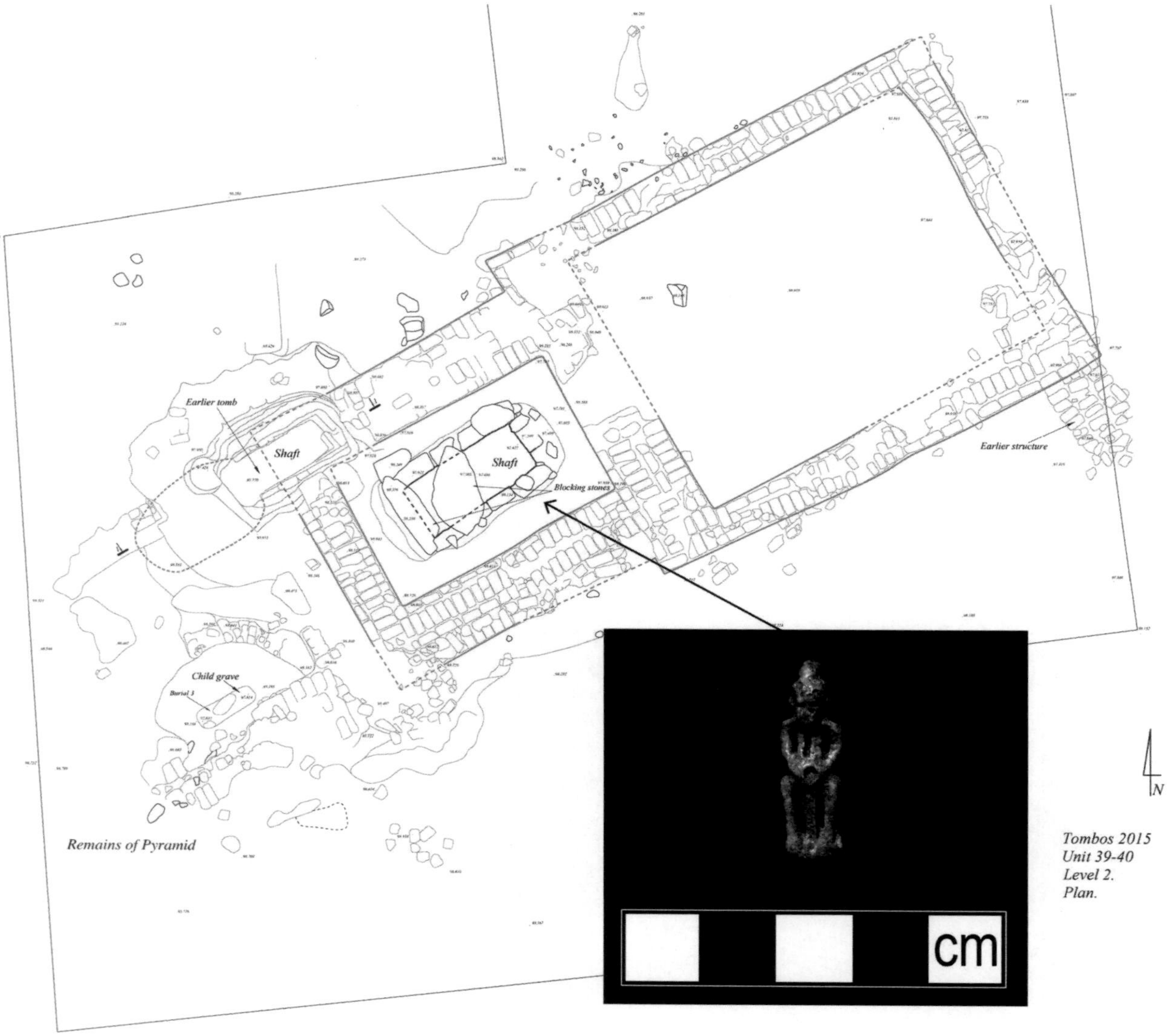

FIGURE 7: Pataikos amulet from a Ramesside or Third Intermediate Period pyramid chapel.

in situ indicating a supine position with head to the west and dating later in the Third Intermediate Period, from 903–810 BCE (radiocarbon date taken from scraps of linen, 98.9% at 2 sigma). The Bes amulet is formed out of blue faience, displaying features that solidify by the Third Intermediate Period. In particular, his protruding tongue and grimacing mouth, potbelly, and feather headdress point towards a later date consistent with the later end of the radiocarbon range. This later style is completed in our example by the loss of a distinct neck and the addition of a moustache and beard.[31] The smaller of the two Pataikos amulets is fairly plain in representation but exhibits the close fitting cap of Ptah and features common to achondroplastic dwarfism. The later, larger Pataikos amulet was rendered by a mas-

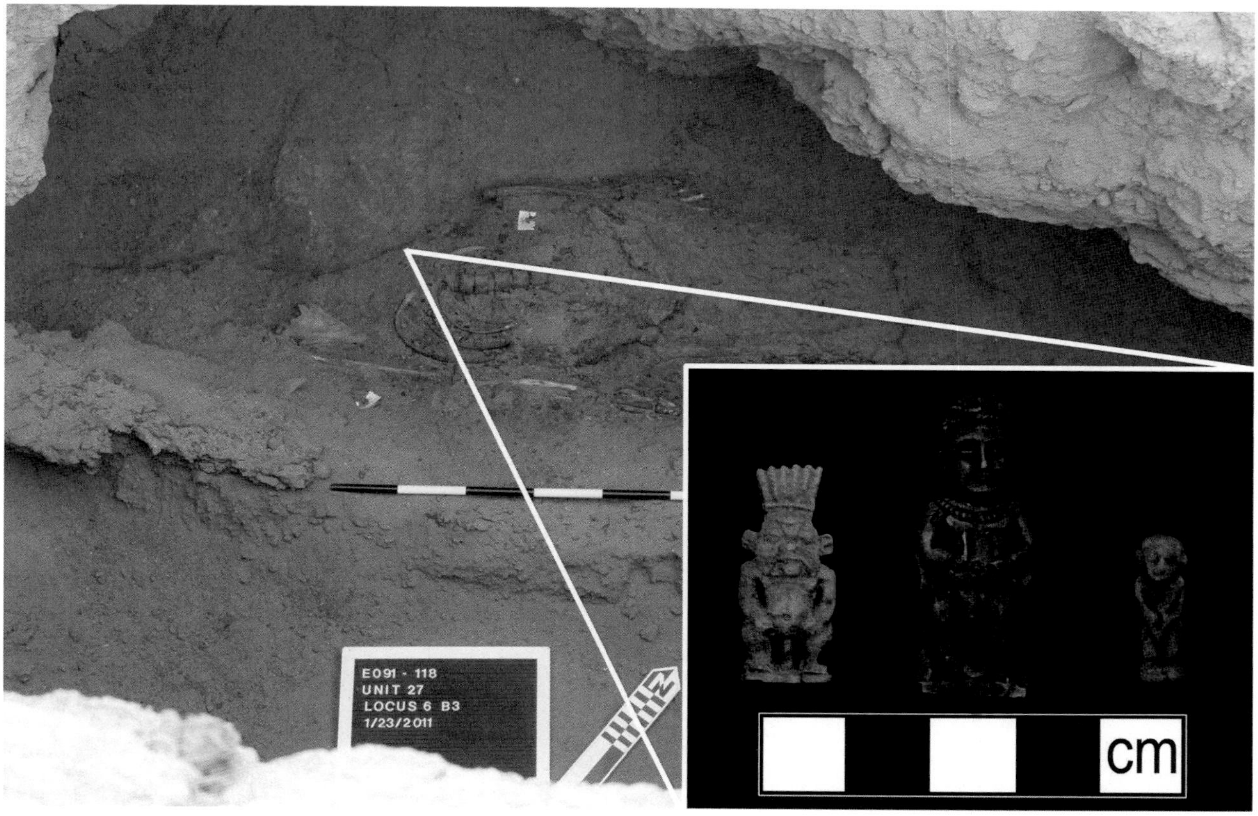

Figure 8: Bes and two Pataikos amulets from a Third Intermediate Period tumulus.

ter of their craft, with even the smallest details evident on the piece. Pataikos stands holding snakes in both of his hands, while adorned by a scarab on his head and an elaborate broad collar around his neck. On the reverse, he is protected by a crouching winged goddess who is often identified as Sakhmet but in this case perhaps represents Isis-Maat. An array of magical symbols was carved on the underside. This elaborated style finds parallels in Late Period Egypt and the Twenty-fifth Dynasty royal cemetery at el-Kurru,[32] about 50 to 100 years later than the end of the radiocarbon range for linen associated with our example.

Lastly, we have one amulet dating to the Twenty-fifth Dynasty, a double-sided figure with a grotesque male figure on one side and an equally grotesque female figure on the reverse (Fig. 9). This amulet also comes from an entangled context, albeit more Egyptian in character than the previous burials. The vaulted east-west oriented mud-brick chamber tomb was located in the older, Egyptian part of the cemetery next to a Twenty-fifth Dynasty pyramid complex. The deceased was supine, head to the west, mummified and placed in a coffin, which was itself placed upon a bed in Nubian style. The Pataikos amulet was found with a group of beads and Egyptian style amulets next to the burial, including a scarab with a cartouche of Shabaka, perhaps thrown there by looters in search of jewelry made of gold or silver. At first glance it would be tempting to identify the figures as Bes and Beset; however, if one examines them more closely, the male figure sports a side-lock of youth, which is commonly found on representations of Pataikos.[33] He also lacks the

Figure 9: Double-sided Pataikos/Sakhmet amulet from a Twenty-fifth Dynasty burial (from left to right: right-side, front, left-side, and rear views).

typical animalistic features associated with Bes. Although represented in a less than goddess-like manner, we believe that the female figure on the reverse is the goddess Sakhmet, who is a known companion of Pataikos and for whom there are parallels at el-Kurru and Meroe.[34]

Discussion

All in all, the iconography of these two deities, as represented in different contexts, provides us with an interesting account of their popularity at Tombos. Given their manner of suspension and wear, both the Bes and Pataikos amulets in our study would almost certainly have been worn by the owner for protection during life and further accompanied them into death. As noted previously, Bes is best known for his primary attributes as an apotropaic deity of the household.[35] He was often called upon for his powers of protection against general evil and hostile entities,[36] and was tied to warfare and victory over one's earthly enemies.[37] More interesting still is the role of Bes as a deity invoked for protection in death. Bes was believed to preside over sleep, given the ancient Egyptian conception of the close relationship between sleep and death.[38] He provided safe passage for the dead during their journey through the underworld,[39] specifically assisting the deceased against demons and the *bau* of other deities.[40] Bes also had connections to lands south of Egypt and to the Eastern Desert, which were seen as the margins of both civilization and the cosmos in the ancient Egyptian worldview, where the daily solar cycle of birth, death, and rebirth took place each day.[41] The liminality of Bes thus shines through with his attributes as a beneficent deity to humans within the earthly household,[42] along with his strong ties with the underworld and its many denizens.[43]

Pataikos parallels many of the same qualities that are associated with Bes in terms of his apotropaic nature for both the living and the dead and his larger association with the cycle of birth, death, and rebirth. Unfortunately, there are no direct references to Pataikoi in written sources, as they were not characters in any known mythic tradition, nor were they incorporated into official texts or iconography. What we know about the attributes of Pataikos as a deity come directly from his iconography, which is primarily amuletic in form.[44] Pataikoi, especially in the form of statuettes and some amulets, may have served as magical charms with strong connections with fertility.[45] More specifically, Dasen suggests that the attributes of Pataikos can be grouped into three categories: 1) Fertility, 2) Creation, 3) Rebirth and Rejuvenation.[46] Pataikoi are often adorned with magical symbols on the base ensuring health and fertility for the owner, including the *wḏ3t*, fish, lotus buds, and lions, among others.[47] This is reflected in the elaborate faience Pataikos in our study dating to the Third Intermediate Period, which has a fish, *wḏ3t*, cat, lotus bud, lion, and newborn hartebeest (Gardiner E9, *ỉw*, *ỉwr*, "conceive"[48]) on the base. Pataikoi are directly linked to the dwarf form of the creator god Ptah and sometimes share a haircut or cap similar to the close-fitting cap of the deity.[49] Lastly, Pataikoi are often connected to rebirth and regeneration through their strong links to solar deities such as Amun-Re and Khepri in the form of a scarab (in our case and other examples placed on the head),[50] Horus as the morning sun god, and Osiris and Sokar as nocturnal sun gods.[51] This strong solar association ties into the daily journey of Re—the cycle of the death and rebirth of the sun each day that was so crucial to Egyptian religious canon. As with Bes, these features link this particular dwarf god to the liminality of the cyclical movements between the world of the living and the dead, as well as the endless cycle of creation, death, and rebirth.

The iconographies of both Bes and Pataikos in amuletic form are thus interesting in their own right, given that they tie both deities to both the realm of the living and the realm of the dead as protectors of humans from perils both natural and supernatural. However, their adoption and adaptation into Nubian religious beliefs and practice highlights their importance as entangled figures transformed by the colonial encounter and the emergence of a new hybrid Kushite culture and dynasty. Both Bes and Pataikos amulets are common in the cemetery at Sanam, the main necropolis for the new Kushite cap-

FIGURE 10: Ornate Pataikos from a Third Intermediate Period tumulus (clockwise from top: side, rear, base, front, and top views).

ital at Napata. As at Tombos, amulets at Sanam reflect a dual emphasis on protection and fertility, life and rebirth.[52] Bes and Pataikos are also common at the large cemetery of Missiminia to the north and far to the south at the early, western cemetery at Meroe,[53] reflecting their spread throughout the Kushite kingdom in the Napatan period. They also appear in a royal context at el-Kurru, where many Bes and Pataikos amulets were found within queens' tombs dating to the reign of Piankhy and his successor Shabaqo (Ku 51–54).[54] Perhaps starting with the adoption of the deity by individual Nubians as in the examples discussed above, the inhabitants of Tombos and other places in Upper Nubia brought these gods into their personal worship on a widespread scale, which we see grow into a much larger religious following as time progresses from colonization during the New Kingdom down into the Twenty-fifth Dynasty and beyond.

In contrast to Bes's continuing role in the household in both Egypt and Nubia, the long-term cultural entanglement that brought Bes southwards also resulted in his transformation into an important deity within the Kushite state theology. Large ceramic statues of Bes and Beset found in a chapel at Kawa[55] and the monumental Bes columns in the Mut temple commissioned by Taharqa at Jebel Barkal (B-300)[56] provide examples of his importance in a formal cult setting, a role unparalleled in Egypt until the Greco-Roman period. The popularity of Bes is mirrored both in Egypt and in Nubia; however, it is within Nubia that we see Bes first rise to such prominence, venerated in grand temples commissioned by the Nubian pharaohs. The incorporation of Bes in Twenty-fifth Dynasty state theology could have set a precedent that influenced his later enhanced role in the *mammisi* of Greco-Roman temples, like Dendara and Philae, as well as the creation of his only temple in Bahariya Oasis.[57]

Concluding Thoughts

From their widespread popularity as deities in personal and household religion within Egypt and Nubia to their incorporation into the Kushite State theology, Bes and Pataikos exemplify a twofold liminal status: 1) They are able to move between the world of the living and the dead on behalf of humankind, and 2) they had equally popular religious trajectories, transcending the borders of Egypt into Nubia, where they further developed and transformed over time. In order to assess the impact of Bes and Pataikos in Nubia, we chose to investigate amulets in the form of Bes and Pataikos found within burial contexts at Tombos, as these small personal items exemplify individualized choices on the part of the Nubians who lived and were buried at this borderland site. By considering the materiality of these objects in the larger scope of the long-standing cultural change that took place between the Egyptians and Nubians, we are able to bring anthropological theory to Egyptology and place these objects within their social and archaeological context, which lends to a fuller picture of their place and significance in Nubian history.

By examining the amuletic forms of Bes and Pataikos—interred with their owners at Tombos—in terms of their iconography, their popularity in personal and household religion, as well as the attributes associated with their protective natures, we are able to tease out a small part of this larger religious entanglement, while at the same time identifying similar trends in their popularity at the personal and household levels. Although of no use to ancient looters, as a few examples in our study show, amuletic forms of Bes and Pataikos were valued by the individuals with whom they were buried or perhaps those who were responsible for preparing the body for burial. Many examples from our study show signs of wear and even significant damage attesting to a personal attachment to these amulets and the styles of Bes and Pataikos clearly mimic amuletic styles from Egypt or perhaps were even imported directly from there. As Silliman points out for the New World encounter, eventually borrowed cultural features such as these two deities are internalized and cease to be foreign, becoming fully integrated into society.[58] This study further highlights the value of amuletic objects with discrete provenience information as well as illuminating the value of investigating the transfer of Egyptian theological concepts beyond Egypt's borders.

When we consider these amulets within their immediate archaeological context and their larger historical and cultural contexts, we are able to conceive a much fuller picture of the importance of these two deities as protectors of the living, through crucial times such as childhood, childbirth, and even warfare; key players in the state ideology with similar connotations of protection and fertility; and their transcendence into death as protectors of their owners, whether Egyptian or Nubian, commoner or king. It is our ultimate hope that this paper will continue to foster meaningful academic dialogue regarding shared religious traditions/deities between Egypt and its larger cultural sphere, while highlighting the entangled nature of these shared ideas and the role that individual choices play in intercultural borrowing.

References

Andrews, Carol A. R. 1994. *Amulets of Ancient Egypt*. Bath: Bath Press.

Arav, Rami and Monika Bernett. 1997. "An Egyptian Figurine of Pataikos at Bethsaida." *Israel Exploration Journal* 47: 198–213.

Arkush, Elizabeth. 2011. "Explaining the Past in 2010." *American Anthropologist* 113: 200–212.

Bosse-Griffiths, Kate. 1977. "A Beset Amulet from the Amarna Period." *The Journal of Egyptian Archaeology* 63: 98–106

Buzon, Michele, Stuart Tyson Smith, and Antonio Simonetti. 2016. "Entanglement and the Formation of the Ancient Nubian Napatan State." *American Anthropologist* 118: 284–300.

Cusick, James G. 1998. "Historiography of Acculturation: An Evaluation of Concepts and Their Application in Archaeology." In J. G. Cusick (ed.), *Studies in Culture Contact: Interaction, Culture Change, and Archaeology*, 126–145. Carbondale: Center for Archaeological Investigations, Southern Illinois University.

Dasen, Véronique. 1993. *Dwarfs in Ancient Egypt and Greece*. Oxford: Clarendon Press.

Dawson, Warren R. 1938. "Pygmies and Dwarfs in Ancient Egypt." *The Journal of Egyptian Archaeology* 24: 185–189.

Dietler, Michael. 2005. "The Archaeology of Colonization and the Colonization of Archaeology: Theoretical Challenges from an Ancient Mediterranean Colonial Encounter." In G. J. Stein (ed.), *The Archaeology of Colonial Encounters: Comparative Perspectives*, 33–68. Santa Fe: School of American Research Press.

——. 2010. *Archaeologies of Colonialism: Consumption, Entanglement, and Violence in Ancient Mediterranean France*. Berkeley: University of California Press.

Dunham, Dows D. 1950. *Royal Cemeteries of Kush, Volume 1: El Kurru*. Cambridge, Massachusetts: Harvard University Press for the Museum of Fine Arts Boston.

——. 1963. *The Royal Cemeteries of Kush, Volume 5: The South and West Cemeteries at Meroe*. Cambridge, Massachusetts: Harvard University Press for the Museum of Fine Arts Boston.

——. 1970. *The Barkal Temples*. Boston: Museum of Fine Arts.

Gardiner, Alan H. 1957. *Egyptian Grammar: Being an Introduction to the Study of Hieroglyphs*. 3rd edition. Oxford: Griffith Institute.

Hawass, Zahi. 2000. *The Valley of the Golden Mummies*. Cairo: American University in Cairo Press.

Hodder, Ian. 2011. "Human-Thing Entanglement: Towards an Integrated Archaeological Perspective." *Journal of the Royal Anthropological Institute* 17: 154–177.

——. 2014. *Entangled: An Archaeology of the Relationships between Humans and Things*. Malden: Wiley-Blackwell.

——. 2014. "The Entanglements of Humans and Things: A Long-Term View." *New Literary History* 45: 19–36.

—— and Angus Mol. 2015. "Network Analysis and Entanglement." *Journal of Archaeological Method and Theory* 23: 1–29.

Knappett, Carl. 2014. "Materiality in Archaeological Theory." In C. Smith (ed.), *Encyclopedia of Global Archaeology*, 4700–4708. New York: Springer.

Liebmann, Matthew and Melissa S. Murphy. 2010. "Rethinking the Archaeology of 'Rebels, Backsliders, and Idolaters.'" In M. Liebmann and M. S. Murphy (ed.), *Enduring Conquests: Rethinking the Archaeology of Resistance to Spanish Colonialism in the Americas*, 3–18. Santa Fe: School for Advanced Research Press.

Lightfoot, Kent G. and Antoinette Martinez. 1995. "Frontiers and Boundaries in Archaeological Perspective." *Annual Review of Anthropology* 24: 471–492.

Lohwasser, Angelika. 2010. *The Kushite Cemetery of Sanam: A Non-Royal Burial Ground of the Nubian Capital, c. 800–600 BC*. London: Golden House Publications.

Malkin, Irad. 2002. "A Colonial Middle Ground: Greek, Etruscan, and Local Elites in the Bay of Naples." In C. L. Lyons and J. K. Papadopoulos (ed.), *The Archaeology of Colonialism*, 151–181. Los Angeles: Getty Research Institute.

Mata, Karim. 2013. "Colonial Entanglements and Cultic Heterogeneity on Rome's Germanic Frontier." In V. G. Koutrafouri and J. Sanders (ed.), *Ritual Failure: Archaeological Perspectives*, 131–154. Leiden: Sidestone Press.

Minas-Nerpel, Martina. 2013. "Ptah-Pataikos, Harpokrates, and Khepri." In E. Frood and A. McDonald (eds.), *Decorum and Experience: Essays in Ancient Culture for John Baines*, 147–150. Oxford: Griffith Institute.

Morkot, Robert G. 2013. "From Conquered to Conqueror: The Organization of Nubia in the New Kingdom and the Kushite Administration of Egypt." In J. C. M. García (ed.), *Ancient Egyptian Administration*, 911–963. Leiden: Brill.

Ogdon, J. R. 1981. "A Bes Amulet from the Royal Tomb of Akhenaten at El-'Amarna." *The Journal of Egyptian Archaeology* 67: 178–179.

Olsen, Bjørnar. 2010. *In Defense of Things: Archaeology and the Ontology of Objects*. Plymouth: AltaMira Press.

Overholtzer, Lisa. 2013. "Archaeological Interpretation and the Rewriting of History: Deimperializing and Decolonizing the Past at Xaltocan, Mexico." *American Anthropologist* 115: 481–495.

Pinch, Geraldine. 1994. *Magic in Ancient Egypt*. Austin: University of Texas Press.

Romano, James F. 1989. *The Bes-Image in Pharaonic Egypt*. New York: The Graduate School of Arts and Sciences.

——. 1998. "Notes on the Historiography and History of the Bes-Image in Ancient Egypt." *The Bulletin of the Australian Centre for Egyptology* 9: 89–101.

Schreiber, Katharina. 2005. "Imperial Agendas and Local Agency: Wari Colonial Strategies." In G. J. Stein (ed.), *The Archaeology of Colonial Encounters: Comparative Perspectives*, 237–262. Santa Fe: School of American Research Press.

Silliman, Stephen W. 2005. "Culture Contact or Colonialism? Challenges in the Archaeology of Native North America." *American Antiquity* 70: 55–74.

——. 2009. "Change and Continuity, Practice and Memory: Native American Persistence in Colonial New England." *American Antiquity* 74: 211–230.

Smith, Stuart Tyson. 2003. *Wretched Kush: Ethnic Identities and Boundaries in Egypt's Nubian Empire*. London: Routledge.

——. 2006–2007. "A New Napatan Cemetery at Tombos." *Cahier de recherches de l'Institut de papyrologie et d'égyptologie de Lille* 26: 347–352.

——. 2014. "Nubian and Egyptian Ethnicity." In J. McInerney (ed.), *A Companion to Ethnicity in the Ancient Mediterranean*, 194–212. New York City: John Wiley and Sons, Inc.

Stein, Gil J. 2002. "From Passive Periphery to Active Agents: Emerging Perspectives in the Archaeology of Interregional Interaction: Archaeology Division Distinguished Lecture AAA Annual Meeting, Philadelphia, December 5, 1998." *American Anthropologist* 104: 903–916.

——. 2005. "Introduction: The Comparative Archaeology of Colonial Encounters." In G. J. Stein (ed.), *The Archaeology of Colonial Encounters: Comparative Perspectives*, 3–31. Santa Fe: School of American Research Press.

Stockhammer, Philipp W. 2013. "From Hybridity to Entanglement, from Essentialism to Practice." *Archaeological Review from Cambridge: Archaeology and Cultural Mixing: Creolization, Hybridity and Mestizaje* 28: 11–28.

van Dommelen, Peter. 2002. "Ambiguous Matters: Colonialism and Local Identities in Punic Sardinia." In C. L. Lyons and J. K. Papadopoulos (ed.), *The Archaeology of Colonialism*, 121–147. Los Angeles: Getty Research Institute.

Ward, William A. 1972. "A Unique Beset Figure." *Orientalia* 41: 149–159.

Weiss, Lara. 2009. "Personal Religious Practice: House Altars at Deir El-Medina." *The Journal of Egyptian Archaeology* 95: 193–208

Welsby, Derek A. 1998. "Survey and Excavations at Kawa: The 1997/8 Season." *Sudan and Nubia* 2: 15–20.

——. 2000. "The Kawa Excavation Project." *Sudan and Nubia* 4: 5–10.

Wilkinson, Richard H. 1994. *Symbol and Magic in Egyptian Art*. London: Thames and Hudson.

——. 2003. *The Complete Gods and Goddesses of Ancient Egypt*. New York: Thames & Hudson.

Notes

1 Andrews 1994, 12; Dasen 1993, 33.

2 Arav and Bernett 1997; Dasen 1993, 47.

3 Dasen 1993, 44; Dawson 1938, 188.

4 Romano 1989, 212.

5 Arav and Bernett 1997, 205.

6 Dasen 1993, 46.

7 Arav and Bernett 1997, 205; Dasen 1993, 47; Dawson 1938, 188.

8 Cusick 1998; Dietler 2005; Liebmann and Murphy 2010 Lightfoot and Martinez 1995; Overholtzer

2013; Schreiber 2005; Silliman 2005; Stein 2002; Stein 2005; generally, Arkush 2011.

9 Malkin 2002; Mata 2013, 131–154; Stein 2002; Stockhammer 2013, 11–28; van Dommelen 2002; generally, Hodder 2011; Hodder 2012; Hodder 2014; Hodder and Mol 2015.

10 Dietler 2010, 9.

11 Dietler 2010; Stein 2005.

12 Buzon et al. 2016; also see Smith 2014, 194–212.

13 Knappett 2014; Olsen 2010, 9.

14 Morkot 2013; Smith 2003.

15 Dasen 1993, 82.

16 Andrews 1994, 79; Bosse-Griffiths 1977, 100; Dasen 1993, 55, 59, 63, 82; Ogdon 1981, 179; Pinch 1994, 44.

17 Wilkinson 2003, 103.

18 Dasen 1993, 60; Ogdon 1981, 179; Pinch 1994, 44; Ward 1972, 149.

19 Dasen 1993, 64; Wilkinson 2003, 103.

20 Dasen 1993, 61; Ward 1972, 149.

21 Bosse-Griffiths 1977, 100; Dasen 1993, 59; Pinch 1994, 44; Ward 1972, 149.

22 Ogdon 1981, 179; Romano 1989, 69–70, 109–110, 147; Wilkinson 2003, 104.

23 Dasen 1993, 67, 73.

24 Dasen 1993, 67, 77.

25 Romano 1989, 20, 110–111; Romano 1998, 89, 98–99.

26 Romano 1998, 96.

27 Ward 1972, 149.

28 Bosse-Griffiths 1977, 105; Pinch 1994, 79.

29 Arav and Bernett 1997, 204; Dasen 1993, 84, 86, 90; Wilkinson 2003, 123.

30 Dasen 1993, 88.

31 Dasen 1993, 58–59; Romano 1989, 128, 135, 153; Romano 1998, 99.

32 Dunham 1950.

33 Arav and Bernett 1997, 204; Dasen 1993, 86, 91–92; Wilkinson 2003, 123.

34 Dasen 1993, 86, 91, 96; Smith 2006–2007.

35 Andrews 1994, 55; Bosse-Griffiths 1977, 104; Dasen 1993, 55, 67, 74, 81–82; Romano 1989, 220; Weiss 2009, 202; Wilkinson 1994, 196–197; Wilkinson 2003, 102–103.

36 Pinch 1994, 44.

37 Dasen 1993, 67, 76, 82.

38 Dasen 1993, 67, 75–76, 82.

39 Dasen 1993, 67, 82.

40 Bosse-Griffiths 1977, 104; Pinch 1994, 44.

41 Dasen 1993, 82.

42 Wilkinson 2003, 102.

43 Dasen 1993, 82.

44 Dasen 1993, 85.

45 Dasen 1993, 89.

46 Dasen 1993, 89.

47 Dasen 1993, 97.

48 Gardiner 1957.

49 Dasen 1993, 89, 91–92; Wilkinson 2003, 123.

50 Minas-Nerpel 2013.

51 Dasen 1993, 89, 91–93, 98.

52 Lohwasser 2010.

53 Dunham 1963.

54 Dunham 1950.

55 Welsby 1998; Welsby 2000.

56 Dunham 1970.

57 Hawass 2000, 169–173.

58 Silliman 2009.

Journal of Ancient Egyptian Interconnections

The B3w of Taweret: Vindictiveness (and Forgiveness) of the Hippopotamus Goddess

Sabrina Ceruti
Civic Archaeological Museum, Milan

Abstract
In Egyptological scholarship, the so-called hippopotamus goddess is traditionally depicted as a completely benevolent being that is the effective apotropaic protectress of women and children. Even though this picture appears quite consistent with most of the documentation, nevertheless in a few textual instances the goddess, more or less explicitly, exhibits a menacing attitude towards the people she is usually thought to protect, even threatening the same children she ought strongly to defend. In the present paper, evidence of this malevolent facet of the goddess is gathered, arguing her more complex nature and role, and a more stratified worship than is commonly claimed. Even in the light of the goddess' long-lasting fortune, such an ambiguous facet of hers makes her perhaps one of the better cases to bring to inquiry into the ancient Egyptians' approach to the transcendental world, their deeply devotional attitude, and even their *timor*, towards it.

Introduction

Although not to be numbered among its major deities, the so-called hippopotamus goddess is nonetheless one of the most long-lived and successful beings of the Egyptian pantheon, her career spanning from the late Old Kingdom, if not earlier, well into the Ptolemaic and Roman periods.[1] In Egyptological scholarship, she is traditionally portrayed as a completely benevolent entity. Almost invariably associated with Bes, she is included among the most popular Egyptian deities, and specifically acknowledged as one of the most favoured household and domestic[2] apotropaic being relating to pregnancy and fertility, thus the patroness of childbirth and childhood.[3]

In view of the overall paucity, and also vagueness, of relevant textual references involving a theological discourse concerning the goddess, the positing of such a role is chiefly based on her iconography and the typology of the items on which her image most frequently recurs, above all starting from the Middle Kingdom onwards. These are mainly amulets and statuettes, scarabs, the Middle Kingdom magical wands and rods, jewellery, and other implements recognized as being primarily connected with protective or healing rituals and practices referring to women—above all of pregnant women, women in labour and puerperae—their newborn babies, and children.[4]

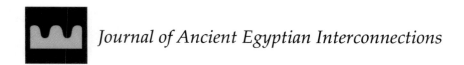

In her more distinctive and recurring frightful image—seemingly hippopotamic but actually hybrid, blending both human and animal components—she could actually embody a very effective apotropaic force. With the rounded belly of a pregnant woman and the heavy breasts of a nursing mother, threateningly standing erect on her lions' paws, holding the *s3*-sign/amulet symbol of protection and/or one or more knives, and, last but not least, exhibiting a fearsome hippopotamus' snarling muzzle and a crocodile's skin on the back, she must have been wielded to ward off whatever potential evil force that could menace mainly pregnancy and childbirth, as well as that might prevent the healing of newborns and infants, and indeed, any vulnerable individual.

However, although such a portrait may be accurate, in light of the most comprehensive evidence related to the deity and also in view of the often scanty reliability—and in many cases the complete lack—of archaeological data (even more so when referring to early excavations),[5] the goddess' status as a household/domestic deity should not be overemphasized,[6] nor should perhaps her role be restricted to the positive and benevolent one sketched above.

Of the already mentioned meagre textual evidence that contributes to defining her nature, there are in fact a few instances in which, more or less explicitly, a very dreadful attitude is attributed to the hippopotamus goddess, this time directed towards the vulnerable individuals whom she ought protect and not towards the hostile powers that might menace them. The evidence of this harmful facet of the goddess has remained largely unnoticed, and even underestimated, in Egyptological scholarship.[7] but it turns out to be indeed prominent for establishing the nature of the goddess, allowing us to construe a more complex character and a more stratified worship and cult of her than the ones commonly stated. These occurrences appear in, and are mainly restricted to, the Ramesside New Kingdom, therefore primarily concerning her name of Taweret,[8] and stem particularly from the Theban milieu, where her worship and cult were seemingly more rooted than elsewhere at that time.

The *B3w* of Taweret, or the Revenge of the Goddess

A small group of documents from the settlement of Deir el-Medina refers to a *b3w (n) T3-wr.t*, i.e., a *b3w*-manifestation of the goddess. Notwithstanding some minor interpretative nuances and, as a consequence, divergent translations into various modern languages, there is so far general agreement relating to the concept of a divine *b3w*. On the most general level, it neutrally designates the capacity of a transcendental being to manifest in the human sphere, that is, the perceptible materialization of its power experienceable as an episode in whatever context and by whatever means. More specifically, it signifies a deity's injurious intervention in a person's life in response to an offence he/she has received: therefore, accordingly, a manifestation of an avenging wrath directed towards the offender, implicitly demanding a show of remorse from him/herself.[9] False oaths seem to be the grounds for this divine anger in some cases, but mostly the motive—evidently a human *hybris*—is left unsaid, nor is it specified what trouble the manifestation has caused, although in some cases it must have been a health issue, such a temporary blindness.[10] The texts implying such a dreadful divine intervention are mostly strictly associated with the sphere of the so-called "personal piety"[11] and refer to it concisely as both *b3w (nṯr) ḫprw*, "a (divine) manifestation come about" (without naming the deity actually concerned), and *b3w (n) D(ivine) N(ame)*, respectively, or in more elaborate inscriptions in which the author proclaims—and warns against—the wrath of such and such a deity as it has been experienced by him/herself. Each of these forms occurs in the instances relating to Taweret herewith concerned, all from the Nineteenth–Twentieth Dynasties.[12]

1: Ostracon Ashmolean Museum 166

The first one is O. Ashmolean Museum 166 (ro. 1–3),[13] a statement before the local law-court in which a certain Nakhtmin[14] reports a theft he suffered by a certain lady Tanehesy[15]. He tells how, while he was sitting in his private chapel on the occasion of a festival of Taweret (named the "Birth of Taweret"),[16] the said lady stole from him one of his *sš*-cakes—clearly an offering to the goddess on her feast day—and how *ḫr ir s3 10 n hrw iw=ś ii r ḏd n=i b3w ḫprw*, "but ten days later she (i.e., Tanehesy) came saying to me: 'a divine manifestation has come about!'" (ro. 2–3).[17]

Although, as a rule, there is no mention of how the manifestation occurred,[18] nor is it explicitly stated that is was indeed her *b3w*, it was evidently the evil manifestation of the goddess herself that Tanehesy experienced in the ten days that elapsed between her theft and her confession (perhaps a significant timing, if the date of the feast were known).[19] And it may have been perhaps the fear of experiencing, in his turn, the same goddess' wrath—for having failed to accomplished his due rituals towards her—that led to Nakhtmin making a public statement, thus exonerating himself before the deity.[20]

Instead of being deduced from events, in the next two instances a *b3w* is openly attributed to Taweret, although, unlike in the previous instance, here the actual context is much less clear. Both are related to a consultation of the so-called wise woman (*t3 rḫ.t*). She was a sort of diviner and/or healer, perhaps as well a sort of magical practitioner, whose in-depth knowledge (*rḫ*) of both human and transcendental matters and the intrinsic link between the two meant one could ask for advice and an explanation of otherwise inexplicable events, in order to find a solution.[21]

2: OSTRACON DEM 1690

In the fragmentary letter of O. DeM 1690,[22] an unnamed man is requested to turn to the wise woman to ask her about an anonymous woman's ocular disease, which someone else (a man?) seems to have already linked to the *b3w n T3-wr.t nb.t-p.t [ỉw=f ḥr]*[23] *ỉr.t r=s ḥr ḥr=f*: "a manifestation of Taweret, lady of the sky, [and it (the *b3w*)] acted against her because of him"(ro. 3–5). Due to the numerous lacunae, other particulars are difficult to grasp. We do not know the reply of the wise woman, whether or not she may have confirmed the suspected *b3w n T3 -wr.t* to be the cause of the trouble; however, the fact remains that Taweret is here explicitly considered to be the one who is probably responsible for the affection of the eyes (temporary blindness?) of the woman in question, and that such a punishment has fallen on the poor woman for the misbehaviour (a false oath?) of someone else, a male person (*ḥr ḥr=f*), somehow linked to her.

3: OSTRACON CAIRO CG 25674

The likewise fragmentary letter of O. Cairo CG 25674[24] parallels the previous one. The *b3w T3-wr.t [nb.t-p.t]* ,[25] "a manifestation of Taweret [lady of the sky]," is here instead mentioned as being the precise reply of the wise woman consulted (ro. 4), here too, by an unnamed male person on the advice of another else, who had previously been told by a woman (wise? the same wise woman?) about the *b3w n Nmty*, "a manifestation of Nemty." The context of the letter is unfortunately far from clear and does not allow a firm interpretation of the circumstances[26] or of the connection—not attested elsewhere, to my knowledge—of the two diverse deities mentioned, if indeed there is any. Nemty is a falcon god who acts primarily as a ferryman to whom is attached a bad reputation: at least by the Late Period sources, he is charged with the mythical episode of beheading of the cow goddess.[27]

4: OSTRACON OIM 16974 VO.

Another possible instance of an evil manifestation of Taweret is to be recognised in the letter of O. OIM 16974 v°, but the text is too poorly preserved to allow a continuous translation.[28] The *nḥt* of Taweret (instead of her *b3w*) is mentioned there (vo. 2) within a context of apparent suffering on the part of the addressee (vo. 4: *m ỉr šn.t ḥ3ty=ṯ m d[ḥr(.t)?]*, "don't question heart with [bitterness(?)]"[29]). Moreover, it is far from clear if this passage—introduced by *ky ḏd* (vo. 1)—could be connected with the letter on the *recto* of the ostracon, which records another consultation of the wise woman, this time regarding two children.[30]

5: OSTRACON DEM 251

A link between (the *b3w* of) Taweret and another deity's *b3w*, only inferable in the above presented O. Cairo CG 25674, is perhaps actually involved in the brief message of O. DeM 251 (ro. 1–4).[31] In this case, an unnamed man commissions to his addressee the making of *wꜥ n <T3?-> wr.t* "a(nother) (statue(ette)/ amulet of Ta?)weret" (ro. 1),[32] because the one of the latter made for him before had been stolen *ḫr ỉry=s b3w Stḫ ỉr=ỉ*, "so it (image)/she (deity) may work a manifestation of Seth against me." Therefore, it was feared the stolen item could impel the evil manifestation of Seth against its previous, and righteous, owner: either by being suitably (i.e., magically) manipulated by a third party, the thief, against its former owner, or simply because this latter could have been considered, somehow, negligent in the care of his holy item and therefore with the pious ties to the being represented by the item.[33] Certainly without his sacred item he could not fulfil the ritual duties attached to it and thus receive protection by means of it. It remains to be seen exactly what kind of item it was and from where it had been stolen. Borghouts, both with philological and contextual arguments, convincingly argued that the term *wr.t/(T3)-wr.t* identifies metonymically a statue(ette) (or amulet?) of the goddess Taweret:[34] might it be a cultic or votive statue(ette) stolen from the owner's house, that is, from his private altar? Or, rather, from a community chapel?[35] The question is of no minor importance, but it seems destined to remain unanswered. What is noteworthy is that the sacred item, metonymically the goddess, was thought to have power over another deity—namely Seth—as a sort of "master of demons." And indeed, the hippopotamus goddess appears endowed with such power in a few slightly later texts, which leads us away from the Deir el-Medina settlement, although we remain in the Theban milieu.

Among the category of dangerous demons listed in the so-called Oracular Amuletic Decrees of the Twenty-first Dynasty,[36] and from which one must be kept safe, are *wrt*-demons. Both female and male, these beings can reveal themselves in various environments, but neither a peculiar iconography nor behaviour is assigned to them.[37] These *wrt*-demons have been cited by some commentators with regard to the *wr.t* of O. DeM 251, and also Borghouts commented on the possible link with the two. Next I would like to underline a particular passage from one such decree that seems to me to be relevant and which strengthens Borghouts' interpretation of the ostracon, here accepted and shared.

6: Papyrus British Museum EA 10251

In the decree for Taahuty of Papyrus British Museum EA 10251, one such female-*wrt* is exceptionally qualified by the definite article and is explicitly named as the foremost of the same category of beings, which, moreover, is here specifically ascribed to the astral milieu. The following is proclaimed: *ỉw=ỉ <r> šd=s m-ḏr.t tꜣ wr.t tꜣ p.t tꜣ ḥꜣ.ty nꜣ wr(.w)t*, "I (the god Khonsu, who emitted the decree) will keep her safe from the hand of *the* demoness (Ta-weret) of the sky, the foremost of the *wrt*-demons" (ro. 32–33).[38] It is noteworthy that here the spelling of the compound *tꜣ-wr.t*, with the egg and cobra classifiers, parallels the name of our hippopotamus goddess: this latter generally displays few graphic variations, and is preferably written without classifier(s) at all, but where present, they are the cobra alone or the cobra and the egg.[39] With the last fullest spelling, the goddess' name appears in the brief label of her image on the Deir el-Medina stele CGT 50062, describing her as *Tꜣ-wr.t tꜣ p.t*, "Taweret of the sky."[40] As isolated as it is, this label could make the connection between the "chief of the *wrt*-demons" of papyrus British Museum EA 10251 and the hippopotamus goddess Taweret be much more than a surmise.[41]

The grounds for such a connection might have been her astral role, i.e., the catasterism of the goddess—well established in the New Kingdom—rather than her commonest epithet *nb.t p.t*, indeed one of the most common epithets for goddesses, which extolls their (great) godhead above all. On the so-called astronomical ceilings of the Theban royal tombs, the image of the hippopotamus goddess stands out among the imperishable stars of the northern sky, embodying the foremost of the circumpolar constellations with the task of firmly holding in its due place the Meskhetiu-Seth constellation (i.e., the Big Dipper/*Ursa Major*), thus preventing him from wandering in the sky and the perversion of the cosmic cycle this would have caused (as related texts tell us).[42] Such an astral image must have been very familiar to the Deir el-Medina workmen in charge of the decoration of the royal tombs, and one might wonder if her astral role could be the grounds of the unusual Taweret's epithet on the stele CGT 50062—later mirrored in the papyrus BM EA 10251—and of the hold she, or rather, her *bꜣw*, was thought to have over Seth in O. DeM 251. Although in the New Kingdom Seth had not yet undergone his quasi-complete demonization into the ultimate evil god he would be from the Third Intermediate Period onward, his role as the possible agent of all kinds of diseases, and even death, was renowned:[43] among others, he was considered the agent of infertility (as an emasculated god), miscarriage, and even forcible rape.[44] The latter are possibly further grounds for his connection with Taweret, otherwise very scanty and ambiguously documented in the Egyptian sources[45] prior to Plutarch's statement about her having been Seth (-Typhon)'s unfaithful concubine.[46] Could Seth be chosen by Taweret as the due agent of her own revenge? The argument risks appearing circular, based on the presumption that the punishment of the deity could be enacted appropriately in the sphere commonly attributed to her exclusive concern, i.e., pregnancy, birthing, and its related phases. But the instances collected here do not appear so confidently related to such circumstances, with the exception of possibly O. OIM 16974 (above, no. 4).[47]

However, other categories of demons can be under the command of the hippopotamus goddess.

7: Louvre E 25479

The three columned text of the back pillar of the votive statuette Louvre E 25479 is one of the most meaningful concerning the goddess (Fig. 1a–b).[48] The statuette was dedicated by two Theban high priests of Amun, probably cousins, in the early Twenty-second Dynasty, and the inscription concerns a goddess' self presentation. At the beginning, in a statement that translates literally her monstrous aggressiveness she says: *ỉnk Rr.t hd m ḫrw=s wnm m*

FIGURE 1: Statuette Louvre E 25479. © Musée du Louvre, dist. RMN—Grand Palais/Christian Décamps.

ḥs=s qꜣỉ ḫrw khb dnỉ.wt, "I am Reret, who attacks with her voice, who devours who presses her, in a loud voice, uttering roars" (col.1).[49] Later on, she specifically qualifies herself as (cols. 2–3):

> *<Tꜣ>-wr.t m sḫm=s ꜥhꜣ.t ḥr jḥt=s dr ꜥwꜣwy (...) ỉnk Ỉpt ḥry-ỉb ꜣḫ.t mk ds<=s> nb-(r)-ḏr nb(.t) nrw ꜥpr <m> ḫprw dndn sbỉw ḥr=f ḫsb ỉnw nt ḫtmyw šmꜣyw ẖr ḏbꜥ=ỉ qdftyw ḥr <ḏd> m pw rf ỉr=n wḏ.n=ỉ mwt r ꜥnḫ,*

> I am (Ta)weret in her might, who fights for her ownership, who repels the demons of prey. I am Ipet on the horizon, whose knife protects the Universal God,[50] the Lady of the fear, of perfect manifestation (*ḫprw*), who beheads his (the Universal God's) rebel-demons. (I) count the duties of the Sealer-demons, the Wanderer-demons are under my control, the demons of death say 'what is it that we should do?' when I have sent death instead of life.

The votive context makes these statements a very epitome of the goddess' apotropaic nature and the means by which she materializes it, but it remains outstanding that she proclaims herself an agent of death instead of life[51], controlling, in her turn, demons of destruction and death, which, if angered —and her *bꜣw*-manifestation testifies she might!— she could unleash not for protection but for vengeance.

8: GRAFFITO DEIR EL-BAHRI 50

Turning back to Ramesside times, we are again faced with the evil nature of Taweret in the Graffito Deir el-Bahri 50, a threat-formula left by a doorkeeper of the temple of Maat in Thebes, named Penpamer, on one of the columns of the Thutmoside temple:[52] *(2)*

ỉr pꜣ nty ỉw=f (3) ftt rn<=ỉ>r rdỉ.t rn=f ỉr n=f (4) Ptḥ m ỉry n ꜥḥꜣ (5) ỉw Sḫm.t m-sꜣ ḥmwt=f ỉw Tꜣ-wr.t (6) <m->sꜣ ẖrdw=f, "as for the one who shall erase <my> name in order to place his name, Ptah shall/may be an opponent to him, (while) Sakhmet shall/may be after his wives, (and) Taweret after his offspring" (ll. 2–6).[53] Taweret is here invoked—even if not named, in a sense, as a *bꜣw*—as an agent of punishment, and her victims are specifically children. Yet, in another, coeval graffito of Deir el-Bahri we find exactly the same sequence of threats, but there the agents are Osiris,[54] Hathor, and Meretseger, the latter two engaged with wives and children, respectively. It is noteworthy that the authors of this curse are two members of the Deir el-Medina village where the two goddesses were prominent.[55] In another threat we again find Sakhmet as the potential persecutor of wives, but Nefertem—Sakhmet's child—as the persecutor of children.[56] Indeed, on graffito Deir el-Bahri 50, Taweret appears in an unusual triad; but, facing the examples just quoted as well as other Ramesside/ Theban threat-formulae, this one may reflect instead a personal divine constellation of the author of the curse—perhaps local and/or based on an association with work duties—rather than a "specialization" of roles of the god/goddesses invoked to protect his pious signature in the temple.[57] Ptah and the lioness goddess Sakhmet are both Memphite gods and, with Nefertem, they fulfil the role of the local triad, but both are present in the Theban area, as well as the hippopotamus goddess. Ptah, frequently bears the epithet "Lord of Maat"—could this be a connection with the author's office in the Maat temple?[58]—and his *bꜣw*-manifestation (after false oaths) is well documented.[59] On the other hand, his consort Sakh-met is the dangerous female deity par excellence in the Egyptian pantheon.[60]

9: Harris Magical Papyrus

Just after Sakhmet, however, Taweret is included in a brief list of dangerous beasts and goddesses to be warded off in a spell for the protection of the herd in the late Ramesside Harris Magical Papyrus. The litany recites: *štb<.tw> rꜣ < n> Tꜣ-wr(.t) ꜥnḫ(.t)*, "May be sealed the mouth of Taweret, the living one." The formula employed is the same for all the members on the list, and is, therefore, not significant for Taweret, being merely a conjuration to render the conjured beings/deities harmless. In the spell we found an obvious allusion to her possible destructive and harmful behaviour towards the living ones—injuries to the herd would imply trouble for them—likely more specifically to her being a devourer (as in her own words on the Louvre statuette, no. 7), even though an explanation for her inclusion in such a context, as well as for her unusual epithet (a *hapax*, to my knowledge), still seems far from clear to me and deserves further investigation.[61]

10: Stele Glasgow EGNN. 683

The *bꜣw* of Taweret is definitely proclaimed in its effectiveness on the Stele Glasgow EGNN. 683 dedicated to the goddess by the guardian Penbuy, who lived at Deir el-Medina in the Nineteenth Dynasty.[62] The text of the stele belongs to the so-called *Bekenntnisbiographien*, in which the author/ devotee acknowledges his/her own misbehaviour and the justness of the punishment consequently doled out by the offended deity, and then proclaims the greatness of the divine clemency finally received.[63] Penbuy does not admit his crime, nor what type of punishment he received from Taweret, but sincerely promises: *ỉw=ỉ r ḥn tꜣ pḥ.tỉ <=ṯ> ꜥꜣ.t n ḫm ṯw n rḫ ṯw ỉw=ỉ r ḏd n ḏꜣm.w n ḏꜣm.w sꜣw=tn r=s ỉrỉ*: "I will let <your> great power be known to those who do not (still) know it and to those who know it. I will tell generation after generation: 'Beware of her!'" (cols. 5–6). And goes on to say: *hrw ḥtp<ỉm=f>* T*ꜣ-wrt ṯꜣỉ ỉb=ỉ rš.w(.t)*, "The day Taweret is pleased, my heart swells with joy" (col. 6); and finally he proclaims: *nw rmṯ nb ntj ꜥnḫ snḏw n Tꜣ-wr.t pꜣ-wn dns bꜣw=s r ḏw n bjꜣ ḫr pꜣ ꜥnḫ pꜣy=s ḥtp*, "Beware, O living men, fear Taweret, for her *bꜣw* (wrath) is heavier than a mountain of metal, but the life is (depend on) her clemency" (cols. 9–10). The goddess is to Penbuy's eyes *tꜣ ꜥn.t ḥtp.tỉ* "the wonderful, when (you are) in a merciful mood"[64] (col. 2), a statement that is also visually translated into the image of the goddess pictured on the stele: that of a beautiful and slender seated woman—*Ỉi.tỉ-nfr.tỉ* she is addressed at the beginning of the hymn (col. 1)— which is one of the rare instances known of a wholly anthropomorphic image of Taweret.[65]

Conclusions

The above collected evidences clearly show that the hippopotamus goddess does not always embody a secure and benevolent protectress of the living. Quite the contrary, in such texts she exhibits a capricious and irascible nature directed towards the very ones she should protect (nos. 1–5; 8) and reveals all the means she can draw on in order to manifest her unfriendly aspect: not only does she wield her own brutish power and weapons (knives), but she could even summon up other gods, namely Seth (no. 5) and bands of demons (no. 7).

This negative character helps to draw a better picture of the goddess in the light of the overall documentation related to her. Certainly, it seems to be the sum of her definite primary, and indeed fundamental, apotropaic nature—she is aggressive in order to protect!—and possibly stems from her being originally a liminal entity, as her very hybrid iconography, which is to be held as the original (being the earliest documented) and likewise bound to be the most long-lived, also seems to attest. The adjective *wr.t*, "great," incorporated into her own name, Taweret, is, maybe, itself liminal, a cross between a common divine epithet (as it is) and a demonic one, at least according to one of the Oracular Amuletic Decrees (no. 6). Through the paper I have constantly referred to her as a goddess, and this is highly consistent for the period concerned in the texts discussed. Such texts reflect Ramesside "personal piety" of the Theban milieu, where she also had a her own cult and appears beside some of the major deities:[66] her inclusion in such "personal" expressions, which reflect the intimate pious spirit and the *timor dei* of the devotees towards their chosen deities,[67] is therefore to be viewed in my opinion as the better reflection of her "career," in a sense, of her "promotion"—of which the Ramesside period seems also the acme—from perhaps more "demonic" origins. Furthermore, as an important corollary—to be further dealt with elsewhere—reflect a complex and wide spectrum of her sway, e.g., her worship being also, and importantly, a male concern [1–2(?), 5, 7–9].[68] Finally, the ambiguous nature of the hippopotamus goddess, in light of her long-lasting fortune, can add some clues to the debate on the definition of demon versus god/godhead in Egyptian religious thought, and left consciously in the background of this paper.[69] Cases of demons who attain a cult, are converted into personal protectors, and thus gain complete godhead are recognizable as mainly Late Period phenomena:[70] in this respect, the case of the hippopotamus goddess appears to be of the utmost interest, because it might be one of the first well documented of this type, her "promotion," in this sense, dating to the Ramesside period (if not even earlier), within the exploit of the "personal piety" phenomenon. On the other hand, even major gods and goddesses have their dual personality: Sakhmet and Seth being prototypical examples, but every god and goddess could be angry and display a demonic—namely, harmful—character.[71] Indeed, dualistic—or rather flexible—as is the Egyptian religious and mythical way of thinking and of viewing the world,[72] it might be ultimately be safer not to seek a definite separation between "demonic" and "godhead," i.e., greater and lesser deities, but instead to think that we are merely faced with the dual/flexible expression of the divine inhabiting the world,[73] more or less great may the deity in concern be.[74]

Acknowledgments

I should like to acknowledge here my gratitude to Kasia Szpakowska (Swansea) for inviting me to contribute to the present volume of proceedings, even though I did not actually participate to the conference from which it arises, and thus affording me the opportunity to develop the topic set forth here. Thanks to Judith for correcting and improving my English and the anonymous reviewer for comments and suggestions. Any errors that may remain are, of course, my own.

References

Assmann, Jan. 1994. "Oracular Desire in a Time of Darkness: Urban Festivals and Divine Visibility in Ancient Egypt." In Ahron R. E. Agus and Jan Assmann (eds.), *Oracular Desire*, 13–29. Yearbook for Religious Anthropology. Berlin: Akademie-Verlag.

Baines, John. 2000. "Egyptian Deities in Context: Multiplicity, Unity, and the Problem of Change" In Barbara Nevling Porter (ed.), *One God or Many? Concepts of Divinity in the Ancient World*, 9–78. Transaction of the Casco Bay Assyriological Institute 1. Casco Bay, ME: Assyriological Institute.

Baines, John and Elisabeth Frood. 2011. "Piety, Change and Display in the New Kingdom." In Mark Collier and Steven Snape (eds.), *Ramesside Studies in Honour of Ken A. Kitchen*, 1–17. Bolton: Rutherford Press.

Barbotin, Christopher. 2007. *Les statues égyptiennes du Nouvel Empire. Statues royales et divines*, vols. 1–2. Paris: Musée du Louvre, Khéops.

Baum, Natalie. 2008. "Les *baou* et leur action sur terre." In Christine Gallois, Pierre Grandet, and Laura Pantalacci (eds.), *Mélanges offert à François*

Neveu par ses amis, élèves et collègues à l'occasion de son soixante-quizième anniversaire, 9–31. Bibliothèque d'étude 145. Le Caire: Institute français d'archéologie orientale.

Bierbrier, Morris and Hermann De Meulenaere. 1984. "Hymne à Taouêret sur une stele de Deir el Médineh." In Rostislav Holthoer and Tullia Linders (eds.), *Sundries in Honour of Torgny Säve-Söderbergh*, 23–32. Acta Universitatis Uppsaliensis Boreas 13. Uppsala-Stockholm: Universitetet; Almqvist & Wicksell.

Blumenthal, Elke. 2011. "Das Schwangere Nilpferd und andere Nothelfergottheiten—Polytheistische Frömmigkeit im Ägyptische Neuen Reich." *THOTs* 6: 9–15.

Bomann, Ann H. 1991. *The Private Chapel in Ancient Egypt*. London—New York: Kegan Paul.

Bommas, Martin. 1998. *Die Heidelberger Fragmente des magischen Papyrus Harris*. Heidelberg: Universitätsverlag C. Winter.

Borghouts, Joris F. 1971. *The Magical Text of Papyrus Leiden I 348*. Oudheidkundige mededelingen uit het Rijksmuseum van Oudheden 51. Leiden: Brill.

——. 1982. "Divine Intervention in Ancient Egypt and Its Manifestation (*Bꜣw*)." In Robert J. Demarée and Jac. J. Janssen (eds.), *Gleanings from Deir el-Medîna*, 1–70. Egyptologischen Uitgaven 1. Leiden: The Netherlands Institute for the Near East.

Brunton, Guy. 1948. *Matmar: British Museum Expedition to Middle Egypt, 1929–1931*. London: B. Quaritch.

Černý, Jaroslav. 1935. *Catalogue général des antiquités du Musée du Caire Nos. 25501–25832. Ostraca hiératiques*, I–II. Le Caire: Institut français d'archéologie orientale.

——. 1939. *Catalogue des Ostraca Hiératiques non littéraires de Deir el Médineh*, IV. Le Caire: Institut français d'archéologie orientale.

Ceruti, Sabrina. 2013. "La percezione del *mostruoso* nell'antico Egitto: il caso della dea-ippopotamo." In Igor Baglioni (a cura di), *Monstra. Costruzione e percezione delle entità ibride e mostruose nel Mediterraneo Antico*, vol. I, 17–28. Religio 1. Roma: Edizioni Qasar.

——. 2017. "The Hippopotamus Goddess Carrying a Crocodile on Her Back: An Iconographical Motif Distinctive of the Late Middle Kingdom." In Gianluca Miniaci, Marilina Betrò, and Stephen Quirke (eds.), *Modelling the Imaginary World of Middle Kingdom Egypt (2000–1500 BC)*, 93–123. Orientalia Lovaniensia Analecta 262. Leuven—Paris—Bristol CT: Peeters.

Cox, Michael J. 2013. *Ba'al and Seth: An Investigation into the Relationship of two Gods with References to their Iconography* (c. 1500-1000 BC). PhD dissertation, Stellenbosch University.

Davies, Benedict G. 1999. *Who's Who at Deir el-Medina: A Prosopographic Study of the Royal Workmen's Community*. Egyptologischen Uitgaven 13. Leiden: Institute of Ancient Near East.

——. 2013. *Ramesside Inscriptions Translated and Annotated: Notes and Comments III: Ramesses II, His Contemporaries*. Chichester: Wiley-Blackwell.

Donker van Heel, Koenraad. 2016. *Mrs. Naunakhte and Family: The Women of Ramesside Deir el-Medina*. Cairo—New York: American University Press.

——, Robert J. Demarée, Ben Haring and Jana Toivari-Viitala (eds.). *The Deir el-Medina Database*. Leiden. < http://dmd.wepwa wet.nl/ >.

Edwards, Iorwerth E.S. 1960. *Hieratic Papyri in the British Museum, Fourth Series: Oracular Amuletic Decrees of the Late New Kingdom*. London: Trustees of the British Museum.

Fischer-Elfert, Hans W. 1993. Review: Gasse, Annie. 1990. *Catalogue des ostraca hiératiques littéraires de Deir el-Medina, Nos. 1676–1774*, Le Caire: Institut français d'archéologie Orientale. *Bibliotheca Orientalis* 50: 125–130.

Frandsen, Peter J. 2011. "Faeces of the Creator or the Temptation of the Dead." In Peter Kousoulis (ed.), *Ancient Egyptian Demonology: Studies on the Boundaries between the Demonic and the Divine in Egyptian Magic*, 25–62. Orientalia Lovaniensia Analecta 175. Leuven—Paris—Walpole, MA: Peeters.

Gabler, Kathrin. 2017. "Stele Turin CGT 50057 (= Cat. 1514) im ikonographischen und prosopografischen Kontext Deir el-Medines: *nb.t pr Mw.t(-m-wjꜣ)* (vi) im Spannungsfeld der Mächte der Taweret und des Seth?" *Rivista del Museo Egizio* 1: 1–34.

Galán, José M. 1999. "Seeing Darkness." *Chronique d'Égypte* 74: 18–30.

Germond, Philipp. 1981. *Sakhmet et la protection du monde*. Aegyptiaca Helvetica 9. Genève: Les Belle-Lettres.

Goebs, Katia. 2002. "A Functional Approach to the Egyptian Myth and Mythemes." *Journal of Ancient Near Eastern Religion* 2: 27–59.

Goecke-Bauer, Maren. 2003. "Untersuchungen zu den 'Torwächetern' von Deir el-Medine." In Jac. J. Janssen, Elisabeth Frood, and Maren Goecke-Bauer, *Wordcutters, Potters and Doorkeepers. Service Personnel of Deir el-Medina Workmen*, 63–153. Egyptologische Uitgaven 17. Leiden: The Netherlands Institute for the Near East.

Goyon, Jean-Claude. 2011. *Le Rituel du* sḥtp Sḫmt *au changement de cycle annuel.* Bibliotèque d'étude 141. Le Caire: Institute français d'archéologie orientale.

Graves-Brown, Carolyn. 2007. "Flint and the Northern Sky." In Thomas Schneider and Kasia Szpakowska (eds.), *Egyptian Stories: A British Egyptological Tribute to Alan B. Lloyd on the Occasion of His Retirement*, 111–135. Munster: Ugarit Verlag.

——. 2018. *Daemons and Spirits in Ancient Egypt*. Cardiff: University of Wales Press.

Griffith, John Gwyn. 1960. *The Conflict of Horus and Seth: A Study in Ancient Mythology from Egyptian and Classical Sources.* Liverpool: Liverpool University Press.

Guermeur, Ivan. 2015a. "Du dualism et l'ambivalence séthienne dans la pensée religieuse de l'Égypte ancienne." In Fabienne Jourdan and Anca Vasiliu (eds.), *Dualismes. Doctrine religieuses et traditions philosophiques*, 63–88. Cluj-Paris: Poliron-Chôra.

——. 2015b. "Un faucon et une chatte dans une recette iatromagique du papyrus de Brooklyn 6-218.2 (col. X + IV, 2–7)." In Magali Massiera, Bernand Mathieu, and Fréderic Rouflet, *Apprivoiser le sauvage—Taming the Wild*, 165–181. Égypte Nilotique et Méditerranéenne 11. Montpellier: Université Paul-Valéry Montpellier 3.

——. 2016. "Encore une historie du sorciere (*š-ˁ-l-ṯ*)? Une formule de protection de la chambra du mammisi (pBrooklyn 47.218.2, x+v$^{2-6}$)." In Sandra L. Lippert, Maren Schentuleit and Martin A. Stadler (eds.), *Sapientia Felicitas. Festschrift für Günter Wittman zum 29. Februar 2016*, 171–189. Montpellier: Équipe "Égypte Nilotique et Méditerranéenne."

Hauser-Wegner, Jennifer. 2001."Taweret." In Donald B Redford. (ed.), *The Oxford Encyclopedia of Ancient Egypt*, vol. 3, 350–351. Oxford: Oxford University Press.

Hoffman, Friedhelm and Joachim Quack. 2007. *Anthologie der demotischen Literatur*. Berlin: LIT Verlag.

Israelit Groll, Sarah. 1992. "A Model of Divine Anger." In Jurgen Osing and E. Koldin Nielsen (eds.), *The Heritage of Ancient Egypt: Studies in Honour of Erik Iversen*, 63–72. CNI Publications 13. Copenhagen: The Carsten Niebuhr Institute Publications.

Iversen, Erik. 1941. *Two Inscriptions Concerning Private Donations to Temples*. Historisk-filologiske meddelelser 27/5. Copenhagen: Munksgaard.

Janssen-Winkeln, Karl. 2005. "Vier Denkmaler einer thebanischen Offiziersfamilie der 22.Dynastie." *Studien zur Ägyptischen Kultur* 33: 125–146.

Jauhiainen, Heidi. 2009. *"Do not celebrate your feast without your neighbours." A Study of References to Feasts and Festivals in Non-Literary Documents from Ramesside Period Deir el-Medina.* Publications of the Institute for Asian and African Studies 10. Helsinki: Helsinki University Print.

Kákosy, László. 1982. "Decans in Late-Egyptian Religion." *Oikumene* 3: 163–191.

Kaper, Olaf. 2003. *The Egyptian God Tutu: A study of the Sphinx-God and Master of Demons with Corpus of Monuments*. Orientalia Lovaniensa Analecta 119. Leuven-Paris-Dudley: Peeters.

Karl, Doris. 2000. "Funktion und Bedeutung einer *weisen Frau* im alten Ägypten." *Studien zur Altägyptischen Kultur* 28:131–160.

Klotz, David. 2013. "A Theban Devotee of Seth in the Late Period." *Studien zur Altägyptische Kultur* 42: 155–180.

Kousoulis, Peter (ed.). 2011. *Ancient Egyptian Demonology: Studies on the Boundaries between the Demonic and the Divine in Egyptian Magic*. Orientalia Lovaniensia Analecta 175. Leuven: Peeters.

Leitz, Christian. 2001. *Magical and Medical Papyri of the New Kingdom: Hieratic Papyri in the British Museum VII.* London: British Museum Press.

—— (ed.). 2002. *Lexikon der ägyptischen Götter und Götterbezeichnungen*, vol. 4. Orientalia Lovaniensia Analecta 113. Leuven: Peeters.

Lesko, Barbara S. 1999. *The Great Goddess of Egypt*. Norman: University of Oklahoma Press.

——. 2008. "Household and Domestic Religion in Ancient Egypt." In John Bodel and Saul M. Olyan (eds.), *Household and Family Religion in Antiquity*,197–209. Malden—Oxford—Chichester: Wiley-Blackwell.

Lucarelli, Rita. 2009. "Popular Beliefs in Demons in the Lybian Period." In Gerard P. F Broekman, Robert J. Demarée, and Olaf E. Kaper (eds.), *The*

Lybian Period in Egypt: Historical and Cultural Studies into the 21st-24th Dynasties, 231–239. Egyptologische Uitgaven 23. Leiden: The Netherland Institute of the Near East.

Luiselli, Maria Michela. 2011. *Die Suche nach Gottesnähe. Untersuchungen zur Persönlichen Frömmigkeit in Ägypten von der Ersten Zwischenzeit bis zum Ende des Neues Reiches.* Ägypten und Altes Testament 73. Wiesbaden: Harrassowitz.

——. 2013. "Images of Personal Religion: An Outline." In Maria Michela Luiselli, Jürgen Mohn, and Stephane Gripentrog (eds.), *Kult und Bild. Die bildliche Dimension der Kultes in Alten Orient, in der Antike und in der Neuzeit*, 13–40. Würzburg: Ergon Verlag.

Mahmoud, Adel. 1999. "Ii-neferti, a Poor Woman." *Mitteilungen des Deutschen Archäologische, Institute Abteilung Kairo* 55: 315–323.

Manassa, Coleen. 2013. "Divine Taxonomy in the Underworld Books." *Archiv für Religionsgeschichte* 14: 47–68.

Marciniak, Marek L. 1974. *Deir el Bahari I. Les Inscriptions hiératiques du temple de Thoutmosis III.* Warsaw: PWN—Éditions scientifiques en Pologne.

Mathieu, Bernand. 1993. "Sur quelques ostraca hiératiques littéraires récemment publiés." *Bulletin de l'Institute français d'archéologie orientale* 93: 335–347.

McDowell, Angela G. 1999. *Village Life in Ancient Egypt: Laundry Lists and Love Songs.* Oxford: Oxford University Press.

Mendel, Daniela. 2005. *Die Monatsgöttingen in Tempeln und im Privaten Kult.* Rites Égyptiens 11. Bruxelles: Brepols.

Meurer, Georg. 2015. *Penbui—Wächter an der Stätte der Wahrheit. Eine prosopographische Untersuchung zu Deir el-Medine in der 19. Dynastie.* Egyptology 24. London: Golden House Publications.

Morschauser, Scott. 1991. *Threat-Formulae in Ancient Egypt: A Study of the History, Structure and Use of Threats and Curses in Ancient Egypt.* Baltimore: Halgo.

Nagy, István. 1992. "La statue de Thouéris au Caire (CG 39194), et la légende de la déesse lontaine." In Ulrich Luft (ed.), *The Intellectual Heritage of Egypt: Studies Presented to L. Kákosy by Friends and Colleagues on the Occasion of His 60th Birthday*, 449–456. Studia Aegyptiaca 14. Budapest: Chaire d'égyptologie.

Nassar, Mohamed A. 2019. "The Wise Woman and the Healing Practice (O.OIM 16974)." *Journal of Ancient Egyptian Interconnections* 24: 41–48.

O'Rourke, Paul. 2015. *A Royal Book of Protection of the Saite Period: pBrooklyn 47-218.49.* Yale Egyptological Studies 9. New Haven: Yale Egyptological Institute.

Porter, Bertha and Rosalind Moss. 1972. *Topographical Bibliography of Ancient Egyptian Hieroglyphinc Texts, Reliefs, and Paintings, Vol. II: Theban Temples.* 2nd edition. Oxford: Clarendon Press.

Quack, Joachim. 1999. "Balsamierung und Totengericht im Papyrus Insiger." *Enchoria* 25: 27–38.

Ritner, Robert K. 2008. "Household Religion in Ancient Egypt." In John Bodel and Saul M. Olyan (eds.), *Household and Family Religion in Antiquity*,171–196. Malden—Oxford—Chichester: Wiley-Blackwell.

——. 2011. "An Eternal Curse upon the Reader of These Lines (with Apologies to M. Puig)." In Peter Kousoulis (ed.), *Ancient Egyptian Demonology: Studies on the Boundaries between the Demonic and the Divine in Egyptian Magic*, 3–24. Orientalia Lovaniensia Analecta 175. Leuven—Paris—Walpole, MA: Peeters.

Sabek, Yasser. 2016. *Die Hieratischen Besucher-Graffiti* ḏsr-ꜣḫ.t *in Deir el-Bahari.* Internet-Beiträge zur Ägyptologie und Sudanarchäologie 18. London: Golden House Publications.

Sadek, Ashraf J. 1984a. "An Attempt to Translate the Corpus of the Deir el-Bahri Hieratic Inscriptions." *Göttinger Miszellen* 71: 67–91.

——. 1984b. "An Attempt to Translate the Corpus of the Deir el-Bahri Hieratic Inscriptions (Part Two)." *Göttinger Miszellen* 72: 65–86.

——. 1987. *Popular Religion in Egypt during the New Kingdom.* Hildesheimer Ägyptologische Beiträge 27. Hildesheim: Gerstenberg.

Stevens, Anna. 2009. "Domestic Religious Practices." In Willeke Wendrich and Jacco Dieleman (eds.), *UCLA Encyclopedia of Egyptology.* Los Angeles: eScholarship. < https://escholarship.org/uc/item/7s07628w >.

Sweeney, Deborah. 2015. "Masculinity, Femininity and the Spirituality of Work at Deir el-Medîna." In Peter Kousoulis and Nicolas Lazaridis (eds.), *Proceedings of the Tenth International Congress of Egyptology, University of Aegean, Rhodes, 22–29 May 2008*, 873–884. Orientalia Lovaniensia Analecta 241. Leuven—Paris—Bristol, CT: Peeters.

Szpakowska, Kasia. 2008. *Daily Life in Ancient Egypt.*

Malden—Oxford: Blackwell.
Te Velde, Herman. 1967. *Seth, God of Confusion: A Study of His Role in Egyptian Mythology and Religion.* Probleme der Ägyptologie 6. Leiden: Brill.
Thiers, Christopher. 2013. "La Chapelle d'Ipet la Grande/Epoeris sur le parvis du temple de Louqsor. Relecture d'une stele kouchite." In Christopher Thiers (ed.), *Documents de théologies thébaines tardives* 2, 149–173. Cahiers Égypte nilotique et Méditerranéenne 8. Montpellier: Université Paul Valéry.
Toivari-Viitala, Jaana. 2001. *Women at Deir el-Medina: A Study of the Status and Roles of the Female Inhabitants in the Workmen's Community during the Ramesside Period.* Egyptologische Uitgaven 15. Leiden: The Netherlands Institute for the Near East.
Tosi, Mario and Alessandro Roccati. 1972. *Stele e altre epigrafi di Deir el Medina n. 50001–n. 50262.* Catalogo del Museo Egizio, Serie II, vol. I. Torino: Edizioni d'Arte Fratelli Pozzo.
Valbelle, Dominique and Emmanuel Laroze. 2010. "Un sanctuaire de Thoutmosis III à la déesse Ipy-Ouret édifié à Karnak par le première prophète d'Amon Menkhéperrêseneb." *Cahiers de Karnak* 13 : 401–428.
van Dijk, Jacobus. 2001. "Ptah." In Donald B. Redford (ed.), *The Oxford Encyclopedia of Ancient Egypt,* vol. 3, 74–76. Oxford: Oxford University Press.
Verner, Miroslav. 1969. "Statue of Taweret (Cairo Museum no. 39145) Dedicated by Pabesi and Several Remarks on the Role of the Hippopotamus Goddess." *Zeitschrift zur Ägyptischen Sprache und Altertumskunde* 96: 52–63.
Vernus, Pascal. 2003. "La piété personnelle à Deir el-Médineh. La construction de l'idée de pardon." In Guillemette Andreu (ed.), *Deir el-Médineh et la Vallée de Rois. La vie en Égypte au temps des pharaons du Nouvel Empire,* 309–347. Paris: Khéops, Musée du Louvre.
Volokhine, Youri. 2014. *Le porc en Egypt ancienne.* Liége: Presses Universitaires.
——. 2016. "La decapitation de la déesse vache." *Égypte, Afrique et Orient* 83: 7–18.
Weiss, Lara. 2015. *Religious Practices at Deir el-Medina.* Egyptologischen Uitgaven 29. Leuven—Leiden: Peeters-Netherland Institute of Ancient Near East.
Wente, Edward. 1990. *Letters of Ancient Egypt.* Atlanta: Society of Biblical Literature.
Wilfong, Terry G. 2013. "The Oracular Amuletic Decrees: A Question of Length." *Journal of Egyptian Archaeology* 99: 295–300.
Winand, Jean, and Stéphanie Gohy. 2011. "La grammaire du Papyrus Magique Harris." *Lingua Aegyptia* 19: 175–245.
Yoyotte, Jean. 2005. "Thouéris." In Pascal Vernus and Jean Yoyotte (eds.), *Bestiaire des pharaons,* 686–697. Paris: Agnès Viénot-Perrin.

Notes

1 For the deity's iconography and career, see an outline in Ceruti 2013 and 2017, 93–97.

2 See the methodological inquiries for such definitions in Ritner 2008, 171–74, 186; Lesko 2008; Stevens 2009; Weiss 2015, 1–26.

3 See, e.g., Sadek 1987, 125–127; Lesko 1999, 275; Wilkinson 2003, 183–186; Szpakowska 2008, 125–126. For some exceptions, see below, n. 7.

4 For the Middle Kingdom types of evidence, see Ceruti 2017, 95–98. To the statues/statuettes there listed (part. 97 fn. 19), is to be added the limestone statue Manchester EGY 270a-b (h. ca. 31 cm).

5 Such a corpus of evidence has been gathered in my unpublished doctoral research mainly focused on the pharaonic period (see Ceruti 2017, 94 fn. 3, to which paper I refer for a discussion in particular on the reliability of the Middle Kingdom documents).

6 See Weiss 2015, 23–27, 107, for the case of Deir el-Medina, certainly pivotal for the deity's worship in the New Kingdom, as most of the evidence related to it comes from there (see also below, n. 62).

7 Exceptions are: Borghouts 1982, 18–19, probably the first to highlight the goddess' "ambiguous role"; Hauser-Wegner 2001, 351: "Taweret could have had a *demonic* [namely, harmful] *aspect*" (brackets and italics added); Yoyotte 2005, 692: "on peut *entravoir* que la Grande pouvait à l'occasion nuire aux humains" (italics added).

8 For the entangled question of the deity's name(s)/identity(ies) as Ipy/Ipet-Reret-Taweret, see an outline with some remarks in Ceruti 2017, 94 fn. 3 (with references).

9 The seminal discussion, with references, is Borghouts (1982), who regards the term as a col-

lective/abstract noun/notion, meaning the *"ba-hood"* of a transcendental being (by nature: a god, a dead person; or by role: the king), with distinctive negative connotations, distinguisable, and therefore nearly independent (although stemming from the same root), from the singular *bꜣ* and the plural *bꜣ.w* (i.e., *"bas"*), and thus proposing for it the differentiated (albeit somehow, artificial) transliteration *bꜣw*. See also Vernus 2003, 317–318; Baum 2008, 22–23 for some remarks to Borghouts' transliteration and concept of the term, which she interprets rather at a psycho/theological level as a "revelation." For the purposes of the present paper, not focussed on the philological/semantic investigation of the concept itself, I still retain Borghouts' transliteration, which, however, fits with the texts here in concern. The expression will survive in the Demotic *b(ʿ)y.t/bw(ꜣ)*, except for one case, only with such a negative sense: see Ritner 2011, 15 (with references).

10 (Temporary) blindness being the punishment for false oath and connected with a deity's *bꜣw*, e.g., on stele BM EA 589 (Neferabu; *bꜣw Ptḥ*): Borghouts 1982, 7; recent translation in Luiselli 2011, 361–363 [G.19.6]. For blindness, real and/or metaphorical: Assmann 1994); Galán 1999; Luiselli 2011, 162–168 (with list of documents); see also Israelit Groll 1992; Mahmoud 1999.

11 The notion is not, however, confined to the "personal piety" sources, but appears also both in magic texts and literary genres (as the *Königsnovelle*). For the "personal piety"—an ever-functioning definition, the topic of which is however still highly debated, and now rather generally approached with expressions such as "practical/personal religion"—see the latest discussions in Baines and Frood 2011; Luiselli 2011 and 2013, 13–40.

12 Some new material has appeared since the study of Borghouts 1982, where first has been collected the core of this small Deir el-Medina dossier about Taweret's *bꜣw*.

13 No date preserved, but ascribed by most to the Nineteenth Dynasty (Ramesses II): lastly in Davies 2013, 401–402 [A.59: as O. Gardiner 166 (older nr.)] with references, to which must be added McDowell 1999, 102 [74.B] and Donker van Heel 2016, 50–51.

14 His identification among the villagers is impossible, as the name is common at Deir el-Medina: Davies 1999, sub index.

15 At least three women with this name are recorded at Deir el-Medina (Davies 1999, index). Donker van Heel 2016, 25, 51, assumes that this might be a further one, identifiable as the first wife of the scribe Qenhikhopshef (i)—the couple would have been childless—who later married the famous Naunakhte (i) (brackets after names, according to Davies 1999).

16 Interpretation first argued by Borghouts (1982, 4, and n. 13), accepted by Davies (2013, 401), and relied upon by Jauhiainen (2009, 154), who interprets this feast day of Taweret—for which the ostracon is presently the sole attestation—as a personal feast.

17 A similar case of theft brought before the local court is referred to in BM EA 65930 (= O. Nash. 1): here a woman who witnessed to a theft, only after experiencing a *bꜣw nṯrw ḫprw* decides to testify to the court that she had seen the crime committed: Borghouts 1982, 4 (nr.1); extensive references in Donker van Heel et al., *The Deir el-Medina Database*.

18 The *bꜣw*-manifestation being an epiphany *per se*, it might be considered a premonitory dream (Davies 2013, 400; Donker van Heel 2016, 50), or perhaps an illness, physical distress (blindness?), or any misfortune she, or someone in her family, could have suffered in those ten days, to which it was believed the confession could put a stop.

19 Borghouts 1982, 5.

20 Borghouts 1982, 5; Davies 2013, 400. Donker van Heel 2016, 51, wonders if, *"after all,"* Nakthmin's charges were instead addressed to the goddess herself.

21 This figure is referred to only in a few ostraca, all from Deir el-Medina: Karl 2000; Toivari-Viitala 2001, 228–231; cf. also Nasser 2019.

22 Fragmentary, written on both sides (ro. 1–7; vo. 1–5), no date preserved, but ascribed to the Nineteenth–Twentieth Dynasties: Mathieu 1993, 335–336; Fischer-Elfert 1993, 126; Karl 2000, 134–135; Toivari-Viitala 2001, 229.

23 Integration of Karl 2000, 134, fn. 26.

24 No date preserved, but ascribed to the Nine-

teenth–Twentieth Dynasties. Text in Černý 1935, 56, 76*, pl. 73; proposed translations: Borghouts 1982, 24; Karl 2000, 137 (the latter reproduced in Toivari-Viitala 2001, 230).

25 Integration of Mathieu 1993, 336 n. 4; cf. Karl 2000, 137.

26 The grounds for the consultation may have been the life/(false) oath of a father/a certain *P3-ìt* (ro. 3). It is likely inferred that both the deities are being pinpointed as an explanation of the man's trouble (with Borghouts 1982, 24), but one should also wonder if the text describes two diverse situations, involving two different male persons (the adviser—referring to his own earlier experience—and the advised) and two distinct divine manifestations, with neither linked to the other.

27 Reconstruction of the mythical episode in Volokhine 2016, 10–11. Nemty (previously read Anty) is the ferryman, e.g., in *The Contendings of Horus and Seth* (P. Chester Beatty I, Ramesside). The god is sometimes assimilated to Horus and, in a case, also to Seth (Te Velde 1967, 113–114): proceeding on the assumption of an actual Taweret and Nemty link, in the light of O. DeM 251 (here, no. 5), one could wonder if the assimilation with Seth is in stake here. Complete references for Nemty in Leitz 2002, 242–244.

28 Unpublished. Transcription: Notebook Černý Mss. 17.107.30. My thanks are due to the Griffith Institute staff (University of Oxford) for providing me with the scan of Černý's transcription on which my translation is based. Its publication (Nasser 2019) issued when the present paper had already been submitted for publication.

29 Černý's conjectural reading (not mentioned in Nasser 2019). For the term *dḥr(.t)* and its generally negative connotation, see O'Rourke 2015, 60 (O).

30 It has been suggested that the ostracon would have been the reply to O. Letellier, concerning a consultation of the wise woman about the death of two children. See Toivari-Viitala 2001, 229; Karl 2000, 134; Nasser 2019; complete references in Donker van Heel et al., *The Deir el-Medina Database*.

31 No date preserved, but ascribed to the Nineteenth–Twentieth Dynasties. Text in Černý 1939, 3, pl. 3. Translations and comments in Borghouts 1982, 15–19; Wente 1990, 141 [n. 182]; McDowell 1999, 102 [n. 74]. Cf. Donker van Heel et al., *The Deir el-Medina Database*.

32 Borghouts 1982, 16–17.

33 Borghouts 1982, 18; McDowell 1999, 102; Baum 2008, 19.

34 Borghouts 1982, 15–19, to whom I refer for thorough discussion. By others the item is considered as an amulet of whatever protecting entity: Edwards 1960, xxii; Baum 2008, 19; Lucarelli 2009, 234.

35 A few statues have been excavated by Bruyère in the settlement (or are ascribed to it by prosopographic data), and they range from few centimetres to the 39.5 cm tall of statue Turin C 526. However, with few exceptions (Louvre E 14377bis, from a tomb: Barbotin 2007, I–II, 178–79, cat. 115), the exact original context is hardly ascertainable. Moreover, the archaeological records seem support the conclusion that in the settlement Taweret was worshipped preferably in votive chapels (Weiss 2015, 106 and fn. 803), as the so-called *Chapelle du Djebel* (Bomann 1991, 42, 69).

36 Mostly of Theban origin, they consist of divine oracle deliberations written on narrow strips of papyrus to be worn as phylacteries by their owners—generally young males and females—for protection: Edwards 1960; Lucarelli 2009, 231–239; Wilfong 2013 (the last two with updated list of documents and bibliography).

37 Edwards 1960, xxii; Lucarelli 2009, 234–235. These demons/demonesses are rarely found outside the Oracle Amuletic Decrees, and the term will survive only with negative meaning in Demotic sources: references in Guermeur 2016, 181. See also below, n. 42. For an apotropaic/positive function attached to an *wr.t* being/goddess, see O'Rourke (2015, 199–200), who also connects her to the various manifestations of the Eye of Re.

38 Edwards 1960, 15.

39 As has been emerged from the collected corpus of evidences relating to the deity, the most relevant variant in its spelling is indeed the presence or absence of the suffix *.t* and its graphic posi-

tion. It is also worth noting that the name *T3-wr*.t will disappear from the hieroglyphic and hieratic sources by the end of the Third Intermediate Period–early Late Period. See the references above, n. 5 and 8.

40 Tosi and Roccati 1972, 100.

41 Already seen in Kákosy 1982, 185; Tosi and Roccati 1972, 100, however, reconnect the label to the commonest of Taweret's epithets, *nb.t p.t*.

42 For an alternative interpretation, stressing the watery essence of the northern sky and its link with the Inundation, see Graves-Brown 2007, 114ff. The constellation actually has various names probably based on diverse mythological traditions (for an overview: Ceruti 2017, 108–112, with references), but for the Deir el-Medina workmen it remains, first and foremost, the image of the goddess known only as Taweret in their performing "personal piety." In the late Ptolemaic Papyrus Insinger, *t3-wry(.t)* is the demoness of the bad influences, the female astrological personification of bad destiny, by whom "one is carried away" and "who causes the end" (P. Insinger, 17,8, 18,7–8; cf. also 18,18, 19,2: see Quack 1999, 28; Hoffman and Quack 2007, 258–259). I wonder if this demoness does not conceal the hippopotamus goddess, still documented in Ptolemaic-Roman times, especially in her astral conception (cf. Ceruti 2017, 94, 108–110). This topic needs further study and is, however, far beyond the limit of the present paper.

43 Mostly documented in medico-magical and funerary texts. For Seth: Te Velde 1967; recently Cox 2013, 31–53 (with bibliography); Guermeur 2015a, 76–83. Anyway, the theory of the complete Late Period demonization and proscription of Seth based on the seminal work of Te Velde (1967) has been recently questioned: see lastly Klotz 2013 (with further references).

44 Te Velde 1967, 28–29, 53–59; Guermeur 2015b, 176.

45 Besides the ostracon O. DeM 251 and the abovementioned astronomical myth, to my knowledge these are: Stele Turin CGT 50057, Ramesside, from Deir el-Medina (lastly: Gabler 2017); Stele Cairo JE 55887, Ramesside, from Matmar (Brunton 1948, 61 n. xi, pl. 50), but without any inscriptions. The hippopotamus goddess rarely appears in medico-magical spells, and never, to my knowledge, in clear connection with Seth.

46 Griffith 1960, 105, reads (with others) Plutarch's statement as the aetiological myth reflecting the negative aspect of the male hippo, incarnation of Seth, versus the positive one of the female hippo, i.e., of Taweret-like images (passing over the fundamental hybridism of the hippopotamus goddess). It is worth noting that Plutarch's text comes much later than the Egyptian quasi-complete demonization of Seth. Cf. also Borghouts 1982, 18–19; Gabler 2017, 7 (although I do not agree with some of the interpretations there expressed, nor with the identification of an early hippopotamus goddess Ipet diverse from the later Taweret [for this topic see above, n. 8]).

47 Regarding O. Ashm. 166 (here, text no. 1), cf. Donker van Heel (2016, 51), who on the basis of his uncertain identification of Tanehesy as a childless woman (see above, n. 15), wonders if the theft were not the woman's attempt to gain closeness with Taweret. However, the author's arguments do not seem convincing.

48 The inscription also pinpoints the three fundamental names attributed to the goddess (see above, n. 8). Last translation: Jansen-Winkeln 2005, 140–146, Taf. 9–11. Here I quote only the passages of the text most relevant for the present topic.

49 In her name of Reret (Sow/Nourisher), here it could also be echoed the occasional identification of the hippopotamus goddess with the sky goddess Nut, in one aetiological and astral myth this latter being described as a sow (*rr.t*) swallowing her piglets, i.e., the decanal stars (*rrw*), in order to give birth to them again. It is worth noting that the "piggishness" of the hippopotamus goddess—and generally of goddesses—is both far from being represented in images and clear: cf. Ceruti 2017, 111–112; Volokhine 2014, 148–153, 154–158. Cf. also Guermeur 2016, 179–181.

50 *mk.(t) nb=s* "who protects her Lord;" she is similarly labelled on the statue Cairo CG 39145. See Verner 1969, 58, but with another reading of the passage, accepted by Nagy (1992, 455) and lastly by Mendel (2005, 35).

51 On the statuette Aberdeen Anthropological Museum 1422 (probably Saite), we find the parallel statement *ʿnḫ mwt m ḫfʿ=ṯ "life and death are in your grasp"* (lastly Mendel 2005, 32–33, with previous references). However, the statuette does not properly portray the hippopotamus goddess here concerned, but rather one of the twelve month-goddesses (namely *ỉmy.t-p.t-Sšm.t-nṯrw*), which are attested by the Late Period onwards. They mostly share with/derive from the hippopotamus goddess their iconography, but not their names, and seem to specify her function on a timing base (Mendel 2005; some notes in Ceruti 2017, 94 fn. 3). In view of the history of the deity that I draw from the collected corpus of documents (see references above, n. 1), I surmise that most of the numerous hippopotamus goddess' amulets datable to the Late and Ptolemaic Period might be related more to this cohort of goddesses (and also to the similar one, of the goddesses of the thirty-six decans) than to the hippopotamus goddess Ipy/Ipet-Reret-Taweret per se.

52 Text in Marciniak 1974, 104 (no. 50): line nr. after him. Translation and transcriptions: Sadek 1984b, 69; Sabek 2016, Graffito 6.

53 I follow Sadek's reading (Sadek 1984b, 69) omitting from the threat-formula proper the last line 7 of the graffito—which implies the name and title *wḥm Jmn-nḫt*—as seemingly inconstant with the curse. Otherwise Sabek (2016, 147) integrates the line into the formula as its line 6, reading "[u]nd Taweret (6) (möge den) *wḥm*-Priester *Jmn-nḫt* (7) und seine Kinder verfolgen": that would mean a curse *ad personam*, highly exceptional for such type of formulae (see Morschauser 1991, *passim*).

54 As the "Lord of the Eternity," in fact he can unleash the Hereafter's demons: see, e.g., Ritner 2011 (mostly for late and Demotic samples).

55 Marciniak 1974, 60 (no. 3); Sadek 1984a, 75–76; Sabek 2016, 270 (Graffito 68).

56 Stele Cairo JE 45327: Iversen 1941, 5–6; for the dreadful character of Nefertem, see Borghouts 1971, 66, n. 94.

57 Morschauser 1991, 138–139.

58 A Penpamer (i) (or Penpai/Penpaesh) is known at Deir el-Medina holding the position of doorkeeper (sc. "of the Tomb"), with a career spanning from (at least) the year 24 of Ramesses III to the year 4 of Ramesses V, and Sabek (2016, 147) tentatively identifies him with the author of the graffito. Indeed, a few Deir el-Bahri graffiti may be ascribed to members of the village (Sabek 2016, 104), yet in any case doorkeepers were not effectively member of the crew, but rather support staff from outside the village: see Goecke-Bauer 2003, 63–153 (with also Penpamer (i) dossier). The temple of Maat lies in the precinct of Montu, at Karnak-Nord (Porter and Moss 1972, 11–13).

59 O. Ashmolean Museum 149 (Karl 2000, 136; Toivari-Viitala 2001, 230); Stele British Museum EA 589 (see above, n. 10). In the Theban area, besides Karnak, where he had his own temple, Ptah was also worshipped (with Meretseger), in a rock-shrine between Deir el-Medina and the Valley of the Queens. For an introduction to the god see van Dijk 2001.

60 Sakhmet is therefore frequently invoked in threats (Morschauser 1991, 140). On the goddess and the requirement of her pacification see Germond 1981; Goyon 2011.

61 Papyrus BM EA 10042 vo., II, 6 = fr. Heidelberg vo., col. II.6. Lastly: Bommas 1998, 44 (with some criticisms of previous interpretations, but without his own proposal); Leitz 2001, 49. For the text date to the late Twentieth Dynasty, see Winand and Gohy 2011, 243, where are underlined both lexical and grammatical singularities, due to the composite nature of the text, which, e.g., presents many lexical *hapax* (Winand and Gohy 2011, 186, 240–243).

62 Bierbrier and De Meulenaere 1984, 23–32; lastly in Meurer 2015, 55–57, Taf. 52 (with complete bibliography): cols. nr. after him. The hymn of the stele and Penbuy's particular devotion to Taweret—to whom he dedicated another stele (Louvre E 16374) and a libation basin (CGT 22031)—would deserve more comments than those allowed by the limits of this paper, and it should also be viewed in the wider context of the goddess' cult at Deir el-Medina, which, in its turn deserves a reappraisal. Here are cited the passages of the hymn most relevant to the present topic.

63 Cf. also Meurer 2015, 6 (with references), and

Blumenthal 2011, 13. Luiselli (2011, 373) assumes the text is rather a prayer to the deity for having children; that is debatable, in my view, according to both the content of the hymn as a whole, and that two son of his seven children (four male and three female) are depicted on the lower register of the stele. On this type of texts and the notion of forgiveness, see Vernus 2003 (cf. also above, n. 10).

64 For this expression see Vernus 2003, 330–332.

65 See above, note 2, especially Ceruti 2013, 22.

66 Above all at Deir el-Medina (see above, notes 6 and 62), but also at Thebes/Karnak (Opet Temple), where her cult was established already in the Eighteenth Dynasty (Valbelle and Laroze 2010), even if it is much more documented for the Late and Ptolemaic periods, both at Karnak, and Luxor (Thiers, 161–163).

67 Even when reflected in an elaborate, literary phraseology: Vernus 2003, 338–340.

68 As the Deir el-Medina documents as a whole attest (above, n. 6 and 62), but also elsewhere. Cf. Sweeney 2015, 884.

69 For the issue see the various approaches lastly in Kousoulis 2011, with further references; cf. Graves-Brown 2018.

70 Ritner 2011, 4, 14; Kaper 2003.

71 Frandsen 2011, 60–61.

72 E.g., Goebs 2002, 27-59; Guermeur 2015a.

73 Cf. Frandsen 2011, 61–62.

74 For a divine taxonomy, see, e.g., Baines 2000, 35–39 (with further references); Manassa 2013.

Journal of Ancient Egyptian Interconnections

MNḤ, "THE BUTCHER" AND LORD OF THE BUTCHER DEMONS

Amr Gaber
Alexandria University

ABSTRACT

This work investigates a demon, Meneh, who is attested from the Middle Kingdom until the Graeco-Roman Period in epigraphic and iconographic evidence. His epithets reflect aggression, ferocity, and violence, which Meneh uses mainly against enemies of the deities. Additionally, he can be a threat to the deceased. However, not only did he have his own cult in the Graeco-Roman temples, but he also had his own clergy. Therefore, this work studies his various aspects *in extenso*. Moreover, newly proposed readings of two of his epithets, as well as the similarity of functions and mutual connection to Osiris, establish his link to the butcher demons.

NAME AND DETERMINATIVES

Meneh, whose name has different variants as *mnḥ*, *mnḥy*, *mnḥwy*, *mnḥw*, *ḥmn*,[1] and *imnḥy*[2] (TABLE 1:1–44), means "the butcher" or "the slayer."[3] His name is often confused with the goddess *mnḥyt*[4] and the god *ḥmn*[5] due to the similarity in writing. Despite the fact that his name is mostly accompanied by a wide array of determinatives, ranging from  (A40),[6]  (A179),[7]  (A199A),[8]  (R8),[9]  (C268B)[10] or  (C39A)[11] to the double determinatives  (A199A)+  (G7C),[12]  (A199A)+  (A40A),[13]  (A199A) +  (R8),[14]  (R8) +  (A40)[15] or  (T30) +  (A40),[16] only one determinative,  (A199A), showing a man holding a knife in one hand, reflects the meaning of his name and duties that he performs, while  (T30) illustrates the tool with which he carries out his duties. Meneh is first attested in the Coffin Texts, where his temple is mentioned in Spell 580, entitled *tm šmw sḫdw*, "not to walk with head looking downwards."[17] In this spell, the deceased proclaims that *iw pr mnḥ sḏ3yt n wnm N pn ḥs swr n ṯn* "(when) the temple of Meneh is sealed, this N will not eat faeces and will not drink (urine) for you."[18] Instead the deceased will live on the two loaves of *ḫnmt*-bread issued from the altar of Re.[19]

ICONOGRAPHY AND ATTRIBUTES

The first surviving representation is in the eighth hour of the Book of *Amduat*, dating to the New Kingdom. Meneh is depicted in the ninth cavern together with three other deities (second place).[20] Each one of them, including Meneh, is represented as a human mummiform standing with a ceremonial beard and a hieroglyphic sign  (S27A) of clothing before them.[21] The text before them narrates: *wnn.sn m sḫr pn mnḫwt.sn m b3ḥ.sn mnw ḥr šꜥy.sn m sšt3 ir in ḥr* "They are like this. Their clothing before them, remaining on their sand as a mystery made by Horus."[22]

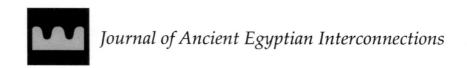

Table 1: Tracing the attestations of Meneh[a] *(continued on next page).*

No.	Writing	Date	Source	Publication	Notes
1	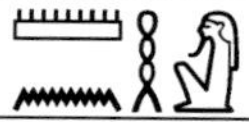	Middle Kingdom	Coffin Text Spell 580	*CT* VI, 159d	Coffin: Beni Hassan Cairo JE 37563b
2		Middle Kingdom	Coffin Text Spell 1100	*CT* VII, 417a	Coffin: Bersheh BM EA 38042
3		New Kingdom	Book of the Dead Chapter 153A	Naville 1908, pl. XV	Papyrus of Youa: Cairo CG 51189
4	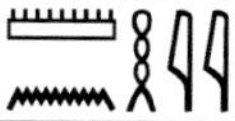	New Kingdom	Book of the *Amduat*[b]	Hornung 1965, 151	Ninth cavern of the eighth hour: deity No. 614
5	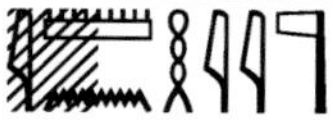	Twenty-fifth Dynasty	Stele of Pi'ankhy; Cairo JE 48862 (+JE 47086 –JE 47089)	Grimal 1981, §16=L.83	Line 83
6	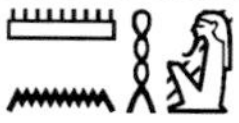	Darius	Hibis Temple	Davies 1953, 10	West door jamb-room VI (K of Winlock)[c]
7	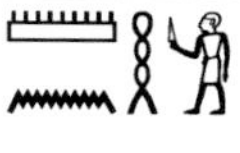	525–530 BCE	Granite Sarcophagus of Ankhhapy, Cairo JE 15011	Cairo CG 29303, 98	Second band of text: exterior face of the body: south-east section
8	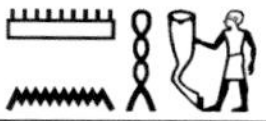	525–530 BCE	Granite Sarcophagus of Djedhor; Cairo JE 15039	Cairo CG 29304, 129	Exterior face of the body: western face: upper band of text
9	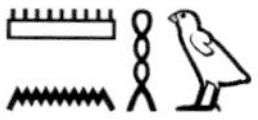	Ptolemaic	Statue of the Museum Lausanne No. Eg. 7	Wild 1954, 182, pls. II–III, col. 4	Fourth column: posterior face: dorsal pillar
10	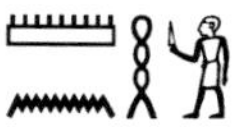	Ptolemaic	A granite statue of a certain Platon; Cairo JE 38033; CK 608 Legrain No. 672.	Coulon 2001, pl. XX	First column on the dorsal pillar of the statue
11	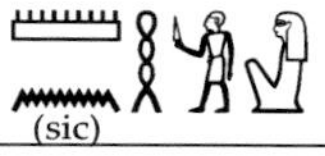 (sic)	Ptolemaic	P. Bremner-Rhind (BM EA 10188)	Faulkner 1933	Col. 20, 21–22
12					Col. 20, 21–22
13					Col. 26, 14
14					Col. 33, 6
15	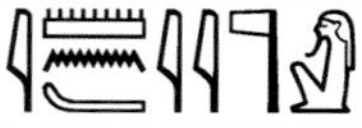	Ptolemaic	Edfu Temple	*E* I, 174, 1	Third register: northern wall: third western chamber
16	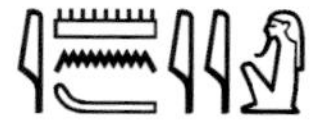	Ptolemaic	Edfu Temple	*E* II, 52, 2	Fourth register: southern wall: second hypostyle hall
17		Ptolemaic	Edfu Temple	*E* III, 301, 15	Western face: third architrave: first hypostyle hall
18	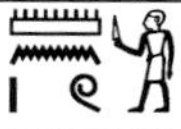 (sic)	Ptolemaic	Edfu Temple	*E* III, 323, 9	Eastern face: third architrave: first hypostyle hall

Notes

[a] The attestation of Meneh in the temple of Medamoud is considered by Leitz as the god's name, making this a designation of the bull. Therefore, it has been excluded from this table. See Drioton 1926, no. 343, 12.

[b] This writing occurs in the tombs of Thutmose III (KV 34), Amenhotep II (KV 35), Sety I (KV 17), Tauseret and Sethnakht (KV 14), Ramesses III (KV 11), and Ramesses V and VI (KV 9). Additionally, it occurs in the tomb of Useramun (TT 61). The text is broken in the tombs of Thutmose I (KV 38) and Amenhotep III (KV 22). See Hornung 1965, Langfassung, 4. bis 8. Stunde, 639.

[c] PM VII, 285 (100), plan on 276; Davies 1953, 16, pl. 10.

Table 1: *(continued from previous page)* Tracing the attestations of Meneh *(continued on next page)*.

No.	Writing	Date	Source	Publication	Notes
19	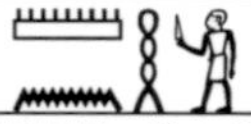	Ptolemaic	Edfu Temple	*E* IV, 84, 11	Second register: western face: exterior: naos
20		Ptolemaic	Edfu Temple	*E* IV, 240, 17	Second register: eastern face: exterior: naos
21	 (?)	Ptolemaic	Edfu Temple	*E* V, 63, 8	Second register: eastern section: south wall: court
22	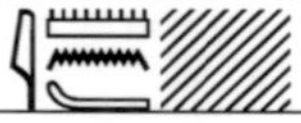	Ptolemaic	Edfu Temple	*E* V, 161, 15	Second register: western section: south wall: court
23		Ptolemaic	Edfu Temple	*E* VII, 119, 2	Girdle wall: outer west face: second register
24	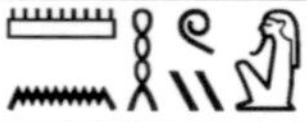	Ptolemaic	Edfu Temple	*E* VII, 280, 12	Girdle wall: outer east face: second register
25	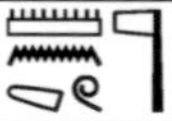	Ptolemaic	Edfu Temple	*E* VI, 159, 4	Third register: western interior wall: girdle wall
26	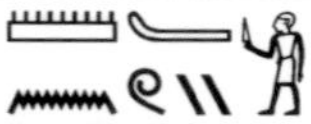	Ptolemaic	Edfu Temple	*E* I, 565, 15	Western wall: eastern staircase: offering bearer no. 3
27		Empty cartouches—Late Ptolemaic	Dendera Temple	*D* XI/I, 59, 3	Room E′ of Chassinat: upper register: exterior lintel: door
28		Empty cartouches—Late Ptolemaic	Dendera Temple	*D* VII/I, 183, 12 *D* VII/I, 196, 5	Eastern wall: eastern staircase. Western wall: eastern staircase.
29		Empty cartouches—Late Ptolemaic	Dendera Temple	*D* VIII/I, 93, 9	Eastern wall: western staircase
30		Empty cartouches—Late Ptolemaic	Dendera Temple	*D* VIII/I, 111, 4	Northern wall: western staircase
31		Empty cartouches—Late Ptolemaic	Dendera Temple	*D* IV, 189, 11	Northern wall: Court of the Chapel of the New Year
32	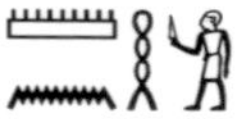	Roman	Dendera Temple	*D* IX/I, 241, 16	Side room III: a scene located above the cornice of the door: exterior of the door
33		Roman	Dendera Temple	*D* XV/I, 155, 13	Exterior of the pronaos: upper lintel: eastern door [G′-I′1]
34	 [d]	Roman	Esna Temple	*Esna* II, 163, 18	Interior face of column B: curtain wall
35	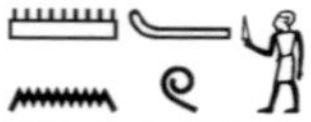	Roman	Esna Temple	*Esna* III, 257A	Upper band of text: column 8
36		Roman	Esna Temple	*Esna* III, 381, 10	A scene on column 17
37		Roman	Esna Temple	*Esna* III, 266, 5	A scene on column 8
38		Roman	Esna Temple	*Esna* III, 268A	Lower band of text: column 8

Notes

[d] There is an unidentified crown on the head of the second determinative. See *Esna* II, 163, 18.

Table 1: *(continued from previous page)* Tracing the attestations of Meneh.

No.	Writing	Date	Source	Publication	Notes
39	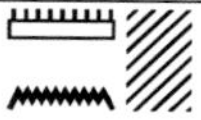	Roman	Esna Temple	*Esna* III, 266, 13	A scene on column 8
40	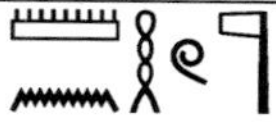	Roman	Asfun block	Farid 1986, 41–43	Block No. 2
41	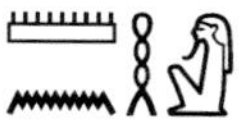	Roman	Asfun block		Block No. 3
42	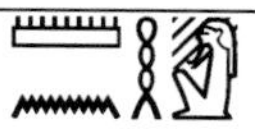	Roman	Block from Tod temple	*Tôd* I, 130, 4	Third register: eastern interior wall: hypostyle hall
43		Roman	Edfu Temple	*Edfu* I, 464, 14	Western side: *Bandeau de la frise*: Hall of Offerings.
44	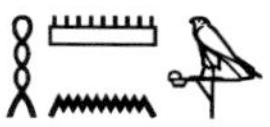	Roman	Hieratic Papyrus Tebtunis (P. Berlin 7808/7810 + P. Louvre AF 11112)	Osing 1998, 285	Papyrus IV [C 2, 17]

In the temple of Hibis at Kharga Oasis, Meneh's depiction dates to the Persian Period. Meneh appears sitting on his knees on a pylon in the guise of a mummified human body. He has the head of a lion with both hands emerge from the bandages and each holds a knife, while the rest of the three deities beneath him are damaged.[23] On the opposite door lintel, there are another four deities, which indicates that Meneh is among guardian deities protecting room VI (K of Winlock).

As a member of the nine dead deities of Edfu, appearing only in the temples of Horus at Edfu (Ptolemaic Period) and Hathor at Dendera (Late Ptolemaic Period/Roman Period), Meneh is depicted in two different forms. The first is a human mummified form.[24] The second is a complete humanoid form, whether sitting on a throne[25] or standing,[26] wearing a short kilt, *nms*-headdress, a wide collar, and holding the *wꜣs*-sceptre in one hand and the *ꜥnḫ*-sign in the other.

In the hypostyle hall of the temple of Esna, Meneh is depicted on a column (no. 8) as a hieracophelic deity wearing the *ḥmḥm*-crown, a short kilt, a short top having straps, wide collar, armlets, and a bracelet in his left hand. He holds in his right hand a knife while grasping the *ꜥnḫ*-sign in the other. The deity stands while being followed by Isis before the Roman Emperor Hadrian/Antoninus Pius, who is spearing a creature (destroyed).[27] The same iconography was depicted again on another column (no. 17) within the temple of Esna, where Meneh while holding a *wꜣs*-sceptre stands behind Khnum-Re in front of the Roman Emperor Trajan, who spears a bull.[28] On a sandstone block found at Asfun el-Mataana,[29] the Roman Emperor Antoninus Aurelius is depicted before Menehwy who wears a sun disc above his head, with the head of a cobra at the front and its tail at the back.[30] On another block, Menehwy wears the *ḥmḥm*-crown before the same emperor.[31] On two other blocks from the same locality (badly damaged), which once formed a single scene, the Roman emperor is depicted before Menehwy, who is shown seated on a throne, wearing a short kilt while holding a knife and a sceptre (damaged) in the right hand and the *ꜥnḫ*-sign in the other. The sceptre of another deity can be seen behind Menhewy.[32] The rest of these four blocks are missing and so the full scene cannot be reconstructed.

Epithets

The epithets of Meneh can be divided sevenfold. The first category echoes his divinity, the second shows his cult centres, the third reveals his role as a butcher, the fourth illustrates his strength and aggression, the fifth connects to his functions, the sixth reflects his iconography, and the seventh shows his control over demons.

The first category reflects his divinity: *nṯr ꜥꜣ* "the great god"[33] and *nṯr nfr* "the good god."[34]

The second specifies the cult centres where he is worshipped or as a lord of foreign localities:

1) *sḥḏ*: This is a locality in Meidum[35] and occurs only in one epithet, *ḫnty sḥḏ* "the foremost of Sehedj."[36]

2) *ḥwt-ḥtp*: this locality is attested in two different epithets, *ꜥšꜣ dmwt m ḥwt-ḥtp* "the one with several of knives in the Mansion of Offerings,"[37] and *nb ḥwt-ḥtp* "lord of the Mansion of Offerings."[38] *ḥwt-ḥtp* is a designation of Esna, the capital of the third nome of Upper Egypt.[39]

3) *ḥwt-bnwy*: It is present in one epithet, *ḥry-ib ḥwt-bnwy* "who resides in the Mansion of the two *bnw*-birds."[40] This is a designation of a temple situated in the region of Esna.[41] It was called *pr-nṯr* "the temple of the god," a place where Shu and Tefnut were worshipped and referred to as the "Children of Re"[42] or the two birds.[43]

4) *ḥwt-bnw*: It is attested in one epithet, *ḥry-ib ḥwt-bnw* "who resides in the Mansion of the *bnw*-birds."[44] This is a designation of a temple called *pr-ḫnm* "the temple of Khnum," situated in the region of Esna.[45] In a text in the temple of Esna, the two designations, i.e., *ḥwt-bnwy* and *ḥwt-bnw*, are mentioned beside each other.[46]

5) *tꜣ-rrt*: It is cited once in *nṯr ꜥꜣ m tꜣ-rrt* "the great god in Dendera."[47]

6) *ḥwt-snfrw*: This locality, which is found in the third nome of Upper Egypt,[48] goes by the modern name of Asfun,[49] and located about 11–12 km to the north of Esna.[50] It is mentioned in two different epithets, *nb ḥwt-snfrw* "lord of the Mansion of Senefru,"[51] and *ḫnt ḥwt-snfrw* "the foremost of the Mansion of Senefru."[52]

7) *ḥwt-ḫnm*: one of the designations of Esna,[53] which is cited in *ḥry-ib ḥwt-ḫnm* "who resides in the Mansion of Khnum."[54]

8) *bḥdw-n-rꜥ*/ *isbt nt rꜥ*: These are two designations for Edfu that are attested in two epithets: *ḥry-ib bḥdw n rꜥ* "who resides in the Throne of Re,"[55] and *ḫnt isbt nt rꜥ* "the foremost of the Throne of Re."[56]

9) Epithet connected to foreign locality: *ḥkꜣ fkḥr* "ruler of Fekher," which is a locality in eastern Africa.[57]

The third category reveals his role as a butcher demon: *ꜥšꜣ dmwt* "the one with several knives."[58] This epithet appears three times in the temple of Esna,[59] two times at Asfun,[60] four times in the temple of Hathor at Dendera,[61] once on a statue from Dios Polis (Thebes east),[62] and once also on a statue from the Karnak Cachette (Cairo JE 38033).[63] Another similar form, *ꜥšꜣ ds*, is mentioned twice in the temple of Dendera.[64] *spd dmt* "sharp of knives" is attested only once in the temple of Dendera.[65] These epithets reflect not only the function that he carries out as a butcher but also his iconography in which he tends to carry one or more knives.

The fourth category illustrates his ferocity, strength, and aggression: *ḥsꜣ* "the fierce one,"[66] *ḳn* "the brave,"[67] *khb* "raging lion,"[68] *khb nḫt* "the strong lion,"[69] *nꜥš dniwt* "who is loud of cry," *pr-ꜥ* "the mighty one,"[70] *bꜣ tkk* "the strong ba."[71] *iṯt m sḫm.f* "who seizes with his power,"[72] *nb šꜥt* "lord of slaughter,"[73] *mꜣi-ḥsꜣ* "the fierce lion,"[74] *tkr pḥty* "mighty in strength,"[75] *wr šꜥt* "great of massacre,"[76] *ꜥꜣ pḥty* "great of power,"[77] *nn ꜥḥꜥ.tw m hꜣw.f* "no one fights in his vicinity,"[78] *ꜥḏ ḳswy.f* "who dismembers his enemy,"[79] *smꜣ ḫꜣkw-ibw* "who slaughters his enemies."[80] As a butcher, the strength of his arms are reflected in these epithets: *ḳn kbty* "strong of arms."[81] and *iṯt ꜥꜥwy.fy* "who seizes with his hands."[82]

The fifth category of the epithets of Meneh is connected to the functions that he undertakes, i.e., protecting deities and localities, defeating harmful beings as well as being an offerer of meat:

1) Killing enemies of Sekhmet and Neseret, who are manifestations of Hathor of Dendera, in order to satisfy them: *mds tpw nw ḫftyw* "who cuts off the heads of the foes."[83] Thus Sekhmet is satisfied: *sḥtp sḫmt m ḫrt.s* "who satisfies Sekhmet with her portion."[84] Furthermore, he cuts off the heads of the enemies of Hathor in order to satisfy her or her manifestation: Nesret (Flame): *ḥsḳ tpw nw ḫꜣkw-ibw*[85] *stpw nw sbiw stptwt m ꜥ ḥtp nbwt m ḫꜣw.sn* "who cuts off the heads of the foes, the pieces of meat of the foes are cut into pieces with the arm, who satisfies the golden one (Hathor) with their meat;"[86] *sḥtp nsrt m*

ḫwdw "who satisfies Nesret with provisions;"[87] *sḥtp nsrt m stpwt ḥꜥw nw ḫftyw ḥsḳ tpw ꜥꜥwy nn wnỉ-mw n wsrt* "who satisfies Nesret with pieces of meat and the bodies of the foes, who cuts off the heads and the hands of those who are hostile to Weseret;"[88] and *sḫm m sbỉw* "who overpowers the rebels."[89] Therefore, Meneh plays an important role in accomplishing the ritual of *sḥtp sḫmt* "satisfying Sekhmet" in the temple of Hathor at Dendera, and subsequently world order is maintained.[90]

2) Defeating the enemies of Re: According to a text in the temple of Dendera, Meneh is *sḫr ḫftyw nw rꜥ* "who overthrows the foes of Re."[91]

3) Slaying Seth, who takes several forms, including that of a bull: A text in the temple of Dendera reads: *smꜣ smꜣw m ꜣbwy nbd* "who slaughters the bulls in the forms of Nebed (Seth)."[92]

4) Protecting Esna: *sḫr sbỉw r pr-nṯr* "who drives away the foes of *pr-nṯr* (Esna),"[93] *mds ky m-ḫnt sḫt* "who kills the enemy before Sekhet (Esna)."[94]

5) Praising Neith in the temple of Esna: *mnḥ ḥr ỉr n.s ỉꜣw* "Meneh to do praise to her (Neith)."[95]

In addition to these functions, there are more attested via other texts:

6) Cutting the head of Apep: Meneh appears in the spell of taking the knife to smite Apep, found in the Book of Overthrowing Apep in Papyrus Bremner-Rhind (P. BM EA 10188). It dates to the early Ptolemaic Period.[96] Apep was stopped with the knife of Meneh (col. 22, 20–21): *nḏrw sp-sn mnḥ sḫr.(ỉ) ḫft n rꜥ m ds.k nḏrw sp-sn mnḥ sḫr.(ỉ) ḫft n pr-ꜥꜣ m ds.k* "Seize, seize, (O) Meneh, I fell the foe of Re with your knife. Seize, seize, (O) Meneh, I fell the foe of Pharaoh with your knife."[97] Another part of the papyrus reads (col. 33, 6–7): *mnḥ ḥry ds.f wr šꜥyt.f ḥr tpw sbỉw.k* "Meneh with his great knife cuts to pieces the heads of those who rebel against you (Re)."[98] In the Coffin Texts (Spell 1100):[99] *nḥm.n N tn sḫtyw ny ꜥḥꜣ m ꜥ.f mnḥ*[100] *spd ꜣt ỉwty ḫs.f* "I have taken the knives of the attacker from him, (even) Meneh, sharp of striking-power, who has not been repelled."[101] This spell is the predecessor of the Book of Overthrowing Apep, which was developed later.[102]

7) Vanquishing a harmful serpent: A text, accompanying a deity called Nekhet (the victorious)[103] in the temple of Horus at Edfu in an offering of *stpwt* "pieces of meat," reads:[104] *tp.k r ḏw ỉwty ꜥꜥwy.fy rdwy.fy dbdb ỉwf.k ḥr msḳ.k mnḥ r.k ꜥšꜣ [dsw] nw ỉmnḥw*[105] *rsyw* "your head is (doomed) to evil, without arms[106] or jambs, your flesh is cut off your leather (because) Meneh is against you, the one with several of [knives] of the southern butchers."[107] The text refers to a malevolent serpent, probably Apep,[108] in the temple of Edfu, who threatens the temple order and against whom Meneh must act. The confusion between the reading of *ḫꜣtyw*[109] and *ỉmnḥw* is probably because both are capable of vanquishing Apep and the uncertainty created by the sign (A199A), which is used in writing both of their names. This uncertainty led Goyon to suggest *ḫꜣtyw*.[110]

8) Providing offerings to the main deity of the temple: A text, accompanying the procession depicted on the northern wall of the western staircase heading towards the roof of the temple of Dendera, reads:[111] *ḫꜣ m ꜣšr m nmt-nṯr m-ꜥ mnḥ ꜥšꜣ dmwt* "one thousand pieces of roasted meat from the divine slaughterhouse of Meneh, the one with several knives."[112] Another text, accompanying a fecundity figure, in the temple of Hathor at Dendera, mentions:[113] *ỉn.f n.t ỉmnḥw ḥry nmt nt rꜥ ḥr stpw nfrw ỉry ꜥ.f ḥtp.t ḥr ỉḫt m ḫrt-hrw ỉr ḫprw.ṯ r mrrt ỉb.ṯ* "he (the king) brings to you (Hathor) Meneh, the chief of the

slaughterhouse of Re, carrying pieces of good meat, made by his hand. She (Hathor) is satisfied because of the offering every day and your manifestation is sustained to love your heart."[114] Another text on the western staircase of Dendera confirms the same role: *ḥry stpwt nw sbiw* "carrying the pieces of meat of the rebels."[115]

The same role exists in the temple of Horus at Edfu, where a text, located on the western wall of the eastern staircase, reads: *in.f n.k mnḥwy ḥry-tp nmt r smꜣ kꜣw nw nmt-nṯr ꜣbwy sbiw.k* "he (the king) brings to you (Horus) Meneh, chief of the slaughterhouse, to slaughter the oxen of the divine slaughterhouse."[116] Another text accompanying the offering bearer reads: *mnḥwy r iwt.f smꜣwty nbḏ m ḫfꜥ.f* "Menehwy at his coming, the confederates of evil are in his fist."[117] A part of the text in the *Bandeau de la frise* of the Hall of Offerings also describes his role among other deities as it states:[118] *ḥmn r stf n.f rꜣ* "Hemen[119] to cut geese for him." This is one of the rare cases in which "Meneh" is written as "Hemen"; Wilson identified the name as a variant of Meneh.[120]

The sixth category of epithets coincides with Meneh's iconography in the temple of Esna: *ꜥꜣ ḥmḥmt* "who is great of *ḥmḥm*-crown (roar),"[121] *ḏrty šps* "the august falcon,"[122] and *bik nṯri* "the divine falcon."[123]

The seventh and last category shows his control over demons, which is reflected through two epithets, both from the temple of Dendera. The readings of the names within these two epithets are not certain. The first epithet, stated by Leitz to be *nb ḫꜣtyw* (?) "the lord of *ḫꜣtyw* demons,"[124] is mentioned twice (Table 2:1–2). Another form of this epithet, *ḥry ḫꜣtyw* (?) "chief of *ḫꜣtyw* demons,"[125] appears only once (Table 2:3). The epithet *ḥry ḫꜣtyw* (?),[126] which was also acquired by Tutu,[127] is a matter of debate among scholars. While Yoyotte translated it as "[chef des] massacreurs"[128] without giving a transliteration, Sauneron read it as *šmꜣyw*.[129] Vernus, Germond, and following them el-Sayed, translated it as "le chef des émissaires."[130] Kaper agrees with Sauneron's reading, describing the sign as an ithyphallic demon with a cat's head and a thick tail, standing on his hind legs and holding a knife.[131] As for the epithets of Meneh, one has 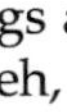 (A199A), which can be used for many demons, such as *hbyw*, *ḫꜣtyw*, *ḥnṯtyw*, *wpwtyw*, *ist*, and *mnḥw* "the butchers."[132] The second epithet, which is written with the sign  (C87) representing a lion-headed deity holding a knife in each hand, can also be used for *(i)mnḥw* and *ḫꜣtyw*.[133] There are three occurrences of two deities having the epithet of a "chief of the *mnḥw* demons." The first is a text engraved above the head of a male fecundity figure at Kom Ombo carrying two trays, one above the other and each having three oxen, and reads:  *inpw ḥry-tp mnḥw* "Anubis, chief of the butcher demons."[134] Both Herbin and Rickert believe that these are the *mnḥw* demons.[135] Another text accompanying a male fecundity figure (head damaged) in the temple of Khonsu at Karnak, which shows that Anubis held the same epithet, has been reconstructed by Rickert as *in.f n.[k inpw ḥry-tp mnḥw]* "he (the king) brings to [you (the deity) Anubis, chief of the butchers]."[136] The third instance shows Horus the Behdetite having the epithet: 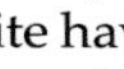 *ḥry mnḥw* "chief of the butcher demons" once, in an offering scene of *rdit ꜥḏ ḥr ḫt* "placing fat on the fire" in the temple of Edfu.[137]

These characteristics lead to two questions: Which reading should be proposed for the epithets of Meneh, and why is *mnḥ* not associated with the *(i)mnḥw* demons instead? The *imnḥ n wsir* "butcher of Osiris" is mentioned in the papyrus of Yuya (P.

Table 2: Epithets of Meneh with unconfirmed readings.

No.	Epithet	Date	Source	Publication	Notes
1		Late Ptolemaic	Dendera Temple	*D* VII/I, 196, 6	C87: a lion-headed deity holding a knife in each hand
2		Late Ptolemaic	Dendera Temple	*D* VIII/I, 93, 9	A199A: A standing man holding a knife in his right hand
3		Late Ptolemaic	Dendera Temple	*D* VIII/I, 111, 4–5	A lion-headed deity holding a knife in his right hand

Cairo CG 51189), dating to the Eighteenth Dynasty,[138] and in Chapter 153A of the Book of the Dead.[139] Furthermore, *mnḥw nw wsir* "the butchers of Osiris" are also cited in the Coffin Texts.[140] Hence, the link between the *mnḥ* and the *mnḥw* demons as both associated with Osiris can be established.[141] Moreover, Meneh is the son of Osiris, as will be seen later.

Elsewhere, I have demonstrated that the *mnḥw* butchers belong to Osiris and they were equipped with sharp knives and painful nails to inflict wounds on Osiris' enemies.[142] They also open the ways before the deceased. Both have similar orthography for their names, can be a threat to the deceased, and have a common function, i.e., vanquishing Apep. Last but not least, both share the same responsibility, as Meneh is called *ḥry nmt nt rʿ* "chief of the slaughterhouse of Re" in the temple of Dendera,[143] which coincides with the epithet of the butcher demons who are called *ḥry(w) nmt nt rʿ* "chiefs of the slaughterhouse of Re," mentioned in the temple of Edfu.[144] Being a son of a certain deity who controls certain demons established a connection between the deity's child and these demons. Tutu, the son of Neith who is associated with the *ḫ3tyw* demons, is the chief of the *ḫ3tyw* demons. Moreover, Anubis the son of Osiris[145] who is associated with the *mnḥw* demons is the chief of the *mnḥw* demons. Furthermore, Horus the Behdetite, who is also called the son of Osiris, is the chief of the *mnḥw* demons.[146] Thus, it is more likely that Meneh, who is the son of Osiris and is associated with *mnḥw* demons, is the chief of the *mnḥw* demons. Accordingly, I propose the reading of the epithets of Meneh as *nb mnḥw* "lord of the butchers" (TABLE 2:1–2) and *ḥry mnḥw* "chief of the butchers" (TABLE 2:3).

SON, WIFE, AND PARENTS

Meneh has a son according to a text accompanying an infant deity in the temple of Esna, which reads: *s3 mnḫ p3 ḫrd ʿ3 wr tpy n mnḥ mnḫ [...] pr m 3st ḫy šps n wnn-nfr*[147] "the excellent son, the child,[148] the first very great child of Meneh,[149] excellent [...] who comes forth from Isis, the august child of Wenen-nefer (Osiris)." Isis, beautiful of eye, and the excellent son are both depicted in front of the Roman Emperor Caracalla who offers a *mnit*-necklace.[150] The son is depicted as a child with a side-lock, wearing the double crown with a lappet at the back, while putting his index finger in his mouth, and holds the *ḥk3*-sceptre, the *nḫḫ3*-flail, and the *ʿnḫ*-sign in his right hand.[151]

Through this text the parents of *mnḥ* are revealed, a relationship confirmed by another text at Esna:[152] *sḫpr ḫrt n it.f wsir s3-3st* "who creates provisions for his father Osiris, son of Isis." Another epithet from Esna stresses the same fact, *pr m 3st s3 smsw n wnn-nfr* "who comes forth from Isis, the eldest son of Wenen-nefer."[153] It would appear that he had a female counterpart called *mnḥt*,[154] who is mentioned following his name in a hieratic papyrus from Tebtunis (P. Berlin 7808/7810 + P. Louvre AF 11112) dating to the second century CE.[155] Due to the fragmentary condition of the papyrus and given the fact that this is her only attestation so far,[156] she remains a mystery.

GOD'S RESPONSE

In return for the Roman emperor's (Trajan's) ritual performed before Meneh in the temple of Esna, i.e., *mds sm3* "stabbing the bull,"[157] Meneh slaughters the emperor's enemies: *di.i h3 bdšw.k r nmt* "I caused that your enemies fall against the slaughterhouse."[158] Moreover, Meneh grants the Roman Emperor Hadrian/Antoninus Pius power against his enemies for the same ritual in another scene:[159] *di.i nḫt ʿʿwy.k r ḥw ḫftyw.(k) dpdp sbiw.k m ds.i* "I gave your arms power to strike your enemies and to cut off your rebels with my knife."[160] Furthermore, as a member of the nine dead deities of Edfu, Meneh appears in two different offering scenes. The first is *wp r3 sp 4* "opening of the mouth four times,"[161] and the second is *irt sntr kbḥ* "burning incense and pouring a libation."[162] Meneh grants Ptolemy IV in return the same: *di.i (n.k)wḥm rnpt mi ḫpri* "I give to you repetition of years like Khepri."[163] Despite the different nature of offerings, Meneh appears in other offering scenes with this group of deities, but his response is not mentioned, as he is not accompanied by a text.[164] During the Twenty-fifth Dynasty, according to a text on the "victory-stele" of Piankhy, the king makes an offering to Meneh. It reads: *m3ʿ.n.f ʿ3bt-ʿ3t n [i]mnḥy ḫnt sḥḏ* "he (the king) offered a great offering to Imnhy the foremost of Sehedj."[165] Moreover, this text reflects the idea that demons were not objects of cults until the Late Period.[166]

PRIESTS

The clergy of Meneh is rarely attested, and there are only two examples mentioning his priests. The first is a *ḥm-nṯr* "priest" for *mnḥ ʿš3-dmwt* "Meneh, the one with several of knives," called Hor-nefer. He is mentioned on a statue dating from the reign of Alexander the Great or the early Ptolemaic Period. The body of this basalt statue is now on display in the Musée des Beaux-Arts de Lausanne (Eg. 7).[167] Another priest/scribe of *mnḥ ꜥšꜣ-dmwt*, Plato Junior, a man of Greek origin from the first century BCE, is attested on a granite statue (Cairo JE 38033).[168]

The King as Meneh's Son or Like Meneh

The king is referred to twice in the temple of Dendera as *sw mi mnḥ* "he is like Meneh," while offering the *ḥnk stpwt* "pieces of meat"[169] before two sacred serpents of Dendera in one scene,[170] and *[ḥnk] ꜣšr* "roast a piece of meat"[171] before Hathor and Horus-sema-tawy in another.[172] The king, while slaughtering an antelope before Montu and Tanenet in the temple of Tod, is called *sꜣ mnḥ*[173] "son of Meneh." In several instances the king has the epithet of Meneh, mainly in connection with a meat offering in the temples of Edfu and Dendera.[174]

Assimilation

According to epigraphic and iconographic evidence, a fecundity figure assimilated into Meneh[175] in the temple of Hathor at Dendera is depicted on the eastern[176] and the western walls[177] of the eastern staircase while ascending towards or descending from the roof. A second fecundity figure assimilated into Meneh is depicted on the eastern[178] and northern[179] walls of the western staircase. The fecundity figure in the four previously mentioned cases is accompanied with his name and epithets after a *ḏd-mdw-in* formula. It is represented in a complete human form, wearing the *nms*-headdress, wide collar, short kilt, and a bull's tail, while carrying a tray laden with pieces of meat among a procession of deities who carry provisions. A third fecundity figure assimilated into Meneh is illustrated on the northern wall of the court of the chapel of the New Year in the temple of Hathor at Dendera. Here Meneh is depicted in a humanoid form wearing a short kilt, *nms*-headdress, wide collar, and a bull's tail, carrying the *šꜥt*-sign in the left hand and a vessel in the other, while a gazelle is represented beside him.[180] On the western wall of the eastern staircase of the temple of Horus at Edfu a fecundity figure assimilated into Meneh is depicted in the guise of a humanoid form wearing the *nms*-headdress, broad collar, short kilt, and a bull's tail, while carrying different pieces of meat.[181] This shows that Meneh participated with his offerings, i.e., pieces of meat, in festivals connected with the roofs of the temples of Edfu and Dendera.

Festivals

Two religious festivals in the calendar of the temple of Esna mention Meneh, who participates in the first festival while the second is his own festival. The first, called *ḥb ẖnm* "festival of Khnum," was celebrated from the first day of the fourth month of the *ꜣḫt*-season until the sixth day, and other deities also participated.[182] The second festival, which was celebrated on the twentieth day of the fourth month of *šmw*-season, was called *ḥb mnḥwy* "festival of Menehwy," and offerings were presented on the altar.[183]

Conclusion

Meneh has been envisaged through his epithets as a bloodthirsty butcher to the enemies of deities such as Hathor of Dendera, his main mission being to slaughter them, dismember and decapitate their bodies, and offer their meat to deities to satisfy them. One enemy, Seth, should be stopped. Another enemy, Apep, must be defeated, otherwise he would jeopardise the stability of the cosmos by attacking the barque of Re in his journey every day. By taking part in the ritual of satisfying Sekhmet, he saves the cosmic order from being endangered. His role as a guardian is attested through his depiction on the door jamb of room VI (K of Winlock) in the temple of Hibis among other deities. As a member of the nine dead deities of the temple of Edfu, not only did Meneh adopt two new iconographies, but he also performed new duties among this group, which appeared in the temple of Dendera as well. Since Anubis and Horus the Behdetite both have the epithets of "son of Osiris" and "chief of the butcher demons," and based on the connection between Meneh and Osiris as Osiris' son, it seems logical to infer that these two epithets, i.e., "lord of the butcher demons" and "chief of the butcher demons," can be possessed by Meneh as well.

Was Meneh entirely a benevolent demon? Texts found on two sarcophagi, of Ankhhapy (Cairo JE 15011)[184] and Djedhor (Cairo JE 15039),[185] dating to 525–30 BCE, read: *n iṯ bꜣ.f imnḥy spd ds* "his ba (deceased) is not seized by Meneh, sharp of knife."[186] This is the only evidence that demonstrates how Meneh could threaten the deceased, and it recalls the danger of the butcher demons towards the deceased.[187] Meneh has both benevolent and malevolent aspects.[188] Despite the threat Meneh can present to the deceased, the benevolent role is predominant in his functions, unlike those of the butcher demons. According to epigraphic and iconographic evidence, it was not until the Graeco-Roman Period that Meneh's cult gained popularity, he had his own festival, and his parents and son were revealed. His cult was active in different geographical localities such as Edfu, Dendera, Esna, and Asfun during the Graeco-Roman Period.

Acknowledgments

This article was written while working as an honorary research associate in the Research Institute for Arts and Humanities (RIAH), College of Arts and Humanities (History and Classics) at Swansea University. I am very grateful for all the facilities provided by the Institute and the support from the members of its staff. I would like to express my appreciation and gratitude to Martina Minas-Nerpel of Universität Trier for all her help and support as my mentor for this post-doctoral position. Special thanks are due to my colleague Kenneth Griffin for reading my article. I am grateful to Alexandria University, where I work as a full-time lecturer, for granting me study leave to conduct postdoctoral research. An abridged version of this article was presented at Demon Things: International Conference on Ancient Egyptian Manifestations of Liminal Entities at Swansea University, 21–24 March 2016.

Abbreviations

AEO Gardiner, A. H. 1947. *Ancient Egyptian Onomastica*, 3 vols. London: Oxford University Press.

Cairo JE Egyptian Museum, Cairo, Journal d'entrée.

CT de Buck, A. 1935–1961. *The Egyptian Coffin Texts*, 7 vols. Oriental Institute Publications 34–87. Chicago: The University of Chicago Press.

D I–V Chassinat, É. 1934–1947. *Le Temple de Dendara*, vols. I–V. Le Caire: Institute français d'archéologie orientale. Vols. II–II, 2nd edition: Le Caire: Institute français d'archéologie orientale, 2004; vol. IV, 3rd edition: Le Caire: Institute français d'archéologie orientale, 2012; vol. V, 2nd edition: Le Caire: Institute français d'archéologie orientale, 2006).

D VI–VIII Chassinat, É. and F. Daumas. 1965–1978. *Le Temple de Dendara*, vols. VI–VIII. Le Caire: IFAO. Vols. VI–VIII, 2nd edition: Le Caire: Institute français d'archéologie orientale, 2006.

D IX Daumas, F. 1987. *Le temple de Dendara*, vol. IX. Le Caire: Institute français d'archéologie orientale.

D X–XII Cauville, S. 1997–2007. *Le temple de Dendara*, vols. X–XII. Le Caire: Institute français d'archéologie orientale.

D XIII–XV Cauville, S. 2007–2008. *Le temple de Dendara*, vols. XIII–XV. <http://www.dendara.net>, accessed 1 January 2014; < https://web.archive.org/web/20080403003327/http://www.dendara.net/download/>, accessed 25 February 2020.

DZA Digitalisiertes Zettelarchiv, < http://aaew.bbaw.de/tla/servlet/S05?d=d007&h=h018 >.

E Chassinat, É. 1892–1985. *Le temple d'Edfou*, 15 vols. Paris—Cairo: Ernest Leroux and Institute français d'archéologie orientale. Vols. I–II, 2nd edition: Cairo, 1987–1990).

Esna Sauneron, S. 1959–1982. *Esna* I–VI; VIII. Le Caire: Institute français d'archéologie orientale.

KO de Morgan, J. et al. 1895. *Kom Ombos. Catalogue des monuments et inscriptions de l'Égypte antique II*. Vienne: Adolphe Holzhausen, Imprimeur de la Cour I. & R. et de l' Université.

LÄ Helck, W., E. Otto and W. Westendorf (eds.). 1972–1992. *Lexikon der Ägyptologie*, 7 vols. Wiesbaden: Harrassowitz.

LD Lepsius, C. R. 1849–1859. *Denkmaeler aus Aegypten und Aethiopien: nach den Zeichnungen der von Seiner Majestät dem Koenige von Preussen Friedrich Wilhelm IV nach diesen Ländern gesendeten und in den Jahren 1842–1845 ausgeführten wissenschaftlichen Expedition*, 12 vols. Berlin: Nicolaische Buchhandlung. (Reprint: Geneva: Éditions de Belles-lettres, 1975.)

LD *Text* Lepsius, C. R. 1897–1913. *Denkmaeler aus Aegyten und Aethiopien: Text*, 5 vols. Edited by E. Naville, L. Borchardt, K. Sethe and W. Wreszinski. Leipzig: J. C. Hinrichs'sche Buchhandlung.

LGG Leitz, C. et al. (eds.). 2002–2003. *Lexikon der*

ägyptischen Götter und Götterbezeichnungen, 8 vols. Orientalia Lovaniensia Analecta 110–116, 129. Leuven: Peeters Publishers.

PM — Porter, B. and R. L. B. Moss. 1960–1981. *Topographical Bibliography of Ancient Egyptian Hieroglyphic Texts, Reliefs, and Paintings*, 7 vols. Oxford: Griffith Institute.

Opet I — de Wit, C. 1958. *Les inscriptions du temple d'Opet, à Karnak* I. Bibliotheca aegyptiaca 11. Brussels: Fondation égyptologue Reine Élisabeth.

SERaT — System zur Erfassung von Ritualszenen in altägyptischen Templen. <http://www.serat.aegyptologie.uni-wuerzburg.de/>, accessed 1 January 2015.

TM — Trismegistos Texts. <www.trismegisto.org>, accessed 1 January 2017.

Tôd — Drioton, E., G. Posener, J. Vandier, and J.-Cl. Grenier. 1980. *Tôd. Les inscriptions du temple ptolémaïque et romain, I. La salle hypostyle, Textes Nos 1–172*. Fouilles de l'Institut français d'archéologie orientale 18/1. Le Caire: Institut francais d'archéologie orientale.

Urk. III — Schäfer, H. 1905. *Urkunden der älteren Äthiopenkönige, Siegesinschrift des Pianchi, Traumstele, Bruchstück Berlin 1068*. Leipzig: J. C. Hinrichs'sche buchhandlung.

Wb — Erman, A. and H. Grapow. 1982. *Wörterbuch der ägyptischen Sprache*, 7 vols. Berlin: Akademie–Verlag.

References

Abdel-Rahman, A. M. 2009. "The Lost Temples of Esna." *Bulletin de l'Institut français d'archéologie orientale* 109: 1–8.

Baines, J. 1985. *Fecundity Figures: Egyptian Personification and the Iconology of a Genre*. Warminster: Aris and Phillips.

Beinlich, H. 2008. *Handbuch der Szenentitel in den Tempeln der griechisch-römischen Zeit Ägyptens: die Titel der Ritualszenen, ihre korrespondierenden Szenen und ihre Darstellungen*, vol. I. Studien zu den Ritualszenen altägyptischer Tempel 3. Dettelbach: J. H. Röll.

Blackman A. M. and H. W. Fairman. 1943. "The Myth of Horus at Edfu: II. C. The Triumph of Horus over His Enemies a Sacred Drama (Continued)." *Journal of Egyptian Archaeology* 29: 2–36.

Carrier, C. 2004. *Textes des sarcophages du moyen empire égyptien, Tome II: spells [355] à [787]*. Monaco: Éditions du Rocher.

Cauville, S. 1999. *Dendara II: Traduction*. Orientalia Lovaniensia Analecta 88. Leuven: Peeters Publishers.

——. 2001. *Dendara IV: Traduction*. Orientalia Lovaniensia Analecta 101. Leuven: Peeters Publishers.

——. 2004. *Dendara V–VI: Traduction [et] index phraséologie, Les cryptes du temple d'Hathor*, I. Orientalia Lovaniensia Analecta 131. Leuven: Peeters Publishers.

Černý, J. 1963. "The True Form of the Name of King Snofru." *Rivista degli studi orientali* 38: 89–92.

Clarysse, W. 2010. "Egyptian Temples and Priests: Graeco-Roman." In A. B. Lloyd (ed.), *A Companion to Ancient Egypt*, vol. I, 274–290. Chichester: Wiley-Blackwell.

Coulon, L. 2001. "Quand Amon parle à Platon (la statue Caire JE 38033)." *Revue d'égyptologie* 52: 85–126.

Daressy, G. 1911. "Un décret de l'an XXIII de Ptolémée Épiphane." *Recueil de travaux relatifs à la philologie et à l'archéologie égyptiennes et assyriennes* 33: 1–8.

Daumas, F. 1952. *Les moyens d'expression du grec et de l'égyptien comparés dans les décrets de Canope et de Memphis*. Supplément aux Annales du Service des Antiquités Égyptiennes, Cahier 16. Cairo: Institut français d'archéologie orientale.

——. 1988. *Valeurs phonétiques des signes hiéroglyphiques d'époque gréco-romaine* I. Montpellier: Université de Montpellier.

Davies, N. de Garis. 1953. *The Temple of Hibis in el Khargeh Oasis, Part III: The Decoration*. Publications of the Metropolitan Museum of Art 17. New York: Metropolitan Museum of Art.

Drioton, É. 1926. *Fouilles de l'Institut français d'archéologie orientale du Caire, année 1926, Deuxième partie: Rapport sur les fouilles de Médamoud, 1926: Les inscriptions*. Fouilles de l'Institut français d'archéologie orientale 4/2. Cairo: Institut français d'archéologie orientale.

Edel, E. 1956. "Beitrage zum ägyptischen Lexikon II." *Zeitschrift für ägyptische Sprache und Altertumskunde* 81: 6–18.

El-Sabban, S. 2000. *Temple Festival Calendars of Ancient Egypt*. Liverpool: Liverpool University Press.

El-Sayed, R. 1982. *La déesse Neith de Sais*. Bibliothèque d'Étude 86/II. Cairo: Institut français d'archéologie orientale.

Farid, A. 1986. "New Roman Blocks from a Hypostyle-Hall found at Asfun El Mata'na." *Studien zur Altägyptischen Kultur* 13: 35–53.

Faulkner, R. O. 1933. *The Papyrus Bremner-Rhind (British Museum no. 10188)*. Bibliotheca aegyptiaca 3. Brussels: Fondation égyptologique Reine Élisabeth.

——. 1937. "The Bremner-Rhind Papyrus: III: D. The Book of Overthrowing ʿApep." *Journal of Egyptian Archaeology* 23(2):166–185.

——. 1938. "The Bremner-Rhind Papyrus: IV. D. the Book of Overthrowing ʿApep." *Journal of Egyptian Archaeology* 24(1): 41–53.

——. 2004. *The Ancient Egyptian Coffin Texts, Spells 1–1185*. Oxford: Aris & Phillips.

Fischer-Bovet, C. 2008. *Army and Society in Ptolemaic Egypt*. PhD dissertation. Stanford University.

Gaber, A. 2015. "A Case of Divine Adultery Investigated." *Journal of the American Research Center in Egypt* 51: 303–327.

——. 2015. "The *Mnḥw* Demons: Benevolent and Malevolent." *Göttinger Miszellen* 246: 31–36.

——. 2015. "The Ten Dead Deities of the Temple of Dendera." *Journal of Egyptian Archaeology* 101: 239–262.

——. Forthcoming. *The Nine Dead Deities of the Temple of Edfu.*

Gabra, G. 1974. "Hemen and Nectanebo I at Mo'alla." *Chronique d'Égypte* 49 (98): 234–237.

Gauthier, H. 1925. *Dictionnaire des noms géographiques contenus dans les textes hièroglyphiques*, Tome II. Cairo: Société royale de géographie d'Egypte.

——. 1927. *Dictionnaire des noms géographiques contenus dans les textes hièroglyphiques*,Tome IV. Cairo: Société royale de géographie d'Egypte.

——. 1928. *Dictionnaire des noms géographiques contenus dans les textes hièroglyphiques* Tome V. Cairo: Société royale de géographie d'Egypte.

——. 1929. *Dictionnaire des noms géographiques contenus dans les textes hièroglyphiques*, Tome VI. Cairo: Société royale de géographie d'Egypte.

Germond, P. 1979. "En marge des litanies de Sekhmet à Edfou: flèches et messagers." *Bulletin de la Société d'égyptologie de Genève* 2: 23–29.

Germond, P. 1981. *Sekhmet et la protection du monde*. Aegyptiaca Helvetica 9. Geneva: Éditions de Belles-Lettres.

Goyon, J.-C. 2006. *Le rituel du sḥtp sḫmt au changement de cycle annuel: d'aprés les architraves du temple d'Edfou et textes parallèles, du Nouvel Empire à l'époque ptolémaïque et romaine*. Bibliothèque d'étude 141. Cairo: Institut français d'archéologie orientale.

Grenier, J.-C. 1977. *Anubis alexandrin et romain*. Études préliminaires aux réligions orientales dans l'empire romain 57. Leiden: E. J. Brill.

Grimal, N. 1981. *La stele triomphale de Pi('ankh)y au Musée du Caire: JE 48862 et 47086–47089*. Études sur la propagande royale égyptienne 1. Mémoires de l'Institut français d'archéologie orientale 105. Cairo: Institut français d'archéologie orientale.

Grimm, A. 1994. *Die altägyptischen Festkalender in den Tempeln der griechisch-römischen Epoche*. Ägypten und das alte Testament 15. Wiesbaden: Harrassowitz.

Hannig, R. 1995. *Grosses Handwörterbuch Ägyptisch-Deutsch. Die Sprache der Pharaonen (2800–950 v.Chr.)*, Kulturgeschichte der Antiken Welt 64. Mainz: Philipp von Zabern.

Herbin, F.-R. 1999. "Trois manuscrits originaux du Louvre: porteurs du Livre des Respirations fait par Isis (P. Louvre N 3121, N 3083 et N 3166)." *Revue d'égyptologie* 50: 149–239.

Hornung, E. 1965. *Das Amduat: Die Schrift des verborgenen Raumes*, Teil 1. Ägyptologische Abhandlungen 7. Wiesbaden: Harrassowitz.

——. 1992. *Texte zum Amduat*, Teil 2: *Langfassung, 4. bis 8. Stunde*. Aegyptiaca Helvetica 14. Geneva: Éditions de Belles-Lettres.

—— and T. Abt. 2007. *The Egyptian* Amduat: *The Book of the Hidden Chamber*. Trans. by D. Warburton. Zurich: Living Human Heritage Publications.

Ibrahim, M. El-Din Abd El-Latief. 1971. *Aspects of Egyptian Kingship According to the Inscriptions of the Temple of Edfu*. Cairo: The General Organization for Government Printing Offices.

Kaper, O. 2003. *The Egyptian God Tutu: A Study of the Sphinx-God and Master of Demons with a Corpus of Monuments*, Orientalia Lovaniensia Analecta 119. Leuven: Peeters Publishers.

Kousoulis, P. I. 1999. *Magic and Religion as a Performative Theological Unity: The Apotropaic "Ritual of Overthrowing Apophis."* PhD dissertation, University of Liverpool.

——. 2000. "The Function of *ḥkꜣ* as a Mobilized Form in a Theological Environment: The Apotropaic 'Ritual of Overthrowing Apophis.'" In Z. Hawass and L. P. Brock (eds.), *Egyptology at the Dawn of the Twenty-first Century: Proceedings of the Eighth International Congress of Egyptologists*, vol. II, 362–371. Cairo: The American University in Cairo Press.

Kurth, D. 1994. *Treffpunkt der Götter. Inschriften aus dem Tempel des Horus von Edfu*. Zürich and München: Artemis Verlag.

——. 2004. *Edfou VII: Die Inschriften des Temples von Edfu, Abteilung I, Übersetzungen 2*. Wiesbaden: Harrassowitz.

——. 2007. *Einführung ins Ptolemäische. Eine Grammatik mit Zeichenliste und Übungsstücken*. Hützel: Backe.

——. 2010. *A Ptolemaic Sign-List: Hieroglyphs used in the Temples of the Graeco-Roman Period of Egypt and their Meanings*. Hützel: Backe.

——. 2014. *Edfou VI: Die Inschriften des Tempels von Edfu, Abteilung I, Übersetzungen, Band 3*. Wiesbaden: PeWe-Verlag.

Leitz, C. 2004. *Quellentexte zur ägyptischen Religion, I: die Tempelinschriften der griechisch-römanischen Zeit*. Einführungen und Quellentexte zur Ägyptologie 2. Münster: LIT Verlag.

Lucarelli, R. 2006. "Demons in the Book of the Dead." In B. Backes, I. Munro and S. Stöhr (eds.), *Totenbuch-Forschungen. Gesammelte Beiträge des 2, Internationalen Totenbuch-Symposiums 2005*, 210–211. Studien zum altägyptischen Totenbuch 11. Wiesbaden: Harrassowitz.

——. 2011. "Demonology during the Late Pharaonic and Greco-Roman Periods in Egypt." *Journal of Ancient Near Eastern Religions* 11: 109–125.

Mariette, A. 1873. *Dendérah: description générale du grand temple de cette ville* Tome IV. Paris: Librarie A. Franck.

Maspero, G. 1914. *Sarcophages des époques persane et ptolémaïque, CGC nos. 29301–29306* vol. I. Cairo: Institut français d'archéologie orientale.

Montet, P. 1961. *Géographie de l'Égypte ancienne, Deuxième partie* 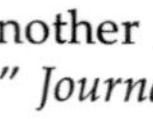 tꜣ šmꜣ, *La Haute Égypte*. Paris: Imprimerie nationale et Librairie C. Klincksieck.

Munro, I. 1994. *Die Totenbuch-Handschriften der 18. Dynastie im Museum Cairo*, Ägyptologische Abhandlungen 54. Wiesbaden: Harrassowitz.

Naville, É. 1908. *The Funeral Papyrus of Iouiya*. Theodore M. Davis' Excavations: Bibân el Molûk V. London: A. Constable and Co., Ltd.

Nims, C. 1952. "Another Geographical List from Medīnet Habu." *Journal of Egyptian Archaeology* 38: 34–45.

Osing, J. 1998. *The Carlsberg Papyri 2: Hieratische Papyri aus Tebtunis I*. The Carsten Niebuhr Institute of Ancient Near East Studies Publications 17. Copenhagen: Museum Tusculanum Press.

Pantalacci, L. 1995. "Compagnie de gardiens au temple d'el-Qal*a*a." In D. Kurth (ed.), *3. Ägyptologische Tempeltagung. Hamburg, 1–5. Juni 1994, Systeme und Programme der Ägyptischen Tempeldekoration*), 187–198. Ägypten und das alte Testament 33(1). Wiesbaden: Harrassowitz.

Rickert, A. 2011. *Gottheit und Gabe: eine ökonomische Prozession im Soubassement des Opettempels von Karnak und ihre Parallele in Kôm Ombo*, Studien zur spätägyptischen Religion 4. Wiesbaden: Harrassowitz.

——. 2014. "Die ökonomischen Prozessionen im Überblick." In A. Rickert and B. Ventker (eds.), *Altägyptische Enzyklopädien. Die Soubassements in den Tempeln der griechisch-römischen Zeit: Soubassementstudien I*, Band 1, 337–360. Studien zur spätägyptischen Religion 7. Wiesbaden: Harrassowitz.

Sass, D. 2014. *Slaughterers, Knife-bearers and Plague-bringers: A Study of the Role and Significance of the ḫꜣ.tyw in Ancient Egyptian Thought*. MA thesis, Macquarie University.

Sauneron, S. 1960. "Le nouveau sphinx composite du Brooklyn Museum et le rôle du dieu Toutou-Tithoès." *Journal of Near Eastern Studies* 19: 269–287.

Shonkwiler, R. L. 2014. *The Behdetite: A Study of Horus the Behdetite from the Old Kingdom to the Conquest of Alexander*. PhD dissertation, University of Chicago.

Smith, H. S. 1979. "Varia Ptolemaica." In J. Ruffle, G. A. Gaballa and K. A. Kitchen (eds.), *Glimpses of Ancient Egypt: Studies in Honour of H. W. Fairman*, 161–166. Warminster: Aris & Phillips.

Takács, G. 2008. *Etymological Dictionary of Egyptian* vol. 3. Handbuch der Orientalistik, Erste Abteilung: Der Nahe und Mittlere Osten 48. Leiden: E. J. Brill.

van der Molen, R. 2000. *A Hieroglyphic Dictionary of Egyptian Coffin Texts*. Probleme der Ägyptologie 15. Leiden: E. J. Brill.

Vandier, J. 1950. *Mo'alla: La tombe d'Ankhtifi et la tombe de Sébekhotep*. Bibliothèque d'Étude 18. Cairo: Institut français d'archéologie orientale.

——. 1955. "Hémen et Taharqa." *Revue d'égyptologie* 10: 73–79.

Vernus, P. 1978. *Athribis: textes et documents relatifs à*

la géographie, aux cultes et à l'histoire d'une ville du Delta égyptien à l'époque pharaonique. Bibliothèque d'Étude 74. Cairo: Institut français d'archéologie orientale.

Vikentiev, V. 1930. *La haute crue du Nil et l'averse de l'an 6 du roi Taharqa: le dieu "Hemen" et son chef-lieu "Hefat."* Recueil de travaux publiés par la Faculté des Lettres de l'Université égyptienne 4. Cairo: Institut français d'archéologie orientale.

von Pfeil-Autenrieth, C. 2008. *Der Gotteslohn für die Pharaonen: Untersuchungen zu den Gegengaben in ägyptischen Tempeln der griechisch-römischen Epoche*. Studien zu den Ritualszenen altägyptischer Tempel 6. Dettelbach: J. H. Röll.

Wild, H. 1954. "Statue de Hor-Néfer au Musée des Beaux-Arts de Lausanne." *Bulletin de l'Institut français d'archéologie orientale* 54: 173–222.

Willems, H. 1990. "Crime, Cult and Capital Punishment (Moaalla Inscription 8)." *Journal of Egyptian Archaeology* 76: 27–54.

Wilson, P. 1997. *A Ptolemaic Lexikon: A Lexicographical Study of the Texts in the Temple of Edfu*. Orientalia Lovaniensia Analecta 78. Leuven: Peeters Publishers.

Yoyotte, J. 1955. "Une étude sur l'anthroponymie gréco-égyptienne du nome prosôpite." *Bulletin de l'Institut français d'archéologie orientale* 55:125–140.

——. 1963. "Études géographiques II. Les localités méridionales de la région memphite et 'le pehou d'Héracléopolis.'" *Revue d'égyptologie* 15: 87–119.

Notes

1 For two cases, for the confusion between *mnḥ* and *ḥmn*, see Table 1:43–44. For the theory that *ḥmn* and *mnḥ* were originally one deity, and that the priests had to invent another deity and split the territories among them, see Farid 1986, 51.

2 This writing is attested only in the Graeco-Roman Period in the temple of Edfu so far. For the *i*-prefix before the name see Edel 1956, 17.

3 *Wb* II, 87, 17; Smith 1979, 162; Wilson 1997, 433. For the different signs used for the writing of his name in the Coffin Texts, see van der Molen 2008, 308; Hannig 1995, 340.

4 Wild 1954, 191.

5 Farid 1986, 50–53. For this deity, see *LGG* V, 150a–b; see also Vandier 1950, 8–13; Nims 1952, 40–1, 45; Vandier 1955, 73–79; LD IV, 27b; Vikentiev 1930, 68; *LÄ* II, 1117, s.v. Hemen; Gabra 1974, 234–237; *AEO* II, 14*–17*; Willems 1990, 43–46.

6 *E* II, 52, 2; *E* III, 301, 15; *E* VII, 280, 12.

7 Cairo JE 15039; Cairo CG 29304, see Maspero 1914, 129.

8 Cairo JE 15011; Cairo CG 29303, see Maspero 1914, 98; *E* III, 323, 9; *E* IV, 84, 11; *E* VII, 119, 2; *D* IX/I, 241, 16; *D* XV/I, 155, 13.

9 On a Kushite Period stele, dating to Piankhy's reign (Cairo JE 48862), for which see Grimal 1981, §16, l.83; *Urk*. III, 26, 83; Yoyotte 1963, 99, 105.

10 *Esna* III, No. 266, 5.

11 *Esna* III, No. 268A.

12 Faulkner 1933, cols. 22, 21; 33, 6.

13 *E* IV, 240, 17.

14 *D* VIII/I, 93, 9.

15 *E* I, 174, 1.

16 Naville 1908, pl. XV.

17 *CT* VI, 195d.

18 The text clearly shows *mnḥ*, but the translation mistakenly mentions it as Hemen. See Faulkner 2004, 470; Carrier 2004, 1360–1361.

19 Faulkner 2004, 470.

20 The three other deities are: Darkness (first), Who keeps off the *Akh*-spirits (third), and Hacker of the Earth (fourth); see E. Hornung and Abt 2007, 270.

21 Hornung 1965, 151, No. 614; Hornung 1992, 639–640.

22 Hornung and Abt 2007, 270.

23 Davies 1953, 10.

24 PM VI, 149 (252)–(255); *E* I, 173, 1–174, 8; *E* IX, pl. 23a; SERaT 900668; PM VI, 143(179); *E* I, 382, 4–15, pl. 31c; *E* XII, pl. 327; SERaT 901588; PM VI, 136 (108)–(109); *E* II, 51, 3–52, 9; *E* IX, pl. 40d; SERaT 901836; *E* III, 323, 5–12; *E* IX, pl. 80; SERaT 900246.

25 PM VI, 130; *E* III, 301, 8–16; *E* IX, pl. 79; SERaT 900345; PM VI, 156 (291)–(294); *E* IV, 83, 4–85, 8; *E* X, pl. 85; SERaT 900637; PM VI, 158 (302)–(305); *E* IV, 239, 13–241, 14; *E* X, pl. 91; PM VI, 126 (43)–(46); *E* V, 61, 17–63, 16; *E* X, pl. 113; SERaT 900974; PM VI, 125 (39)–(42); *E* V, 160, 12–

162, 6; *E* X, pl. 117; SERaT 900855; PM VI, 166 (328)–(333); *E* VII, 118, 4–119, 9, pl. 167; SERaT 901369; PM VI, 167 (337) – (344); *E* VII, 279, 16–281, 2, pl. 175; SERaT 901262; PM VI, 44 (XX); *D* XI/I, 58, 11–59, 8; *D* XI/II, pl. 39; SERaT 111692; *D* IX/I, 241, 9–19; SERaT 110192; *D* XV/I, 155, 5–14, pl. 62; SERaT 111937.

26 *D* XIV/I, 205, 8–206, 9, pl. 164; SERaT 111954.

27 *Esna* III, No. 266; PM VI, 112. The text states that the ritual is "killing sacrificial animal." See also SERaT 600078.

28 *Esna* III, No. 381; PM VI, 112; SERaT 600096.

29 It was built on the ancient village of *ḥwt-snfrw* or *ḥsfn*; see Farid 1986, 49.

30 Farid 1986, 41, fig. 4, pl. 6.

31 Farid 1986, 42–43, fig. 5, pl. 6.

32 Farid 1986, 45, figs. 9–10, pl. 7.

33 *E* VII, 280, 12; *D* VIII/I, 111, 4; *Esna* III, No. 381, 10.

34 *Esna* III, No. 268A.

35 Grimal 1981, 92, no. 276; see also Montet 1961, 197–198; Montet 1960, 58; Gauthier 1928, 44. For *sḥḏt n mḥ3t-t3wy* in a decree dating to year 23 of the reign of Ptolemy V, see Daressy 1911, 4 (9); Daumas 1952, 168; Yoyotte 1963, 100–103.

36 Stela Cairo JE 48862; *Urk*. III, 26, 83; Grimal 1981, 92 (no. 276); Yoyotte 1963, 99; *LGG* V, 862a.

37 *Esna* II, No. 55, 5; *Esna* III, No. 266, 5.

38 *Esna* III, No. 268A; *LGG* III, 694a.

39 Gauthier 1929, 115–116.

40 *Esna* III, No. 266, 5.

41 Gauthier 1927, 67.

42 This is the same designation of the nine dead deities of the temple of Horus at Edfu, for which see Gaber, forthcoming. The ten dead deities of Dendera have the same epithet. See Gaber 2015, 248.

43 *Esna* V, 8. For this temple, see Abdel-Rahman 2009, 5–6; El-Sayed 1982, 643, doc. 1050.

44 *Esna* III, 268A; *Esna* III, No. 381; 10–11.

45 *Esna* V, 7.

46 *Esna* II, No. 55.

47 *D* VII/I, 183, 12; DZA 20.793.820.

48 Montet 1961, 49.

49 Gauthier 1927, 126.

50 *AEO* II, 12*–17*; *LÄ* III, 90, s.v. Hut-Snofru; see also Černý 1963, 89–92.

51 *Esna* III, No. 381, 10; *LGG* III, 694b–c.

52 *Esna* III, No. 257A.

53 Gauthier 1927, 120.

54 *Esna* III, No. 266, 13.

55 *E* VII, 119, 2; Kurth 2004, 212.

56 *E* IV, 249, 17.

57 *Esna* III, No. 257A; Gauthier 1925, 163; *LGG* V, 508c. For *ḥḳ3 fkḫr* as an epithet for Montu-Re-Horakhty, see *D* IX/I, 244, 5; *LGG* V, 393c–394a.

58 *LGG* II, 222a–b.

59 *Esna* III, No. 266, 5, No. 268A, No. 381, 10; L*D*, Text, IV, 31(y).

60 Farid 1986, 41–44, figs. 4–5, pl. 6; *Esna* V, 50, footnote (b), 377.

61 *D* VII/I, 183, 12; DZA 20.793.820; *D* VII/I, 196, 5; DZA 20.793.760; *D* VIII/I, 93, 9; DZA 20.793.830; *D* VIII/I, 105, 1; 196, 5.

62 See Wild 1954, 193. The body of the statue is now in Lausanne, Musée des Beaux-Arts (Eg 7), see TM 48399.

63 CK 608, see http://www.ifao.egnet.net/bases/cachette/ck608; TM 113837, see www.trismegistos.org/text/113837; Coulon 2001, 88, 90, 93 (k)

64 *D* VIII/I, 86, 5–6; *D* VIII/I, 111, 4; *LGG* II, 222b.

65 *D* VIII/I 111, 4. This is also an epithet of Amun; see *LGG* VI, 286a.

66 *Esna* III, No. 268A; *LGG* V, 478b.

67 *Esna* III, No. 381; *LGG* VII, 214a.

68 *Esna* III, No. 266, 6.

69 *Esna* III, No. 257A; *Esna* III, No. 268A; *LGG* VII, 292c–293a.

70 *D* VII/I, 196, 5; *D* VII/I, 183, 12; DZA 20.793.820; *D* VIII/I, 93, 9; DZA 20.793.830; *Esna* III, No. 257A; *LGG* III, 55c–56b.

71 *D* VII/I, 183, 13; DZA 20.793.820; *D* VII/I, 196, 6; DZA 20.793.760; *D* VIII/I, 93, 9; DZA 20.793.830; *LGG* II, 705c–706c.

72 *D* VII/I, 183, 12–13; DZA 20.793.820; *D* VIII/I, 111, 5. For *i͗tt m pḥty.f*, see *D* VIII/I, 93, 9–10; DZA 20.793.830; *Esna*, No. 381; *LGG* I, 633b.

73 *D* VIII/I, 93, 9; DZA 20.793.830; *LGG* III, 747c–

748a.

74 *D* VIII/I, 111, 5; *LGG* III, 211a–212a.

75 *D* VII/I, 196, 5; DZA 20.793.760; *LGG* VII, 441c–442b.

76 *D* VII/I, 196, 5–6; DZA 20.793.760; *LGG* II, 462a–b.

77 *Esna* III, No. 381.

78 *Esna* III, No. 381; *LGG* III, 481a.

79 *Esna* III, No. 381, *LGG* II, 239b–c.

80 *Esna* III, No. 381; *LGG* VI, 323c.

81 *D* VIII/I, 111, 4–5; *LGG* VII, 218c–219a.

82 *D* VII/I, 196, 6; *LGG* I, 628a.

83 *D* VII/I, 183, 13; DZA 20.793.820; *LGG* III, 473b.

84 *D* VII/I, 183, 13; DZA 20.793.820; *D* VIII/I, 93, 10; DZA 20.793.830; *LGG* VI, 471a–b.

85 *D* VIII/I, 111, 5–6; *LGG* V, 489a.

86 *D* VIII/I, 111, 5–6.

87 *D* VII/I, 183, 14–15; DZA 20.793.820; *D* VIII/I, 93, 11; *LGG* IV, 353a–354b.

88 *D* VII/I, 196, 7; DZA 20.793.830.

89 *D* VII/I, 196, 6; DZA 20.793.830; *LGG* VI, 540a–b.

90 For the importance of this rite, see Germond 1981, 252. For the rite itself, see Goyon 2006.

91 *D* VIII/I, 111, 5; *LGG* VI, 579a–b.

92 *D* VII/I, 196, 6–7; DZA 20.793.830; *LGG* VI, 326c.

93 *Esna* III, 268A; *LGG* V, 522c–523a.

94 *Esna* III, 268A; *LGG* V, 862a–b.

95 *Esna* II, 163, 18.

96 TM 48496.

97 Faulkner 1933, col. 22, 21–22; Faulkner 1937, 168; DZA 20.793.750.

98 Faulkner 1933, col. 33, 6–7; Faulkner 1938, 53; DZA 20.793.840.

99 *CT* VII, 417a.

100 For the uncertain reading of this word as *tm* "leader (?)," see Carrier 2004, 2280–2281.

101 Faulkner 2004, 157.

102 Kousoulis 1999, 24; Kousoulis 2000.

103 For other attestation of Nekhet in the temple of Edfu, see *E* III, 33, 6; *E* VI, 329, 11–12; *E* VIII, 126, 4. Nekhet, who usually appears as one of a group of nine deities, is represented among eight deities in this scene only due to the lack of space. Each one of these deities including Nekhet is represented as a falcon-head deity wearing the short kilt and the bull's tail while holding a knife in the right hand and a spear in the left hand. See *E* X/II, pl. CXLV.

104 PM VI, 160 (308)–(311); SERaT 901130; *E* VI, 159, 4; *E* X/II, pl. CXLV; Beinlich 2008, 119.

105 See Goyon 2006, 57, footnote 4. Kurth follows Goyon's reading, for which see Kurth 2014, 274.

106 For the same description of serpents, see Goyon 2006, 56, footnote 8.

107 *E* VI, 159, 4. For the reading of *ḫꜣtyw rsyw*, which is attested only once, see *LGG* V, 637c. See Kurth 1994, 243; Kurth 2014, 274.

108 Kurth 2014, 274.

109 For the *ḫꜣtyw* in charge of slaying Apep, see Faulkner 1938, 43.

110 See Goyon 2006, 57, footnote 4.

111 *D* VIII/I, 104, 15–105, 1; *D* VIII/II, pl. DCCXLIV.

112 For a similar text, without mentioning the name of the demon, see *D* IV, 205, 13–14; Cauville 2001, 336–337.

113 *D* IV, 189, 11; Cauville 2001, 306–307.

114 *D* IV, 189, 11; Cauville 2001, 306–307.

115 *D* VIII/I, 86, 5–6; DZA 20.793.850.

116 *E* I, 565, 15.

117 *E* I, 555, 8.

118 *E* I, 464, 14; DZA 25.792.840.

119 As mentioned before, *ḥmn* is often confused with *mnḥ*.

120 Wilson 1997, 467.

121 *Esna* III, No. 266, 6; *LGG* II, 34b–c.

122 *Esna* III, No. 257A; *LGG* III, 635b–c.

123 *Esna* III, No. 268A.

124 *D* VII/I, 196, 6; DZA 20.793.760; *D* VIII/I, 93, 9; DZA 20.793.830; *LGG* III, 712a.

125 *D* VIII/I, 111, 4–5; *LGG* V, 372c–373a.

126 *ḥry ḫꜣtyw* is attested as a royal epithet in an offering scene of *ḥnk mꜣʿt* "giving maat" in the temple of Edfu; see *E* IV, 76, 2. Chassinat suggested that the sign used with the royal epithet was a jackal-headed deity and that, despite the chiseling, he

could still see the head and the nose. See *E* IV, 76, footnote 1. The jackal-headed determinatives are associated with the *šmꜣyw* demons, for which see *Wb* IV, 471. SERaT reads this epithet as *ḥry-ḫnṯtyw* "chief of the *ḫnṯtyw* demons." See SERaT 900604.

127 It appears on a block from Athribis; see Kaper 2003, 260 (R-38).

128 Yoyotte 1955, 136.

129 Sauneron 1960, 272, footnote 22.

130 Vernus 1978, 200, doc. 170, pl. 34; Germond 1979, 27, footnote 16; el-Sayed 1982, 485, doc. 685.

131 Kaper 2003, 28, 260 (R–38).

132 Blackman and Fairman 1943, 21, no. 6. For *ḫꜣtyw* and *ḫnṯtyw*, see Kurth 2010, 7; Kurth 2007, 131. For *ḫꜣtyw*, see Sass 2014, 25–27. For *mnḥ*, see Leitz 2004, 154. For all of these readings, see Daumas 1988, I, 32. For *mnḥ*, see *E* VI, 142, 12; Wilson 1997, 433.

133 For *ḥnwt šmꜣyw*, see *D* VI, 40, 1; S. Cauville 2004, 308. For the reading of *ḥnwt imnḥw*, see Daumas 1988, 109. Leitz read it as *wpwtyw*, but the reading is not certain. See *LGG* V, 173b.

134 See *KO* 66 (right). For examples where the king has the epithet of *mnḥ*, "the butcher." see Ibrahim 1971, 137–`28.

135 Herbin 1999, 197, footnote 104; Grenier 1977, 21; Rickert 2011, 83, pl. 17. As for Leitz, he reads it as *ḥry-tp mniww* "chief of the shepherds." See *LGG* V, 394b. For another attestation of this epithet in the temple of Edfu with uncertain reading, see *E* II, 168, 8.

136 *Opet* I, 224 (left); Rickert 2011, 83, pl. 16; Rickert 2014, 357.

137 See *E* V, 146, 9. For the reading of *ḥrj ḫnṯtyw*, see SERaT 900823.

138 Dating to the reign of Amenhotep III, see TM 134267.

139 Munro 1994, pl. 58. Cairo CG 51189. See Quibell 1908, 68; Naville 1908, pl. XV.

140 *CT* VII, 133f; *LGG* III, 305b.

141 For the *mnḥw* demons, see Gaber 2015, 31–36.

142 For the functions of the *mnḥw* butchers, see Gaber 2015, 31–36.

143 *D* IV, 189, 11; Cauville 2001, 306–307.

144 *E* I 470, 1; *E* IX, pl. 35c; DZA 26.863.530; Gaber 2015, 31–36.

145 For Anubis as son of Osiris, see Gaber 2015, 318–320.

146 For Horus the Behdetite as the son of Osiris, see Shonkwiler 2014, 143, 158, 203, 302, 473.

147 *Esna* VI/I, No. 523, 10–11.

148 *LGG* VI, 81a.

149 *LGG* II, 18c.

150 SERaT 600143; Beinlich 2008, 311.

151 *Esna* VI/I, 143.

152 *Esna* III, No. 381.

153 *Esna* III, No. 257A.

154 For the reading as *ḥmnt* and not *mnḥt*, see Osing 1998, 285–286, pl. 29 (C 2, 17).

155 TM 56095.

156 Leitz reads the name as *mnḥt*: see *LGG* III, 305c.

157 SERaT 600096.

158 *Esna* III, No. 381, 13.

159 SERaT 600078.

160 *Esna* III, No. 266, 9.

161 SERaT 900668; Beinlich 2008, 330.

162 SERaT 901836; Beinlich 2008, 509.

163 *E* I, 173, 1; DZA 20.793.800; *E* II, 52, 2; DZA 20.793.810.

164 These god's responses are not a part of a recent study. See von Pfeil-Autenrieth 2008.

165 Grimal 1981, 88.

166 See Lucarelli 2011, 110.

167 The head is now in New York, Metropolitan Museum of Art (Egyptian), MMA 1980.422. TM 48399; see www.trismegistos.org/text/48399; Wild 1954, 182, pls. II–III.

168 TM 113837; Clarysse 2010, 284; Coulon 2001, 88, 90, 93 (k). It appears that the policy of the Ptolemies was to concentrate administrative, military, and religious power among the same families. See Fischer-Bovet 2008, 297.

169 Beinlich 2008, 119.

170 SERaT 110355; *D* II, 165, 5, pl. CXLIII; Cauville 1999, 250–251.

171 Beinlich 2008, 121.

[172] SERaT 110986; *D* VII/I, 160, 12; *D* VII/II, pl. DCLXII.

[173] *Tôd* I, 130, 4.

[174] For *kꜣ dšr stp ḫpšwy.fy*, see SERaT 900228; *E* III, 178, 15. For *ḥrw-ʿ (?) stpw*, see SERaT 900646; *E* IV, 128, 12. For *mꜣỉ mꜣ-ḥḏ*, see SERaT 901140; *E* VI, 142, 12. For *ṯs-ỉḫt*, see SERaT 110655; *D* III, 185, 12–13. For *ḥw-ʿ r stpw*, see SERaT 110558; *D* VI, 36, 2. For *wḏꜣt*, see SERaT 110605; *D* VI, 143, 3–4. See also Ibrahim 1971, 137–138; Wilson 1997, 433.

[175] For other fecundity figures assimilated into Amun, Re and Hapy, see Baines 1985, 259–260.

[176] *D* VII/I, 183, 12–15; DZA 20.793.820; *D* VII/II, pl. DCLXXI.

[177] *D* VII/I, 196, 5–7; *D* VII/II, pl. DCLXXXVI; DZA 20.793.760. See also Mariette 1873, pl. 16; see also Yoyotte 1963, 105.

[178] The deity has a ceremonial beard. See *D* VIII/I, 93, 9–11; *D* VIII/II, pl. DCCLXXXVII.

[179] A gazelle is represented standing beside Meneh, for which see *D* VIII/I, 111, 4–6; *D* VIII/II, pl. DCCLXI.

[180] *D* IV, pl. CCXCIX.

[181] *E* IX, pl. XXXVIII (1).

[182] *Esna* II, No. 55, 5; S. El-Sabban 2000, 162; Grimm 1994, 56–57; Farid 1986, 53.

[183] *Esna* II, No. 77, 17; *Esna* V, 6–7; El-Sabban 2000, 168; Grimm 1994, 140–141.

[184] TM 109510. Cairo CG 29303, see Maspero 1914, 98.

[185] TM 109514. Cairo CG 29304, see Maspero 1914, 129.

[186] *LGG* VI, 286a–b.

[187] For the different threats of the butcher demons towards the deceased, see Gaber 2015, 31–36.

[188] For other demons having both aspects, see Pantalacci 1995, 187–198; Lucarelli 2006, 210–211.

Journal of Ancient Egyptian Interconnections

The Guardians of Menekhibnekau: Chapter 144 of the Book of the Dead in the Shaft tomb of Menekhibnekau at Abusir

Renata Landgráfová
Czech Institute of Egyptology, Charles University, Prague

Abstract
Although the Saite-Persian shaft tomb of Menkehibnekau at Abusir is more conservative in its decoration programme than that of Iufaa, it nonetheless contains several interesting and unusual features. One such element of decoration is Chapter 144 of the Book of the Dead with its vignette on the southern (entrance) wall of the burial chamber. While the placement of Pyramid Text snake spells at such locations for apotropaic/guardian functions is well known, demonic gate-guardians have so far been found only here. The vignette, moreover, uses the three-dimensional feature of the entrance to the burial chamber as the depiction of its "gates," thus stressing even more the dual function of the BD 144 demons as both underworld gate guardians and guardians of the burial chamber of Menekhibnekau.

The Shaft Tomb of Menekhibnekau

The shaft tomb of general Menekhibnekau[1] is one of the three hitherto explored large tombs on the Saite-Persian cemetery in the northwestern part of the Abusir necropolis. It is located to the south of the tomb of Iufaa[2] and roughly contemporaneous with it (the entire Abusir shaft tomb cemetery apparently having been built within a short period of about 50 years).[3]

Decoration Program and Texts

While the decoration of the burial chamber of Menekhibnekau is less extensive than that of Iufaa[4] and consists basically of the standard program of the coeval shaft tombs, it still contains several interesting and unusual elements, such as the personifications of the hours of day and night[5] and the guardian demons with Chapter 144 of the Book of the Dead, which is the topic of the present study.

BD 144 in the Shaft Tomb of Menekhibnekau

Chapter 144 of the Book of the Dead, with its accompanying vignette, covers the entire south (entrance) wall. It is divided into two horizontal registers, with the top register containing the demons of gates 1–3 and the lower one the demons of gates 4–7. The sections pertaining to each gate are divided from one another by vertical lines and have a uniform setup: under the identification of the gate in a line of text at the top are three demons (standing, sitting, or squatting), with their titles and names inscribed in a column of text before each of them. The text of the chapter is inscribed in 33 columns under the vignette, around the arched entrance leading to the burial chamber. The very bottom part of the wall has been left blank.

The Vignette

In the following section, the images of the demon

guardians and their accompanying texts are described and analyzed in detail.

FIGURE 1: The first gate of BD 144 in the burial chamber of Menekhibnekau.

The guardians of THE FIRST GATE have the following forms: a standing ram-headed man, a seated man holding a kid, and a standing baboon-headed man holding a stalk with an ear of corn in his hand. The text reads:

ꜥr.t tpj.t rn n jr.j-ꜥꜣ=s sẖd-ḥr.w ꜥšꜣ-jr.w jr.j=s smt[6] *smj jm=s swh-ẖrw*[7]

The first gate. The name of its doorkeeper is "One with inverted faces, Numerous of forms," of the one who guards it, "Hearer," and of the one who reports in it, "Roaring of voice."

FIGURE 2: The second gate of BD 144 in the burial chamber of Menekhibnekau.

The guardians of THE SECOND GATE have the following forms: a seated man with a ram's head, a hippopotamus standing Tweret-like on its hind legs, holding a dagger, and a standing baboon-headed man holding a stalk with an ear of corn in his hand. The text reads:

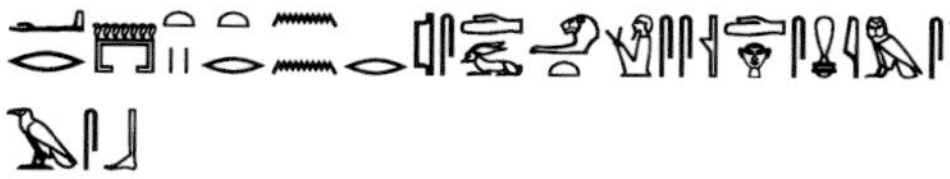

ꜥr.t sn.nwt rn n jr.j-ꜥꜣ=s dwn-ḥꜣ.t jr.j=s sḳd-ḥr smj jm=s ꜣsb

The second gate. The name of its doorkeeper is "He with extended forehead," of the one who guards it, "Watchful of face," and of the one who reports in it, "Burning one."

FIGURE 3: The third gate of BD 144 in the burial chamber of Menekhibnekau.

The guardians of THE THIRD GATE have the following forms: a man with a turtle in place of the head, a standing man with the head of a lion, and a standing baboon-headed man holding a stalk with an ear of corn in his hand. The text reads:

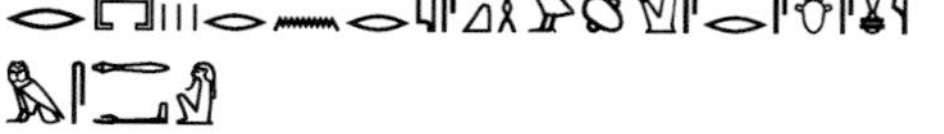

ꜥr.t 3.t rn n jr.j-ꜥꜣ=s ḳḳ ḥw<ꜣꜣ.t> jr.j=s rs-jb smj jm=s ꜥꜣ

The third gate. The name of its doorkeeper is "Eater of putrefaction," of the one who guards it, "He with alert heart," and of the one who reports in it, "Great one."[8]

FIGURE 4: The fourth gate of BD 144 in the burial chamber of Menekhibnekau.

The guardians of THE FOURTH GATE have the following forms: a standing ram-headed man, a standing man, and a standing baboon-headed man holding a stalk with an ear of corn in his hand. The text reads:

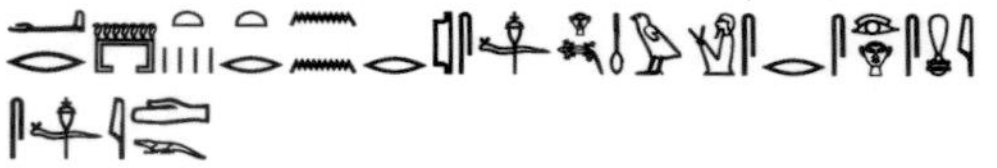

ʿr.t 4.t rn n jr.j-ʿ3=s ḥsf-ḥr ʿš3-ḫrw jr.j=s rs-ḥr smj jm=s ḥsf jd

The fourth gate. The name of its doorkeeper is "Repulsive of face, Many-voiced," of the one who guards it, "Alert of face," and of the one who reports in it, "Punisher of the Angry one."

FIGURE 5: The fifth gate of BD 144 in the burial chamber of Menekhibnekau.

The guardians of THE FIFTH GATE have the following forms: a seated Bes-faced man holding two animal shanks in his hands, a standing man with the head of a cow, and a standing baboon-headed man holding a stalk with an ear of corn in his hand. The text reads:

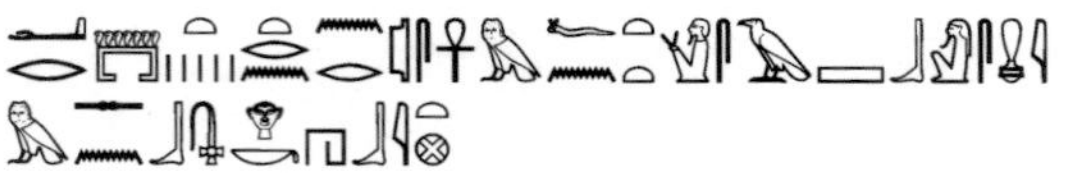

ʿr.t 5.t rn n jr.j-ʿ3=s ʿnḫ m fnṯ(.w) jr.j=s 3šb.w smj jm<=s> znb-ḥr khb jt[9]

The fifth gate. The name of its doorkeeper is "He who lives on worms," of the one who guards it, "Burning one," and of the one who reports in it, "Destructive of face, Raging of onslaught."

FIGURE 6: The sixth gate of BD 144 in the burial chamber of Menekhibnekau.

The guardians of THE SIXTH GATE have the following forms: a standing ram-headed man, a standing man with the head of a lion, and a standing baboon-headed man holding a stalk with an ear of corn in his hand. The text reads:

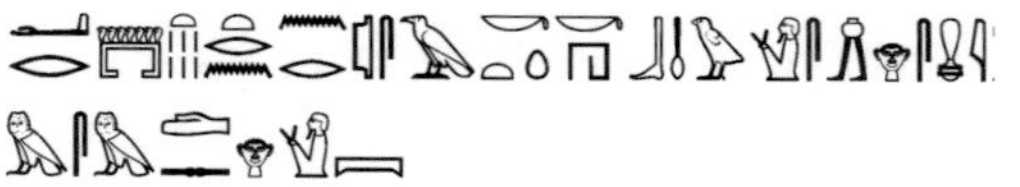

ʿr.t 6.t rn n jr.j-ʿ3=s 3k[10]*-t khb-ḫrw jr.j=s jnj-ḥr smj jm=s mdz-ḥr s3-p.t*

The sixth gate. The name of its doorkeeper is "Attacker of bread, Violent of voice", of the one who guards it, "Face-bringer", and of the one who reports in it, "Sharp-faced, guardian of the sky."

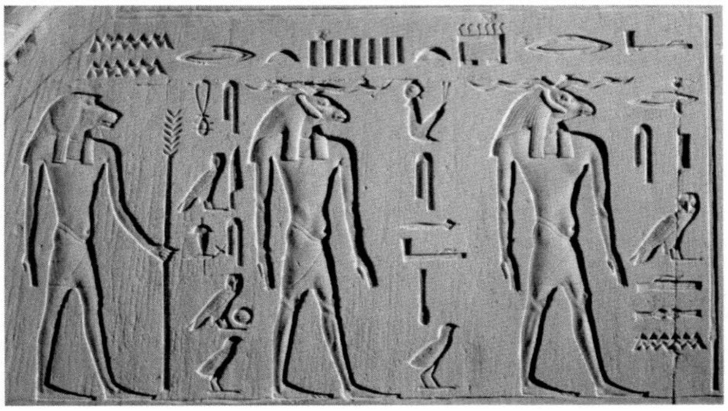

FIGURE 7: The seventh gate of BD 144 in the burial chamber of Menekhibnekau.

The guardians of THE SEVENTH GATE have the following forms: a ram-headed man, a standing ram-headed man, and a standing baboon-headed man holding a stalk with an ear of corn in his hand. The text reads:

ʿr.t 7.t rn n jr.j-ʿ3=s mds<=s>n jr.j=s ʿ3-ẖrw smj jm=s ẖsf ẖmj.w

The seventh gate. The name of its doorkeeper is "He who crushes <th>em," of the one who guards it, "Loud-voiced," and of the one who reports in it, "Punisher of attackers."

THE VIGNETTE OF BD 144 OF MENEKHIBNEKAU IN CONTEXT OF OTHER ATTESTATIONS OF BD 144V

Menekhibnekau's representations show all three guardians for every gate, each identified by a name, although they do not exactly correspond to any known representation of gates and guardians in the known vignettes of BD 144.[11] The range of these representations is very wide, but they can be divided into basic groups according to the number and nature of the guardians represented and the presence (and form) or absence of representations of the individual gates. The database of the Totenbuchprojekt[12] contains 107 papyri of BD 144 with vignette. Three main types (each with subvariants) can be identified: Vignette Type I consists of a row of standing or striding demons with no gates represented, vignette Type II shows 7 gates (each with a demon inside) and 1 or 2 (other) demon(s) standing behind each gate, and vignette Type III shows 7 gates usually in its upper part, divided from the demons below them, which are usually in pairs, by the identifications of the gates and guardians. The subvariants manifest in differing numbers of demons and types of their heads, the exact nature of the gates represented (usually their frieze), and the relative position of the vignette and chapter text. The 107 attestations are distributed among these three types somewhat unevenly, with a slight but clear preference of Type I (29% are of Type I, 18% are of Type II, 16% of Type III, and 13% cannot be identified due to damage of the papyrus). It is also interesting to look at the historical distribution of the vignette types. TABLE 1 shows the situation for the 76 attestations on papyri.

The table clearly shows that on papyri, vignette Type III, i.e., the arrangement of gates in the upper part of the chapter text and the demons (usually in pairs) below, represents the early version of the vignette: of the 17 New Kingdom papyri with BD Chapter 144V recorded in the Totenbuchprojekt database, 12 have vignette Type III, 1 vignette Type I, and in 4 cases the nature of the vignette cannot be ascertained due to damage. Vignette Type I appears to be the simplified, shortened form (without gates), which could be employed at any time when required, as it is attested from the New Kingdom to the Ptolemaic Period. Vignette Type II represents the late type, appearing (on papyrus) in the Late Period at the earliest and culminating in the Ptolemaic Period. The papyrus versions show a development from a bound arrangement (in vignette Type III, the gates have to stand in an ordered form next to each other, the whole vignette forming a tall rectangle) to a freer one (the gates of vignette Type II can be arranged in many different forms and can fill all kinds of available space). For the mummy wrappings, the situation is similar: out of the 21 examples which could be checked in the Bonn Totenbuchprojekt archive,[13] 12 vignettes are of Type I, 4 are of Type II, and 5 are so damaged that the vignette type could not be determined with certainty. Since 17 of these are Ptolemaic, 3 date to the Late Period, and 1 between the Late and early Ptolemaic Periods, the absence of Vignette Type III corroborates the evidence of the papyri. The even greater prevalence of Type I than in the case of the papyri may be explained by the greater difficulty in drawing more complex shapes on the bandage, as well as by greater space (specifically height) restrictions.[14] Perhaps this

TABLE 1: Temporal distribution of vignette types on papyri (source: Totenbuchprojekt Bonn archive < http://totenbuch.awk.nrw.de >, accessed 28 June 2017).

	I	II	III	UNCLEAR
New Kingdom	1[a]	–	12[b]	4[c]
Third Intermediate Period	1[d]	–	1[e]	1[f]
Late Period	4[g]	–	–	2[h]
Late Period/Ptolemaic	4[i]	4[j]	–	–
Ptolemaic	19[k]	14[l]	–	8[m]
Roman	–	14[n]	–	–
Σ	29	19	3	15

NOTES

a P. New York Amherst 16.

b P. London BM EA 10489, P. Hannover 1970.37 (P. Brocklehurst 2), P. Triest 12089 a–d, P. Kairo CG 51189, Martin Schøyen Collection (MS 1638), Oslo (formerly), P. Leiden T 2 (SR), P. London BM EA 10477, P. London BM EA 9913, P. Mailand, Ospedale Maggiore (P. Busca), P. Paris Louvre N. 3074, P. Privatsammlung Varga, P. Turin 8438.

c P. London BM EA 9900, P. London BM EA 9953 A, P. Moskau I, 1b, 1060 A (A+B) und B, P. Princeton Pharaonic Roll 5.

d P. London BM EA 10014.

e P. Kairo CG 40007 (J.E. 26229, S.R. IV 980).

f P. London BM EA 10554 (P. Greenfield).

g P. Köln P. Colon. Aeg. 10207, P. London BM EA 10558, P. Vatikan 38611 (P. Vatikan 54), P. Vatikan 48832 (P. Vatikan 1, N. 16).

h P. Kairo J.E. 95841 (S.R. IV 939) [1], P. Paris Louvre N. 3091.

i P. London BM EA 10539 + 10700 + 10733, P. London BM EA 9912, P. London BM EA 9944, P. Privat MacGregor.

j P. Chicago OIM 9787 (P. Ryerson), P. Leiden L.XII.2, P. New York MMA 35.9.20, P. St. Petersburg 3531.

k P. Berlin P. 10477, P. Berlin P. 10478 A-N, P. Cologny CV, P. Hildesheim RPM 5248, P. Kairo J.E. 32887 (S.R. IV 930), P. Leiden T 1 (CI), P. London BM EA 10097, P. London BM EA 10098, P. London BM EA 10479, P. Mailand E. 1023, P. Manchester Hieratic 3, P. Paris Louvre N. 3079, P. Paris Louvre N. 3081, P. Paris Louvre N. 3084, P. Paris Louvre N. 3144 + N. 3250 + N. 3198, P. Paris Louvre N. 5450, P. Privatsammlung Paris 3, P. Turin 1791, P. Wien Vindob. Aeg. 65.

l P. Berlin P. 3149 + 14376, P. Detroit 1988.10, P. Dublin MS 1669, P. Hohenzollern-Sigmaringen I, P. Kairo CG 40029 (J.E. 95837, S.R. IV 934), P. Paris Louvre N. 3129 + E. 4890 B, P. Lausanne 3389, P. Leiden T 16 (AMS 41), P. Wien ÄS 3862 (3856-58, 3864, 3866-69) + 10159, P. London BM EA 10257, P. New York Amherst 34, P. Paris Louvre N. 3088, P. Paris Louvre N. 3089, P. Paris Louvre N. 3248.

m P. Kairo J.E. 95859 (S.R. IV 958), P. Leiden T 17 (AMS 19), P. Paris Louvre N. 3090 + N. 3206 + N. 3198, P. Paris Louvre N. 3151, P. Vatikan 38598 (P. Vatikan 57), P. Vatikan 38602 (P. Vatikan 28), P. Wien ÄS 3852 (No. 6), P. Chicago OIM 10486 (P. Milbank).

n P. Paris Louvre N. 3279.

is also the reason for the presence of a special variety of vignette Type I on mummy wrappings, not seen on papyri: 7 (?)[15] pairs of standing demons, each pair following a symbolic representation of an opened door-jamb.[16]

However, the situation becomes somewhat more complex when we look at the vignettes of BD 144 found in monumental context (see TABLE 2).[17]

Most of the monumental examples feature vignettes of Type I, but, interestingly, the earlier examples show variations. The vignettes of TT 353 and TT 41 show the "mummy-wrapping" variant of vignette Type I, i.e., standing demons following "gates" represented by opened door jambs. Perhaps even more interesting is the vignette of the Abydos temple of Ramesses II,[18] which represents a transitory variant with features of all three vignette types: the chapter is presented in a table of sorts, the upper half of which contains seven rectangles filled in part with text and in part with one squatting demon per rectangle (the future gates with squatting demons of Type II). The entire tabular setup of the image corresponds to the usual setup of vignette Type III,

TABLE 2: Monumental attestations of BD 144V.

ATTESTATION ID	DATE	OWNER	VIGNETTE TYPE
TT 353[a]	18th Dyn.	Senenmut	I (variant)
TT 41[b]	19th Dyn.	Amenemope	I (variant)
Abydos temple[c]	19th Dyn.	Ramesses II	I/II/III
QV 66[d]	19th Dyn.	Nefertari	I
Block Cairo JE 88131[e]	22nd Dyn.	Sheshonq	I (variant)
Tanis[f]	22nd Dyn.	Osorkon II	III
Sarcophagus CG 29315[g]	Ptolemaic	Djehutiirdis	II
Dendera temple[h]	Ptolemaic–Roman		I

NOTES

a Saleh 1984, 77; photo by Karl H. Leser at < https://www.maat-ka-ra.de/german/personen/senenmut/sen_t353.htm >, accessed 3 May 2017).

b Assmann 1991, 145–146 and pl. 64.

c Abdelrahiem 2006, 14–15.

d Hawass 2006, 241–245.

e Badawi 1957, pl. VII.

f Roulin 1998, 245–246.

g Maspero 1914, 78-101 and pls. XXVII-XXIX.

h Cauville 1997, 344–346 and pl. 192.

whereas the 7 pairs of standing demons in the lower part of the table correspond to one of the most usual variants of Type I. Perhaps we are seeing the birth of both vignette Type II and the "mummy wrapping" variant of Type I in these early monumental examples. The reasons that triggered these changes are unclear, but they might lie both in the spatial aesthetics of tomb and temple walls and the impossibility of directly transferring a (papyrus) original onto a stone surface.[19]

But let us return to the vignette of Menekhibnekau, the setup of which seemingly does not correspond to any of the three types identified here. While the demons are depicted in clearly delimited groups of three and one of the three is often seated or squatting, no gates are represented. However, this apparent inconsistency can be resolved when the entire composition of the wall is considered: the guardian-groups are arranged around a real "gate" of sorts, the entrance to Menekhibnekau's burial chamber, which they guard alongside their respective gates of the underworld.[20] Menekhibnekau's vignette thus can be considered to have a single, three-dimensional representation of a gate, which is to be "read" seven times. Table 3 shows the resulting situation.

With its three-dimensional representation of the gate(s), Menekhibnekau's vignette of BD 144 falls well within the range of the innovative monumental variants. At the same time, this unusual representation of the gate(s) ensures that the demons serve not only as the guardians of netherworld gates but also as guardians of (the tomb of) Menekhibnekau.

The Text of BD 144 of Menekhibnekau

Unlike the vignette, the text of the chapter, inscribed on the southern wall of the burial chamber of Menekhibnekau, is a relatively standard composition.[21] As it contains several interesting features and has not been published so far, a preliminary translation is included here alongside the treatment of the vignette.

(1) *ḏd-mdw*[22] *j ꜥrr.wt 7.t jpw jr.w ꜥrr.wt ḥr wsjr s.w ꜥrr.wt=sn* (2) *j smj.w ḫr(.t) tꜣ.w n wsjr rꜥ nb wsjr mnḫ-jb-nkꜣ.w pn rḫ tn* (3) *rḫ rn=tn*

To be recited: "O you 7 gates and you who watch over Osiris, who guard your gates! O you who report the affairs of the lands[23] to Osiris daily! This Osiris Menekhibnekau knows you and knows your names.

ntf ms m rꜣ-stꜣ.w dj{t}(.w) sꜣḫ n{=k} <nb> ꜣḫ.t sꜥḥ wsjr mnḫ-jb-nkꜣ.w pn (4) *m p mj ꜥb wsjr šsp wsjr mnḫ-jb-nkꜣ.w pn kꜣj m rꜣ-stꜣ.w*

He is one who was born in Rosetau, to whom was given the transfiguration of <the lord> of the horizon. This Osiris Menekhibnekau is noble in Buto as Osiris is pure. This Osiris Menekhibnekau receives acclaim[24] in Rosetau.

sšm (5) *nṯr.w ḥr ꜣḫ.t m šnw.t*[25] *ḥꜣ wsjr wsjr mnḫ-jb-nkꜣ.w pn* (6) *wꜥ jm m sšm.w=sn wsjr mnḫ-jb-nkꜣ.w pn ꜣḫ nb ꜣḫ.w ꜣḫ jr{t}* (7) *wsjr mnḫ-jb-nkꜣ.w pn sw(t) pw wn.t(j)=f(j)*

Table 3: Overview of features of vignette types and the vignette of Menekhibnekau.

	I	II	III	Menekhib-nekau
Gates	–	+	+	+ (3D)
Demons per Gate	2	3	2	3
Seated Demons	–	+	+	+
Demon Heads	standardized	varying	standardized	varying

When the gods are led through the horizon as the suite behind Osiris, this Osiris Menekhibnekau is one of them as their leader. This Osiris Menekhibnekau is an *akh*, lord of *akhu*. The *akh* whom this Osiris Menekhibnekau made, it is he who shall exist.[26]

wsjr mnḫ-jb-nkꜣ.w pn (ḥr) jr.t ꜣbd smj (8) *m smd.t*

This Osiris Menekhibnekau performs the monthly (new-moon) festival and reports at the half-monthly (full-moon) festival.

j dbn wsjr mnḫ-jb-nkꜣ.w pn <ḥr> jr.t ḥr.w jr.j-ꜥ ḏḥwtj m <g>rḥ ḏꜣ=f (9) *p.t m mꜣꜥ-ḫrw dd swꜣ wsjr mnḫ-jb-nkꜣ.w pn m ḥtp sḳd=f m wjꜣ* (10) *n rꜥ*

O, this Osiris Menekhibnekau encircles the Eye of Horus,[27] an assistant of Thoth at night! May he cross the sky in triumph! Cause that this Osiris Menekhibnekau may pass in peace as he sails in the barge of Re!

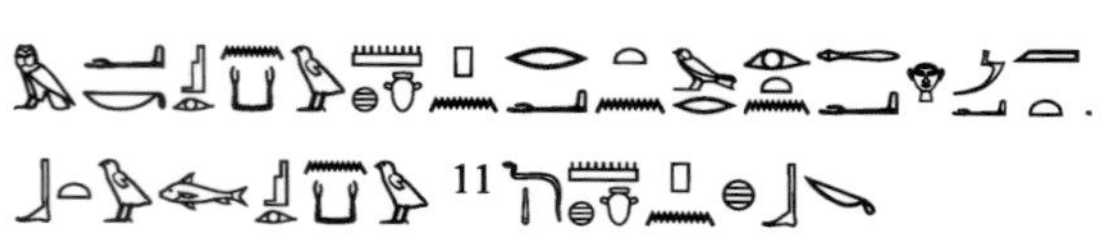

mk<.t> wsjr mnḫ-jb-nkꜣ.w pn rdj.t (j)n wr jr.t (j)n ꜥꜣ ḥr mꜣꜥ.t bw.t wsjr mnḫ(11)*-jb-nkꜣ.w pn ẖb*

The protection of this Osiris Menekhibnekau is that which has been given by the Great and made by the Mighty because of *ma'at*. Annihilation is *bwt*[28] to this Osiris Menekhibnekau.

mk.t wsjr mnḫ-jb-nkꜣ.w pn mk.t ḥr.w-sms.w-rꜥ (12) *jr.t n=f jb=f nn nḏr* (13) *wsjr mnḫ-jb-nkꜣ.w pn* (14) *n<n> ḫsf=f ḥr ꜥrr.wt* (15) *wsjr mnḫ-jb-*(16) *nkꜣ.w pn ꜥpr rw.tj*

The protection of this Osiris Menekhibnekau is the protection of Hor-the-eldest-Re,[29] which his heart has made for him. This Osiris Menekhibnekau shall not be seized, he shall not be held back at the portal, for this Osiris Menekhibnekau is one whom Ruti equipped.

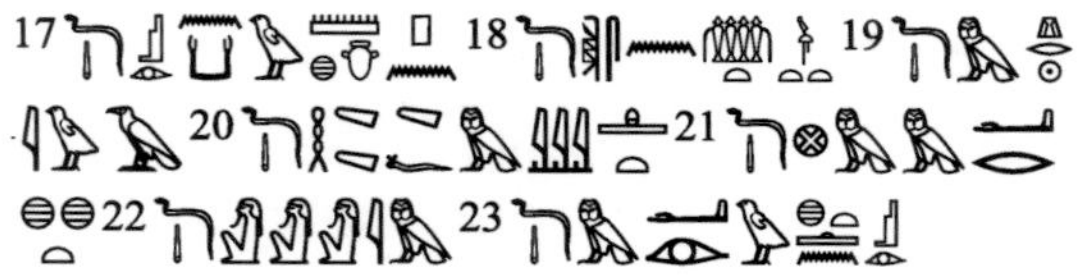

(17) *wsjr mnḫ-jb-nkꜣ.w pn* (18) *šms(.j) n ḫn.tj-jmn.tjw* (19) *m ḥr.t-hrw jw ꜣ*(20)*ḥ.w=f m sḫ.t-ḥtp* (21) *m-m rḫ.w-ḫ.t* (22) *{j}m-*(23)*m jr.w-ḫ.t n wsjr*

This Osiris Menekhibnekau is a follower of Khentyimentu in the course of the day. His acres are in the Field of Offerings among the knowledgeable ones, and among those who perform ritual activities for Osiris.

wsjr mnḫ-jb-nkꜣ.w pn sš jr.j-ꜥ n ḏḥwtj m-m <jr>.w ḥtp.w jw (24) *wḏ jnpw jm.j ḥtp.w wsjr mnḫ-jb-nkꜣ.w pn m ꜥ=f nn jṯ sw m ꜥ=f jn jmj.w* (25) *ḥꜣḳ*

This Osiris Menekhibnekau is an assistant scribe of Thoth among those who make offerings. Anubis, who is with the offering, assigned <the offerings of> this Osiris Menekhibnekau in his hand. 'There is no one who shall seize it from his hand,' say the plunderers.

wḏꜣ wsjr mnḫ-jb-nkꜣ.w pn m{j}[30] *ḏsr ꜣḫ.t n.t p.t*

This Osiris Menekhibnekau traverses in the secluded area of the horizon of heaven.

sr wsjr mnḫ-jb-nkꜣ.w pn (26) rꜥ ḥr ꜥrrw.t ꜣḫ.t ḥꜥꜥ r=f nṯr.w m ḫsf wsjr mnḫ-jb-nkꜣ.w pn jw stj-nṯr (27) r=f n pḥ sw nbḏ n {rꜥ}<ḫ>m sw jr.jw ꜥrrw.wt

This Osiris Menekhibnekau announces Re at the portal of the horizon, and the gods jubilate over him at approaching this Osiris Menekhibnekau. God's scent pertains to him, the evil one shall not reach him, the guardians of the gates shall not overthrow him.

wsjr mnḫ (28) jb-nkꜣ.w pn štꜣ-ḥr m-ẖnw ꜥḥ ḥr p.t zḫm nṯr r nw sbꜣ.w (29) pḥ.n wsjr mnḫ-jb-nkꜣ.w pn jm=f m-ḫt ḥw.t-ḥr.w

This Osiris Menekhibnekau is secret of face within the palace in heaven, the sanctuary of the god at these gates, which this Osiris Menekhibnekau has entered behind Hathor.

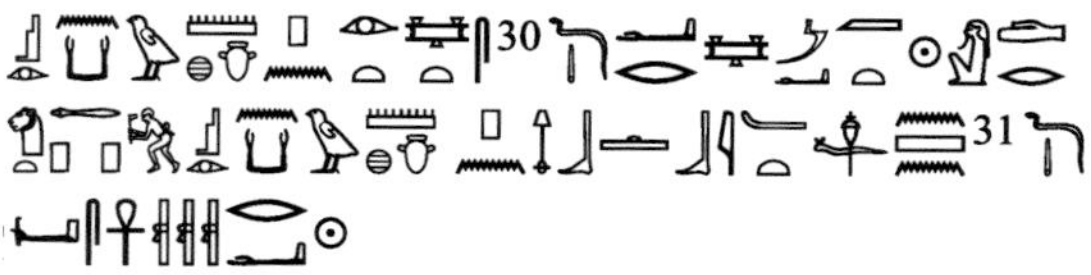

wsjr mnḫ-jb-nkꜣ.w pn jr{.t} wꜣ.t s (30) ꜥr mꜣꜥ.t <n> rꜥ dr pḥ.tj ꜥꜣpp wsjr mnḫ-jb-nkꜣ.w pn wbꜣ bjꜣ ḫsf nšn (31) sꜥnḫ jz.w rꜥ

This Osiris Menekhibnekau is one who makes way, lifts up Maat <to> Re and repels the power of Apep. This Osiris Menkehibnekau is one who pierces the firmament, punishes the stormy one and nourishes the crew of Re.

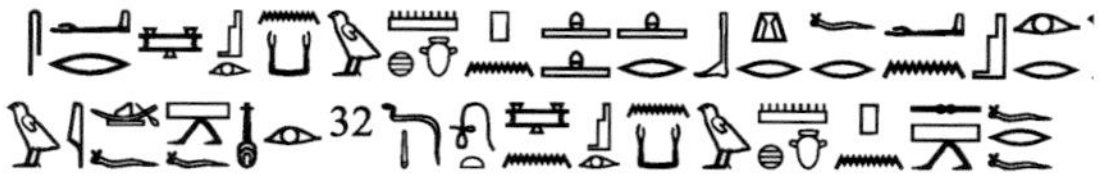

sꜥr wsjr mnḫ-jb-nkꜣ.w pn ḥtp.w r b(w) ẖr=f rdj.n wsjr <j>r wjꜣ=f šm=f nfr jr (32) wꜣ.t n wsjr mnḫ-jb-nkꜣ.w pn zš=f r=f

This Osiris Menkehibnekau lifted offerings to the place that is under him, when Osiris caused his barge to make its beautiful course. Make way for this Osiris Menekhibnekau, so that he may pass!

jw ḥr n wsjr mnḫ-jb-nkꜣ.w pn wr=f m wrr.t (33) ntf nb nṯr.w[31] mnḫ-jb-nkꜣ.w pn ḥtt m ꜣḫ.t wr js ḥr=tn ḥr=tn <n>hs=tn jr wꜣ.t n nb=tn mnḫ-jb-nkꜣ.w pn mꜣꜥ-ḫrw

The face of this Osiris Menekhibnekau is great with the Wereret-crown. He is the lord of gods. This Menekhibnekau is a Baboon[32] in the horizon, indeed one great over you. May you fall, watchers! Make way for your lord, this Menekhibnekau, justified!"

Alongside the vignette, the text of Chapter 144 ensures that Menekhibnekau is protected and allowed transfiguration and a safe passage into the next life. He proclaims that he knows the guardians depicted over the text and demands them to grant him passage. He proclaims to be fully transfigured, purified and able to defeat anyone who might threaten him, including Apep, and take up his place in the following of Osiris and on the barge of Re. The entire composition of Chapter 144 of the Book of the Dead of Menekhibnekau has thus found an ideal placement on the entrance wall of the burial chamber, where the entrance serves both as a three-dimensional representation of the underworld gates guarded by the demons, and a real passage between this world and the next.

Acknowledgments

The work was supported from European Regional Development Fund-Project "Creativity and Adaptability as Conditions of the Success of Europe in an Interrelated World" (No. CZ.02.1.01/0.0/0.0/16_019/

0000734) and by the Charles University Progress project Q11 - Complexity and resilience: Ancient Egyptian civilisation in multidisciplinary and multicultural perspective. The author would like to thank Ladislav Bareš for continuous support and Silvia Einaudi and Louise Gestermann for information on ongoing projects (Padiamenope and Montemhat).

Abbreviations

LGG IV Leitz et al. 2002a
LGG V Leitz et al. 2002b
TLA Thesaurus Linguae Aegyptiae < http://aaew.bbaw.de/tla/ >

References

Abdelrahiem, Mohamed. 2006. "Chapter 144 of the Book of the Dead from the Temple of Ramesses II at Abydos." *Studien zur Altägyptischen Kultur* 34: 1–16.

Assmann, Jan. 1991. *Theben III: Das Grab des Amenemope*, Mainz am Rhein: Philipp von Zabern.

Badawi, Ahmad. 1957. "Das Grab den Kronprinzen Scheschonk, Sohnes Osorkon's II. und Hohepriesters von Memphis." *Annales du Service des antiquités de l'Égypte* 54: 153–177.

Bareš, Ladislav. 2009. "Personifications of the Day- and Night-Hours in the Tomb of Menekhibnekau at Abusir—A Preliminary Notice." In Petra Maříková Vlčková, Jana Mynářová, and Martin Tomášek (eds.), *My Things Changed Things. Social development and Cultural Exchange in Prehistory, Antiquity, and the Middle Ages*, 16–24. Prague: Charles University in Prague, Faculty of Arts.

——, Jiří Janák, and Renata Landgráfová. Forthcoming. "The Iconography of Late Period Shaft Tombs at Abusir." In Joachim Friedrich Quack and Daniele Luft (eds.), *Praktische Verwendung religiöser Artefakte*. Tübingen: Mohr Siebeck.

——, and Květa Smoláriková. 2008. *Abusir XVII: The Shaft Tomb of Iufaa*. Prague: Czech Institute of Egyptology, Faculty of Arts, Charles University in Prague.

—— and ——. 2011. *Abusir XXV: The Shaft Tomb of Menekhibnekau*. Prague: Czech Institute of Egyptology, Faculty of Arts, Charles University in Prague.

Cauville, Sylvie. 1997. *Le Temple de Dendara: les chapelles osiriennes*. Caire: Institut français d'archéologie orientale.

Frandsen, Paul J. 1998. "On the Avoidance of Certain Forms of Loud Voices and Access to the Sacred." In Willy Clarysse, Antoon Schoors, and Harco Willems (eds.), *Egyptian Religion the Last Thousand Years*, Part II, 975–1000. Orientalia Lovaniensia Analecta 85. Leuven: Peeters.

Griffin, Kenneth. 2017. "Towards a Better Understanding of the Ritual of the Hours of the Night (Stundenritual)." In Elena Pischikova (ed.), *Tombs of the South Asasif necropolis: New Discoveries and Research 2012–14*, 97–134. Cairo: The American University in Cairo Press.

Hawass, Zahi. 2006. *Bilder der Unsterblichkeit: die Totenbücher aus den Königsgräbern in Theben*. Mainz am Rhein: Philipp von Zabern.

Iskander, Sameh and Ogden Goelet Jr. 2015. *The Temple of Ramesses II in Abydos, Volume 1: Wall Scenes*. Atlanta: Lockwood Press.

Janák, Jiří and Renata Landgráfová. 2017. "The Book of Snakes from the Tomb of Iufaa at Abusir."In Katalyn Anna Kóthai (ed.), *Burial and Mortuary Practices in Late Period and Graeco-Roman Egypt: Proceedings of the International Conference held at Museum of Fine Arts, Budapest, 17–19 July 2014*, 111–122. Budapest: Museum of Fine Arts.

Kockelmann, Holger. 2008. *Untersuchungen zu den späten teotenbuch-Hanschriften auf Mumienbinden Bd. I, Die Mumienbinden und Leinenamulette des memphitischen Priesters Hor*. Wiesbaden: Harrassowitz.

Landgráfová, Renata, Filip Coppens, Jiří Janák, and Diana Míčková. 2017. "Myth and Ritual in the Burial Chamber of the Shaft Tomb of Iufaa at Abusir: Snakes and Snake-like Beings." In Miroslav Bárta, Filip Coppens, and Jaromír Krejčí (eds.), *Abusir and Saqqara in the Year 2015*, 613–626. Prague: Czech Institute of Egyptology.

—— and Diana Míčková. Forthcoming. "Purification of the Whopper: The Royal Purification Ritual in the Shaft Tomb of Iufaa." In Miroslav Bárta, Filip Coppens, and Hana Vymazalová (eds.), *XI. Tempeltagung—The Discourse between Tomb and Temple*. Wiesbaden: Harrassowitz.

Leitz, Christian et al. 2002a. *Lexikon der ägyptischen Götter und Götterbezeichnungen, Bd. 4*, nbt–h. Orientalia Lovaniensia Analecta 113. Leuven: Peeters.

—— et al.. 2002b. *Lexikon der ägyptischen Götter und Götterbezeichnungen, Bd. 5*, ḥ–ẖ. Orientalia Lovaniensia Analecta 114. Leuven: Peeters.

Lucarelli, Rita. 2010. "The Guardian-demons of the

Book of the Dead." *British Museum Studies in Ancient Egypt and Sudan* 15: 85–102.

Maspero, Gaston. 1914. *Sarcophages des époques persane et ptolémaïque (CG 29301–29323)*. Caire: Institut français d'archéologie orientale.

Quirke, Stephen. 2013. *Going out in Daylight*—prt m ḥrw *the Ancient Egyptian Book of the Dead Translation, Sources, Meanings*. London: Golden House Publications.

Roulin, Gilles. 1998. "Les tombes royales de Tanis: analyse du programme décoratif." In Philippe Brissaud and Christiane Zivie-Coche (eds.), *Tanis. Travaux récents sur le Tell Sân El-Hagar. Mission Française des fouilles de Tanis 1987–1997*, 193–273. Paris: Noêsis.

Saleh, Mohamed. 1984. *Das Totenbuch in den thebanischen Beamtengräbern den Neuen Reiches*. Mainz am Rhein: Philipp von Zabern.

Sherbiny, Wael. 2017. *Through Hermopolitan Lenses: Studies on the So-called Book of Two Ways in Ancient Egypt*. Probleme der Ägyptologie 33. Leiden: Brill.

Verhoeven, Ursula. 1971. *Das Saitische Totenbuch der Iahtesnacht*. Bonn: Rudolf Habelt.

Notes

1 Bareš and Smoláriková 2011.

2 Bareš and Smoláriková 2008.

3 Bareš and Smoláriková 2011, 81–82.

4 The inscriptions of the shaft tomb of Iufaa are still being studied and analyzed by the Czech team and their full publication is in preparation. For partial studies see: Bareš et al. forthcoming; Janák and Landgráfová 2017; Landgráfová et al. 2017; Landgráfová and Míčková forthcoming.

5 Bareš 2009; for an online edition of the hours of the day of the Stundenritual, of which Menekhibnekau's version only includes small excerpts for each hour, see Erhart Graefe's Das Stundenritual < http://www.uni-muenster.de/IAEK/forschen/aeg/proj/laufend/stundenritual.html > (accessed 31 May 2017); a complete study of the hours of the night is being prepared by Kenneth Griffin, see Griffin 2017.

6 The name varies between *smt* "Hearer" and *smtmt* "Eavesdropper," see Abdelrahiem 2006), 5.

7 This is unusual; the name usually appears as *hꜣ-ḫrw* "Loud-voiced" or variants (Abdelrahiem 2006, 6).

8 The name of this demon differs greatly, but the meaning is usually close to "Cursing one" (Abdelrahiem 2006, 7).

9 Lemma *ꜣd*, TLA lemma 342

10 Lemma *jkj*, TLA lemma 32420.

11 The names and especially the representations of the guardians are far from constant across the attestations of BD 144; see Lucarelli 2010, 87.

12 Totenbuchprojekt Bonn < http://totenbuch.awk.nrw.de > (accessed 31 May 2017).

13 The two examples from the Simonian collection (Simonian 2 and 4) could not be checked.

14 See, for example, the mummy wrappings of Hor, Kockelmann 2008, pls. 1–12. In the case of Hor, the height varies between 6 and 18.7 cm, see Kockelmann 2008, 55. The vignettes of Hor show also that wrapping height was indeed a problem for the ancient Egyptians, or at least for the maker of this particular copy, as the tops of the vignettes are sometimes missing due to the copyist's mistaken estimation of available space, see Kockelmann 2008, 175.

15 The vignette is never completely preserved.

16 M. Cairo S. V. IV 690 a, M. Turin 1870, M. Memphis 1994 4.17.

17 Parts of the guardian-demon sequence of the Book of the Dead (BD 144–147) are frequent in monumental context, but the exact setup of BD 144 is relatively rare; see Lucarelli 2010, 86; also Saleh 1984, 77–81.

18 For a recent photograph and line drawing of the vignette, which is located at the entrance to chapel G of the temple, see Iskander and Goelet Jr. 2015, 309–310.

19 Compare, for example, the frequently tabularized funerary and ritual texts on the tomb and sarcophagus walls of the shaft tomb of Iufaa with the "plaintext" papyrus versions; see Coppens et al. forthcoming.

20 In the same manner, these guardians are employed to guard other areas in underworld or funerary contexts; see Lucarelli 2010, 89-91.

21 Compare now with Quirke 2013, 324–329. The chapter is especially frequent in Late and Ptole-

maic Periods, Quirke 2013, 324.

22 *ḏd-mdw* appears at the beginning of every column and thus performs merely a decorative (and perhaps partially iterative) function here. It is thus not transliterated or translated in the remainder of the text.

23 Probably "two lands" is meant here, as in P. Nu, 23 (*tꜣ.wj*). There is great confusion here in the various versions of the Book of the Dead, and besides *tꜣ.wj* and *tꜣ.w*, *ꜥꜣ.wj*, "the two doorjambs," appears frequently (e.g., P. Iahtesnakht, Verhoeven 1993, 275 and n. 5; P. Turin Museo Egizio 1791).

24 The various versions of BD 144 differ greatly in the writing of this word, other interpretations include *kꜣy.w* "others," see Verhoeven 1993, 275 and n. 8. Quirke 2013, 325, reads "reverence" in line with our present interpretation.

25 Written in a very unusual way, with *sn* (T22) signs instead of *šn* (V7), probably due to misreading of a hieratic version.

26 This meaning is confirmed by the CT 1042 version of this section, where it is followed by "the *akh* whom this N denounces, he is not existent" (in the translation of Sherbiny 2017, 191).

27 Earlier versions of BD read *dbn wsjr N ḥr jr.t ḥr.w* (see e.g., P. Nu; Quirke 2013, 325); in the CT the eye of Horus is in the hand of Thoth (Sherbiny 2017, 191). The Saite versions are rather consistent in having the deceased circulate the eye of Horus, i.e., *dbn wsjr N jr.t ḥr.w*; see Verhoeven 1993, 275 and n. 14.

28 For the nature of *bw.t*, see, e.g., Paul J. Frandsen ("Certain forms of loud voices and access to the sacred") in Frandsen 1998, 975–1000, esp. 996–999.

29 *LGG* V: 290: *ḥr-smsw* as Amun-Ra or Ra-Harakhty, exactly this connection not present; there is a *ḥr-wr-rꜥ*, *LGG* V: 251, of which one attestation is written ambiguously and can be read either as *ḥr-wr-rꜥ* or *ḥr-smsw-rꜥ*). Alternatively Horus, the eldest of Re.

30 This is the simplest possible emendation, but perhaps one should emend *mj* <*ḥr.w m*> *ḏsr* … "traverses, like Horus, the secluded area...."

31 Or this is the determinative, and a word is missing. Alternate versions have *nb wsr.t*.

32 See *LGG* IV, 813. This word is problematic in the other attestations of this BD chapter. In P. Nu, it is *hr* "to be content" (Quirke 2013: 327); P. Iahtesnakhte has *hꜣ.tj* "jubilating" (Verhoeven 1993, 107*), which U. Verhoeven interprets as erroneous writing of *hr* (Verhoeven1993: 277 and n. 4). While here very clear, the word *ḥṯt* "baboon"is probably a reinterpretation of a word that became corrupt through recopying.

Journal of Ancient Egyptian Interconnections

Liminal Sources of Dangerous Powers: A Case of the Black Ram

Nika Lavrentyeva
Pushkin State Museum of Fine Arts

Ekaterina Alexandrova
Russian State University for the Humanities

Abstract
This article proposes a semiology-inspired model for the description of "demonic characters." In this model, an image of a mythological character is seen as a kind of sign with a twofold plane of expression because Egyptian signifiers combine visual and verbal components. Each of these components could be expressed through text and/or display, as in the case of the "Lord of Power" described verbally in the Pyramid Texts and depicted visually in the Book of Two Ways as a Black Ram. An incarnation of the pharaoh in the Pyramid Texts, in the Book of Two Ways the "Lord of Power" is one of the "judges" threatening the deceased. Viewed from different perspectives (e.g., inhabitants of the Netherworld, the pharaoh, the noble deceased, the sun-god), the Black Ram and related characters of the later sources seem to be dangerous and hostile creatures not as much "by nature" but by context and situation in which the solar energy exists in a particular moment and to whom it is opposed. More generally, this essay shows that characters often perceived as demonic genetically can possess positive divine, even solar, energy, which in some contexts can receive dangerous, aggressive manifestations.

The absence of substantial narratives is a much-discussed feature of Egyptian religious texts.[1] This is especially the case with lower mythology or demonology full of minor deities[2] of intricate appearance and composite names. The long and compound names of these creatures often allude to a mythological situation that sometimes stays obscure to us. Such names can be labeled as "folded mythologemes"[3] representing in a compact way some mythological episode which otherwise could be extended to a narrative.

As John Baines and Katja Goebs have argued, "such narratives are often not attested in the record since they were likely transmitted orally."[4] Spells from medical or funeral contexts available to us were meant to be effective by merely actualizing proper mythological events and facts and not to explain or communicate these events and facts to someone unaware.[5] However, sometimes we are quite lucky to unfold these mythologemes and trace these elusive narratives through correlation of images and mythemes scattered throughout different monuments. We are going to share one such investigation dealing with the "Lord of power," portrayed as a black ram.

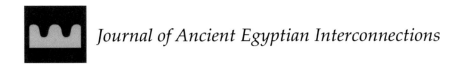

The character in question represents the broad cluster of the inhabitants of the Netherworld, specifically those who are dangerous and repelling for the living and the dead. Pyramid Texts[6] spell 255 gives a good example of Egyptian notion of an image and allows explication of a structure of demonic image in particular:[7]

PT 255

ꞽ ḫbḏ pw
ḫbḏ ḳdw
ḫbḏ ꞽrw

O Hateful one,
Hateful of nature (character)
Hateful of form

The address to this quite abstract character begins with vocative. It specifically marks the first part of this passage as a verbal component and thus we relate it here to the Egyptian category of name (*rn*). The other two categories seem to represent opposition of a character's nature (*ḳdw*) and its visible manifestation (*ꞽrw*). We can associate these categories with semantic (signified) and visual components of a demonic image. In these terms, we can outline the process of our interpretation of religious texts as follows: sources give us names and visible manifestations of dangerous creatures (two-fold signifiers), and we are trying to clarify their nature (signified). For the purpose of analysis, we label visual and verbal components of a demonic image as "icon" and "mytheme." Each of these receives its realization through text and/or display.

At the Predynastic sources all aspects of demonic image are expressed through display without any textual complement. Decorated ceramics, slate palettes and small-sized sculptures present various desert animals and reptiles—the typical incarnations of danger and destructive powers of chaos. In the Pyramid Texts—the first extensive textual corpus fixed at the end of the Fifth Dynasty—dangerous entities, on the contrary, are realized through textual medium only.

PT 287

nnꞽ-mwt=f
nnꞽ-mwt=f
ꞽ=k rr m nn
ꞽ=k rr m nn
Mꜣꞽ ṯfꞽ

Weariness-of-his-mother,
Weariness-of-his-mother,
You are really as that
You are really as that
LION, be off!

PT 299

ḏd-mdw
ḏt r pt SPꜣ-ḥrw r tꜣ
ṯb.t Ḥr šꜣs=f
nb ḥwt, kꜣ ṯpḥt
šnṯ n šnṯ=ꞽ
nht Wnꞽs nht=f
ḫtt Wnꞽs ḫtt=f
gmy Wnꞽs m wꜣt=f
wnm=f n=f sw mwmw

Recitation:
Cobra, to the sky! Horus's CENTIPEDE, to the earth!
Horus is with sandalled feet when treading on
The Lord of Enclosure, the Bull of the Cavern
šnṯ-snake, do not oppose me!
Unas's sycomore is his sycomore,
Unas's stick is his stick:
Anyone whom Unas finds in his way
He will devour

PT 254

GFWT=*f* ZNT-TP.W
swꜣ Wnꞽs ḥr=ṯn m ḥtp

You, his APES WHO CUT OFF HEADS,
Let Unas pass by you in peace!

In these examples, icons and mythemes are easily distinguishable in different kinds of references to "demons." Determinatives and phonetic denotation of such creatures as lions, centipedes, and apes are iconic in nature in that they appeal to realistic, natural images. These images are different from those of slate palettes only by medium—verbal versus display. In terms of the scheme outlined above we regard them as an icon (*ꞽrw*)—visual component of "demonic image."

However, the Pyramid Texts introduce a new dimension to the demonic image by characterizing names such as "Hateful one" in our first example and "Belligerent-of-Face" in the next passage:

PT 251

i ḥrw-wnwt
tp-ꜥ.w-Rꜥ
ir.y wꜣt n Wnis
swꜣ Wnis
m-ẖnw pẖr.t nt ꜥḤꜣW-ḤR

O you in charge of hours,
Who precede Re,
Make way for Unas!
Let Unas pass
Within the circuit of those BELLIGERENT-OF-FACE!

These references are quite obscure but seem to have themes of aggression and fear in their core. As a token of some mythological context and a kernel of a possible mythic narrative, such names could be labeled as mythemes.

For the first time, real interplay of textual and visual representation of the Netherworld and its inhabitants occurs in the Middle Kingdom on the magical wands and in the Coffin Texts, in the Book of Two Ways[8] in particular. We still can see quite simple examples of icons (in depictions of snakes, rabbits) and mythemes (in names such as "Terrifying," "Trembling," "Burning" [CT 1041]). However, a distinctive feature of demonic images in the Book of Two Ways is the proliferation of characters that are hybrid, or *mixamorph*[9] in appearance (combining nature of several beings—mammals, reptiles, humans) and have compound names ("folded mythologemes"). For example, CT 1076 refers to characters "He-who-spits-Hapi" (*bš-ḥpy*) and "He-who-eats-his-mothers" (*wnm-mwt=f*). Nevertheless, the texts accompanying these characters are still concise. It is the distribution of these creatures that allows us to make a step further in understanding the nature of their dangerous powers.

In the Book of Two Ways, the majority of "demonic" characters are shown in the vignette with a map of ways of the Netherworld. Two non-overlapping bending roads—by water and by land—are inhabited by demons living in their curves. There is a lake of flame between the roads excluding any possibility to change the road. However, both of these ways lead to the same destination: the palace of Osiris in Abydos.

In accompanying texts the focus is on the description of the overall situation and the space in which these dangerous creatures are located. They guard the gates and the bends of the road. In iconic dimension (*irw*) there are many snakes among them, e.g., *ꜥftt*-snakes (CT 1034). Most of the names (mythemes) describes the hostility and aggression of these characters: "He-who-destroys-by-his-face" (CT 1033), "He-who-punishes-the-destroyer" (CT 1037), and "Cutting-those-who-are-loud-of-voices" (CT 1053).

It is interesting to note that the water path (CT 1038–1053) adjoining the lake of fire is inhabited by demons often of fiery nature: "Flaming" (*ꜣšbw*), "Wakeful" (*rsy-ḥr*), "Fluctuating flame" (*nhd-ns*) (CT 1044; cf. also CT 1039, 1041, 1045, 1053).[10] The land road (CT 1055–1067), which curves and obstacles are formed by water flow, lakes, and marshes, is guarded by the creatures living mostly in or by the water (CT 1061, 1062, 1064). Fire in the first case and water in the second can form an opposition to the substance of the safe roads (water and land respectively) and represent the chaos. Falling into it in the context of the Netherworld is comparable (or synonymous) to being unjustified and means eternal death: "you shouldn't pass on it" (CT 1053).[11] Thus, guards and gatekeepers, located on the border of the cosmos and chaos, are the representatives and embodiment of the latter.[12] They are depicted and referred to in terms of icons and mythemes associated with chaos—the element of danger—in that particular situation.

In their intricate appearances and names, characters of the Book of Two Ways form a visual embodiment of the liminal state and transition, which are always fraught with danger. In the hands or feet of certain keepers guarding the portals and turns of the road, there are long, sharp knives, threatening the deceased. The images of these creatures often lack well-defined form (CT 1070–1071): their heads are placed on the body, devoid of imagery—they do not have the typical "stands" of anthropomorphic and zoomorphic bodies.[13] The editors of the Book of the Two Ways thus tried to portray the mysterious, invisible, and formless otherworld beings. This lack of the body (some in CT 1070–1071, and some on the map vignette) as well may be a consequence of the danger for the deceased. The creatures belonging to "other world" in the funerary texts sometimes are shown not in the full form, but as "crippled" or schematized.[14] The body not adapted to movement or the lack of it emphasizes also the literal "attachment" of these creatures to their place of dwelling. Thus the "Lords of offerings" inhabiting the "House of Judges" are shown as scarabs on threadlike veins-legs (CT 1070).

The "House of Judges" is located next to the image of Ro-Setau. This is a place that in the Egyptian sacred topography is thought to be a corridor (CT 1035). Here the deceased is subjected to the greatest number of hazards, among them being the "Lords of power". CT 1071 was created to help the deceased to pass them by:

CT 1071

q3-sṯ3w.w rn=f pw
ʿpr.w
r n sw3 ḥr snw nt ḫr=f
nb-3t rn=f pw
nhs.w
ink q-ḫrw m 3ḫt
wr=ṯn is
ḥr.jw=ṯn nhs.w
ir w3.t n nb=ṯn
Ink pw
bs.w rn=f pw
r n sw3 ḥr=f snw nt ḫr=f
sḏ.t-ḥr rn=f pw
nb.w-wsr.wt
iw ḥr ink m wr
pḥ.y=i m wrrt
ink nb-wsr.tjw
h3.sf- ir.w rn=f pw
r n sw3 ḥr snw nt ḫr=sn
m33=sn m-ḥr.t w3.wt
ḥ3=f-ḥr rn=f pw
nbw-n3w rn=f pw
ink ḥms ḥr ir.t-ḥr tp.y-ḫmt
wḏ-mdw m snw n Ḏḥwty
mk.tw ink pw mk.tw Ḏḥwty

High-of-winds (*q3 -sṯ3w.w*)—is his name.
Equipped!
This is a spell for passing him by and those who are under his authority
LORD OF POWER ***(nb-3t)***—is his name
Awakened!
I am—High-of-voice in the horizon
greater than you
Down on your faces, you awakened!
Give the way to your lord!
It's me
Flaming (*bs.w*)—is his name
Utterance to pass him by, and those who are under his rule.
Fire-faced (*sḏ.t-ḥr*)—is his name.
Lords of strength (*nb-wsr.t*)!
My face—is the (face of) the Great One,
my power—is in the crown Wereret:
I'm the lord of strengths (*nb-wsr.tjw*)
Tired by his forms (*h3.sf-ir.w*)—is his name.
This is a spell for passing him by, and those who are under his rule
They see the way forward.
His-hindhead-is-in-front (of him)—is his name (he-whose-face-is-turned-back)
The-lord-of-flame/complaints (*nbw-n3w*)—is his name.
I sit at the Eye of Horus as the first of three,
to judge the Two for Thoth.
My protection is the protection of Thoth

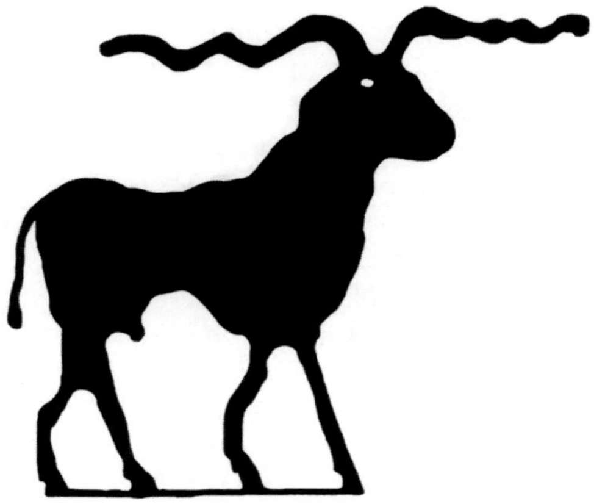

FIGURE 1: The "Lord of power." From CT 1071.

The "Lord of power"—mighty creature—of this spell is depicted as a black ram, or rather, his silhouette filled with black paint (FIG. 1). He is one of the judges in this scene.

An image similar in its iconic and mythemic representation appears already in the Pyramid Texts, in the spell 246, as one of the forms acquired by the deceased pharaoh:

PT 246

mꜣ ꜥḥꜥ.t Wnis pn m bꜣ
ꜥb.wy tp=f smꜣ.wy
n ṯwt is zi km
zꜣ zit km.t
ms.w zit bꜣḳ.t
snḳ.w fd.t wꜣp.t
ii r=ṯn ḥr ḫsbḏ-ir.ty
sꜣ=ṯn ḥr dšr-ir.ty
mr-ꜣt
n ḫsf bꜣ=f

Behold arising of this Unas as a ram
Two wild-bull horns on his head
For you are a BLACK RAM
Son of a black ewe,
Born by a white ewe,
Suckled by four sheep!
Blue-eyed Horus has come against you
Beware of Red-eyed Horus!
With hurtful power,
Whose might cannot be opposed

This spell is located in the passage between the Funeral Chamber and the Antechamber allowing us to relate these themes of danger and aggression of the sacred character with his liminal state.

Another Pyramid Texts spell also mentioning the "Lord of power" allows us to shed additional light on formation of an image of "a black ram":

PT 255
ir tm=k dr=ṯw ḥr st=k...
iw.kꜣ wnis ḥr=f wr pw
nb-ꜣt
wsr m nkn ir.t im=f
rdi.kꜣ[=f nsr ny ir.t=f]
pḫr=s ḥꜣ=ṯn

If you do not remove yourself from your place
...
Unas will turn his face into the Great One
The Lord of Power,
Who grew strong through the injury which was done to him.
[He] will give [the flame of his eye]
So that it surrounds you

The term *nkn* designates the Horus's mutilation as opposed to Seth's mutilation (*iy*), which were received by them in the mutual conflict. Thus, damage mentioned in the spell is the blinding of Horus. For example, in ritual spells the Eye of Horus is characterized by an epithet "because of which he (that is, Horus) darkened (*kk.t*)" (PT 74). During his lifetime, the pharaoh was considered as an incarnation of the god Horus and a son of the sun god.[15] Thus, the mythological situation of blinding and treatment of Horus represents one of the basic models describing the resurrection of the pharaoh, which is his transition from a condition of death to eternal life in the world of gods. However, being of a solar nature, the pharaoh in his condition of death, seems to appear also as the "darkened" sun in the image of the Black Ram (a dark solar being)[16] in addition to Horus with Red Eyes—the damaged Eye and at the same time the Eye radiating with heat of the desert.[17] Remaining in this state, the pharaoh threatens the cosmic order, and that is the focus of the further formulas of PT 255. This spell also shows how this power of mutilation turns into power protective for the pharaoh aimed to gain him a place in the Netherworld and by this resolving the dangerous liminal state itself. It should be noted especially that both Pyramid Texts spells mentioning the "Lord of power" are connected to purification and thus are protective spells. Spell PT 255, in particular, contains a note about burning incense, and its flame is associated with the heat of the Eye of Horus.

In this case, the liminal state of the pharaoh represented through the image of Horus with the damaged Eye is the source of the dangerous power, which threatens to destroy the world if the pharaoh is not given the place in the sky. Here the binary opposition of cosmos and chaos is represented by the opposition of light and darkness. In the image of the black ram, a solar creature is painted in the color of darkness and danger. We can trace this iconic motif further in several visual stems during the later periods.

During the New Kingdom in the "royal version" of the Book of Amduat[18] the image of the black ram appears several times. The middle register of the third hour shows a character *šfy* (232).[19] He is depicted as a human figure wrapped in a knee-length coat with ram's horns on his head. His name, however, is written with the sign of a head and torso of a black ram. Being one of the main characters in the barque *pꜣḫt*, he may represent one of the forms of the hidden sun.

In the upper register of the fifth hour, there is a

zooanthropomorphic character with the head of a black ram. His name is *bꜣ pf jrj-mwt.w*, "The soul who belongs to the damned" (355). In front of him holding in her hands the sign "dead" (*mwt*) stands a goddess, "The demolishing one, who cuts the damned to pieces" (356). This scene seems to demonstrate the darkness of the damned souls who have not prepared for the light and rebirth.

In the middle register of the eighth hour Tatenen is shown as a ram (598–601). The creatures of this hour are crying out to the god with the "voices of mysterious rams" in the ground where the "Horus hid the gods."[20] When the god continuing his way leaves them, they are enveloped by the darkness. In the lower register of this hour a zooanthropomorphic god with a ram head is named *nb rḫyt*, "Lord of *Rekhit*-people" (605).

In all these cases from the Book of Amduat the mentioning of a black ram is connected with the hidden souls of those who are damned to remain in the ground, in the dark. These images as well as presence of the black ram among judges and executioners in the Coffin Texts suggest an association with the image of the "shadow" of the sun as the "Sun-destroyer." Apparently in the later iconography of these characters they will have the form of the "black sun," which take all the attacks of evil forces against the sun god upon itself. It "absorbs" all the evil and sin[21] during the judgment protecting the deceased as a good companion of the sun god.

The image of the "black sun" occurs, in particular, in the tombs of the New Kingdom. One example is in the tomb of Irunefer (TT 290) at Deir el-Medina in a scene illustrating Chapter 92 of the Book of the Dead. Going forth to light, the deceased is strong, illuminated by the sun, and his shadow is free. Shadows of those who want to harm him will be captured in the Netherworld, in the darkness. By the exit of the tomb the "darkness" is shown in the form of a black sun, which will absorb all the evil plotted against the justified deceased.[22] In the papyrus of Ani (also made for his burial at Deir el-Medina) the text of this chapter mentions some villains residing in the Duat (in the flesh of Osiris), and threatening the deceased:

> BD 92
> *ỉḫḫ.w r ḥr.w=sn*
> *ỉmy.w ʿwt Wsỉr*
>
> And the darkness will cover their faces,
> those who are in the flesh of Osiris

The word "darkness" is written with a surprising determinative of the shining sun. Thus this icon depicts a "shining" black sun, portraying a dark place for sinners.

We can point out that the presence of the black solar creature or black sun itself is closely connected with a situation of "the judgment in the Netherworld." Initially in the Pyramid Texts the deceased enters the Netherworld as an alien being threatening the cosmic balance by his liminal state. To be appeased he claims a definite position in the afterlife. Recognition of this right and granting him a "place" by the god in itself functions as pacification of the dead and turns his aggressive, destructive energy into the merit of protection of the cosmic order. Later monuments show the black sun as a character who devours evil and sin of damned souls and in this way protects the beatified dead and the cosmic order in the whole during and after the judgment of Osiris and going forth by the day.[23]

These cases show that characters often perceived as demonic genetically possess positive divine, even solar, energy, which in some contexts can receive dangerous, aggressive manifestations. Aggressive manifestations are connected to chaos or violation of the cosmic order *mꜣʿt*, and connection to the border between cosmos and chaos is reflected both in appearance and in the name of the demon. The nature of the being was often defined not only by his character but also by properties of the border between cosmos and chaos at which it resides—that is how in a certain situation the chaos is represented: for example, as darkness, desert, fire, watery abyss, marsh. Regarding the character as positive or negative depends on the "point of view":

- of inhabitants of the Netherworld viewing the furious pharaoh;
- of the pharaoh viewing the hostile character usurping his place in the sky;
- of the dead approaching the terrible guard ;
- of the solar god protected by these terrible guards from intrigues of evil forces.

It is noteworthy to point out that the other component of demonic image of the black ram-mytheme *nb* ꜣt in later periods is sometimes associated with such fighting solar god as Horus of Behdet, illustrating the ambiguity of this character as dangerous and protective at the same time.[24]

Thus, the Black Ram seems to be a dangerous and hostile creature not as much by nature but by context and situation in which the solar energy exists in a particular moment of time and to which character it is opposed. Particularly this mythological image (the "Lord of power" depicted as the Black Ram) portrays the solar energy in a liminal and therefore dangerous state.

Structuring a demonic image in terms of icon and mytheme as its components and their specific realizations through text and display proved to be very helpful when applied in comparative analysis of the sources of different historical periods and executed in different materials and techniques.

References

Abbas, Eltayeb Sayed. 2010. *The Lake of Knives and the Lake of Fire: Studies in the Topography of Passage in Ancient Egyptian Religious Literature*. Oxford: Archaeopress.

Allen, James P. 2013. *A New Concordance of the Pyramid Texts: 5th and 6th Dynasty*. Brown University.

Berlev, Oleg. 2003. "Two Kings—Two Suns—on the Worldview of the Ancient Egyptians." In Stephen Quirke (ed.), *Discovering Egypt from the Neva: The Egyptological Legacy of Oleg D. Berlev*, 19–35. Berlin: Achet-Verlag.

de Buck, Adrian. 1935. *The Egyptian Coffin Texts*. 7 vols. Chicago: University of Chicago Press.

Chegodaev, Mikhail A. 2001. "Horus-Without-Eyes-On-His-Brow (An Essay on the Interpretation of the Name) / Хор-Без-Глаз-На-Его-Челе (опыт интерпретации имени)." In *Ancient Orient: Unity and Peculiarity of Cultural Traditions / Древний Восток: общность и своеобразие культурных традиций*, 24–32. Moscow: SIAS.

Eyre, Christopher. 2002. *The Cannibal Hymn: A Cultural and Literary Study*. Liverpool: Liverpool University Press

Goebs, Katja 2013. "Egyptian Mythos as Logos: An Attempt at a Redefinition of 'Mythical Thinking." In Elizabeth Frood and Angela McDonald (eds.), *Decorum and Experience: Essays in Ancient Culture for John Baines*, 127–134. Oxford: Griffith Institute.

——. 2008. *Crowns in Egyptian Funerary Literature: Royalty, Rebirth, and Destruction*. Oxford: Griffith Institute.

Hellum, Jennifer. 2001. *The Presence of Myth in the Pyramid Texts*. PhD dissertation, University of Toronto.

Hermsen, Edmund. 1991. *Die zwei Wege des Jenseits. Das altägyptische Zweiwegenbuch und seine Topographie*. Frieburg, Schweiz: Universtätverlag; Göttingen: Vandenhoeck & Ruprecht.

Hornung, Erik. 1963. *Das Amduat—Die Schrift des verborgenen Raumes—Teile / Bände I und II. Teil 1: Text / Teil 2: Übersetzung und Kommentar (herausgegeben nach Texten aus den Gräbern des Neuen Reiches)*. Wiesbaden: Otto Harrassowitz.

Hornung, Erik. 1994. "Black Holes Viewed from Within: Hell in Ancient Egyptian Thought." *Diogenes* 42(165): 133–156.

Hornung, Erik and Theodor Abt. 2007. *The Egyptian Amduat. The Book of the Hidden Chamber*. Translated by David Warburton. Zurich: Living Human Heritage Publications.

Hussein, Angela Murock. 2010. "Beware the Red Eyed Horus: The Significance of Carnelian in Egyptian Royal Jewelry." In Zahi Hawass, Peter Der Manuelian, and Ramadan B. Hussein (eds.), *Perspectives on Ancient Egypt: Studies in Honor of Edward Brovarski*, 185–190. Cairo: American University in Cairo Press.

Ivanov, Vyacheslav V. 1988. "Lower Mythology / Низшая мифология." In *Myths of the World / Мифы народов мира*, vol. 2, 215–217. Moscow: Sovetskaya Encyclopedia.

Kanawati, Naguib. 2005. "Decoration of Burial Chambers, Sarcophagi and Coffins in the Old Kingdom." In Khaled Daoud, Shafia Bedier, and Sawsan Abd el-Fatah (eds.), *Studies in Honor of Ali Radwan*, vol. 2, 55–71. Cairo: Supreme Council of Antiquities.

Laboury, Dimitri. 1998. "Fonction et signification de l'image égyptienne." *Bulletin de la Classe des Beaux-Arts de l'Académie Royale de Belgique, 6e série* 9: 131–135.

——. 2013. "L'artiste égyptien, ce grand méconnu de l'Égyptologie." In Andreu Guillemette (ed.), *L'art du contour. Le dessin dans l'Égypte ancienne*, 28–35. Paris: Musée du Louvre.

Leitz, Christian and Dagmar Budde. 2002. *Lexikon der ägyptischen Götter und Götterbezeichnungen*. 7 vols. Dudley, MA: Peeters.

Lotman, Jurij M. and Julian Graffy. 1979. "The Origin of Plot in the Light of Typology." *Poetics Today*

1(1/2): 161–184.

Lucarelli, Rita. 2010. "Demons (Benevolent and Malevolent)." In Jacco Dieleman and Willeke Wendrich (eds.), *UCLA Encyclopedia of Egyptology*. Los Angeles: eScholarship. < http://escholarship.org/uc/item/1r72q9vv>, accessed 10 October 2019.

Manassa, Colleen. 2008. "Sounds of the Netherworld." In Benedikt Rothöhler and Alexander Manisali (eds.), *Mythos & Ritual: Festschrift für Jan Assmann zum 70. Geburtstag*, 109–135. Münster: LIT Verlag.

Mathieu, Bernard. 1996. "Modifications de texte dans la pyramide d'Ounas." *Bulletin de l'Institut français d'archéologie orientale* 96: 289–311.

Posener, Georges. 1970. "Sur l'emploi euphémique de *ḫftj(w)* 'ennemi(s).'" *Zeitschrift für Ägyptische Sprache* 96(JG): 30–35.

Redford, Susan and Donald B. Redford. 2005. "The Cult and Necropolis of the Sacred Ram at Mendes." In Salima Ikram (ed.), *Divine Creatures: Animal Mummies in Ancient Egypt*, 164–98. Cairo; New York: The American University in Cairo Press.

Sethe, Kurt. 1908. *Die Altaegyptischen Pyramidentexte nach den Papierabdrucken und Photographien des Berliner Museums*, vol. 1. Leipzig: J. C. Hinrichs'sche Buchhandlung.

Tefnin, Roland. 1991. "Éléments pour une sémiologie de l'image égyptienne." *Chronique d'Egypte* 66 (131–132): 60–88.

Waardenburg, Jacques. 2011. *Classical Approaches to the Study of Religion: Aims, Methods, and Theories of Research: Introduction and Anthology*. Berlin: De Gruyter.

Wengrow, David. 2014. *The Origins of Monsters: Image and Cognition in the First Age of Mechanical Reproduction*. Princeton: Princeton University Press.

Notes

1 See, for example: Hellum 2001; Eyre 2002, 1–6.

2 Distinctions such as "higher" vs. "lower" mythology or "major" vs. "minor" deities can be traced back to the beginnings of comparative mythology. See, for example: Waardenburg 2011, 9–13. Concerning characters of Egyptian texts, this distinction helps to highlight the fact that there is no strict boundary between gods and "demons" in Egypt (as well as any special designation of a demon as such) as noted, among others, by Rita Lucarelli (2010). A useful point concerning "lower mythology" is made by V. V. Ivanov, who distinguishes it in accordance with the higher degree of involvement of "minor" supernatural beings in everyday life of common people (1988, 216). It seems noteworthy that this mode of interaction, together with local instead of universal importance of its outcomes, can result in texts describing contacts with genies and demons being closer to folklore than to substantial mythological narratives.

3 Chegodaev 2001.

4 Goebs 2013, 132.

5 Cf. "Such a narration does not aim to inform any particular reader of something of which he is unaware; rather it is a mechanism which ensures the continual flow of the cyclical processes in nature itself" (Lotman and Graffy 1979, 162).

6 Spells of the Pyramid Texts are cited in accordance with Sethe 1908 and with respect to Allen 2013.

7 Here we are talking about an image in a broad sense as discussed, among others, by Laboury (1998). It is hard to draw a definite line between text and image in Egyptian representations. In fact, investigation in semiology of Egyptian image by Tefnin (1991) seems to show that Egyptian practices of signification are a hard case for European semiology. To begin with, an Egyptian sign should be regarded not as twofold (signified and signifier) but as threefold because Egyptian signifiers are twofold themselves, combining visual and verbal components. In what follows, we are trying to adjust this semiology-based attitude to emic Egyptian categorization. Sensitivity of Egyptian culture to this aspect of artistic representation seem to surface, for example, in designation of artist as *sš ḳdwt*. In the term itself ambivalence of textual and visual is expressed, and in the context of working process it also relates to representation of initial design. Cf. Laboury 2013. This process of realization of an idea actually mirrors signification in terms of semiology. In this respect, PT 255 is especially useful as it shows all aspects of representation. It is noteworthy that the character in question is not necessary a demon: it is someone who was in the shrine but is demanded to free the place

for the pharaoh. So, whoever this character is in this spell, his identity is construed anew from the beginning as someone hateful and thus deserving such a violent attitude.

8 De Buck 1935–1961; Hermsen 1991.

9 Wengrow 2014. This term is commonly applied in Russian tradition of art history; see, for example, Kononenko 2002.

10 The exact statistics here are problematic, as not all texts are devoted to description of gatekeepers (acquiring offerings is also important) and not all of the latter are specified in terms of fire/water opposition; symbols of danger such as knives and loud voice are applied, as well. All these characteristics are accumulated in CT 1053 that sums up this path and is designated among others as "Spell for passing on the path of the fiery ones" (CT VII, 305f).

11 See also Abbas 2010.

12 Cf. Lotman and Graffy 1979, 167:

> It is not difficult to notice that characters can be divided into those who are mobile, who enjoy freedom with regard to plot-space, who can change their place in the structure of the artistic world and cross the frontier, the basic topological feature of this space, and those who are immobile, who represent, in fact, a function of this space.
>
> Looked at typologically, the initial situation is that a certain plot-space is divided by a single boundary into an internal and an external sphere, and a single character has the opportunity to cross that boundary; this situation is now replaced by a more complex derivative. The mobile character is split up into a paradigm-cluster of different characters on the same plane, and the obstacle (boundary), also multiplying in quantity, gives out a sub-group of personified obstacles—immobile enemy-characters fixed at particular points in the plot-space.

13 Wengrow 2014, 56.

14 Such as hieroglyphic mutilation in PT and CT; cf., for example, Mathieu 1996. These practices were also applied to elite tombs and coffins decoration; cf. Kanawati 2005.

15 Berlev 2003.

16 Although solar interpretation of this passage may be somewhat hypothetical, association of rams with the sun god and of a black ram as his night form in particular are well known from later periods. Cf. Redford and Redford 2005. Particularly noteworthy is proposed association of oracular practices related to the Ram of Mendes with homophony of *sr* "ram" and *sr* "foretell," as in the spell in question this very designation is used.

17 Cf. Hussein 2010.

18 Hornung 1963.

19 Hornung and Abt 2007.

20 Manassa 2008.

21 Posener 1970, 30–35.

22 See also Hornung 1994.

23 In this context, noteworthy is the remark of K. Goebs concerning analogies between violent characters of the Pyramid Texts Cannibal spell and later texts, judges of the Declaration of Innocence in the Book of the Dead (chapter 125A), in particular: "one may wonder whether these 'demons' did not originally belong in the context of the solar cycle, and might even represent manifestations of the sungod himself" (Goebs 2008, 224 n. 567). It seems that such comparisons give an interesting perspective on the evolution and transformation of Egyptian sacred literature through centuries. See also Lotman and Graffy 1979 for the evidence for the splitting of characters in the process of evolution of linear narratives.

24 Leitz and Budde 2002, vol. III, 559.

Journal of Ancient Egyptian Interconnections

Baba and the Baboon Demons

Rita Lucarelli
University of California, Berkeley

Abstract
Baba is a rather obscure god, occurring in magical texts since the time of the Pyramid Texts as well as in later ritual and mythical texts where he manifests as baboon or dog. This study analyzes in particular the baboon form of Baba in connection with the baboon-guardian demons in the netherworld, as they occur in mortuary compositions attested on coffins, papyri, and statues from the Middle Kingdom onward.

Baboons in Ancient Egyptian Religion and Cults

The significant role that baboons and monkeys play in ancient Egyptian everyday life and religion is well known, thanks to the numerous illustrations and textual mentions that we have of these animals as household pets or as divine incarnations.[1]

Many deities, all of them male, could manifest in particular as baboons, and, since the earliest times, they played an especially central role in the royal cult. A baboon god called *ḥḏ wr*, the "Great White One," is identified with the king already in the Pyramid Texts, while there are various religious depictions that let us think that baboons were also involved in the cult of the living king.[2] On the ivory tablet of Serkhemet (1st Dynasty) from his tomb in Abydos, a baboon sits on some kind of stool, while on a limestone slab from the Saqqara tomb 3507 (3rd Dynasty) a baboon sits on the throne of Maat before two kings dressed in short *heb sed* cloaks, wearing red crowns on their heads, and holding *wꜣs* staves in their left hands and *hts* staves in their right hands. Baboons were also widely recognized as worshippers of the sun and as a manifestation of the sun god Re himself.[3]

Many baboon entities are an integral part of funerary scenes decorating papyri and tomb walls. They belong to that variegated series of netherwordly inhabitants and guardian gods and demons, to which, for instance, belong the four baboons squatting around the Lake of Fire with flaming braziers in spell 126 of the Book of the Dead as a symbol of purification through fire: their *bwt* "disgust" is *ỉsft* and they are invoked to chase away *ḏw*, namely, two concepts related to the sphere of cosmic and social evil.[4]

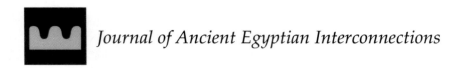

Finally, the god Thoth is often depicted as a squatting baboon, and baboons were also a manifestation of the moon god Khonsu and of Hapy, one of the Four Sons of Horus. Most of the depictions of baboons and baboon-like deities occurring in the ancient Egyptian sources are generally related to Thoth and to his multiple roles within the ancient Egyptian mythological accounts and religion. Among them is, for instance, Isden/Isdes, which occurs especially in temple scenes of the later periods, although its name is already attested in the Coffin Texts.[5] Isden is an example of how even "minor deities" in the shape of a baboon have a long history of attestations. However, Isden and the baboons more closely related to Thoth were not the only divine baboons occurring in religious texts and depictions, especially when we look at funerary literature.

Baba: Not All Baboons Are Thoth

Sexual potency and prowess was a main aspect of baboons, and it seems to be also the main characteristic of the baboon god *Bꜣbi*, according to the primary spelling of the name in the Pyramid Texts, or *Bꜣbꜣ*, as it mainly occurs in the texts of the New Kingdom, or *Bebon* if we use the Greek spelling attested in Plutarch.[6]

Baba[7] does not seem to have had his own temples, similar to Bes and to other divine entities that some scholars call "minor gods"[8] or that could be defined as apotropaic gods with demonic traits, if we agree to consider ancient Egyptian demons as liminal entities not having a cult on earth, a difference from the main gods.[9] However, although Baba does not seem to have benefitted from a cult, in the earliest sources he seems to be associated to the concept of kingship of Upper Egypt and El-Kab, while in later sources he seems to compete with Thoth, possibly also in relation to local cults in the area of Heracleopolis Magna.[10]

Our knowledge of this demonic god is based on a number of funerary and ritual texts and on a few related images of a baboon or of a hybrid human god with the head of a baboon or dog.[11] None of these sources says much on the god's whereabouts, however, only mentioning Baba's role in relation to main gods (Thoth, Ra, or Osiris) and to the deceased. No recent studies have followed up on a few articles published in the last few decades, which were all based on Derchain's first study of the god that appeared in *Revue d'Égyptologie* in 1952.

I believe that in order to re-assess Baba's role within ancient Egyptian religion, it would be important to reconsider its occurrences within a wider context, namely, comparing them with references to other baboon-like demonic entities of the netherworld, which may be related more to Baba and to his role of apotropaic deity in the netherworld than to the most famous baboon-god, Thoth. In other words, we could say that, similar to the case of other animals incarnating important deities,[12] not all baboons have to necessarily be seen as manifestations of or being related to the sphere of a main god such as Thoth. The animal and hybrid manifestations of the ancient Egyptian divine and demonic beings are many and diverse, but at the same time we need to take in consideration that often one same animal was employed as symbol of different supernatural beings.

Baba in the Pyramid Texts

The first textual occurrences of Baba, as already mentioned, date back to the Pyramid Texts. In Pyramid Text spell 549,[13] which concerns the king's entering of the sky and the opening of the sky's door, we learn that Babi can manifest with red ears and scarlet-colored anus:

> Recitation: Back, Babwi (*Bꜣbwi͗*) with red ears and scarlet anus,
> You have ferried to your mouth the haunch belonging to your Reput (goddess of the sedan chair [?]) (rather than one belonging to you).[14]

The color red seems to be a trait distinguishing the baboon from other monkeys, of which he is the king, as we will learn from another spell of this corpus (see below). In this spell Baba seems to be one of menacing guardians of the sky's door whom the deceased king has to ward off in order to pass; in a rather ambiguous way, the spells seems to allude to Baba having stolen the meat from *Rpw.t/rpy.t*, a not well-attested goddess probably carried in a palanquin.[15]

Bꜣbwi͗ is very probably the oldest writing of the entity's name, while the other writings could be defective forms of it.[16]

A further attestation of Baba's appearance and function as guardian of the sky comes from Pyramid Text spell 320, where Babi is called "Lord of the Night-Sky" and *kꜣ i͗ꜥn.w* "the Bull of the Apes"; the king clearly wishes to obtain this god's power in the afterlife:

Recitation:[17]
Now that Unis has swept away the night and Unis has sent off the hour-stars,
the controlling powers (*sḫm.w*) will appear and privilege Unis as Babi.
Unis is the son of her who does not know (him): she bore Unis to yellow-face, Lord of the night skies.
(He is) your greater, Lords! Hide yourselves, O *rekhyt*-populace (subjects), before Unis.
Unis is Babi, the Lord of the night sky,
The Bull of Baboons (*kꜣ iꜥn.w*), in whose absence one lives.

In PT 278, one of the spells copied in the pyramid of Unis against inimical beings and in particular reptiles,[18] Baba's apotropaic power is revealed to be effective against snakes and the god's spit is used as magical technique against the reptile while Baba meets the "Foremost of Letopolis" *ḫnty ḫm*:[19]

Babi has stood up to meet the Foremost of Letopolis (*ḫnty ḫm*),
Let the (poison) spit stop the one whose trampling is desired, you whose trampling is desired.
You are released, *wfi*-snake: let Unis be protected.

Baba in the Coffin Texts and the Book of the Dead

Baba's important role as god of the underworld continues in the main two collections of funerary texts from the Middle Kingdom (Coffin Texts) and the New Kingdom (The Book of the Dead). Most of the occurrences in the Coffin Texts are generally then transmitted in the Book of the Dead.[20] In the Coffin Texts, Seth is mentioned as the "deceased's protection" (*CT* VII, 161), while the role of Baba as guardian of the sky's door, which we have seen being prominent in the Pyramid Texts, does not play a central a role anymore when the god is mentioned in the later spells. Spell 42 and spell 99 of the Book of the Dead mention, however, the god's protection of the solar boat through the identification of the god's body parts with parts of the boat (*CT* V, 87–88/ Book of the Dead spell 99A) and of parts of the deceased's body (Book of the Dead spell 42).[21]

In the Book of the Dead, it is, however, Baba's most ferocious and fearful aspect that becomes more prominent, besides the new spelling of his name, which includes the use of a peculiar hieroglyphic with the white crown on a stand  and could be the relics of a royal cult of Baba as primordial king of Upper Egypt.[22]

Its iconography alludes not only to a baboon, as in the Pyramid Texts, but also to a hybrid god with an anthropomorphic body and a dog head. The dog-like appearance of Baba and the similarity with Seth will also be relevant in the later documents of the Ptolemaic Period, as in Papyrus Jumilhac (see below).

In spell 125 of the Book of the Dead, in particular in the address to the judges of the netherworld (spell 125C) as attested in the papyrus of Nu,[23] it is said that this dangerous god lives on human entrails and that the deceased seeks protection from him during the day of the judgment:

Rescue me from Baba, who lives on the entrails of the Great One
On this day of the great count

In spell 18 of the Book of the Dead, Baba is also represented as baboon in the vignette of the so-called "Tribunal of Naref."[24] The deceased declares himself "true of voice" against his/her enemies before ten tribunals in different places and times and in front of Thoth. In this spell Baba is paired to the other netherworld judges, among which are also the main gods of creation, such as Osiris, Shu, and Ra:

The Great Tribunal of Naref
Is Ra, Osiris, Shu, Baba
The night of the mysteries of the great forms[25]

In spell 63A of the Book of the Dead, which is a later version of a composition found in the Coffin Texts[26] "for drinking water, and not burning by fire," the deceased claims identity first with the oar needed to ferry the gods, then with Baba, who is said to be "the first son of Osiris." The role of the rightful heir of Osiris is the focus of this spell, where therefore Baba enters a mythical context:

I am Baba, first son of Osiris,
The one to whom every god has joined,
Within his eye in Iunu[27]

A probable reference to Baba is also found in spell 93, a spell for "not letting a man be carried to the east in the underworld." The impotence or fatigue as a condition of the deceased is transformed in the status of erection of the sexually active god, here being the phallus of Ra, according to the tradition of Baba as a virile male deity possessing a divine phallus, which goes back to the Pyramid Texts.

Finally, Baba occurs also in a peculiar composition that is mainly composed on the basis of the Book of the Dead, namely the so-called Ritual of the Hours of the Night, occurring on coffins and on temple and tomb walls starting from the 18th Dynasty (the earliest source dates to the reign of Hatshepsut) until the Roman Period. Baba occurs in a number of variants of this interesting composition, in the Eighth Hour of the Night (which includes also spell 28 of the Book of the Dead) especially in the 25th Dynasty tomb of Karakhamun (TT 223) in the South Asasif.[28]

In the Eighth Hour of the ritual, it is said:

> Recitation by the Eighth Hour of the Night, "the One Who is in Charge of Disturbances is her name, she stands for Baba"[29]

In the tomb of Karakhamun, moreover, Baba occurs as manifestation of the deceased also in the so-called "Hour Watch hymn" opening the text, whereas other versions of this hymn mention Geb instead. This could be a mistake in writing the names of the two gods, Geb and Baba ( and ), as noted by Griffin, but we cannot be sure that instead Baba is the name meant when Geb is also attested.[30]

Baba in Ritual and Texts of the Ptolemaic Period

Besides appearing in the main collections of funerary texts as mentioned above, Baba occurs also in a few ritual and magical texts dated to the Ptolemaic Period. In an offering text from Edfu,[31] which is on "presenting figs and honey," it is said:

> You go out from your trial, since you are true of voice, and Babi, the enemy, is in his carnage

The passage in Edfu refers to the demonization of Baba in the later periods, similar to what happens to Seth, with whom Baba can be now identified.

The demonization of Baba is especially outlined in the so-called Papyrus Jumilhac of the end of the Ptolemaic Period,[32] on the myths and legends of the 17th and 18th nomes of Upper Egypt. In one of the mythological episodes of this peculiar papyrus, Baba steals the belongings of Ra and then lies and accuses Thoth of being the one guilty of such bad behavior.[33] Ra, however, recognizes Thoth's innocence and condemns Baba, while a vengeful Thoth then performs a very aggressive ritual of magic on Babi while he is sleeping with a woman.

In this papyrus Baba is the last of a series of dogs, each of which has a different color and is associated to a deity:

> As for the red dog, his face is black and the part which is below his eyes is deeply hollow in its orbit, with yellow eyebrows (?). His eye is... and his glimpse is terrifying. He appears as Baba[34]

The mythological episode of Papyrus Jumilhac having Thoth and Baba as contenders is also mirrored in two texts carved on the pronaos and library walls of Edfu[35] as part of a series of conjurations of Seth and where Baba could be seen as an hypostasis of the former; or conversely, the contention between Thoth and Baba could be interpreted as a myth in its own.[36]

In the demotic magical papyrus of Leiden and London, a guardian of the netherworld is mentioned, called *Bꜣ Bꜣw*,[37] which Griffith-Thompson translates as "Soul of Souls."[38] This guardian-like being is also addressed with epithets applying to Baba as well in the Pyramid Texts, namely "bull of the night" and "son of Nut," and his role is also one of opening the doors of the sky, similar to Baba in the Pyramid Texts.[39] Therefore, instead of translating this name as "Soul of Souls," as Griffith-Thompson originally did in the publication of the manuscript, we could recognize in this text a later attestation of Baba, which shows how the earliest characterization of the god in the Pyramid Texts did not become lost until the latest periods.[40]

From the examples mentioned above, I believe that there is a certain coherence in the occurrences and representations of this demonic deity from the earlier to the later periods; his shape is either that of a baboon (at least until the Middle Kingdom) or of a dog/dog-headed god and his character is mainly apotropaic and potentially aggressive as guardian of the door of the sky at the beginning of his existence, while he becomes fully demonized and dangerous, and also assimilated with Seth, in the occurrences of the Ptolemaic and Roman Period. Furthermore, in Plutarch's *De Iside et Osiride*, in Ch. 49, *Bebon* is represented as a form or companion of Typhon and it is said that his name indicates restraint or hindrance, because the power of Typhon resists "the deeds which proceed in good order and pursue a worthy end."[41]

Baboon Guardian-demons of the Netherworld

I think that the existence of some protective guardian-demons of the netherworld depicted on magical objects and papyri could be related to the same sphere of action of Baba and of his primordial manifestation as baboon. Protective divine figures in the form of a baboon are attested since the Middle Kingdom, if we consider the magical ivory wands (so-called apotropaia or, more recently, birth tusks) where baboon-like figures occur frequently (Fig. 1) as protectors.[42]

Guardian-like baboons and monkeys with knives are also part of the demonic army depicted in the Book of the Two Ways and later in the spells of the Book of the Dead originating from Middle Kingdom compositions (Fig. 2).[43] These protective baboon-demons from the Middle Kingdom continue to play an important role in the tombs and in the funerary equipment during the New Kingdom and later, with attestations on papyrus, coffins, and tomb walls.[44] Baboons become among the most popular animals associated with the series of guardian figures protecting the body of Osiris/the deceased and decorating the exterior sides of later wooden coffins and stone sarcophagi.

Especially interesting is the motif of two squatting baboons preceded by a standing monkey with whom they seem to form a triad, which are found attested starting from the 19th Dynasty on a variety of funerary monuments, from coffins to stone sarcophagi, as well as on tomb and temple walls (Fig. 3). The earliest attestation of these guardian-like baboons is on the royal sarcophagus of Merenptah, which was then usurped by Psusennes in Tanis; they are part of a series of guardian figures that have been already studied because of their widespread occurrences

Figure 1: Ivory wand fragment from the "tomb of the magician" of the Ramesseum. Drawing from Quibell et al. 1898, pl. III.2a (Quirke 2016, 97; courtesy of Stephen Quirke).

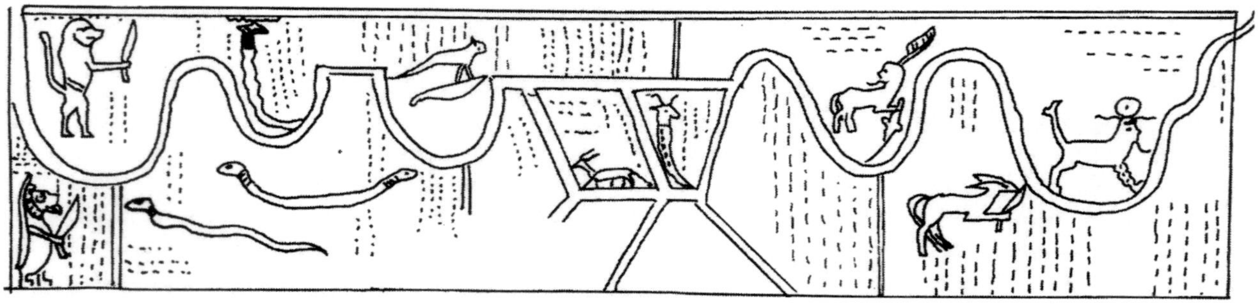

Figure 2: Book of the Two Ways, coffin of Sep. Drawing from Lacau 1903, pl. LV (Quirke 2016, 464; courtesy of Stephen Quirke).

FIGURE 3: Vignette from the sarcophagus of Merenptah. Detail from Montet 1951, pl. LXXXVI (Volokhine 2019, 279; courtesy of Youri Volokhine).

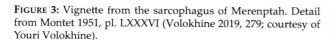

FIGURE 4: Vignette of the First Mound in Spell 149 from Papyrus BM EA 10097 (unpublished; photograph courtesy of Malcom Mosher).

(also on statues) since their appearance on Merenptah's coffin.[45] Particularly interesting are the new occurrences of the triad found on the stone sarcophagi of Iufaa, Menekhibnekau, and Nekau from Abusir (26th/27th Dynasties).[46] The names of the two seated baboons, *sḫd-ḥr* "The One with Upside Down Face" and *db-ḥr.k* "The Hippopotamus-faced," are well-known epithets for guardian-demons since the Middle Kingdom; they occur in the Book of the Two Ways and in its later version, spell 144 of the Book of the Dead.[47] In spell 144, moreover, as attested in particular in the tomb of Menekhibnekau at Abusir, at least one guardian for each gate that the deceased has to pass is baboon-headed.[48]

An even more minacious baboon guardian-demon equipped with knives occurs in the later version (starting with a papyrus of the 21st Dynasty and especially in the Ptolemaic papyri) of spell 149 of the Book of the Dead. He is the guardian of the second of the 14 mounds of the netherworld described in the spell (FIG. 4), the main topic of which is "knowing the mounds and their inhabitants."[49] The second hill has the form of the hieroglyph *ḏw* for mountain; the caption added near the hill in the 18th Dynasty papyri says: "the god within it: Ra-Horakhty;" therefore we may consider this hieroglyph as a representation of the horizon as well.

In the later version of this spell, the vignette is enriched, beside the representation of the mysterious *i͗ꜣwt* "the mounds," with a series of demonic guardians; the guardian of the second hill always occurs in form of a baboon,[50] although in a few variants we can see a crocodile-headed demon, which still, however, has the body of a monkey.[51] His body, leaning forward, resembles that of an animal and has a tail; in a few cases the animal head is instead associated with a human body. The text associated with this section of the vignette of spell 149 deals with the topographic description of the Field of Rushes as one of the place where the solar boat passes by; a few parallel passages occur already in Coffin Texts 159–161 and in spell 109 of the Book of the Dead. The deceased presents himself as "tireless paddler of the boat of Ra," who can find his way in the place since he knows its measures and whereabouts:

> I am the Lord of wealth in the Field of Reeds.
> O Field of Reeds, whose walls are of iron,
> whose barley grows 7 cubits tall,
> whose grain ears are 2 cubits,
> its stalk 5 cubits.
> *Akhw*-spirits of 7 cubits in their length reap them beside Horakhty ...
> *Akhw*-spirits of 9 cubits in their length reap them beside the eastern powers.[52]

As in the case of the other texts describing each mound in this spell, there is not a clear and direct connection of the text with the demonic figure represented in the vignette. However, a baboon-headed being would fit well as protector of the sun god and of his journey in the solar boat, as described in the text. Since one of the main functions of Baba, as we have discussed above, was to be protector of the sun god in the boat similar to Seth, we may assume that this baboon-guardian demon is related more to the sphere of Baba than to that of Thoth. Moreover, the bowing body position, which is the most peculiar trait of this baboon, recalls fully the hamadryas baboon, the exact species that Baba seems to represent, rather than the often hybrid (baboon or ibis-headed) figure of Thoth.[53]

In conclusion, I think that the figure and character of Baba as a baboon god, which is also his earliest form of appearance in the Pyramid Texts, has inspired a series of baboon-like demonic entities acting as guardians of the netherworld and connected to the protection of the deceased as well as of the sun god during his daily journey. The presence of these demons show how the role that baboons play in the ancient Egyptian religion is much more varied and relate to the world of demonic netherworldly guardians as well, beside to that of the main deities.

Ancient Egypt is not an isolated example of how these fascinating animals have been seen as divine or demonic entities with a protective function; Hindu stories of the monkey army of the monkey main god Hanuman that occur in the Ramayana are some among many examples;[54] guardian monkeys occur in Buddhist temples as well, as protectors of the statues of the Buddha. Baboons and monkeys play various roles as netherworld spirits also in modern African religions.[55]

The intriguing figure of Baba, as well as the baboon demons, guardians of the netherworld, could be therefore interpreted as the ancient Egyptian expression of awe towards this wild animal, whose central role as male god or demon in polytheistic world religions is undeniable.

Abbreviations

CT de Buck 1935–1961
LGG Leitz 2002–2003

References

Allen, James P. 2015. *The Ancient Egyptian Pyramid Texts*. 2nd edition. Edited by Peter Der Manuelian. Writings from the Ancient World 38. Atlanta: SBL Press.

Allen, Thomas George. 1960. *The Egyptian Book of the Dead: Documents in the Oriental Institute Museum at the University of Chicago*. Oriental Institute Publications 82. Chicago: The University of Chicago Press.

Altenmüller, Brigitte. 1975. *Synkretismus in den Sargtexten*. Göttinger Orientforschungen, 4. Reihe: Ägypten 7; Synkretistische Erscheinungen in der altägyptischen Religion 2. Wiesbaden: Harrassowitz.

Aufrère, Sydney. 2001. "À propos du chien Bébon, d'Anubis et de l'adultère." *Égypte, Afrique et Orient* 23: 23–28.

Bareš, Ladislav. 2010. "Procession of Deities and Demons on the Inner Sarcophagus of Iufaa." In Hedvig Győry (ed.), *Aegyptus et Pannonia IV: Acta Symposii anno 2006*, 1–12. Budapest: Ibisz Bt.

Bruyère, Bernard. 1959. *La tombe no. 1 de Sen-nedjem à Deir el Médineh*. Mémoires publiés par les membres de l'Institut français d'archéologie orientale 88. Le Caire: Institut français d'archéologie orientale.

Chassinat, Émile 2009. *Le temple d'Edfou VII*. 2nd edition. Mémoires publiés par les membres de la Mission archéologique française au Caire 24. Le Caire: Institut français d'archéologie orientale.

Clère, Jacques J. 1986. "Deux groupes inédits de génies-gardiens du quatrième prophète d'Amon Mentemḥat." *Bulletin de l'Institut français d'archéologie orientale* 86: 99–106.

D'Antoni, Diletta. 2013–2014. "Il Dio Isdes. Unpublished paper, Università di Bologna." Unpublished paper, Università di Bologna. < https://www.academia.edu/17308055/The_god_Isdes >, accessed 9 January 2020.

Darnell, John Coleman and Colleen Manassa Darnell. 2018. *The Ancient Egyptian Netherworld Books*. Writings from the Ancient World 39. Atlanta: SBL.

de Buck, A. 1935–1961. *The Egyptian Coffin Texts*, 7 vols. Chicago: University of Chicago Press

Derchain, Philippe. 1952. "Bébon, le dieu et les mythes." *Revue d'égyptologie* 9: 23–47.

——. 1963. "Nouveaux documents relatifs à Bébon (*bꜣbꜣwj*)." *Zeitschrift für ägyptische Sprache und Altertumskunde* 90: 22–25.

Díaz-Iglesias Llanos, Lucía. 2017. *Naref and Osiris Naref: A Study in Herakleopolitan Religious Traditions*. Zeitschrift für ägyptische Sprache und Altertumskunde—Beihefte 3. Berlin—Boston: De Gruyter.

Edel, Elmar. 1956. "Beitrage zum ägyptischen Lexikon III." *Zeitschrift für ägyptische Sprache und Altertumskunde* 81: 68–76.

Griffin, Kenneth. 2017. "Toward a Better Understanding of the Ritual of the Hours of the Night (Stundenritual)." In Elena Pischikova (ed.), *Tombs of the South Asasif Necropolis: New Discoveries and Research 2012–14*, 97–134. Cairo—New York: The American University in Cairo Press.

——. 2018a. "The Ritual of the Hours of the Night on the Coffins of Heresenes and Nespaqashuty from Deir el-Bahari." In Z. E. Szafrański (ed.), *Deir el-Bahari Studies* 2, 183–244. Polish Archaeology in the Mediterranean 27/2. Warsaw: Warsaw University Press.

——. 2018b. "A Preliminary Report on the Hours of the Night in the Tomb of Karakhamun (TT 223)." In Elena Pischikova, J. Budka, and K. Griffin (eds.), *Thebes in the First Millennium BC: Art and Archaeology of the Kushite Period and Beyond*, 59–70. GHP Egyptology 27. London: Golden House Publications.

Griffith, F. Ll.. and Herbert Thompson. 1904–1909. *The Demotic Magical Papyrus of London and Leiden*, 3 vols. London: Grevel.

Griffiths, J. Gwyn. 1970. *Plutarch's De Iside et Osiride: Edited with an Introduction, Translation and Commentary*. Cambridge: University of Wales Press.

Groves, Colin. 2001. *Primate Taxonomy*. Washington, DC: Smithsonian Institution Press.

Ismail, Fatma Talaat. 2019. *Cult and Ritual in Persian Period Egypt: An Analysis of the Decoration of the Cult Chapels of the Temple of Hibis at Kharga Oasis*. Yale Egyptological Studies 12. New Haven: Yale Egyptology.

Kemboly, Mpay. 2010. *The Question of Evil in Ancient Egypt*. GHP Egyptology 12. London: Golden House.

——. 2017. "Grappling with the Notion of Evil in Ancient Egypt." In Richard Jasnow and Ghislaine Widmer (eds.), *Illuminating Osiris: Egyptological Studies in Honor of Mark Smith*, 173–180. Atlanta: Lockwood Press.

Kurth, Dieter. 1992. "Bebon und Thot." *Studien zur Altägyptischen Kultur* 19: 225–230.

Lacau, Pierre. 1903. *Catalogue génerale des antiquités égyptiennes du Musée du Caire (Nos 28001–28086). Sarcophages antérieurs au nouvel empire* I. Le Caire: Institute français d'archéologie orientale.

Leclant, Jean. 1961. *Montouemhat: quatrième prophète d'Amon, Prince de la ville*. Bibliothèque d'étude 35. Le Caire: Institut français d'archéologie orientale.

——. 1962. "Les génies-gardiens de Montuemhat." In Anonymous (ed.), *Древнии мир: сборник статей. Академику Василию Васильевичу Струве*, 104–129. Moskv: Izd. Vostočnoj Literatury.

Leitz, Christian. 1994. "Auseinandersetzung zwischen Baba und Thoth." In Heike Behlmer (ed.), *... Quaerentes scientiam: Festgabe für Wolfhart Westendorf zu seinem 70. Geburtstag überreicht von seinen Schülern*, 103–117. Göttingen: Seminar für Ägyptologie und Koptologie.

——. 2004. "Deities and Demons." In Sarah I. Johnston (ed.), *Religions of the Ancient World*, 392–396. Cambridge, Mass.: Belknap Press.

Leitz, Christian (ed.). 2002–2003. *Lexikon der ägyptischen Götter und Götterbezeichnungen*, 8 vols. Orientalia Lovaniensia Analecta 110–116, 129. Leuven: Peeters.

Lucarelli, Rita. 2010. "Demons (Benevolent and Malevolent)." In Jacco Dieleman and Willeke Wendrich (eds.), *UCLA Encyclopedia of Egyptology*, Los Angeles. < https://escholarship.org/uc/item/1r72q9vv >, accessed 15 January 2020.

——. 2012. "The So-called Vignette of Spell 182 of the Book of the Dead." In Rita Lucarelli, Marcus Müller-Roth, and Annik Wüthrich (eds.), *Herausgehen am Tage: gesammelte Schriften zum altägyptischen Totenbuch*, 79–91. Wiesbaden: Harrassowitz.

——. 2015. "The Inhabitants of the Fourteenth Hill of Spell 149 of the Book of the Dead." In Ludwig D. Morenz and Amr El Hawary (eds.), *Weitergabe: Festschrift für die Ägyptologin Ursula Rößler-Köhler zum 65. Geburtstag*, 275–291. Wiesbaden: Harrassowitz.

Meurer, Georg. 2002. *Die Feinde des Königs in den Pyramidentexten*. Orbis Biblicus et Orientalis 189. Freiburg—Göttingen: Universitätsverlag—Vandenhoeck and Ruprecht.

Montet, Pierre. 1951. *La nécropole royale de Tanis* 2. Paris: [s.n.].

Mosher, Malcolm JR. 2010. "An Intriguing Theban Book of the Dead Tradition in the Late Period." *British Museum Studies in Ancient Egypt and Sudan* 15: 123–172.

Robins, Gay. 2007. "The Decorative Program in the

Tomb of Tutankhamun (KV 62)." In Zahi A. Hawass, and Janet E. Richards (eds.), *The Archaeology and Art of Ancient Egypt: Essays in Honor of David B. O'Connor*, vol. 2, 321–342. Le Caire: Conseil suprême des antiquités de l'Égypte.

Sherkova, Tatiana A. 2003. "Seven Baboons in One Boat: The Interpretation of Iconography in the Context of the Cult Belonging to the Temple at Tell Ibrahim Awad." In Zahi Hawass and Lyla Pinch Brock (eds.), *Egyptology at the Dawn of the Twenty-first Century: Proceedings of the Eighth International Congress of Egyptologists, Cairo, 2000*, vol. 2, 504–508. Cairo—New York: American University in Cairo Press.

Stadler, Martin Andreas. 2009. *Weiser und Wesir: Studien zu Vorkommen, Rolle und Wesen des Gottes Thot im ägyptischen Totenbuch*. Orientalische Religionen in der Antike/Oriental religions in Antiquity 1. Tübingen: Mohr Siebeck.

Quibell, J. E., R. F. E. Paget, and A. A. Pirie. 1898. *The Ramesseum and the Tomb of Ptah-Hetep*. British School of Archaeology in Egypt and Egyptian Research Account 2. London: Bernard Quaritch.

Quirke, Stephen. 1993. *Owners of Funerary Papyri in the British Museum*, Bd. 92. British Museum Occasional Papers 52. London: British Museum Press.

——. 2013. *Going out in Daylight*—prt m ḥrw*: The Ancient Egyptian Book of the Dead: Translation, Sources, Meaning*. GHP Egyptology 20. London: Golden House.

——. 2016. *Birth Tusks: The Armoury of Health in Context—Egypt 1800 BC*. Middle Kingdom Studies 3. London: Golden House Publications.

Reed, Daniel B. 2003. *Dan Ge performance: Masks and Music in Contemporary Côte d'Ivoire*. Bloomington: Indiana University Press.

Tabona, Shoko. 2007. *Karanga Indigenous Religion in Zimbabwe: Health and Well-being*. Burlington: Ashgate.

Vandier, Jacques. 1952. "La légende de Baba (Bébon) dans le papyrus Jumilhac (Louvre E. 17110)." *Revue d'égyptologie* 9: 121–123.

——. 1961. *Le Papyrus Jumilhac*. Paris: Centre national de la recherche scientifique.

Voloukhine, Youri. 2019. "Un couple de singes redoutables." In Sandrine Vuilleumier and Pierre Meyrat (eds.), *Sur les pistes du désert, Mélanges offerts à Michel Valloggia*, 265–280. Gollion: Infolio.

von Bissing, Friedrich Wilhelm. 1952. *Die altafrikanische Herkunft des Wortes Pavian-Babuin und sein Vorkommen als Gottesname in altägyptischen Texten*. Sitzungsberichte der Philosophisch-historischen Klasse der Bayerischen Akademie der Wissenschaften zu München, Jahrgang 1951. Heft 6, Schlussheft. München: Verlag der Königlich Bayerischen Akademie der Wissenschaf.

Waitkus, Wolfgang. 1987. "Zur Deutung einiger apotropäischer Götter in den Gräbern im Tal der Königinnen und im Grabe Ramses III." *Göttinger Miszellen* 99: 51–82.

Ward, William A. 1977. "Lexicographical Miscellanies." *Studien zur Altägyptischen Kultur* 5: 265–292.

Wolcott, Leonard T. 1978. "Hanuman: The Power-Dispensing Monkey in North Indian Folk Religion." *The Journal of Asian Studies* 37 (4): 653–661.

Notes

1 Two main species of monkeys that were imported from the south since there were no native monkeys in Egypt occur in images and texts; these are the so-called vervet or green monkey and the hamadryas baboon. The olive baboon with dog-like muzzle (*Papio anubis*) occurs as well in some sources. For a classification of baboon and monkey species, see Groves 2001. In ancient Egyptian, there are also different terms to distinguish at least between a green monkey (*gf*), an olive baboon (*ꜥnr*), and a Hamadryas baboon (*iꜥn*). A study of a sketch of a baboon on ostracon, which includes a detailed overview on baboon types present in the ancient Egyptian sources, has been produced by Patricia Podzorski and is in the course of publication. I wish to thank the author for access to her unpublished paper.

2 See Sherkova 2003, 505.

3 Among many similar depictions, see the baboons represented worshipping the boat of the sun in the famous scene depicted in the tomb of Sennedjem in Deir el Medina and representing the vignette of Spell 110 of the Book of the Dead: Bruyère 1959, pl, XIX.

4 On the concept of "evil" in ancient Egypt, see Kemboly 2010 and 2017.

5 For a list of occurrences of Isden/Isdes, see *LGG* I, 558–560. See also the D'Antoni 2013–2014. For the role of Isdes in temples, see Ismail 2019, 84–86.

6 On the origin of the name of the god, its variant and many hypotheses of interpretation, see Leitz 1994, 109, fn. 38; Derchain 1952; Derchain 1963. Currently, these three studies are also still the main references for any investigation on the character and history of attestations of the god Baba; here only a few among the numerous sources mentioned in these articles, which are relevant for a comparison with the baboon-demons, will be discussed, while for a more exhaustive overview on Baba, one should still consult those articles.

7 "Baba" will be the conventional transcription of the name used in this article, because the spelling of the god's name varies constantly in the sources that will be mentioned.

8 See, for instance, Leitz 2004.

9 Lucarelli 2010.

10 For the relationship between Baba and Thoth, see Kurth 1992; Derschain 1952, 30–32. For the differentiation between these two gods according in particular to P. Jumilhac, see Leitz 1994.

11 For the representation of Baba as a dog rather than as baboon in sources of the New Kingdom and later, see Leitz 1994; Aufrère 2001; see *LGG* II, 736–738 for an overview of occurrences of Baba in both forms. In this article the focus will be only on the occurrences of Baba as baboon.

12 See the case of Anubis and the jackal gods, as discussed in Arnaud Quertinmont's article in this volume.

13 The translations of the Pyramid Text passages in this article follow the edition of Allen 2015. PT 549 corresponds to Allen's Pepi 496, a spell against the guardians of the sky's door, and is similar to Unis PT 218, where it is said: "Pull back, Baba's penis! (i.e., the door bolt, according to Allen) Open, sky's door! You sealed door, open a path for Unis on the blast of heat where the gods scoop water" (Allen 2015, 60). Allen translates Baba with "Baboon" and in the glossary defines Baba as "god representing the baboon species," (p. 426) without, therefore, considering the later occurrence of Baba as dog-headed god.

14 Allen 2015, 173.

15 Ward 1977.

16 Edel 1956, 74–76; Derchain 1963, 22.

17 Translation adapted from Allen 2015, 61 (Unis 225).

18 Allen 2015, 52 (Unis 184).

19 *LGG* V, 846.

20 For the Coffin Text occurrences, see Derchain 1952 and 1963; Altenmüller 1975, 56–57.

21 Derchain 1952, 36–37. In Spell 42 (Quirke 2013, 119): "My penis is that of Baba;" in Spell 99A (Quirke 2013, 221): "The patches on the mouth of Baba are its cords, the tail which I made Seth tail is its ties, the uppers of Baba are the ropes."

22 Derchain 1952, 9. On the different writings of Baba's name and their occurrences, see *LGG* II, 736–738.

23 Quirke 2013, 273.

24 Spell 18's main topic is about the tribunals of the netherworld and Thoth; together with Spells 19 and 20, it includes appeals to this god for the justification of the deceased; see Quirke 2013, 69–79 and Stadler 2009, 320–343. On Naref as a mythological and cultic toponym related to the Herakelopolitan territory and religious tradition, see Díaz-Iglesias Llanos 2017, 59-62 for the discussion on this gloss in Spell 18.

25 Quirke 2013, 72.

26 *CT* 359 (V, 12–14) and 361 (V, 15–16).

27 Quirke 2013, 151–152.

28 The Ritual of the Hours of the Night is being studied by Kenneth Griffin, whom I wish to thank for pointing out to me Baba's presence in the composition and sharing the results of his study (Griffin 2017). For the Ritual of Hours on two *qrsw*-coffins, see Griffin 2018a. For the ritual in the tomb of Karakhamun, see Griffin 2018b.

29 Griffin 2017, 118; Griffin 2018a, 206.

30 Griffin 2018b, 66.

31 *Edfou* VII, 169, 11–15, 3 (west wall) (Chassinat 2009).

32 Papyrus Louvre E 17110; Vandier 1961.

33 On this episode, see Vandier 1952, 121–123.

34 Papyrus Jumilhac XVI, 7.

35 Kurth 1992.

36 Kurth 1992 compares the episodes in Papyrus Jumilhac with the occurrences in the temple of Edfu, to show how Baba's role as enemy of Thoth is not to be interpreted as Baba being a Sethian manifestation.

37 Derchain 1952, 46.

38 Griffith and Thompson 1904–1909, vol. 1, 159.

39 For an overview on the epithets of Baba in the Pyramid Texts, see Meurer 2002, 214–218.

40 However, see *LGG* II, 678, where the many occurrences of the divine epithet *Bꜣ-Bꜣw* are collected, including the one in the Leiden-London magical papyrus mentioned above. It shows how this epithet can apply to a number of different deities in various funerary and ritual texts.

41 Fort the passage from Plutarch and the other Greek occurrences of *Bebon*, see von Bissing 1952, 10-–13. For the English translation of the passage in Plutarch's work: Griffiths 1970.

42 See, for instance, the example found in the so-called tomb of the magician at the Ramesseum: Quirke 2016, 100. Quirke (2016, 364–368) also describes the baboon variants found on other magical objects, the majority of which are related to Thoth and hold a *wedjat*-eye or a torch as a symbol of the New Year flood. I would, however, consider the baboon with a torch to be other than Thoth, since it is rather reminiscent of the four demonic baboons of the Lake of Fire in Spell 126 of the Book of the Dead. A very few motifs of a baboon with knife, not necessarily to be connected with Thoth, do exist as well on birth tusks (Quirke 2016).

43 See Quirke 2016, 463-478, for a review of baboons and other guardian figures in the Book of the Two Ways, which can be compared to the similar motifs on birth-tusks. See in particular pp. 464-465 for the depiction of a standing baboon with knife on the coffin of Sep (FIG. 2), identified as *ꜥꜣ ḥr ḫsf ꜣtw* "great of face, who repels the crocodile," a name that will be transmitted then also to one of the guardians in Spell 144 of the Book of the Dead.

44 Among the protective guardian-baboons on tomb walls are those of the *Amduat*, in particular the nine kneeling baboons arranged in a tableau in the First Hour of the composition: see Darnell and Manassa Darnell 2018. They occur also on the west wall of the tomb of Tutankhamon (KV 62), although twelve in number, probably in relation to the hours of the night; see Robins 2007, 327–328.

45 Waitkus 1987; Leclant 1962; Leclant 1961, 114–115; Clère 1986. Very recently, Youri Voloukhine (2019) published a thorough analysis of this couple of baboons. I wish to thank him for sharing this paper with me prior to its publication.

46 See the article of Ladislav Bareš in this volume and Bareš 2010.

47 For a thorough analysis of these names, their variants on different monuments and their similarity and relationship with other demonic names of guardians on statues and coffins, see the recent study of Voloukhine 2019.

48 See the article of Renata Landgráfova in this volume. I wish to thank Renata Landgráfova, Ladislav Bareš, and Jiří Janák for providing useful information on their studies of these sarcophagi.

49 On Spell 149, see Quirke 2013, 357–364; on the demons depicted in the hills, see Lucarelli 2015.

50 See, for instance, BM 10097 in FIG. 4 (Early Ptolemaic Period). I wish to thank Malcom Mosher for providing the photo of this papyrus. See Quirke 1993, n.158; Mosher 2010.

51 See, for instance, P. Ryerson in Allen 1960, pl. XLVII.

52 See Quirke 2013, 358–359.

53 A standing baboon with knife occurs also in the vignette of Spell 182 of the Book of the Dead in the papyrus of Muthetepti (BM EA 10010), with a clearly protective function towards the deceased's mummy. See Lucarelli 2012.

54 See Wolcott 1978.

55 See Tabona 2007, 40: the *shavi regudo* is a baboon spirit in the indigenous religion in Zimbawe,

which is involved in ritual dancing. In the Ivory Coast, monkey masks represent spirits that appear in dreams and are used in ritual performance (Reed 2003).

Journal of Ancient Egyptian Interconnections

The Impact of the Manifestation of Demoniacal Winds on Terrestrial Life: The Role of Demon Gangs in Dispersing the *Ꞽꜣdt-rnpt*

El Zahraa Megahed
Fayoum University, Egypt

Abstract
Ꞽꜣdt-rnpt is the most recurrent impact upon people on earth that is identified with the role of demon gangs of Sekhmet. The manifestation of demons to spread the *ꞽꜣdt-rnpt* is remarkably associated with the blowing of pathogenic air, an argument that raises the hypothesis of a miasmatic role of demons as manifested winds. This article enlightens some aspects of the relation between the manifestation of demons and the blowing of winds carrying disease. These aspects are principally entailed in a selection of texts from the Edwin Smith Papyrus and Papyrus Leiden I 346, and in the Calendars of Lucky and Unlucky Days.

Introduction

From the Middle Kingdom, demon gangs of Sekhmet manifest in texts as the messengers of Sekhmet, harbingers of the *ꞽꜣdt-rnpt*.[1] *Ꞽꜣdt-rnpt* has a very broad sense as a generic term of "annual pestilence, misery, woes, calamity, and/or dire affliction."[2] As a demonic impact, *ꞽꜣdt-rnpt* is a typical role that demon gangs exercise on mortals in everyday life.[3] It is defined in this article as a personified harmful force that is capable of performing any disaster or series of disasters, of which the epidemic or incurable diseases are the most notable.[4]

Identified as harbingers of the *ꞽꜣdt-rnpt*, demon gangs of Sekhmet are known as sickness-demons where morbid winds are attributed to them.[5] It is not strange that demons are identified with winds. Winds have some characteristics that can be classified as demonic because of their close resemblance to the nature of demons.[6] Similar to demons, winds represent an invisible phenomenon, but there are several indications to their existence. They can be felt through their warmth or coldness. They can be heard, and the voice may be frightening. Sometimes they had an odor that can be easily smelled. Their course can be easily realized in the movement of treetops and other things.[7] Another common aspect between winds and demons is their relationship to the Sun-god. As the sun moves accompanied by winds, the Sun-god comes and goes with demons who secure his night journey. In mythology, the wind bears the Sun-god and opens his way in the sky.[8] As messengers of the Sun-god, demons are *wpwtyw ḫꜣḫw sỉnw sḫs.sn mỉ šwt nt ḫt* "swift, nimble messengers that they may run like a body's shadow."[9] Winds are also strong and fast, and their strength has destructive effects that can be recognized with the falling or scattering of things and with striking passengers.[10] Considering their effects, they are both associated with bringing diseases.[11] As winds can cause fires to flame,[12] demons are also known as agents of Sekhmet who destroy her enemies by burning them by her flames.[13]

This paper highlights a selection of texts to explain the possible hypotheses about the correlation between demons gangs of Sekhmet and the winds bearing the *ỉ3dt-rnpt*. The oldest of our sources is the Edwin Smith Papyrus from the 2nd Intermediate Period, where we find a text from a medical case on the recto that contains surgical treatise. It corresponds to the directions that the physician should consider during his diagnosis of diseases caused by demoniacal winds. From the same papyrus, we present other texts from the magical incantations against the annual threat of the *ỉ3dt-rnpt* preserved on the verso. Another source is the Book of the Festival of the Last Day of the Year in the Papyrus Leiden I 346, a magical text from the Nineteenth Dynasty. The text of this book serves as a magical protection against the threat of demon gangs of Sekhemt as bringers of the *ỉ3dt-rnpt*. The main third source is the Calendars[14] either in version C or in version S,[15] dating back to the Ramesside era. In Calendars, the omens are foretold by comparing cosmological phenomena to the occurrence of some mythological events. In this context, the manifestation of winds, either to disturb navigation in the Nile, to spread diseases, to cause foul weather, or even to circulate refreshing winds, are related to a coinciding activity of demons. As the days of the year are all precisely declared in the calendars, the wind that is supposed to blow on the cited day is easily identified. This identification is helpful to understand the disease that the winds/demons may cause on the identified days.

Demons Intermingle in the Sky with Winds Causing *Ỉ3dt-rnpt* as an Incurable Disease

In Calendars, I *prt* 19 (15 Hathor), winds spread the *ỉ3dt-rnpt* where diseases of an irremediable nature are expected. The winds on this day are suggested to refer to the manifestation of demons. In S, rt. 14, 9-15, 1:

> *ỉw ṯ3w m pt m hrw pn šbnw n sw ỉ3dt-rnpt mwtw ꜥš3w ḥbsw m-ḫnw n.f ỉr sw3.f ḥr ỉrt nb nn snb.f m ḫ3yt ỉmyw.f*
>
> The wind in the sky in this day is mixed with the *ỉ3dt-rnpt*, many dead are hidden within it. If it passes by anyone, he will not recover from the disease which is in him.[16]

On this day of the year, November 22nd, the country is expected to be completely free of the water of the flood.[17] Exhalations carrying plague are suggested to come out from carcasses of animals drowned during the Nile flood. A hypothesis interprets the incurable nature of the disease. The manifestation of winds in such an environment will evidently spread the contagion. It is of interest here to note that the action of the wind is determined by the verb *sw3* "to pass by."[18] This verb is known in a variety of texts as an act that describes the motion of demon gangs, especially their movement in winds to spread the threat of the *ỉ3dt-rnpt*.[19] Thus, it would not be strange to suggest that the blowing of the wind in the text describes the proceeding of demons to disperse the *ỉ3dt-rnpt*. On the same day, I *prt* 19, in the second almost identical version of Calendars in C,[20] *nṯrw ꜥ3w* "great gods" are mentioned instead of *ṯ3w* "winds" while they do the same role. Both *ṯ3w* and *ntrw* suggest an implied reference to demons. In Calendars, demons, especially *ḫnṯtyw* "butchers" and *ḥrytyw* "those who cause terror," are commonly designated as *nṯrw*[21] and *ṯ3w*.[22]

Another similar content is attested in Calendars, C, vs. 4, 5 (II *šmw* 20, 16 Paremoude). In this text, the coming of the dead bearing disease is accompanied, like the previous text, with the coming of winds/demons:

> *ỉw mwtw ꜥš3w ỉỉt.sn m sbyt ṯ3w ỉmỉ.k prỉ m ṯ3w nb m hrw pn*
>
> Dead are numerous, they come in headwinds. You shall not go out in any wind on this day.[23]

The prohibition against going out in winds refers apparently to the threat of disease.[24] It can be suggested that the *sbyt ṯ3w* refer to the manifestation of demons. This assumption considers that the term *sbyt* may also refer to a hostile action of an opposite wind.[25] It is noteworthy here that the gang *ḫnṯtyw* is mentioned on another day in Calendars (I *3ḫt* 4) to go in *sbỉw ṯ3w* "headwind".[26]

A similar text to the previous text of Calendars, I *prt* 19 is attested in the prognosis of a medical case from the recto of P. Edwin Smith where diseases are caused by demonic winds. According to the prognosis, physicians "should distinguish him (the patient) from the one afflicted because of something that has entered from outside."[27] By the end of the spell, the things entering from outside are defined in a gloss (rt. 4, 16–17):

> *ỉr ꜥḳt m-rwty ṯꜣw pw n nṯr n rwty m(w)t rꜣ-pw ỉn sꜥḳt n ḳmꜣmt ḥꜥw.f*
>
> As for "something that enters from outside": it is the wind of a god (i.e., demon) of the outside, or a dead man by making entry, not something that his body creates.[28]

Like the text of the Calendars, I *prt* 19, winds are attributed here to demons, designated also as *nṯr(w)*, and to the dead.[29] The winds cause similarly an irremediable disease that should be distinguished from other types of disease that may be cured by normal medical intervention. The *rwty* "outside" can be then assimilated to the "sky" mentioned in I *prt* 19 as the source from which the winds carrying demons come. *rwty* is the chaotic area outside the two-horizon-lion,[30] the non-human sphere from which gods and demons interact with people. The *rwty* is supposed to be inhabited by demon gangs as the area between the mortals and the beyond.[31] In P. Leiden I 346, I, 14–II, 1, demons are also suggested to intermingle with *ỉꜣdt-rnpt* in the sky to spread the contagion:

> *šmꜣyw sbyw m-m [ỉꜣ]d[t] rnpt Wꜣḏyt sḥtp.tỉ swꜣw ꜥ[r]w n ỉmyw šmꜣyw [ỉry]yw-spw n ỉmn-rn.f*
>
> .... the wanderers who go amidst *ỉꜣdt-rnpt*! Wadjet is pacified! (O) *swꜣw* who mount up to those-who-are-in-wanderers! The breaths (lit. [Those-who-cr]eate-feat) are in the air (lit. whose-name-is hidden)!

Although the text does not explicitly mention the identification of demons as winds, we suggest the existence of this relation. The motion of the *šmꜣyw* to *sbyw* "go amidst" the *ỉꜣdt-rnpt* can be suggested to evoke the action of the demonic winds to intermingle with the *ỉꜣdt-rnpt* in the sky as mentioned above in the text of Calendars I *prt* 19. In this regard, *ỉmyw-šmꜣyw* "those who are in *smꜣyw*" can be assumed to designate the *ỉꜣdt-rnpt*. The term *ꜥr* is then used to describe the movement of *swꜣw* to "to mount up (to the sky)"[32] full of the *ỉꜣdt-rnpt* to propagate it.[33]

The role of the pathogenic air in this etiological process is evident in the text. *Ỉmn-rn.f* refers to the hidden nature of the air.[34] As the explicit pronouncing of the name of the air may convey the influence of its essence, it seems that the nomination *ỉmn-rn.f* is intended to keep it inactive.[35] The term *ỉmn* is written here with a tired man with his arms sinking to ground from exhaustion 𓀇 (Gardiner Sign List A7). This determinative, commonly used in the sense "weary, weak, tire, faint, or to be soft,"[36] describes the tiredness character of pathogenic air to the hidden potentialities of winds.[37]

Ỉryw spw and *ỉmn-rn.f* can be translated in light of the just following text of P. Edwin Smith, vs. 18, 11–14, as puns that designate respectively pathogenic breaths and winds bearing demons. Accordingly, it can be suggested that *ỉryw spw* and *ỉmn rn.f* correspond respectively in their connotations to *nfw* and *nšny*. This proposition can explain the nature of the breaths of demons as a feat that they create to transmit disease to people.[38]

The following part will present more texts to explain how demons/winds proceed to disperse the contagion until arriving to people on earth.

Demons Spread Winds Widely, Cause Storms to Rage, and Disperse Contagious Breaths

In the second spell of P. Edwin Smith, vs. 18, 11–14, demons provoke *ṯꜣw* "winds," *nšny* "storms," and *nfw* "breaths" as a sequence of tasks in a process of etiology:

> *ky (rꜣ) n ḫsf ṯꜣw n dḥrt ḫꜣytyw nḏstyw wpwtyw-Sḫmt ỉḫtw ḫꜣytyw nn pḥ wỉ nfw r swꜣ swꜣw r nšny r ḥr.ỉ*
>
> Another (spell) for opposing wind of malady of slaughterers, the minor gods, the messengers of Sekhmet. Retreat slaughters! The breaths shall not reach me until the passersby pass by at the storm (far) from me (lit. my face).[39]

The reading of the text assumes that the three terms *ṯꜣw*, *nšny*, and *nfw* define three different aspects of air as a pathogenic medium. It is implied that the real impact is expected to affect people through the *nfw*, following to the coming of *ḫꜣtyw* in *ṯꜣw* and *swꜣw* in *nšny*. For this reason, the aim of the protection is to prevent the nfw from touching the man. It may be of interest here to observe that the occurrence of the breaths is negated in a future tense, while the storms are mentioned in a present tense. It can be then assumed that the threat of the epidemic affects people through the *nfw* as the air of the winds or the breath of demons.[40] Thus, the *swꜣw* are charmed to pass in the *nšny* without letting the *nfw* reach people, while the *ḫꜣtyw* are addressed to retreat, most probably to evoke the recession of winds. The contagion will then transmit to people causing the state of malady *dḥrt*.[41] A similar idea is mentioned in the first spell of P. Edwin Smith, vs. 18, 8–9, where the pathogenic agent *dḥrt* is transmitted to people in the *nfw* "breath" of *ṯꜣw* "winds (of demons)": "you have saved me from every *dḥrt*, etc. of this year in the *nfw* of every evil *ṯꜣw*." *dḥrt*, known also as "(the plague)-bitterness," defines the morbid state of the person infected by an etiological wind.[42] *dḥrt* is known to be controlled by the *wꜥb* priest of Sehkmet;[43] the role of this priest in purification is typical to expel the miasma.[44]

The text reveals another aspect concerning the significant association between *nšny* "storms"[45] and the *swꜣw*. It is interesting to note that the threat of the *iꜣdt-rnpt* is launched by the *ṯꜣw* "winds" of the *ḫꜣtyw*. Subsequent to the latter, the *swꜣw* gang comes to agitate the wind by raging *nšny* in roads and passages. It can be established that the role of *swꜣw* in the process of proceeding the winds comes consequent to other gangs, namely *ḫꜣtyw* in P. Edwin Smith, vs. 18, 8–9, 12, and *šmꜣyw* in P. Leiden I 346, I, 14. In these two spells, *ḫꜣtyw* and *šmꜣyw* are implied to start the threat of the *iꜣdt-rnpt*, while the *swꜣw* sweep it in roads and junctions nearby people.[46] This assumption could be linked with the sense of the name of *swꜣw* as "passers-by."[47] Another derivative from the same root may refer to the nature of *swꜣw* to exist in the surroundings: *sww* "entourage (of someone), vicinity."[48] This proposition can find its justification in P. Edwin Smith, vs. 19 (1–2) in an incantation for the protection against the *iꜣdt-rnpt*. In this spell, the *swꜣw* are cited as propagators of *nšny* in the roads

ink wḏꜣ m wꜣt swꜣw ḥwi.tw.i irf wḏꜣ.kwi iw mꜣꜣ.n.i nšny ꜥꜣ nsrt twy m wdi m.i ink pri m nšny ḥr.ti r.i

I am the healthy one in the way of the passers-by. So shall I be smitten, while I am healthy? I have seen the great storm. You flame, do not shoot in me! I am the one who has come forth out from the storm. Be far from me!

Like the previous of P. Edwin Smith, vs. 18, 11–14, this text correlates also between *swꜣw* and *nšny* "storms." Herein, the connotations of the term *ḥwi* can help in revealing some of the mystery about the relation between demons and winds. It can be suggested that demons use winds as their tool by which they strike the passengers.[49]

Nsrt "The Flame-goddess"[50] as one of the manifestations of Sekhmet may suggest *nšny* as hot desert winds or igniting ones.[51] However, it is more convincing that the aspect *Nsrt* is evoked to describe the figure of burling inflammation. Regarding this hypothesis, Leitz assimilated the symptoms of being hurt by arrows, especially the traces left on the skin, to those caused by the bubonic plague.[52] *wdi* can refer then to the inflammation caused by the bubonic plague[53] as a probable equivalent of the *iꜣdt-rnpt*. In this context, the connotations of the verb *wdi* "to shoot (arrows)"[54] are significant. *wdi* describes the action of Sekhmet to send her demons as if arrows[55] are shot.[56]

Concerning the way of shooting the arrows, its source is most probably associated with the mouth of Sekhmet by means of her word. It has been suggested that the notion of winds in ancient Egypt is similar to the *logos* of the Greeks.[57] However, it can be suggested that Sekhmet shoot demons as if arrows from her mouth through her fiery breath.[58] In the Book of the Festival of the Last Day of the Year in P. Leiden I 346, I, 3–6, *ḫꜣtyw* are designated as *styw ššrw.sn m rꜣ.sn* "Those who shoot their arrows from their mouths."[59] The dispersal of disease from the mouths of demons in the form of arrows may describe how the breath of demons is affected by their identity as pathogenic arrows of Sekhmet.[60] In this text, the impact of demons to spread their pathogenic breaths is also correlated to the manifestation of winds. There is a series of designations that implicitly qualify the notion of demons as winds.[61] They are *wpwtyw m-ḫt spꜣwt* "the messengers who are everywhere in the provinces."[62] The last epithet describes the nature of winds to surround people far and wide. Another designation is *sḫsw ḫt tꜣ* "who hurry through the land,"[63] where the rapidity of demons qualifies the ubiquitous nature of winds and their capacity to exist everywhere in the provinces. In this respect, the role of demons can be interpreted in the light of the Galen's theory of miasma.[64] This concept connected epidemics with miasma and corrupted air where demons generate pestilence through exhalations of their pernicious effluvium into the atmosphere.

Conclusion

The texts, discussed in this paper, emphasize the link between demons, winds, and the *ỉ3dt-rnpt*. The threat of the last, identified as irremediable disease, is dispersed by demons when winds are active in the sky. In other words, winds laden with epidemic represent an exhorting environment that agitates demon gangs of Sekhmet. The argument that can be established from the ensemble of texts suggests that demons and pathogenic winds superimpose with each other in the sky. The role of demons is then to manifest as the blowing of winds to spread them on a large scale everywhere around people. While passing in winds, demons transmit the contagion and the pathogens from their mouths through their morbid breaths. It seems that the role of demon gangs has a complementary nature in which each of them is entrusted with achieving a certain task. It seems that *ḫ3tyw* "Executioners" and *šm3yw* "Wanderers" spread the winds, while *sw3w* "Passers-by" cause the storms to rage.

As propagators of morbid winds and exhalations,[65] the role of demon gangs of Sekhmet is interpreted as refering to a miasmatic theory of disease in which the practice of magical treatment is gathered with an anticipated recognition of infection.[66] The theory is held in a context that considers the physical impact of miasma on people. The role of demons serves, then, to justify the incurable nature of the epidemic by attributing it to mythological causes, as the work of demons.

In this context, demon gangs of Sekhmet are identified as the mythical-religious explanation of the *ỉ3dt-rnpt*. The interpretation of the role of demons of Sekhmet to bring disease is evident in religion where demons, *ỉ3dt-rnpt*, winds, and diseases are all sent and controlled by Sekhmet and her priest.[67] It is of interest to note that morbid winds are described as arrows bearing diseases when they are sent by Sekhmet or by her demons. As messengers of Sekhmet, demons acquires the attributes of their mistress, behaving as she does to spread diseases through winds.[68] Winds and diseases are thus not only sent by Sekhmet, they are also the work of her demons.

A Bibliographic Note for Sources of Texts and Their Translation

The transliteration and the translation of texts are made by the author; otherwise, the reference is mentioned in a footnote.

Abbreviations:

CT de Buck, Adriaan. 1935–1961. *The Egyptian Coffin Texts*, 7 vols.. Chicago: The University of Chicago Press.

LGG Leitz 2002a–f.

Wb Erman and Grapow 1926–1930.

References

Allen, James. 2005. *The Art of Medicine in Ancient Egypt*. New York: Metropolitan Museum of Art.

Aufrère, Sydney. 1985. "Le cœur, l'annulaire gauche, Sekhmet et les maladies cardiaques." *Revue d'égyptologie* 36: 21–43.

Bardinet, Thierry. 1995. *Les papyrus médicaux de l'Égypte pharaonique*. Paris: Fayard.

Blumenthal, Elke. 1970. *Untersuchungen zum ägyptischen Königtum des Mittleren Reiches. I: Die Phraseologie*. Abhandlungen der Sächsischen Akademie der Wissenschaften zu Leipzig, Phil.-hist. Klasse, Band 61, Heft 1. Berlin: Akademie-Verlag.

Bommas, Martin. 1999. *Die Mythisierung der Zeit. Die beiden Bücher über die altägyptischen Schalttage des magischen pLeiden I 346*. Gottinger Orientforschungen IV/37. Wiesbaden: Harrassowitz.

Borghouts, Joris F. 1971. *The Magical Texts of Papyrus Leiden I 348*. Oudheidkd Meded Rijksmus Oudheiden 51. Leiden: Brill.

Breasted, James H. 1930. *The Edwin Smith Surgical Papyrus. Volume 1: Hieroglyphic Transliteration with Translations and Commentary*. Oriental Institute Publications 3. Chicago: University of Chicago Press. Reissued 1991 with a foreword by T. A. Holland.

Caminos, Ricardo A. 1954. *Late-Egyptian Miscellanies II*. London: Oxford University Press.

Edwards, Iorwerth E. S. 1960. *Hieratic Papyri in the British Museum, 4th Series. Oracular Amuletic Decrees of the late New Kingdom*. London: British Museum.

Erman, Adolf and Hermann Grapow (eds.). 1926–1930. *Wörterbuch der Ägyptischen Sprache*. Berlin—Leipzig: Von Quelle & Meyer.

Faulkner, Raymond. 1962. A *Concise Dictionary of Middle Egyptian*. Oxford: Griffith Institute.

Flessa, Nicolas. 2006. *"(Gott) schütze das Fleisch des Pharao." Untersuchungen zum magischen Handbuch pWien Aeg 8426*. Corpus Papyrorum Raineri Archeducis Austriae 27. München: K. G. Saur.

Germond, Philippe. 1981. *Sekhmet et la protection du monde*. Aegyptiaca helvetica 9. Geneva: Éditions de Belles-Lettres.

Ghalioungui, Paul. 1968. "La notion de maladie dans les textes égyptiens et ses rapports avec la théorie humorale." *Bulletin de l'Institut français d'archéologie orientale* 66: 37-48.

Goyon, Jean-Claude. 2006. *Le Rituel du* sḥtp Sḫmt *au changement du cycle annuel. D'après les architraves du temple d'Edfou et textes parallèles, du Nouvel* Empire à l'époque ptolémaïque et romaine. Bibliothèque d'étude 141. Le Caire: Institut Français d'Archéologie Orientale.

Gutbub, Adolphe. 1977. "Die Vier Winde im Tempel von Kom Ombo (Oberägypten), Mit einem Beitrag von A. Gutbub über die vier Winde in Ägypten." In O. Keel (ed.), *Jahwe-Visionen und Siegelkunst: eine nueu Deutung de Majestätsschilderungen in Jes 6, Ez 1 und 10 und Sach 4. Stuttgart Bibelstudien 84/85*, 328–353. Stuttgart: Katholisches Bibelwerk.

Hannig, Rainer. 2006. *Ägyptisches Wörterbuch II. Mittleres Reich und Zweite Zwischenzeit*. Kulturgeschichte der antiken Welt 112. Mainz am Rhein: Philippe von Zabern .

Herbin, François. 2004. "Un texte de glorification." *Studien zur Altägyptischen Kultur* 32: 171–204.

Hornung, Erik. 1991. *Der Ägyptische Mythos von der Himmelskuh: Eine Ätiologie des Unvollkommen*. Orbis Biblicus et Orientalis 46. 2nd edition. Freiburg—Schweiz: Universitätsverlag; Gottingen: Vandenhoeck & Ruprecht.

Koenig, Yvan. 1979. "Un revenant inconvenant? (Papyrus Deir el-Medineh 37)." *Bulletin de l'Institut français d'archéologie orientale* 79: 103–119 (with 2 plates).

Kuhlmann, Klaus. 1976. "Göttereigenschaften." In Wolfgang Helck and Eberhard Otto (eds.), *Lexikon der Ägyptologie*, Band 2, 679–683. Weisbaden: Otto Harrassowitz.

Kurth, Dieter. 1975. *Den Himmel Stützen, die "ṯwꜣ pt" Szenen in den ägyptischen Tempeln der griechisch-römischen Epoche*. Rites Egyptiens II. Bruxelles: Fondation égyptologique Reine Élisabeth.

——. 1980. "Luft (Luftgott)." In Wolfgang Helck and Eberhard Otto (eds.), *Lexikon der Ägyptologie*, Band 3: 1098–1102. Weisbaden: Otto Harrassowitz.

——. 1986. "Wind." In Wolfgang Helck and Eberhard Otto (eds.), *Lexikon der Ägyptologie*, Band 6: 1266-1272.

Leitz, Christian. 1994. *Tagewählerei. Das Buch* ḥꜣ.t nḥḥ pḥ.wy ḏt *und verwandte Texte*. Ägyptologische Abhandelungen 55. Wiesbaden: Harrassowitz.

——. 1999. *Magical and Medical Papyri in the New Kingdom Hieratic Papyri in the British Museum*, 7th series. London: British Museum Press.

——. 2002a–f. *Lexikon der ägyptischen Götter und Götterbezeichnungen*, 6 vols. Orientalia Lovaniensia Analecta 110–115. Leuven, Dudley, MA: Peeters.

Lichtheim, Miriam. 1973. *Ancient Egyptian Literature I: The Old and Middle Kingdoms*. Berkeley—Los Angeles—London: University of California Press.

Lopez, Jesús. 1972. "Naufragé, col. 36–37 et 105–106." *Revue d'égyptologie* 24: 111–115.

Loprieno, Antonio. 1984. "Sprachtabu." In Wolfgang Helck and Eberhard Otto (eds.), *Lexikon der Ägyptologie*, Band 5: 1211–1214. Weisbaden: Otto Harrassowitz.

Lorton, David. 1993. "God's Beneficent Creation: Coffin Texts Spell 1130, the Instructions for Merikare, and the Great Hymn to the Aton 125." *Studien zur Altägyptischen Kultur* 20: 125–155.

Lucarelli, Rita. 2010. "Demons (Benevolent and Malevolent)." In Jacco Dieleman and Willeke Wendrich (eds.), *UCLA Encyclopedia of Egyptology*. Los Angeles: eScholarship. <https://escholarship.org/uc/item/1r72q9vv>.

——. 2011. "Demonology during the Late Pharaonic and Graeco-Roman Periods in Egypt." *Journal of Ancient Near Eastern Religions* 11: 109–125.

Meeks, Dimitri. 1977. *Année lexicographique Egypte Ancienne 1*. Paris: Cybèle.

——. 1978. *Année lexicographique Egypte Ancienne 2*. Paris: Cybèle.

——. 1979. Année *lexicographique Egypte Ancienne 3*. Paris: Cybèle.

——. 2011. "Demons." In Donald B. Redford (ed.), *The Oxford Encyclopedia of Ancient Egypt*, vol. 1. Oxford: Oxford University Press.

Megahed, Elzahraa. 2016. *The Role of Malevolent Demon Troops with the Livings in Ancient Egypt*. PhD dissertation, Lyon 2 University.

Guglielmi, Waltraud. 1976. "Flachs." In Wolfgang Helck and Eberhard Otto (eds.), *Lexikon der Ägyptologie*, Band 2: 256–257. Weisbaden: Otto Harrassowitz.

Meyrat, Pierre. 2012. *Les papyrus magiques du Ramesseum: Recherches sur une bibliothèque privée de la fin du Moyen Empire*. PhD dissertation, Genève University.

Nunn, John. 1996. *Ancient Egyptian Medicine*. Norman: University of Oklahoma Press.

Nyord, Rune. 2009. *Breathing Flesh: Conceptions of the Body in the Ancient Egyptian Coffin Texts*. Copenhagen: Museum Tusculanum.

Parkinson, Richard. 2009. *Reading Ancient Egyptian Poetry: Among Other Histories: From 1850 BC to the Present*. Malden, MA: Wiley-Blackwell.

Rondot, Vincent. 1989. "Une Monographie Bubastite." *Bulletin de l'Institut français d'archéologie orientale* 89: 249–270.

Roquet, Gérard. 1973. "Espace et lexique du sacré : autour du nom du 'ciel' en vieux nubien." *Bulletin de l'Institut français daarchéologie orientale* 73: 158–159.

Steuer, Robert O. and John B. de C. M. Saunders. 1959. *Ancient Egyptian and Cnidian Medicine: The Relationship of Their Aetiological Concepts of Disease*. Berkeley—Los Angeles: University of California Press.

Strawn, Brent A. 2005. *What is Stronger than a Lion? Leonine Image and Metaphor in the Hebrew Bible and the Ancient Near East*. Orbis Biblicus Orientalis 212. Fribourg: Academic Press—Göttingen: Vandenhoeck.

Szpakowska, Kasia. 2009. "Demons in Ancient Egypt." *Religion Compass* 3(5): 799–805.

te Velde, Henk. 1967. *Seth: God of Confusion: A Study of His Role in Egyptian Mythology and Religion*. Leiden: Brill.

——. 1975. "Dämonen." In Wolfgang Helck and Eberhard Otto (eds.), *Lexikon der Ägyptologie*, Band 1: 980–984. Weisbaden: Otto Harrassowitz.

Thomas, Elizabeth. 1959. "Ramesses III: Notes and Queries." *Journal of Egyptian Archaeology* 45: 101–102.

von Bomhard, Anne-Sophie. 2008, *The Naos of the Decades: From the Observation of the Sky to Mythology and Astrology*. Oxford: Oxford Centre for Maritime Archaeology.

von Deines, Hildegard and Wolfhart Westendorf. 1961. *Wörterbuch der Medizinischen Texte, Grundriß der Medizin der Alten Ägypter VII-1*. Berlin: Akademie-Verlag.

von Lieven, Alexandra 2002. *Der Himmel über Esna. Eine Fallstudie zur Religiösen Astronomie in Ägypten, Eine Fallstudie zur Religiösen Astronomie in Ägypten*. Ägyptologische Abhandlungen 64. Wiesbaden: Harrassowitz.

Vernus, Pascal. 1981. "Omina calendériques et comptabilité d'offrandes sur une tablette hiératique de la 18e dynastie." *Revue d'égyptologie* 33: 94–95.

——. 1982–1983. "Etudes de philologie et linguistique (II)." *Revue d'égyptologie* 34: 115–128.

Valloggia, Michel. 1976. *Recherche sur les "messagers" (wpwtyw) dans les sources égyptiennes profanes*. Geneva—Paris: Librairie Droz.

Verhoeven-van, Ursula. 1984. *Grillen, Kochen, Backen im Alltag und im Ritual Altägyptens: ein lexikographischer Beitrag*. Rites Egyptiens IV. Bruxelles.

Westendorf, Wolfhart. 1966. *Papyrus Edwin Smith: Ein medizinisches Lehrbuch aus dem alten Ägypten: Wund- und Unfallchirugie Zaubersprüche gegen Seuchen, verschiedene Rezepte*. Bern—Stuttgart: Hanz Huber.

——. 1975. "Atem." In Wolfgang Helck and Eberhard Otto (eds.), *Lexikon der Ägyptologie*, Band 1, 517–518. Weisbaden: Otto Harrassowitz.

——. 1999. Handbuch der altägyptischen Medizin. HdO 36/1. Leiden—Boston—Köln: Brill.

Wilkinson, Richard. 2003. *The Complete Gods and Goddesses of Ancient Egypt*. Cairo: American University in Cairo Press.

Wilson, Penelope. 1991. *A Lexicographical Study of the Texts in the Temple of Edfu*. PhD dissertation. Liverpool University.

Yoyotte, Jean. 1968. "Une théorie étiologique des médecins égyptiens." *Kêmi: Revue de philologie et d'archéologie égyptienne et coptes* 18: 79–84.

——. 1980–1981. "Héra d'Héliopolis et le sacrifice humain." *Annuaire de l'École pratique des hautes-études, 5è section—sciences religieuses* 89: 31–102.

Zandee, Jan. 1960. *Death as an Enemy*. Leiden: Brill.

——. 1963. "Seth als Sturmgott." *Zeitschrift der Ägyptischen Sprache* 90: 144–156.

Zivie, Alain-Pierre. 1984. "Regen." In Wolfgang Helck and Eberhard Otto (eds.), *Lexikon der Ägyptologie*, Band 5: 201–206. Weisbaden: Otto Harrassowitz.

Notes

1 The oldest source that cites the role of gangs of Sekhmet as heralds of the *ỉꜣdt-rnpt* is the Papyrus Ramesseum XVII (pBM EA10770), a priestly text to conjure the dangers of the year. Its content is similar to the famous P. Leiden I 346: Meyrat

2012, s.v. P. Ramesseum XVII, frame III: fragment A, x+7; frame III: fragment B/2, x+5; frame III: fragment C+D, 6. Another source from the same period is the story of the Eloquent Peasant in P. Berlin 3023, B1, 149-150, in which the threat of the messengers is cited in a metaphor: Lichtheim 1973, 169ff; Parkinson 2009, 302.

2 Erman and Grapow 1926 (= *Wb* 1), 35 (16–18); Faulkner 1962, 9; Hannig 2006, 81c; Wilson 1991, 73–74, s.v. *ỉ3dt-rnpt*.

3 There is no fear of the threat of *ỉ3dt-rnpt* in the hereafter; for more about the dangers in the hereafter: Zandee 1960, *passim*, esp. ix–xvii.

4 Yoyotte 1968, 83; Germond 1981, 291–292; Megahed 2016, 442; 446ff.

5 Westendorf 1999, 373–374.

6 In this article, the term "demons" is used to refer to "demons gangs of Sekhmet."

7 Kurth 1986, 1266(B).

8 Kurth 1975, 70f.; for the eastern winds and its role with the Sun: Gutbub 1977, 340.

9 Hornung 1991, 16.

10 Kurth 1986, 1266(B).

11 Kurth 1986, 1267(D); von Deines 1961, 965; Meeks 1977, 77.4893.

12 Kurth 1986, 1266(B); Verhoeven 1984, 187–188.

13 Goyon 2006, 63; 67; 89; 95(14); Yoyotte 1980–1981, 43–44.

14 "Calendars" is used in this article as an abbreviation to refer to Calendars of Lucky and Unlucky Days.

15 "C" and "S" refer respectively to the two versions of Calendars of Lucky and Lucky Days: Papyrus Cairo JE n° 86637 and the Papyrus Sallier IV (BM 10184).

16 The translation is made after the reading of Leitz 1994, 212-3.

17 Leitz 1994, 134, 212.

18 Erman and Grapow 1930 (= *Wb* 5), 60(8)–61(20); Faulkner 1962, 216; Hannig 2006, 675.

19 For details about the demonic connotations of the verb *sw3* "als tätigkeit von krankheitsdämonen": Leitz 1994, 213(d); Megahed 2016, 352 cites: "In the corpora [P. Edwin Smith, vs.18, 13; vs. 19, 20; Calendars, P. C, rt. 22; Calendars, P. S, vs. 15, 1], the term *sw3* figures as a hostile action of demons, it qualifies their movement in winds to spread the threat of the *ỉ3dt-rnpt*." *sw3* is also mentioned in P. Wien Aeg 8426: Flessa 2006, 42; 49 (= 2nd spell, lines 9).

20 Rt. 22, 3–4.

21 Calendars, I *3ḫt* 4, II *3ḫt* 25 and II *prt* 24: Leitz 1994, 96 (n° 4); 364. The term *nṯrw* designates demons in Calendars as a kind of linguistic taboo: Loprieno 1984, 1214; von Deines & Westendorf 1961, 491. *Nṯrw* identifies the very nature of demons as minor divinities: te Velde 1975, 981; Meeks, 2001, 375.

22 In Calendars, winds upon earth are regarded as emanations or reflections to the conflict between Re and Apophis in which demon gangs acting as the agents of Re, especially *ḫnṯtyw* and *ḫrytyw*, are identified with the east winds that prevail over the west winds that are identified with the *msw-bdšt* as the agents of Apophis: Leitz 1994, 96–97.

23 The translation is made after the reading of the text by Leitz 1994, 364.

24 See the argument about the mention of disease on the same day in Coptic and Arabic almanacs: Leitz 1994, 364.

25 From the same root is *sbyt* "headwind": Erman and Grapow 1929 (=*Wb* 4), 89.1; Bommas 1999, 59(n° 69).

26 Leitz 1994, 17.

27 Allen 2005, 79.

28 For similar translation: Vernus 1982–1983, 123, fn. 54; compare also Allen 2005, 79.

29 The *ỉ3dt-rnpt* is commonly cited in texts in a comprehensive view of animism where it is attributed not only to demon gangs but also to several malevolent divinities, disembodied dead of humans and animals from the two genders, malignant beings, etc. Breasted 1930, 376; von Deines 1961, 21–22; Westendorf 1999, 375.

30 Westendorf 1966, 45, n° 17.

31 Szpakowska 2009, 799. Distinguished by their very nature as "wanderers," demons gangs are assumed to wander between the beyond and the earth: Lucarelli 2010, 3.

32 Wilson 1991, 304, s.v. *ʿr*.

33 For the verb *ʿr* as the action of the disease to penetrate the body of the patient: Bommas 1999, 59–60, footnote 148.

34 For the play on words between the hidden nature of the air and the name *ỉmn rn.f*: Erman and Grapow 1926 (= *Wb* 1), 84(2); Kuhlmann 1977, 680; Nyord 2009, 400; Caminos 1954, 49; 153.

35 Nyord 2009, 399.

36 Gardiner Sign List A7.

37 Bommas 1999, 61(n° 75).

38 For the verb *ỉr* as the demonic action of the *ḥry-tyw* identified as demonic winds: Calendars, C, vs. VI, 13; as the action of the *ḫ3tyw*: von Bomhard 2008, 46. Demons are designated as *ỉryw-šʿt* "Those-who-carry-out-massacre": Leitz 2002a (=*LGG* 1), 511c, s.v. *ỉrw-šʿt* [1]. Demons are gods of the Book of *ỉrw(t)* "Duties": Edwards 1960, 96(14).

39 For a similar translation of the text: Allen 2005, 107.

40 Vernus 1982–1983, 121, 123. For *nfw* "breath of air" or "wind"': Erman and Grapow 1927 (= *Wb* 2), 250 (15–18); Hannig 2006, 407; Westendorf 1975, 517(A). *nfw* as a variant of *ṯ3w*: Kurth 1980, 1098. For the interpretation of *nfw* as exhalations: Bommas 1999, 60, footnote 150. *nfw* "souffle miasmatique": Germond 1981, 44–45 (n° 26); 76; 219; Goyon 2006, 88(12). *nfw* appears in *CT* VII, spell 1141g as a personified demon "Les démons des miasmes": Meeks 1978, 78.2084.

41 In the Naos of Decades, *dḥrt* is associated with breathing air while the sky is full of winds: von Bomhard 2008, 149.

42 Westendorf 1999, 387; 388; Vernus 1981, 94–95; Vernus 1982–1983, 121–122.

43 Vernus 1982–1983, 121. *dḥrt* as a demonical effect is translated "morbific air": von Bomhard 2008, 103; 288.

44 Germond 1981, 304–309.

45 For the meteorological sense of *nšny* to denote the raging of foul weather in storms: Faulkner 1962, 140. *nšny* as storms and thunders: Kurth 1986, 1266ff; te Velde 1967, 25; Lorton 1993, 126 (fn. 6); Leitz 1999, 37. *nšny* "The raging one" as a Sethian epithet of meteorological conotations: Zandee 1963, 147; Leitz 1994, 273; 346; 368; 384.

46 Lucarelli 2010, 4.

47 Hannig 2006, 675; Bardinet 1995, 518.

48 Erman and Grapow 1929 (= Wb 4), 62 (4–9); Wilson 1991, 1436, s.v. *sww*; Meeks 1979, 79.2464.

49 Meyer 1977, 256. *ḥwỉ* as the action of weapons: Wilson 1991, 1120–1121, s.v. *ḥw*. The variants *ḥwỉ* and *ḥwt* identify the action of rain to hit passengers: Roquet 1973, 158–159; Zivie 1984, 202 (3). The waves of sea also *ḥwỉ* "strike": Erman and Grapow 1928 (= *Wb* 3), 48-49; Lopez 1972, 111.

50 Leitz 2002d (= *LGG* 4), 353–354 [28].

51 Brent 2005, 260; Wilkinson 2003, 181. Sekhmet as a desert goddess who send epidemics with winds: Blumenthal 1970, 98 (B 6.13). *ṯ3w* is interpreted to evoke the fire sent by Sekhmet in the Book of Glorifying the Dead: Herbin 2004, 193 (II, 4–6).

52 Bommas 1999, 40; Leitz 1994, 207-208, n°2(3) evokes the sense of the Arabic term for the "plague": *taʿün* (طاعون) as a derivative from the Arabic verb *taʿana* (طعن) "to stab."

53 Nunn 1996, 59–60.

54 Faulkner 1962, 72; Thomas 1959, 102.

55 In *CT* II, spell 149, 237b, demons of Sekhmet are designated as arrows: Bommas 1990, 40, note 31; cf. pLeiden I 347, V, 2: "Sekhmet didn't shoot her Arrows against me." Meanwhile, the Twenty-second Dynasty at Bubastis, the form of a troop of "Seven Arrows": Rondot 1989, 249ff., esp. 264–267; Lucarelli 2011, 121–122.

56 In the *sḥtp Sḫmt* ritual, *wdỉ* describes the action of sending miasmatic breaths: Goyon 2006, 86 (text 9, lines 13-14); 88(n°12). For the connotations of *wdỉ nfw*: Rondot 1989, 256 (n. f); *wdỉ* is the inimical action of demonic entities to put disease or any kind of evil into the person: Borghouts 1971, n° 2 (fn. 5); Koenig 1979, 110 (g; e).

57 Ghalioungui 1968, 40; for details about this argument and their evidence in texts: Megahed 2016, 177, s.v. *mdwt*; 235, s.v. *šsrw*.

58 For the fiery breath of Sekhmet, Wilson cites that the *sḫm* scepter is "offered to Nephthys in her

capacity as a fire breathing goddess who is thus equated with Sakhmet": Wilson 1991, 1600, s.v. *sḫm*; cf. a dangerous place in *CT* IV, 329k is called "The fiery breath from the mouth of *Sḫmt*": Zandee 1960, 214.

59 Leitz 2002f (= *LGG* 6), 681c, s.v. *stw-šsrw.sn-m-rꜣ.sn*[1].

60 For the dispersal of diseases through the mouths of demons: Aufrère 1985, 29. Demonic entities cause death through their morbid breaths identified with verb *tpỉ* "to breathe," a term that is also related to actions done by the mouth, such as "to spew out" or "to be spat upon": Erman and Grapow 1930 (= *Wb* 5), 296 (3–4); Faulkner 1962, 298. Gods seize people in the act of taking a breath: Edwards 1960, 54 (39).

61 Von Lieven 2000, 24 (fn. 82); Bommas 1999, 36; 41.

62 Leitz 2002b (= *LGG* 2), 366b. *wpwtyw-m-ḫt-spꜣwt* as an indication for the astral manifestation of demons who would be seen in the sky from different locations on earth: von Lieven 2000, texts 400 and 406; Valloggia 1976, 56 (§108.4). The expression *m-ḫt spꜣwt* explains the sense of spreading effects everywhere: Herbin 2004, 186 (footnote 63).

63 Leitz 2002f (= *LGG* 6), 588c, s.v. *sḫsw-ḫt-tꜣ*.

64 It is held that Galen's concept built upon the knowledge of the ancient Egyptian medical school: Steuer and Saunders 1959, 68f.

65 For the role of disease carried by breaths in the ancient Egyptian etiological theory: Yoyotte 1968, 79ff, esp. 82; Vernus 1982–1983, 121ff.; cf. the argument about the similarity of the impact of winds in ancient Egypt to the "pneuma" of the Greeks: Ghalioungui 1968, 40. The belief of the ability of winds and breaths to cause disease is strikingly still kept in nowadays Egyptian popular heritage; the expressions " لفحة هوا " in the sense of "blight of air" and " أخذ هوا " in the sense of "he took air" are common to express that someone is ill because of being exposed to air. The verb "اتنفس" "a breath affected him" and the term " منفوس " "being affected by a breath" are used to describe the condition of someone suffering from troubles that are commonly understood as the effect of an evil being: Ghalioungui 1968, 40.2; 41.1.

66 Nunn 1996, 49.

67 Germond 1981, 290–291. Cf. in the ritual of *sḥtp Sḫmt*, Sekhmet launches the threat of the *iꜣdt-rnpt* by sending winds, Germond 1981, 289.

68 Vernus 1981, 94 (fn. 16).

Journal of Ancient Egyptian Interconnections

Symbolae Sacrae: Symbolic Formulae for Protection and Adoration within the Quarries of Gebel el-Silsila

Maria Nilsson
Department of Archaeology and Ancient History, Lund University

Abstract
Within the quarries of Gebel el-Silsila is a vast amount of unique symbolic representations: stylized iconographic and pseudo-scripted signs and marks that to some extent signify deities and their protection against demons, evil and mishaps. Like written protective formulae, these marks were placed within the quarries to symbolically safekeep the ancient workers and express gratitude once the work had been completed. This paper aims to present a selection of quarry marks that can be associated with the metaphorical world of the ancients (chiefly early Roman), with focus on assigned protective deities, the ever-assimilating daemon Shaï, apotropaic figures, and marks used for protection, adoration, respect, and gratefulness. It is an attempt to broaden the perspective of traditionally accepted ancient apotropaia and to incorporate superstitious representations communicated by a group of hardworking quarrymen at Gebel el-Silsila. The material presented is based on preliminary conclusions.

Introduction

The ancient site (including sandstone quarries) of Gebel el-Silsila lies approximately 65 km north of Aswan and is divided into east and west sides by the Nile at its narrowest point. Like many other sites in the Nile Valley, the rock and quarry faces of Gebel el-Silsila were attractive to rupestral inscribers over several millennia, the results ranging from Epipalaeolithic petroglyphs to modern graffiti, such as "Vive la France" written by one of Napoleon's scientific members. The epigraphic documents with which the current paper will be concerned are primarily located on the eastern side of the Nile, dispersed over six quarries, chronologically spanning from the Ramesside period to the reign of Emperor Claudius. Documents included here are part of a larger corpus which comprises over 5,000 quarry marks and over 800 Greek, Demotic, and Latin texts.

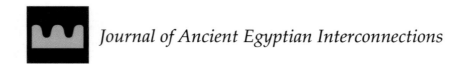

Friedrich Preisigke and Willhelm Spiegelberg incorporated in their 1915 publication a register of Egyptian deities attested in Greek and demotic inscriptions at Gebel el-Silsila.[1] Included therein are the Egyptian gods Amun, Hathor, Horus, Isis, Khnum, and Montu, the *genius loci* Pachimesen, and the obscure anguiform deity Shaï/Psais.[2] Since its start in 2012 the Swedish-led archaeological project has added numerous inscriptions and some divine names to those previously documented, many of which have been abbreviated as "quarry marks."[3] Gods added to the previously recorded list of deities include Bes, Min, Thoth, Tutu, and the Greek goddesses Tyche and Athena.[4] The aim here is to present a selection of quarry marks, focusing on those representing assigned protective deities, apotropaic figures, and marks used for protection, adoration, respect, and gratefulness. It is an attempt to broaden the perspective of traditionally accepted ancient apotropaia and to incorporate superstitious representations communicated by a group of hard-working men within the quarries of Gebel el-Silsila. The material presented is based on preliminary conclusions.

Terminological Issues

With the increased academic attentiveness to "pseudo script"[5] and non-textual marking systems,[6] quarry marks have been recognized for their symbolic, non-literal character, included under the thematic corpus of "identity marks" together with graphic signs on seals, ceramic vessels, ostraca, and graffiti in temples and tombs.[7] Quarry marks appear in abundance throughout Egypt, located within the quarryscape and on extracted blocks placed within monuments, and sandstone ostraca, but similar to other graphic signs they had not been studied systematically (until now), consequently resulting in plausible misconceptions of their significations. Summarising: three main categories of signification have been proposed previously, including practical signs used for transportation and positioning,[8] linguistic application,[9] and religious purposes.[10] Terminology and definitions, trivial as they may appear, are direct results of the interpretation of meaning and function, and are intertwined in possible misconceptions. Based on the over 5,000 marks documented and studied at Gebel el-Silsila, it appears that all three categories are accounted for, some simultaneously. However, if so, how shall the marks be designated?

Influenced by his linguistic premise, George Legrain was vigilant and elusive in designating the marks as "inscriptions," "peculiar characters," and "mark or inscription."[11] Spiegelberg inconclusively described them as "Zeichnungen," "Symbole," "Zeichen," and "Steinmetzmarken."[12] Others simply defined the marks as "graffiti," or, without further reasoning, entitled the marks as "quarry marks."[13] In actuality, this inconclusive trend remains: Caminos,[14] Klemm and Klemm,[15] and the author of the current paper favour the generic term "quarry mark," which is considered to encompass all non-textual, historical markings (disregarding prehistoric rock art) at Gebel el-Silsila simply because the marks, regardless of signification or type of execution, are all located within or adjacent with a quarry.

The sporadic reference to "graffiti"[16] is here considered inappropriate as its etymological significance (*graffiato* "scratched") habitually refers to any kind of textual or graphic inscription scratched, engraved, carved, scribbled, painted, or drawn.[17] In this sense, graffiti may range from simple scratched marks, *dipinti* or *tituli picti*, to extravagant painted scenes, and thereby encompass a vast group. Moreover, graffiti are habitually considered spontaneous, informal, arbitrary, ephemeral, and unsophisticated creations, and therefore treated with less respect and attention compared with more formal epigraphic documents.[18] The quarry marks at Gebel el-Silsila may appear personal and non-official, but they were well prepared, some with preparatory guide- or gridlines drawn prior to incision, and spatially they are well arranged. Text and pictorial representations coexisted, and were produced correspondingly, consistently supporting the message communicated within the larger epigraphic context. Seen in the light of the current paper, it can also be asked if the quarry marks indeed should be considered informal when addressing the divine pantheon in a more profound statement, also recalling that the workers were sent out on behalf of the official temple for which the stone was extracted. Certainly, it is essential to acknowledge the symbolic impact of an ancient quarryman thanking the local god or demon for his protection by engraving a mark or text, visible and forever viewable within the very landscape he desired to be protected from.[19]

Taking it one step further, "graffiti," if following Peden's category of "a form of [written] communication that is invariably free of social restraints,"[20] cannot be applied to either quarry marks or texts at Gebel el-Silsila, as the inscribers were not only aware of preexisting rupestral activity, but they also conformed to certain rules with regard to the text *and* graphic formulae they applied. Furthermore, spatially, ancient graffiti have been tacitly defined by scholars as graphic or textual representations that occur in unpredicted locations, without any easily explainable reason for the modern viewer.[21] However, what appear to a modern viewer as unexpected had most likely a sensible explanation for the ancient inscriber.[22] In this respect, a modern viewer may find him/herself amazed, but perplexed, when endeavouring to comprehend why ancient inscribers engraved their epigraphic memorandum 40 m above the current ground. Still, what today appears as a straight-cut vertical cliff was once a step-system with extended platforms from which the blocks were extracted and lowered down.[23] Obviously, the inscriber was not pending in thin air, but stood steadily on the cliff. As the steps were extracted, the men were provided with new, fresh surfaces to communicate their messages—at times a formula expressing gratefulness to endure—for which there are texts and images all over the full heights and widths of each quarry face.

Form and Style

The quarry marks' stylistic forms are individually comparable with hieroglyphs, Greek letters, concrete images such as zoomorphic and anthropomorphic figures, architectural components, boats and technical sketches, cosmic representations, fauna, weaponry and tools, abstract geometrical patterns, and a few unidentified characters. They were carefully engraved with a single or double outline, predominantly in sunken relief. Examples of bas-relief and *dipinti* exist too. They rarely appear as singular marks, but rather in series containing up towards twenty marks. Generally, they measure between 10 cm up to 175 cm in height. They are present in all cardinal directions, over the full heights and width of the quarry faces within all Roman quarries at Gebel el-Silsila, although with higher occurrence in quarries Q24, 34–37, at times over 200 marks on one quarry face, or over 3,000 marks within one quarry!

New Interpretations

Taking into consideration the enormous size of Gebel el-Silsila, it is not unexpected to find a multiplicity of marking systems that were used for miscellaneous purposes, having manifold and simultaneous meanings, and applied during different chronological periods. However, from at least the 19th Dynasty, and indubitably during the Graeco-Roman period, an orientation is noticeable towards a sense of superstitious, apotropaic or religious images, indicating that different deities were regarded as local protectors of different quarries.[24] Thus far, approximately twenty deities have been identified within the quarry marking system, of which some are concrete depictions of Bes, Harpocrates, Horus, Min, Ptah, Shaï, Thoth, Tutu, and a figure that may have been envisioned as a representation of the anguiform demon Abraxas.[25]

As an alternative to the clearly identifiable depictions of deities, although often used simultaneously and occasionally located adjacently, a series of gods and demons were displayed within the quarries in a more emblematic form, i.e., a deity was signified by a stylistic symbol that emphasised a characteristic personal element, and often gathered from traditional iconography.[26] Additionally, there are lapidary references, adorations, and dedicatory formulae (Greek, Latin, and Demotic) addressing divine beings.

Table 1 is a simplified diagram displaying the spatial distribution of emphasized quarry marks at Gebel el-Silsila, while Table 2 shows established associations between quarry (origin), ascribed deities and demons (text and image), and temple (destination). Deities or demons that are represented pictorially and without either clarifying texts or further iconography, or archaeological context may be difficult to analyse in the terms of why they were chosen as an object to illustrate. This being so, the interpreter is confined to their traditional mythological roles and religious significance as documented elsewhere, preferably within a parallel environment. One aforesaid example is the dwarf-god Bes, who was depicted twice as complete anthropomorph and in several abbreviated forms revealing only his face/mask.

Bes—Protector of Human and Divine

Thus far, the earliest indication of an apotropaic marking repertoire is found in a quarry (GeSE.Q23) situated in the central part of the east bank. Adjacent quarries were exploited during the 18th and 19th Dynasties respectively, and, based on its displayed quarrying technique, ceramic fragments, and contiguous quarry marks, it is reasonable to suggest a 19th Dynasty *terminus post quem* for this motif. The depiction shows Bes, characteristically facing forward with a protruding tongue, exaggerated eyes, rounded ears, an accentuated navel, and a triangular-shaped tail between his legs.[27] He wears his notable feather plumage and holds a tambour. The half-meter-tall figure is situated on a west-facing part of the quarry. No supporting texts or adjoining images were documented.

When the Romans under Tiberius later resumed work in an adjacent quarry (GeSE.Q24) they reproduced the dwarf-god in a simplified style with less iconographical details compared with the previous example.[28] There were no defining associated texts or comparable images found within this quarry to explain the significance of placing Bes there.

The Main Quarry, Q34C, displays in total five representations of Bes-figures from the time of Emperor Augustus (27 BCE–AD 14 CE), divided into 1) anthropomorphs, and 2) Bes-masks. One of the more enigmatic figures is an anthropomorphic representation of a Bes-figure holding Roman keys (Fig. 1). He is positioned in a standing pose, oriented

Table 1: Spatial and chronological distribution of quarry marks at Gebel el-Sisila East.

Chronological Key: 18th, 19th = Dynasties; L = Late Period; G = Greek; R = Roman				
Quarry No. (GeSE)	**Relative Date of Quarry**	**Number of Quarry Marks**	**Characteristic/ Emphasized Mark(s)**	**Textual Inscriptions**
Q12	G–R	25		X
Q13	G–R	15	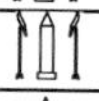	X
Q14	18th, G–R	8		X
Q15[a]	18th, G–R	6		
Q19	18th, L–R	13	 Roman Eagle	X
Q20	19th–R	11	  	
Q21	19th–L	12	  	
Q22[b]	19th–L	35	  	
Q23	19th–L	11		
Q24	18th, G–R	109	 	
Q26	18th, G–R	3	No emphasised mark	
Q27	L	12		
Q28	L–R	2		
Q31	19th, G–R	26	No emphasised mark	X
Q32	19th	14		
Q33	19th, G–R	26	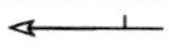 temple furniture	X
Q34	19th, G–R	3,090+95[c]	(N)   (S)	X
Q35	R	176	 	X
Q36	R	21		
Q37	R	335	  	X
Q38	G–R	1		
Q39	G–R	6	Uncategorised	X
Q40	G–R	5	Figure of Amun(?) 	X
Q46	19th–R	7		X
Q48	18th–R	2	No emphasised mark	X

Notes

[a] Includes three marks recorded on boulders above the quarry.

[b] Fifteen marks have been recorded within Quarry 22, but the total number given here also includes marks located in an adjacent wadi with a series of rocky outcrops where another 20 marks were found.

[c] Ninety-five quarry marks were recorded on extracted blocks left within the quarry.

TABLE 2: Spatial and chronological distribution of quarry marks at Gebel el-Sisila East.

QUARRY MARK	IDENTIFIED DEITY	QUARRYING FOR THE "TEMPLE OF [...]"	"QUARRY OF [...]	IDENTIFIED GEOGRAPHIC DESTINATION	QUARRY NO. (GESE)
	Bes	–	–	–	Q23
	Harpocrates	Montu	Montu	Medamoud	Q24
	Pachimesen	Horus Behedet	Horus, Hathor, Pachimesen	Edfu	Q34. A–D
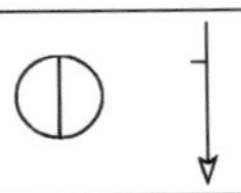	Hathor, Horus (and Harsomtus)	–	Hathor, Horus, Harsomtus	Dendera	Q34. C6–15
	Bes	–	Hathor, Horus, Harsomtus	Dendera	Q34. C12–15
	Khnum	Khnum	Amun	Esna	Q34.S
	Isis; Min	Isis	Min	Coptos	Q35
	Isis	–	–	–	Q36
	Isis	Isis	Amun	Coptos	Q37

towards the right/south. The engraving was produced with a metal tool in a single outline. The face displays traditional characters of Bes-figures, including wide eyes, a large and flat nose, protruding ears, and projecting tongue. Unconventionally, the figure is depicted with regular, straight legs. Three Roman keys are depicted in the figure's immediate context; one is handheld in front of the figure, another resting on the figure's shoulders, and a third—unattached to the figure—slightly below to the left. An ambiguous iconographic element is located to the figure's right, possibly representing a bird or a wing. The pictorial context includes a figure of Harsomtus.

The Roman keys, consisting of a looped lower terminus/handle and one row of three to four teeth, also appear as individual quarry marks, always located in a pictorial context containing lined circles, harpoons, and imagery associated with Horus, Hathor, or Harsomtus (tutelary deities of Dendera). The key is here interpreted as an abbreviation symbol for Bes.

In addition to the complete anthropomorphic representations of Bes, there are various illustrations of almost circular faces, generally known as Bes-masks (FIG. 2),[29] all depicted with emphasised eyes and nose, protruding ears, and occasionally pointed hair. At first, these images appear smiling with a large, open mouth, but as representations of Bes, this smile should be seen as a protruding tongue, and the pointed hair as his feather crown.

The representations may indicate that the dwarf-god had a role as a protector of quarrymen, conceived to prevent them from mishaps during their work, keeping them safe from dangerous vipers and cobras in his role as defender of evil.[30] Comparable examples found outside of Gebel el-Silsila were found in Hatshepsut's limestone quarry at Qurna[31] and in the sandstone quarry of el-Kilh support such generalization.[32] However, none of these illustrations brought forward any additional information of as to why Bes was favoured by quarrymen.

Returning to Gebel el-Silsila, contextual, intriguing references to Harpocrates as the son of Montu and Raet-tawi have been documented in quarry

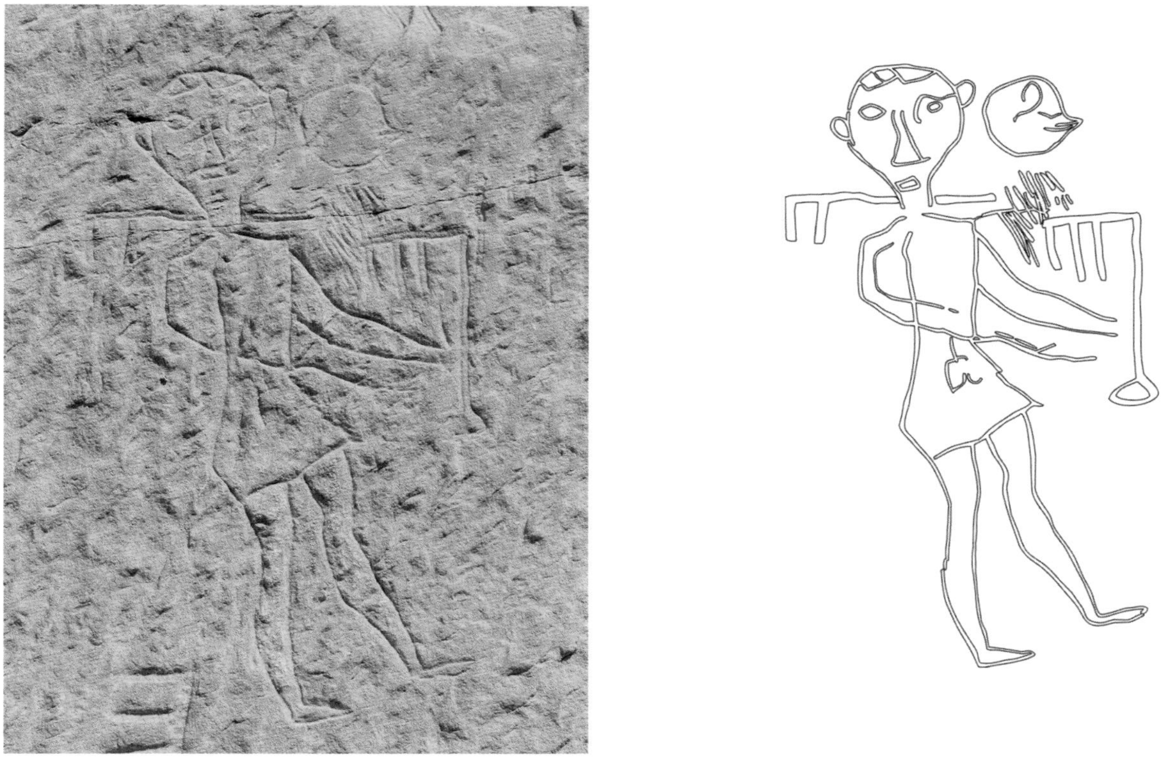

Figure 1: Anthropomorphic representation of a Bes-figure holding Roman keys. .

Figure 2: Example of a so-called Bes-mask as represented at Gebel el-Silsila.

GeSE.Q24, and to Harsomtus, son of Horus and Hathor, in quarry GeSE.Q34C, plausibly indicating also more symbolic reasoning for Bes' presence there, to take the role as the protector of the divine youngster.[33] The Main Quarry, furthermore, presents complete iconographic representations of the young Harsomtus in a barge, and the only known example of a "Cippus" engraved into a quarry face,[34] both incised adjacently with Bes-masks. For the understanding of the comprehensive iconographic repertoire displayed in quarry partition GeSE.Q34C, the Bes-figures present a window into the apotropaic signification, i.e., protection per se, and also as supportive evidence in determining the predestined final destination of the stones extracted: Dendera for Q34C and Medamoud for Q24.[35]

Min—Shaï of the Mountain

Min is found in iconographic form in two quarries (GeSE.Q34-35) dated to the reigns of Augustus/Tiberius and Claudius, respectively.[36] One illustration shows an anthropomorph located approximately 14 m above the current ground level in quarry GeSE.Q34S.[37] It shows an abridged ithyphallic standing figure facing left. Its details are limited to a body, head, legs, arms and phallus, with no indicative context to suggest signification.

Appreciatively, the second example is supplemented with a demotic inscription, located on a vertical, east-facing surface, approximately 1.5 m above the ground level within GeSE.Q35 (Fig. 3).[38] The depiction is meticulous in its decoration and skilfully carved: it shows an engraved ithyphallic, mummified figure of Min in the standing position, legs together, facing right/north: he holds a flagellum, wears a pectoral and collars around his neck, and is depicted with a beard and crowned with the double feather plume. The demotic text describes him as "Min, the great god" in "year 10 of Claudius, Thoth 1, the beginning of the year." The scene displays a *sḫn*-shrine connected to a *sḫnt*-pole, which gives emphasis to the bull aspect of Min and the ritual of climbing the Min-pole.[39] Even though Min's assimilation with Kamutef habitually signifies fertility, its alternative meaning is preferred here, linked with the New Year as cited in the demotic text. The small clover-like illustrations (which do not appear elsewhere) were perhaps intended to characterise lettuce. Min's role within this quarry was a *genius loci*, the "Shaï of the Mountain."

Although Min's role has been clarified, his abbreviation symbol—quarry mark—remains ambiguous and obscure. While having semiotic resemblances with a stylized bow and arrow, it can best be described as a D-shape with a horizontal line running through it. One example is located below the Min-scene mentioned above, but it generally appears as an isolated motif. It was also documented as a single mark on a stone ostracon found on the floor in GeSE.Q35. At present, there is no convincing correlation between form and significance of the quarry mark other than its link with Min, possibly accentuating his ithyphallic form.

The quarrymen turned to Min for his protective aspect, stressed in his association with Shaï, the good demon of the mountain. As the god of wild places, Min was a plausible god to call upon for protection, similar to Min-Pan in the Eastern Desert.[40]

Shaï—O Fortune!

Preisigke and Spiegelberg considered the rather abstract deity Shaï a protective being generally associated with the Alexandrian Agathos Daimon.[41] As such, "Shaï" was chiefly applied as an epithet or determinative to stress a vigilant aspect of another, more dominant god. However, Shaï also appears, albeit rarely, as an alone-standing entity, defining "Good Fate of the quarry,"[42] and being included in the formula "may the beautiful name remain here before Shaï."[43]

Shaï also appears as graphic representations. One image shows a risen, partially coiled serpent facing right/east, wearing a solar disk upon its head. The snake surmounts a standard-like object as a figurehead attached to the high, curved bow of a large barque.[44] The terminus of the barque's stern is shaped as an antelope's head, and a large, single steering oar is fastened to the hull, operated from a cabin. A series of oars is illustrated below the stern. The barque itself is moored to a quay. Contextual iconography includes a harpoon, and two unpublished demotic texts were dedicated to (Shaï-)Pachimesen.[45]

As a protective force, the "Good Fate of the quarry" does not require further explanations as to why the workers required this divine being's presence.

Pachimesen—Harpooning His Enemy

The name "Pachimesen" has previously been translated as "He of the uplifting of the harpoon,"[46] but it rather reads "Pachois, the Harpooner,"[47] and its semiotic structure advocates an association with Horus as the Lord of Mesen ("Harpoon City"),[48] as

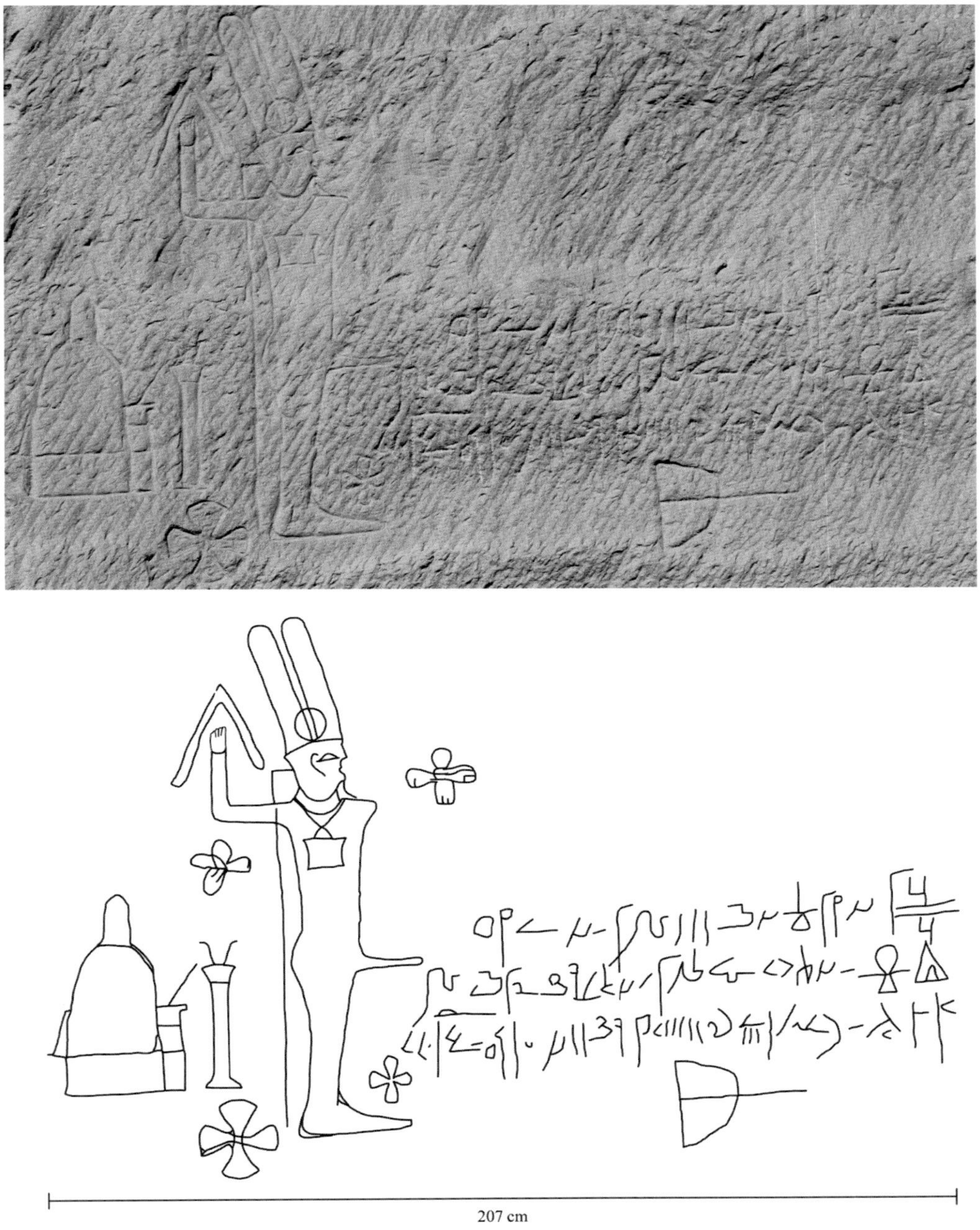

Figure 3: Original and facsimile of scene with "Min, the great god" in year 10 of Claudius.

well as being related to Horus the child (the Harpooner).[49] Within GeSE.Q34 numerous texts are dedicated to Pachimesen, and recent field-work has revealed that the workers expressed their devotion to this divine patron also by means of a quarry mark, symbolised with a toggle harpoon.[50]

The quarry mark corpus in GeSE.Q34A–D is dominated by harpoons, which make up more than half of the total number of marks. For example, the eastern partition's 739 harpoons constitute 47% of the total amount of marks there. The harpoon is habitually grouped with other harpoons, hourglasses, and lined circles. The combination of a harpoon and a lined circle may be used as indication of a predestined temple area; as such arrangement is documented also within sandstone blocks at Dendera.[51]

The harpoon is also represented as an iconographic element in a larger composition, held by anthropomorphic, falcon-headed figures. These figures are repeatedly represented wearing Roman attire and occasionally the double crown. One example depicts a falcon-headed anthropomorph, crowned and seated on a throne with a snake curled behind his shoulder while harpooning a crocodile below the throne: this is the only known representation of a "Cippus" within a sandstone quarry.[52] Other examples exclude the anthropomorph completely, leaving a representation of a harpoon inserted into the back of a crocodile (FIG. 4). Together, these illustrations clarify the harpoon's signification as a symbol of Pachimesen and an abbreviated form of the characteristic victorious scene of Horus defeating evil in which the harpoon is his symbol.[53] For the same reasons, it may be theorised that the falcon-headed Roman legionnaires[54] represent Pachimesen too when situated within this quarry. Reading the quarry mark as an identity mark of Pachimesen there are literary hundreds of attestations of how important the daemon's protection was for the workers. It should be added that the stone extracted from this quarry was intended mainly for the Temple of Horus in Edfu[55] and in parts for early Roman structures at Dendera (Mammisi, unfinished enclosure wall, and the eastern gate).[56]

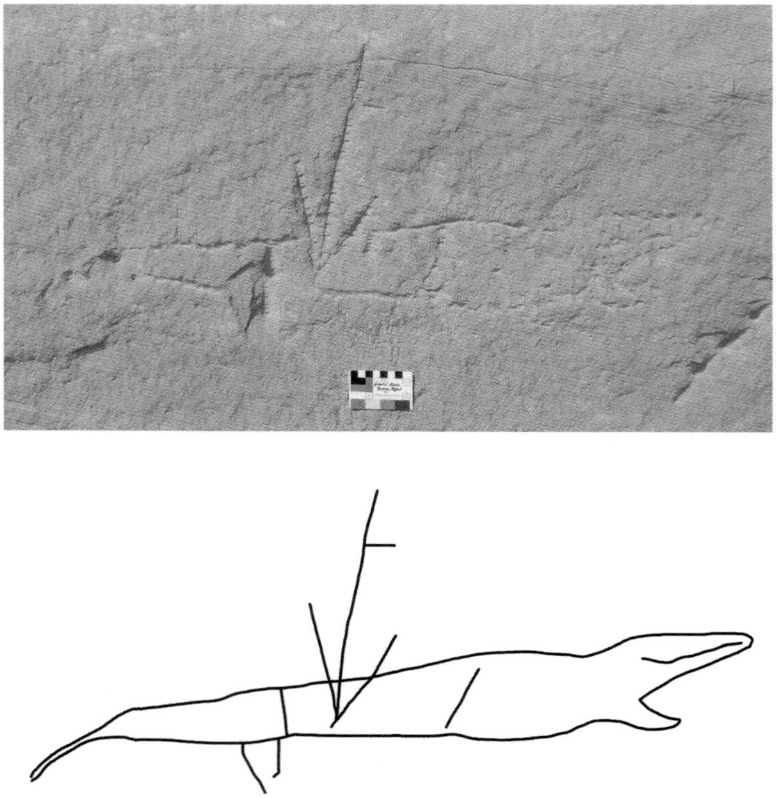

FIGURE 4: Original and facsimile of a quarry mark showing a harpooned crocodile.

Isis—Milking the Gods

In addition to the prominent Min scene mentioned above, GeSE.Q35 displays a pictorial repertoire dominated by *situlae*, a recognised attribute of mother-goddesses, principally Isis.[57] In contrast to her "quarry- and temple-sharing" divine spouse, Min, Isis was not depicted as a complete anthropomorph in the quarry but was commemorated instead by several textual dedications, including a *proskynema*-inscription (GeSE.Q35.C.In.5) dated to "year 9, 1 Mesore" of Claudius (23 July 23 CE), which pronounces a quarry worker as the "craftsman of Isis."[58] The inscription is not only bordered by two *situlae*, but their signification is emphasised in the Greek word γλα ("milk"), written adjacently to the *situlae* (Fig. 5).

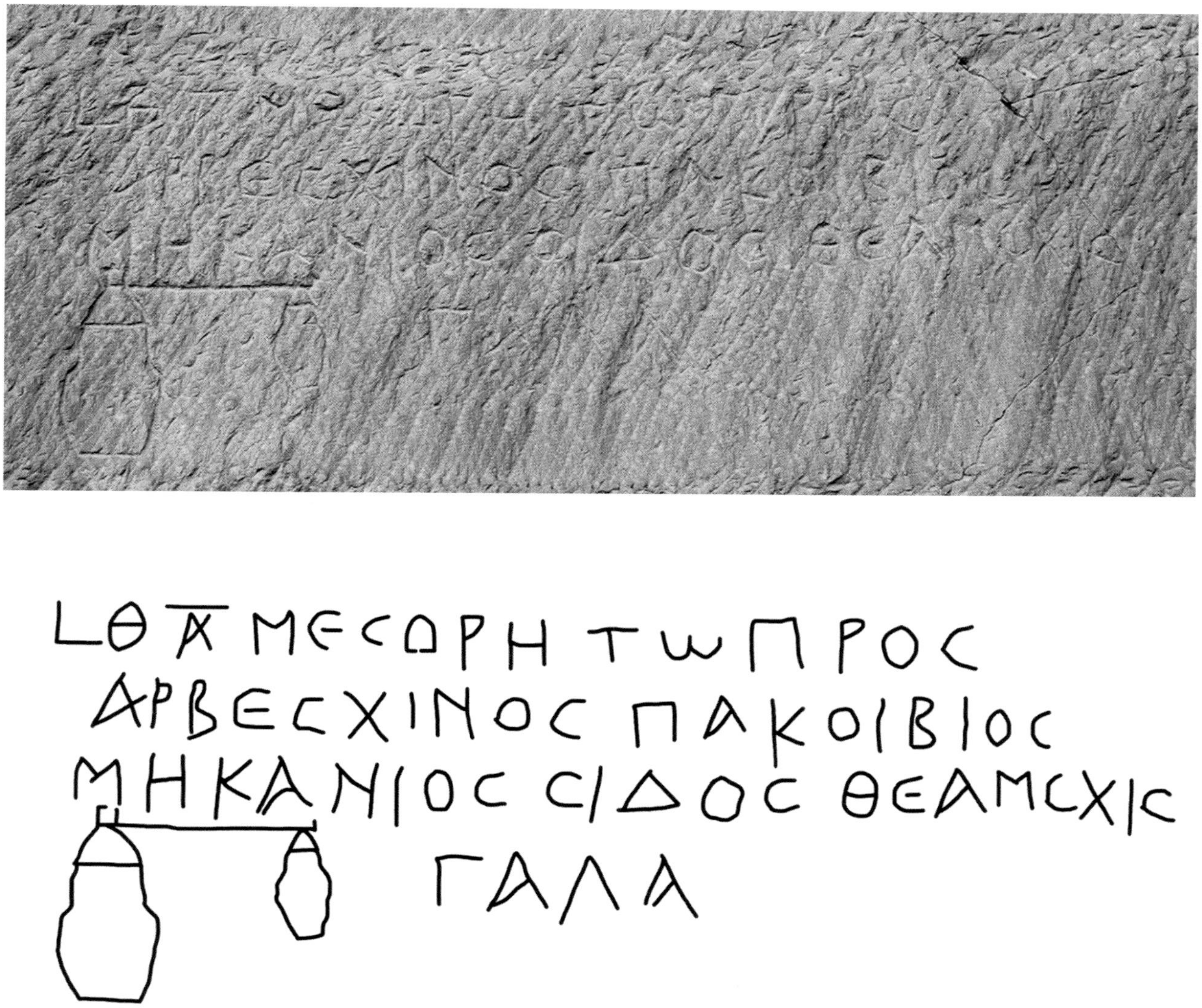

Figure 5: Proskynema-inscription from the reign of Claudius with two situlae depicted to the left. The vessels are described to contain milk.

Associated with the textual dedication[59] and graphic *situlae* is an anguiform represented thrice within the quarry. They show a risen, somewhat arched, schematic serpent crowned with a blooming water lily. One of the examples is located next to a Greek signature.[60] The text itself makes known no signification of the serpents, but combined with dedications to Isis, the profession "workman of Isis," and the *situla*, as well as temporal and archaeological details indicating Coptos as the intended temple destination for the stone,[61] it may be postulated that the *situla* here defines Isis as the Lady of Coptos residing in Gebel el-Silsila and protecting the quarrymen.

Khnum (Chnoubis)—Protector or "Merely" God

Epigraphic references to Khnum are limited to the southern partitions of GeSE.Q34, including its associated Nile-side quay. The quarry mark repertoire is chiefly represented by stone vessels (Gardiner's W9; *ẖnm*), ankhs, and offering tables (Fig. 6). The quarry dates to the reigns of Augustus and Tiberius.[62]

The repertoire includes 157 ankhs, 128 vessels, and 79 offering tables, together making up 68% of the total amount of quarry marks displayed.[63] Similar to other quarry marks acting as abbreviation symbols, the context has to be explored in order to understand their signification(s). An illuminating

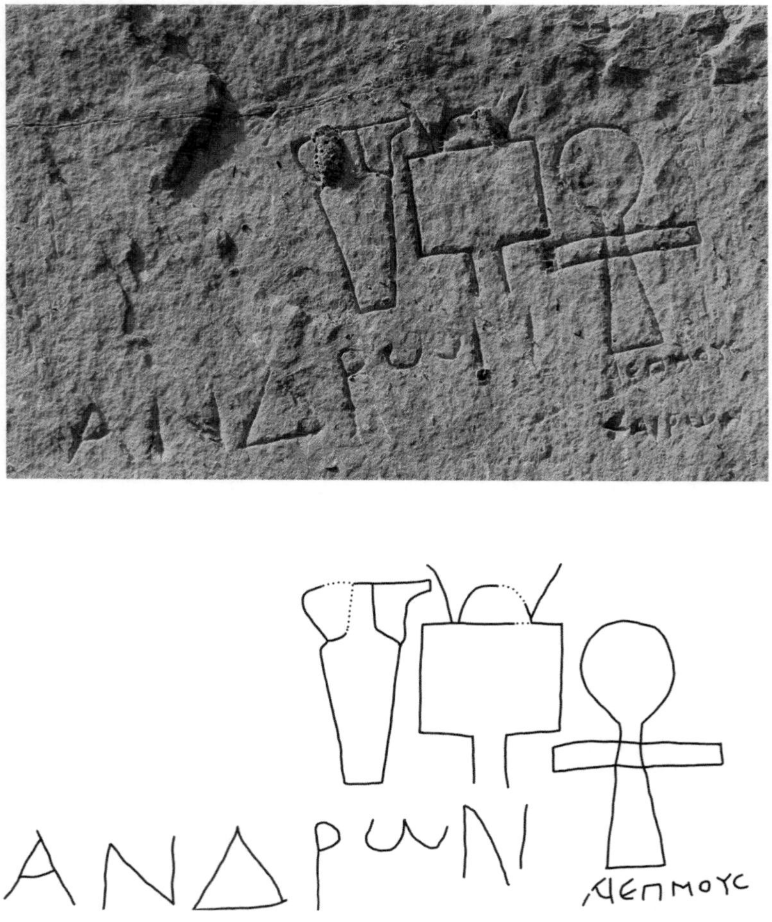

Figure 6: Example of quarry mark composition containing the stone vessel, which symbolised the god Khnum. Below the marks is a Greek signature belonging to an Andron.

candidate is found in the depiction of rams, shown zoomorphically, with curled horns and in a striding position.[64] Incorporating inscriptions, Greek and demotic texts make reference to Khnum in dedications and adorations and within the professions listed for individuals ("overseer of the work for Khnum" and "superintendent of the Temple of Khnum").[65] Moreover, a demotic inscription describes that the workers extracted stone for the construction of a "Temple of Khnum."[66] Tying the variables together, the vessel and ram are always located on quarry faces that also speak of Khnum.

Iconographically, Khnum is illustrated with a potter's wheel and sporadically holds a vessel containing the sacred Nile water; the god's connection with the vessel can be further clarified as the vessel marks the first hieroglyphic sign in the name of Khnum.[67] The vessel, as a consequence, may be symbolically associated with Khnum or with individuals working on behalf of the god and, thus, functions as an abbreviation symbol identifying a deity.

Tutu—Benevolent Defeater

Gebel el-Silsila displays several depictions of Tutu. A more prominent illustration[68] shows the sphinx-god in a lying position, facing south/right, holding a sword in his paws and wearing a crown upon his head. His body surmounts a snake. Another (unpublished and fragmentary) scene shows a lion-sphinx standing in a barge/boat. The lapidary context includes the name in demotic (Tutu) and Greek (Totoes/Tithoes). It may be argued that the inscriptions refer to a personal name rather than the deity,[69] but when written, the name is never followed by a patronym supporting this.

Although he was considered a dangerous demon, feared more than loved, the representations of Tutu in the quarry were likely to address the deity as a benevolent protector.[70] However, Tutu's signification within the quarry was not limited to one role. Indeed, his presence, discloses the predetermined destination for extracted blocks, as he forms a triad with Khnum and Neith (described as "Athena"),[71] suggesting Esna as the final destination.

Malevolent Anguiforms—Defeat the Demon!

Above was explored the positive character of divine protectors and demons of Good Fate, preventers of mishaps, and residing divinities of temples and quarries. However, the quarry mark repertoire also displays defeated snakes, sometimes in a form of a symbolic enigma or rebus, best represented in Figure 7: the scene includes three iconographic elements: a bird (ostrich or ibis), a horned viper, and an ankh. The bird is stood triumphant, surmounting a horned viper, with the life-sign located to their right. The scene

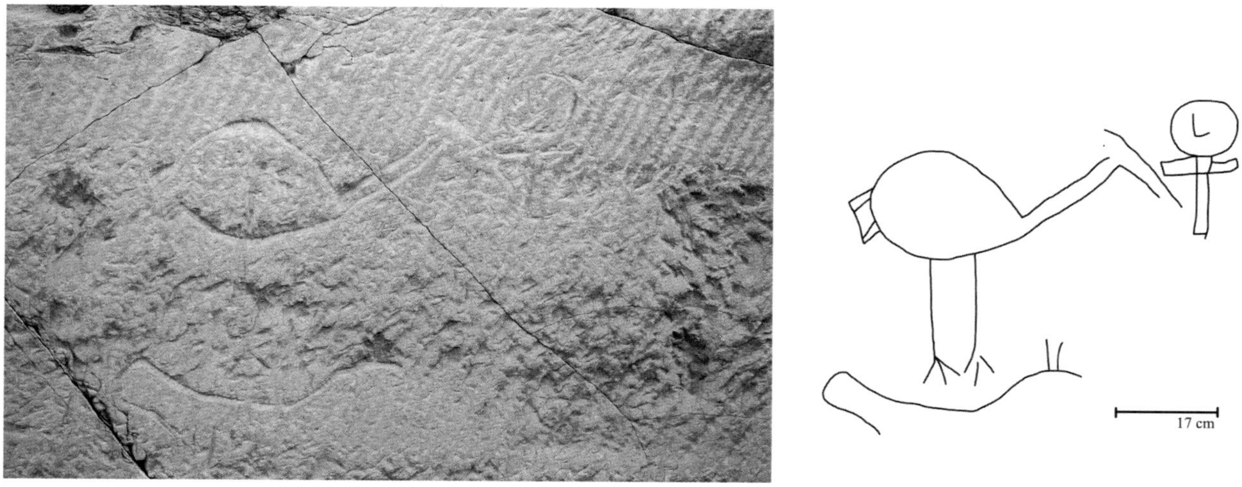

Figure 7: Quarry mark example of a rebus: a large bird (ostrich or perhaps ibis) stands victorious above a horned viper. To the right is the sign of life.

reasonably refers to a true event in which the bird fed on vipers,[72] and through its association with Thoth (ibis) or Amun (ostrich) had an apotropaic value in communicating the workers' plea to the god for protection or, alternatively, their gratitude after enduring the daily threat embedded in their milieu each day. The already mentioned depiction of Tutu recalls the theme of a predator surmounting a snake as a sign of tutelary force.

LIMINAL CREATURES

"AKEPHALOS," OR, RATHER, AN ANTHROPOFIED *ꞽIJ.Ṯ*-KNIFE

Gebel el-Silsila displays within its unique quarry mark register an extraordinary representation of what at first may appear as an *akephalos* (FIG. 8)—a headless (and armless) creature facing right/south with a centrally placed large eye and defined legs/feet—located approximately 15 m above the ground level at GeSE.Q34F2, which is equally home to the representations of Tutu and Khnum mentioned above. The illustration is situated within a rupestral context of signatures and *proskynemata*, and various graphic representations with an early Imperial Roman date (Augustus/Tiberius). Two unpublished adjoining inscriptions reveal two names, although they do not clarify the signification of the object. The pictorial context primarily focuses on iconography associated with the tutelary deities of Esna.

1. UNPUBLISHED GREEK INSCRIPTION GESE.Q34.F2.IN.61:

1. ΠΑΜ[...]
1. Παμ[ῆνες]
1. Pamenes

Commentary: Although unfinished, it may be postulated that the signature was intended as Pamenes, which is documented in demotic form at

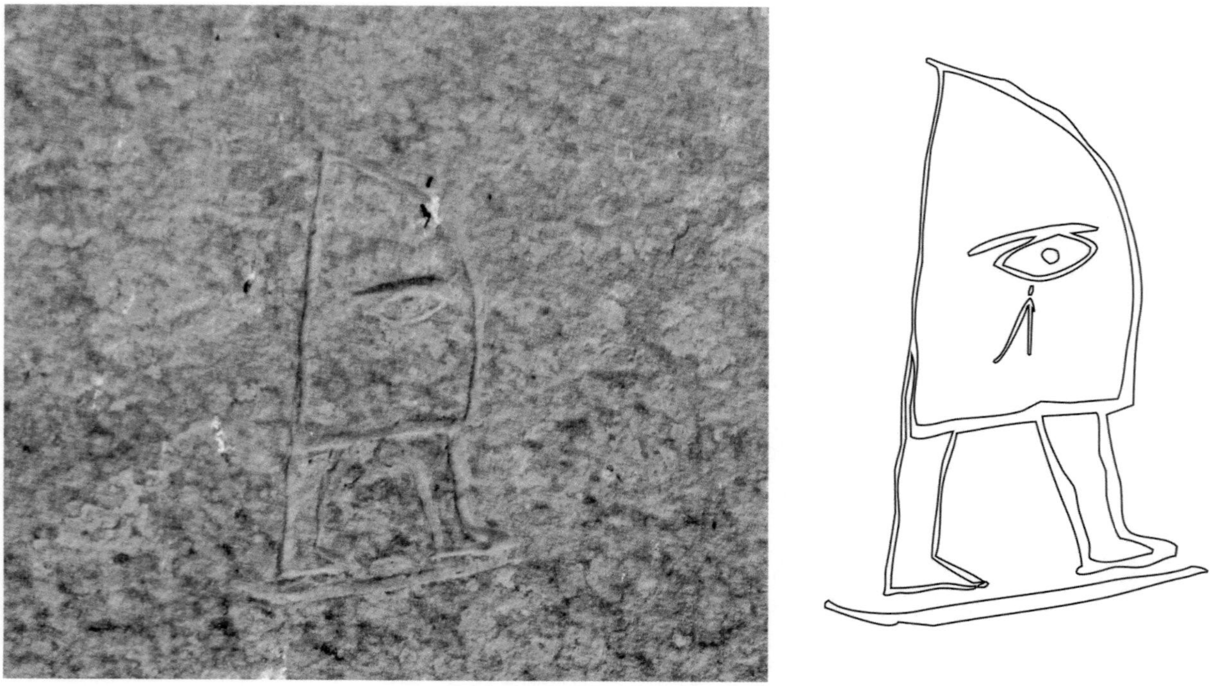

FIGURE 8: An *akephaos* or an anthropofied ceremonial knife?

adjacent GeSE.Q34.F3.[73] The text is located too high (c. 16.5 m) to measure its details.

2. Greek inscription GeSE.Q34.F2.In.62:

1. ΟΡCΕΝΟΥΦΟC ΠΑΧΝΟΥΒΙΟC
1. ᾿Ορσενουφ(ί)ος Παχνουβίος
1. (The proskynema) of Orsenouphos (son of) Pachnoubios

Commentary: The text is located too high (c. 15 m) to measure its details.[74] The spelling of Orsenouphios with an ending omicron instead of iota and omicron has no previous attestations. "Osenouphios," however, is attested at Gebel el-Silsila. "Pachnoubis" TM Name variant 12676 of "Pachnoumis", TM Name 674.

Without descriptive context, an identification of the figure must be found elsewhere, which is found at the eastern external wall, third register, of nearby Kom Ombo Temple (*Kom Ombos* II, 938).[75] The scene illustrates Sobek, fronted by a lion-headed wand to the left, and Haroeris, fronted by a monumental *ỉj.t*-knife to the right, the two objects being separated by a central hymn. The main object here is the monumental knife, oriented towards the left/south, facing Sobek. The knife stands on a small pedestal, depicted with a *Wḏꜣ.t*-eye and acting individually as a personification. The knife is attested again as a hieroglyphic sign in the hymn, and in two other scenes at Kom Ombo (*Kom Ombos* I, 138, 276), presented as an individual being rather than being limited to describing qualities of Haroeris.[76]

Martina Minas-Nerpel recently presented a summary and analysis of offering scenes in which the *ỉj.t*-knife is presented, incorporating reference from the Temples of Shenhûr, Philae, and Qus in addition to the Kom Ombo scenes.[77] She also adds a limestone stela from the Ägyptische Museum und Papyrussamlung in Berlin (ÄM 17549) that depicts Horus or Haroeris as a legionary accompanied by an individual *ỉj.t*-knife. She concluded that the *ỉj.t*-knife is closely associated with Haroeris in his role as combatant against Ra's enemies. However, while the knife is associated with Haroeris, Minas-Nerpel suggests that the object itself is a female personification, presumably of Hathor through the role as the Eye.[78]

Whether the knife can be interpreted as male or female here, it is plausible that it represents Haroeris, supported by adjacent depictions of Roman legionnaires. Haroeris may have been called upon for the protection and wellbeing of the quarrymen (plausibly by Pamenes and Orsenouphos) working or patrolling the area. Their wish, however, may not have lasted throughout the season, as a large section of the quarry wall collapsed during antiquity, halting all labour, after which extraction work was never resumed.

Anguiform Anthropomorph—Abraxas?

Located some 2 m above a ledge and c. 20.5 m above the ground level is an anthropomorph (Fig. 9a) depicted with avian facial features and dressed as a Roman legionnaire. This unpublished figure holds a shield in his left hand and a spear in his right hand. The character is represented in motion, plausibly running, or, alternatively, with snake-like legs (anguiped). Adjacent unpublished texts place the illustration towards the end of Augustus' reign.

There are various alternatives for signification. Firstly, if regarded an anguipede, it possesses similarities with later representations of Abraxas, the avian anguipede in Roman armour.[79] Many are the discussions on Abraxas' origin[80] and the signification of anguipedes, but few have considered an assimilation between the armed Horus and the anguiform Shaï. Such integration would be adequate in the pantheon at Gebel el-Silsila, in which Shaï often appears assimilated with the main god of the quarry.[81] However, identification with Abraxas becomes superfluous if considering the beak as belonging to a falcon rather than a cock.[82]

A second interpretation, which is preferred here, is presented if considering the figure within its context, including Figure 9b: Located immediately to the left of the anthropomorph is a rectangular illustration enclosing a Bes-mask depicted with characteristic facial features of the dwarf-god. The encompassing rectangle is internally segregated through a perpendicular line and two overlapping horizontal lines, which may signify the quarry (levels or blocks). Attached to its right is another rectangle, standing on its short end and intersected by two crossed diagonals. Based on its architectural

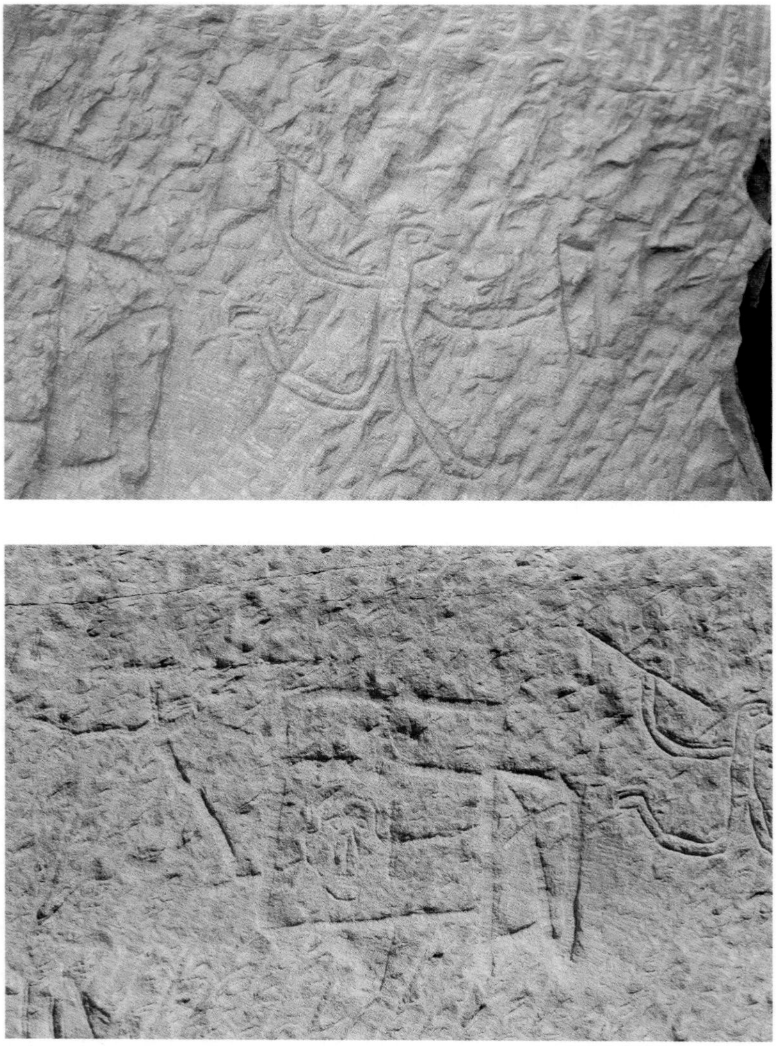

Figure 9: The running anguiform deity of Gebel el-Silsila in a complex scene perhaps representing the ceremonial opening of the quarry.

similarities with its physical surrounding, this smaller rectangle is likely to represent the very physical ledge into which the depiction has been engraved. In conclusion, it is here advocated that the illustration was intended to depict the physical quarry from which stone was extracted to construct a sacred building.[83]

Combining the representations—the physical quarry and the anthropomorph interpreted as a divine legionnaire (Horus/pharaoh)—a working thesis may be presented: It is generally known that the pharaoh, or a representative thereof, performed several rituals when constructing a new temple.[84] However, the individual quarries at Gebel el-Silsila were considered representatives of the temples for which stone was extracted.[85] It may, consequently, be argued that a form of ritual was performed already at the time of extraction. Thus, if the illustration of the "running" falcon-god is considered as representing the pharaoh, and its pictorial context as the physical quarry, could the scene signify a ritual devoted to the commencement of a new temple? Such a ritual may then, arguably, have included aspects of the pharaoh marking the area, or even "running" around the boundary markers to a certain extent comparable with rituals of the *heb-sed*.[86]

Concluding Remarks

This paper aimed to present a selection of quarry marks that can be associated with the metaphorical world of the ancients with focus on assigned protective deities, apotropaic figures, liminal beings, and marks used for protection, adoration, respect, and gratefulness. Included herein was a selection of a complex and diverse marking system at Gebel el-Silsila, the study of which is still in process. It has been acknowledged that the marks can be attributed with at least three different functions, including practical, linguistic, and religious meanings, which often were applied simultaneously. Evidently the "symbols" had a more profound and multifaceted significance than previously thought. A selection of the marks appears to have been used as abbreviations for deities and demons, while others were used as determinatives. Within the larger study of these marks, it is evident that the quarries were regarded as microcosms of the temple structure to which stone was extracted, containing the original divine "essence" later transformed into a sanctuary. The quarries housed not only the main god but also the entire triad, as summarised in Table 3.

However, identifying the individual deities of the triads is very similar to putting together a jigsaw puzzle, where all aspects of epigraphy and archaeology must be considered. Assembled, the puzzle reveals a wide array of religious applications and beliefs, but above all they express the workers' collective need for divine protection in their daily journey through a harsh and dangerous quarryscape. Each day they faced disastrous risks related to the extraction of the blocks that were earmarked for one or another of the sacred edifices of Upper Egypt. But also, they were constantly threatened by the forces of Mother Nature: the natural fauna in the form of snakes, crocodiles, and hippopotami constantly lurked nearby, and the men were close to defenceless against nature's forces such as sandstorms, extreme heat, and the yearly flooding.

Gods and demons were addressed in metaphorical formulae as either tutelary *genii loci* or as the object to be defeated. While representations of protective divinities are elaborated, defeated demons are depicted in a most simplified form. The examples included here indicate a complex religious or superstitious system, which reflects the fundamental life of a regular worker—to stay alive. For this they expressed their faith and asked for divine protection and uttered their gratefulness for safekeeping after completing a season. With horned vipers being a constant feature on site, and seen as demons of their

Table 3: Roman quarry marks series (east bank) and their relation with divine triads.

Quarry Mark Series	Divine Father	Divine Mother	Divine Child	Quarry No. (GeSE.) Geographic Destination
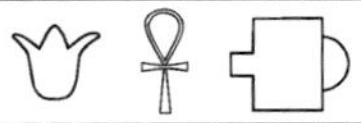	Montu	Raet-tawi	Harpocrates	Q24 Medamoud
	Pachimesen/ Horus the Elder	Hathor	Harsomtus	Q34.N Edfu and Dendera
	Khnum	Neith	Tutu	Q34.S Esna
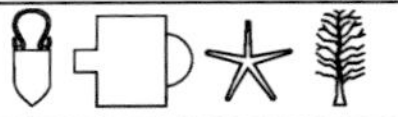	Amun-Min	Isis	Harpocrates	Q35 Coptos
	Amun-Min	Isis	Harpocrates	Q36 Coptos
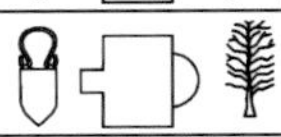	Amun-Min	Isis	Harpocrates	Q37 Coptos

time, it is easy to relate to the workers' choice in praying that the treacherous ally would remain beneficent. As the saying goes, "keep your friends close, but keep your enemies ['demons'] closer..."

Acknowledgements

I would like to express my gratitude to the entire Gebel el-Silsila team and to the financial patrons of the project, without whom this research would not be possible: Vetenskapsrådet (#2015-00291); Gerda Henkel Stiftung (#AZ 58-V-15; AZ 47/v/18); National Geographic Society (HJ-103R-17); Vitterhetsakademin (Enboms stiftelse); Magnus Bergvalls stiftelse; Längmanska stiftelsen; Lars Hiertas Minne; and Helge Ax:son Johnsons stiftelse, and all private patrons. Of course, I am also thankful to the Permanent Committee and the Ministry of Antiquities, Dr. Anani, Dr. Waziri, and Mr. Abdel Moniem, for allowing the team to continue the archaeological work at Gebel el-Silsila. As all previous publications, this paper is a result of complete cooperation—from start to end—with Mr. John Ward, assistant director to the project. Thus, thank you, John, for your support, ideas, discussions, and never-failing encouragement!

Abbreviations

CDD	Johnson 2001.
Kom Ombos	de Morgan et al. 1895–1909.

References

Arnold, Felix. 1990. *The Control Notes and Team Marks: The South Cemetery of Lisht*, vol. 2. New York: Metropolitan Museum of Art.

Aston, David. 2009. "Theban Potmarks—Nothing Other than Funny Signs? Potmarks from Deir el-Medineh and the Valley of the Kings." In B. J. J. Haring and O. E. Kaper (eds.), *Pictograms or Pseudo Script? Non-textual Identity Marks in Practical Use in Ancient Egypt and Elsewhere: Proceedings of a Conference in Leiden, 19-20 December 2006*, 49–65. Leiden: Brill.

Baird, J. A. 2011. "The Graffiti of Dura-Europos: A Contextual Approach." In J. A. Baird and Claire Taylor (eds.), *Ancient Graffiti in Context*, 65–66. New York and London: Routledge.

—— and Claire Taylor. 2011. "Ancient Graffiti in Context: Introduction." In J. A. Baird and Claire Taylor (eds.). *Ancient Graffiti in Context*, 4–5. New York and London: Routledge.

—— and —— (eds.). 2011. *Ancient Graffiti in Context*. New York and London: Routledge.

Blackman, A. M. and H. W. Fairman. 1944. "The Myth of Horus at Edfu: II. C. The Triumph of Horus over His Enemies: A Sacred Drama (Concluded)." *Journal of Egyptian Archaeology* 30: 5–22.

Bonner, Campbell. 1950. *Studies in Magical Amulets: Chiefly Graeco-Egyptian*. Ann Arbor: University of Michigan Press.

Budka, Julia, Frank Kammerzell, and Sławomir Rzepka (eds.), *Non-Textual Marking Systems in Ancient Egypt (and Elsewhere)*. Lingua Aegyptia Studia Monographica 16. Hamburg: Widmaier Verlag.

Caminos, Ricardo and Thomas G. H. James. 1963. *Gebel es-Silsilah*, vol. 1*: The Shrines*. London: Egypt Exploration Society.

Chaniotis, Angelos. 2011. "Graffiti in Aphrodisias: Images—Texts—Contexts." In J. A. Baird and Claire Taylor (eds.), *Ancient Graffiti in Context*, 193–196. New York and London: Routledge.

Finnestad, Ragnhild. 1983. *Image of the World and Symbol of the Creator*. Studies in Oriental Religions 10. Wiesbaden: Harrassowitz.

Fronczak, Maria and Sławomir Rzepka. 2009. "'Funny Signs' in Theban Rock Graffiti." In Petra Andrássy, Julia Budka and Frank Kammerzell (eds.), *Non-textual Marking Systems, Writing and Pseudo Script from Prehistory to Modern Times*. LingAeg Studia Monographica 8, 159–178. Göttingen: Hubert and Co.

Gosline, Sheldon. 1992. "Carian Quarry Markings on Elephantine Island." *Kadmos* 31: 43–49.

Griffiths, John Gwyn. 1958. "The Interpretation of the Horus-Myth of Edfu." *Journal of Egyptian Archaeology* 44: 75–85.

Hahn, Johannes . 2013. "Graffiti." In Roger S. Bagnall, Kai Brodersen, Craige B. Champion, Andrew Erskine, and Sabine R. Huebner (eds.), *The Encyclopedia of Ancient History*, 2974–2975 Oxford: Wiley-Blackwell.

Haring, B. J. J. 2000. "Towards Decoding the Necropolis Workmen's Funny Signs." *Göttinger Miszellen* 178: 45–58.

——. 2009. "Workmen's Marks on Ostraca from the Theban Necropolis: A Progress Report." In B. J. J. Haring and O.E. Kaper (eds), *Pictograms or Pseudo Script? Non-Identity Marks in Practical Use in Ancient Egypt and Elsewhere: Proceedings of a Conference in Leiden, 19-20 December 2006*, 143–167. Leiden: Brill.

——. 2017. *From Single Sign to Pseudo-Script. An Ancient Egyptian System of Workmen's Identity*

Marks. Leiden: Brill.

—— and O. E. Kaper (eds.). 2009. *Pictograms or Pseudo Script? Non-Identity Marks in Practical Use in Ancient Egypt and Elsewhere: Proceedings of a Conference in Leiden, 19-20 December 2006*. Leiden: Brill.

Harrell, James A. and Per Storemyr. 2013. "Limestone and Sandstone Quarrying in Ancient Egypt: Tools, Methods, and Analogues." *Marmora* 9: 19–43.

Jaritz, Horst. 1980. *Elephantine III. Die Terrassen von den Tempeln des Chnum und der Satet. Architektur und Deutung*. Deutsches Archäologisches Institut Kairo 32. Mainz am Rhein: Archäologische Veröffentlichungen.

Johnson, Janet H. (ed.). 2001. *Chicago Demotic Dictionary*. Chicago: The University of Chicago. < https://oi.uchicago.edu/research/publications/demotic-dictionary-oriental-institute-university-chicago >, accessed 22 May.2005.

Kaper, Olaf E. 2003. *The Egyptian God Tutu: A Study of the Sphinx-God and Master of Demons with a Corpus of Monuments* (OLA 119). Leuven: Brill.

Klemm, Rosemarie and Dietrich Klemm. 2008. *Stones and Quarries in Ancient Egypt*. London: British Museum Press.

Kraemer, Bryan. 2013. "Bes." In Roger Bagnall, Kai Brodersen, Craige Champion, Andrew Erskine, and Sabine Huebner (eds.), *The Encyclopedia of Ancient History*, 1102–1103. Chichester: John Wiley and Sons.

Kucharek, Andrea. 2012. "Gebel el-Silsila." In Willeke Wendrich (ed.), *UCLA Encyclopedia of Egyptology*. Los Angeles: eScholarship < https://escholarship.org/uc/item/2x73c8bz >.

Kurth, Dieter. 1999. "Esna." In: Kathryn A. Bard (ed.), *Encyclopedia of the Archaeology of Ancient Egypt*, 295. New York: Routledge.

Legrain, George. 1906. "Inscriptions in the Quarries of el Hôsh." *Proceedings of the Society of Biblical Archaeology* 28: 17–26.

Mairs, Rachel. 2011. "Egyptian 'Inscriptions' and Greek 'Graffiti' at El Kanais in the Egyptian Eastern Desert." In J. A. Baird and Claire Taylor (eds.), *Ancient Graffiti in Context*, 158–159. New York—London: Routledge.

Meeks, Dimitri. 1991. "Dieu Masqué, dieu sans tête." *Archéo-Nil* 1: 5-15.

Minas-Nerpel, Martina. 2017. "Offering the *ij.t*-knife to Haroeris in the Temple of Isis at Shanhûr." In Richard Jasnow and Ghislaine Widmer (eds.), *Illuminating Osiris: Egyptological Studies in Honour of Mark Smith*, 259–276. Atlanta: Lockwood Press.

Morgan, Jacques de, Urbain Bouriant, Georges Legrain, G. Jéquier, and A. Barsanti. 1895–1909. *Kom Ombos I–II*. Catalogue des monuments et inscriptions de l'Égypte antique, première série Haute Ègypte 3. Vienne: Adolphe Holzhausen.

Nilsson, Maria. 2014. "Pseudo Script in Gebel el Silsila—Preliminary Results of the Epigraphic Survey 2012." In Kelly Accetta, Renate Fellinger, Pedro Lourenço Gonçalves, and W. Paul van Pelt (eds.), *Current Research in Egyptology 2013: Proceedings of the Fourteenth Annual Symposium*, 122–141. Oxford: Oxbow Books.

——. 2015a. "Non-textual Marking Systems at Gebel el Silsila: From Dynastic Signifiers of Identity to Symbols of Adoration." In Julia Budka, Frank Kammerzell, and Sławomir Rzepka (eds.), *Non-Textual Marking Systems in Ancient Egypt (and Elsewhere)*. Lingua Aegyptia Studia Monographica 16, 81–105. Hamburg: Widmaier Verlag.

——. 2015b. "Anguiform Graffiti in the Roman Quarries at Gebel el Silsila." *Journal of Intercultural and Interdisciplinary Archaeology* 2015 (2): 85–96.

——. 2018. "Quarry Marks in Gebel el-Silsila: Signifiers of Gods and Men Alike?" In B. J. J. Haring, K. van der Moezel, and D. Soliman (eds.), *Decoding Signs of Identity: Egyptian Workmen's Marks in Archaeological, Historical, Comparative and Theoretical Perspective*, 113–136. Leiden—Leuven: Peeters.

—— and Adrienn Almásy. 2015. "Quarrying for Claudius, Protected by Min: Reflections on a Small Quarry in Gebel el Silsila East." *British Museum Studies in Ancient Egypt and Sudan* 22: 87–110.

——, Ahmed Faraman, and Abdel Moniem Said. 2019. "Some Rock Inscriptions from Gebel el-Silsila." *Journal of Egyptian Archaeology* 104(1): 71–79.

—— and John Ward. 2014. "Quarry Marks in Partition B, Main Quarry at Gebel el Silsila: Remarks on Their Meaning and Function." *Journal of the Society for the Study of Egyptian Antiquities* 39: 139–178.

—— and ——. 2016. "Pictorial Representations at Gebel el Silsila—A 10 000 Year Long Repertoire."

In G. Capriotti Vittozzi (ed.), *Archaeological Heritage & Multidisciplinary Egyptological Studies 3: Proceedings "Italian Days in Aswan,"* 167–183. Rome: Istituto di Studi sul Mediterraneo Antico.

—— and ——. 2017. "Five 'New' Deities in the Roman Pantheon at Gebel el-Silsila." *Journal of Ancient Egyptian Interconnections* 14: 22–30.

—— and ——. 2019. "Mason or Priest? A Comparison between Graeco-Roman Signs on Magical Amulets and Symbols in Egyptian Quarries." In K. Endreffy, Á. M. Nagy, and J. Spier (eds.), *Magical Gems in Their Contexts: Proceedings of the International Workshop Held at the Museum of Fine Arts, Budapest 16–18 February 2012*, 217-236. Studia Archaeologica 229. Roma: "L'Erma" di Bretschneider.

——, ——, and Adrienn Almásy-Martin. 2019. "Quarrying for Augustus: Gebel el-Silsila as a Source for Early Roman Monuments at Dendera." *Journal of Ancient Egyptian Interconnections* 23: 1–77.

——, ——, Sarah K. Doherty, and Adrienn Almásy. 2015. "Gebel el Silsila: Field Report from the Main Quarry." *Journal of Intercultural and Interdisciplinary Archaeology* 2015(2): 147–192.

Nilsson, Martin P. 1951. "The Anguipede of Magical Amulets." *The Harvard Theological Review* 44: 61–64.

Peden, Alexander J. 2001. *The Graffiti of Pharaonic Egypt: Scope and Roles of Informal Writings (c. 3100–332 B.C.).* Leiden—Boston—Köln: Brill.

Petrie, W. M. Flinders. 1888. *A Season in Egypt. 1887.* London: Field and Tuer.

Preiskge, Friedrich and Wilhelm Spiegelberg. 1915. *Ägyptische und griechische Inschriften und Graffiti aus den Steinbrüchen des Gebel Silsile (Oberägypten) —nach den Zeichnungen von Georges Legrain.* Strassburg: K.J. Trübner.

Quaegebeur, Jan. 1975. *Le dieu égyptien Shaï dans la religion et l'onomastique*. Louvain: Presses Universitaires de Louvain.

Romano, J. F. 1998. "Notes on the Historiography and History of the Bes-image in Ancient Egypt." *Bulletin of the Australian Centre for Egyptology* 9: 89–105.

Rossi, Carina. 2003. *Architecture and Mathematics in Ancient Egypt.* Cambridge: Cambridge University Press.

Sakr, Faiza Mahmoud. 2007. "New Foundation Deposits of Kom el-Hisn." In Jean-Claude Goyon and Christine Cardin (eds.), *Proceedings of the Ninth International Congress of Egyptologists*, vol. 2, 1657–1672. Orientalia Lovaniensia Analecta 150. Leuven: Peeters.

Savigny, Jules-César. 1805. *Histoire naturelle et mythologique de l'ibis*. Paris: Allais.

Sayce, Archibald. 1907. "Excavations at Gebel Silsila." *Annales du Service d'antiquités de l'Égypte* 8: 97–105.

Shonkwiler, Randy L. 2014. *The Behdetite: A Study of Horus the Behdetite from the Old Kingdom to the Conquest of Alexander*. PhD dissertation, University of Chicago.

Smith, Mark. 1999. "Gebel el-Silsila." In Kathryn A. Bard (ed.), *Encyclopedia of the Archaeology of Ancient Egypt*, 396. London: Blackwell.

Sweeney, Deborah. 2002. "Gender and Conversational Tactics in the 'Contendings of Horus and Seth.'" *Journal of Egyptian Archaeology* 88: 141–162.

Uphill, Eric. 1965. "The Egyptian *Sed*-festival Rites." *Journal of Near Eastern Studies* 24: 365–383.

Wainwright, G. A. 1935. "Some Celestial Associations of Min." *Journal of Egyptian Archaeology* 21: 152–170.

Ward, John and Maria Nilsson 2015. "Mallets, Chisels, Sledges and Boats: The Art of Quarrying at Gebel el Silsila." In Massimiliano S. Pinarello, Justin Yoo, Jason Lundock, and Carl Walsh (eds.), *Current Research in Egyptology: Proceedings of the Fifteenth Annual Symposium*, 59–72. Oxford: Oxbow Books.

Witt, R. E. 1997. *Isis in the Ancient World*. Baltimore—London: Johns Hopkins University Press.

Notes

1 Preisigke and Spiegelberg 1915.

2 Quaegebeur 1975, 94.

3 See, for example, Nilsson 2014; Nilsson 2015a; Nilsson 2015b; Nilsson 2018; Nilsson and Almásy 2015; Nilsson, Ward, Doherty, and Almásy 2015; Nilsson and Ward 2014; Nilsson, Ward, and Almásy-Martin 2019. For a synopsis of visitors' graffiti and rock art at Gebel el-Silsila, see Nilsson and Ward 2016, and Nilsson, Faraman, and Said 2019.

4 Nilsson and Ward 2017.

5 E.g., Haring and Kaper 2009.

6 Budka et al. 2015.

7 Aston 2015; Fronczak and Rzepka 2009; Haring 2000; 2009; 2017.

8 Arnold 1990; Aston 2015.

9 Gosline 1992; Legrain 1906.

10 Preiskge and Spiegelberg 1915, 4; Jaritz 1980. For a summary of previous interpretations and classifications, see Nilsson 2015a.

11 Legrain 1906. He was, furthermore, incorrect in stating that no marks were located on the rocks or surfaces outside the quarries. The current team has, quite the opposite, located several marks located on natural rock surfaces in various locations outside the quarries, including on the mountain plateau and strategic lookouts, by the river, and on stone ostraca found within structures.

12 Preisigke and Spiegelberg 1915, 4.

13 Petrie 1888, 17 with pl. XIX; Sayce 1907.

14 Caminos and James 1963, iv.

15 Klemm and Klemm 2008.

16 Kucharek 2012.

17 Hahn 2013.

18 Hahn 2013, 2; Baird and Taylor 2011.

19 Cf. Mairs 2011, 158–159.

20 Peden 2001, xix, xxii.

21 Chaniotis 2011, 193–196; Baird 2011, 65–66.

22 Baird and Taylor 2011, 4–5.

23 See, for example, Harrell and Storemyr 2013; Ward and Nilsson 2015.

24 Nilsson 2013, 2015a, 2015b; Nilsson and Almásy 2015; Nilsson, Ward, Doherty and Almásy 2015; Nilsson and Ward 2017.

25 For a comparison with representations of Abraxas on magical gems, see Nilsson and Ward 2019.

26 Nilsson 2015a, 95–96.

27 Nilsson 2015a, 93, with fig. 18.

28 Nilsson 2015a, 94, with fig. 20.

29 E.g., see Meeks 1991, 5–15.

30 E.g., Romano 1998, 89–105 with pls. 17–21.

31 Nilsson 2015a, 94 with fig. 19.

32 Klemm and Klemm 2008, 175–176 with fig. 263.

33 For a brief summary see Kraemer 2013, 1102–1103.

34 Nilsson 2015a, 100–101 with figs. 26a–b.

35 The extensive quarry mark repertoire in each quarry and their relation with marks displayed within exposed, undressed blocks within the temple structure at Dendera and Medamoud will be dealt with individually and elsewhere. For Dendera see Nilsson, Ward and Almásy-Martin 2019.

36 For Claudius, see Nilsson and Almasy 2015, 87–110; for Augustus/Tiberius see Preisigke and Spiegelberg 1915, 23; Nilsson, Ward and Almásy-Martin 2019.

37 Nilsson and Ward 2017, 22–23 with no. 1.

38 Nilsson and Almasy 2015, 89–91, no. 1.

39 Wainwright 1935, 152–170.

40 For an interpretation of Pan graffiti in El Kanais, see Mairs 2011.

41 Preisigke and Spiegelberg 1915, 6; Quaegebeur 1975, 160–161.

42 So far, eleven documented demotic texts contain the name 'Shaï' without an additional divine name.

43 Nilsson and Ward 2014, 160 (translation by A. Almásy).

44 Nilsson 2015b, 6 with no. 1.

45 Inventory numbers GeSE.Q34.AS.In.11 and GeSE.Q34.AN.In.13.

46 Smith 1999, 396; Preisigke and Spiegelberg 1915, nos. 228, 230–231, 248.

47 *CDD* M: 235 (= Johnson 2001).

48 Griffiths 1958, 76.

49 Shonkwiler 2014, 314.

50 Nilsson 2014, 129–130.

51 Together with John Ward, the current author has documented quarry marks within the temple structures since 2007 and is currently preparing a publication on these relationships. Petrie 1888, 17, associates Dendera with the quarries of el-

Hosh, based on the prominent position of this marking combination there. However, neither Petrie nor Legrain (1906) took into consideration the overall context, for which GeSE.Q34C6–15 can be pinpointed as a source of at least a part of the Dendera structure. See Nilsson, Ward, and Almásy-Martin 2019.

52 Cf. Nilsson 2015a, 100–101 with figs. 26a–b. Due to the finding of the other crocodile mark, the item held in the figure's hand, previously interpreted as a sceptre, was re-examined and reinterpreted as a harpoon.

53 E.g., Sweeney 2002, 154; Finnestad 1983, 15; Blackman and Fairman, 1944, 5–22.

54 Bonner 1950, 124.

55 Nilsson 2015a, 95–96.

56 For the relation between GeSE.Q34C6-15 and Dendera, see Nilsson, Ward and Almásy-Martin 2019.

57 Witt 1997, 55.

58 Nilsson 2015a, 99.

59 Nilsson and Almásy 2015, 94–95 (no. 6) with figs. 8a–b: Adoration |of Pakoibis son of Paweris |for the greatest god among the gods of |the quarry of Isis (?) |year 8 of Claudius, Thoth 19.

60 Nilsson and Almásy 2015, 93–94 (no. 5) with figs. 7a–b: "Harbeschinis son of Petephibis |year 6 of Claudius."

61 Nilsson and Almásy 2015, 97.

62 For example, see Nilsson, Ward, Almásy and Doherty 2015, nos. 26–27.

63 Nilsson 2015a, 96–98.

64 Nilsson 2013, 131–132 with fig. 10.11.

65 Nilsson 2015a, 97; Preisigke and Spiegelberg 1915, nos. 98, 100, and 102.

66 Nilsson 2015a, 97.

67 Kurth 1999, 295; Preisigke and Spiegelberg, nos. 112, 131, and 133.

68 Nilsson and Ward 2017, no. 5.

69 Kaper 2003, 19, 179, 193.

74 Nilsson, Ward, Doherty and Almásy 2015, no.

70 Kaper 2003, 201–204.

71 Nilsson, Ward, Almásy, and Doherty 2015, no 25.

72 Although Egyptian mythology habitually depicts and describes the ibis as a snake-eater, it was clarified already by Savigny 1805 that they merely ate snake eggs. Instead, it is more likely that the true *aves* depicted was a shoebill stork. The author would like to thank John Wyatt for intriguing discussions and for providing information regarding avian depictions and signification in ancient Egypt.

73 Preisigke and Spiegelberg 1915, no. 145.

11.

75 De Morgan et al. 1895–1909.

76 Cf. *Kom Ombos* I, 131, 144–145.

77 Minas-Nerpel 2017, 259–276.

78 Minas-Nerpel 2017, 263 describes the *Wḏꜣ.t*-decorated *ỉj.t*-knife as a personification of Hathor based on the feminine determinative used for the *ỉj.t* in the hymn.

79 See, e.g., Bonner 1955, chapter IX, esp. 123–124.

80 See, for example, Nilsson 1951, 61–64.

81 For Min see Nilsson and Almásy 2015, no. 1.

82 Still, one could remain equally hesitant to the identification of the beak as belonging to a cock on all magical gems (especially when without a comb) when obverses reveal figures of Harpocrates on a water lily. See, e.g., Bonner 1955, 127–128 with n. 20.

83 Various forms of technical sketches are preserved within the quarries of Gebel el-Silsila, including a description of how to lower an obelisk block from its origin, some 20 m above the current ground level. See Nilsson 2014, 157–158 with fig. 6; Nilsson 2015a, 92–93 with figs. 16a–b and 17.

84 E.g., Sakr 2007, 1657–1672; alternatively Rossi 2003, chapter 4.

85 Nilsson and Ward 2017, 24–25.

86 Uphill 1965, 365–383.

Journal of Ancient Egyptian Interconnections

A Particular Depiction of Anubis from the Tomb of the Sculptor Nakhtamun (TT 335): Is Anubis a Demon?

Arnaud Quertinmont
Royal Museum of Mariemont

Abstract
We know how flexible the Egyptian iconographic system is and the limitations of our modern classifications, especially in regard to gods, spirits and demons. This paper reviews the god Anubis' particular and completely distinctive iconography shown in the tomb of sculptor Nakhtamun (TT 335). Analysis of this means we can tackle the depictions of armed guardian-demons, particularly those in Chapters 145 and 146 of the Book of the Dead.

In March, 2016, Swansea University launched the database for Demon Things—The Ancient Egyptian Demonology Project, Second Millennium BCE.[1] This tool, which is essential for people taking an interest in demons and liminal beings, aims to gather various Egyptian entities into a single catalogue. It seems relevant at this juncture to consider the god Anubis' particular and completely distinctive iconography shown in the tomb of sculptor Nakhtamun (TT 335).[2] Examination of this will shed light on the flexibility of the Egyptian iconographic system and the limitations of our modern classifications, especially in regard to gods, spirits, and demons.[3]

The funerary complex of Nakhtamun dates from the Nineteenth Dynasty and was discovered by Bernard Bruyère at the Deir el-Medina site on the 16th of January, 1925. It originally consisted of a courtyard, a chapel and a network of underground rooms. The latter is composed of three chambers. The first two (A and B) are at the same level and are dedicated to depictions of the family of the deceased and offerings placed there at the time of the funeral ceremony. The third chamber (C), which is at a lower level, is the actual burial vault itself. When you are in Chamber B and you look towards the passage leading to Chamber A, you can see that it is surmounted by a double representation of Anubis (Fig. 1). The god appears in a hybrid canine-headed human form, sitting and wielding a knife. He is under a rectangular structure topped by a *khekeru* frieze. It is indubitable that the text attributes both of these depictions to Anubis. Hence, the one on the right is, "Anubis, who is at the head of the divine pavilion, who is upon his mountain, master of the West… in the necropolis" (*ỉnpw ḫnty sḥ nṯr tpy ḏw.f nb ỉmnt ... m smt*), while the one on the left is, "Anubis, who is in *wt*, the great god, lord of the sacred country, providing protection in the place of eternity" (*ỉnpw*

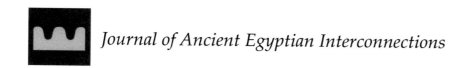

Figure 1: Nakhtamon's Tomb. © Thierry Benderitter—Osirisnet.

ỉmy-wt nṯr nfr nb tꜣ ḏsr ỉrj.k sqw m st ḥḥ). The name of Osiris Nakhtamun, now partially destroyed, is seen between the two figures. It has to be noticed that the tomb kept several particular depictions of the Anubis (i.e., with a ram's head).[4]

It is not unusual to find an image of the god guarding a passageway. Many examples are well known, such as in the tombs of Queen Nefertari (QV 66),[5] Sennefer (TT 96),[6] or Pashed (TT 3).[7]

In these cases, Anubis is usually depicted in an animal form, lying down with head raised and alert, and hanging his tail. This is the classic image that can be found on the intrados (inner curve of an arch) or lintels of certain steles or on components of coffins and sarcophagi. What is unusual, however, is to find a hybrid image of the god sitting, armed with a knife, and guarding a passageway. In order to ascertain what sort of image we are dealing with, it is worth going back over Anubis' functions and iconography.

Anubis: Functions and Types of Iconography

Although posterity only seems to have preserved the memory of three canine divinities, Anubis, Wepwawet, and Duamutef, sources also confirm the existence of a certain Sed, Khentyamentiu, and Hereret, to name but a few others.[8] Several studies have conducted research into these, some of a general nature,[9] others focusing on specific aspects associated with the Meroitic and Mediterranean world.[10] Let us briefly go over some important concepts connected with Anubis and the functions attributed to him that will help us have a better understanding of the iconography in Nakhtamun's tomb.

Anubis, the Greek rendering of the Egyptian name *ỉnpw*, is chiefly known for being in charge of mummification and his involvement in the scene of the last judgment which occurs in the Book of the Dead. However, study of the texts, his epithets, and depictions provides a more complex picture.[11] Although he is one of the most ancient Egyptian deities,[12] it is hard, if not impossible, to arrive at the truth concerning Anubis at the beginning of Egyptian history. At the most, we know that originally he was the only deity allowed to be depicted at the entrance of mastabas;[13] he was in charge of providing for the dead, for assuring a good burial, and he was responsible for the afterlife.[14]

It was only at the end of the Fifth Dynasty and the beginning of the Sixth that Anubis was incorporated into the Osiris myth and lost his pre-eminence to Osiris, who replaced him in the offering formulae.[15]

It was also in this era that Osiris supplanted and absorbed the canine god of Abydos, Khentyamentiu. [16] It is understood that even the personality of Anubis, along with his theology, evolved over time. If we were briefly to summarise his fields of activity, it might be said that he is principally involved in three contexts: funerary, judicial, and pastoral.

The first field, which is the best known, is linked with the funerary realm. In this context, Anubis plays the role of practitioner and facilitator of rebirth. He assists embalmers and priests as *jmy w*, "He who is in the place of embalming" and as *ḫntj sḥ nṯr* "He who is at the head of the divine pavilion." He watches over the mysteries of mummification and the metamorphoses of the deceased as *ḥrj-sštꜣ* "Master of Secrets." This latter epithet resonates wonderfully with the Anubis on the casket from Tutankhamun's tomb. [17] He is also guardian of tombs and necropoleis, as is indicated by his name, Anubis *nb tꜣ ḏjsr* "Lord of the Necropolis," *tpj ḏw-f* "He who is upon his mountain," and some other epithets naming specific necropoleis, such as Gebelein and Asyut.[18]

The dog-headed entity's second field of competence is judicial.[19] When the deceased reaches the Hall of Two Truths (or Maat), Anubis acts as *sr-ḏꜣḏꜣt*, the judge of the court. Indeed, being invested with this responsibility, he announces the arrival of the deceased and proceeds with weighing his heart. His role in Osiris' funeral also had a judicial nature. It turns out that the oldest son was ultimately responsible for providing for the funeral. As practitioner, Anubis assumed this responsibility and acted for Horus. It is perhaps this aspect that identifies Anubis as Osiris' son, born of adultery. He is the king's son but, as he was illegitimate, he had no right to the throne. Horus alone, the son and rightful heir, would have this primacy. [20]

Perhaps this clue should be linked with a philological hypothesis relating to the use of the vocable *inp* to designate young royal princes. [21] Once the mummification was completed and Osiris had been buried, his mortal remains needed to be protected. That is why Anubis put together a group of fourteen guardians (2x7) in charge of protecting the body (chapter 17 of the Book of the Dead).[22] It was then the responsibility of the heir to rehabilitate his father's memory. So, Horus took the title of Harendotes, "Horus the protector of his father," and pursued Seth and his disciples. It should also be noted that Anubis was involved in scenes of the king's rejuvenation and, thus rebirth, in which Anubis is depicted by a lunar disc.[23]

The third field, which is less known, appears in the Ptolemaic era and relates to the god's pastoral function. There is mention of this at some temples, such as at Kom Ombo, Dendera, and Edfu. In those instances, Anubis is shown in connection with cattle as the Lord of Milk Cows,[24] Guardian of Herds, or Chief of Butchers.[25] These functions, which might come as a surprise, seem to be already present in the Pyramid Texts.[26] Moreover, if the Jumilhac Papyrus is to be believed, this may explain the connection between the canine and Hesat, the celestial cow-goddess. She was worshipped in Atfih, on the border of the Seventeenth nome of Upper Egypt, the Cynopolitan nome in which Anubis was the Tutelary Deity. [27]

As we can see, the god's field of action is more complex than it appears to be at first glance. Immediately, we find ourselves faced with a recurring problem when we deal with Egyptian religion,[28] namely, the limitations of our modern classifications. Egyptian thought is characterised by religious polymorphism and a plethora of approaches. Certain aspects and ideas may contradict one another but are not mutually exclusive and do not cancel each other out. Each of the features added to the file must be taken into consideration and, like so many different perspectives, allows us to get that bit closer to the divine essence.[29]

In the present case, that is to say, Nakhtamun's tomb, it seems evident that we are in a funerary context and thus it is Anubis' role as guardian (*ḫnty sḥ nṯr tpy ḏw.f*) and protector (*irj.k sqw m st ḥḥ*) that is highlighted.

Now, let us turn to the god's iconography. With the exception of one unique example in which Anubis is portrayed as having an entirely human appearance,[30] he is usually depicted either in hybrid form with a man's body and a canine head or in a completely animal appearance.[31] The latter is also adopted by another canine god, Wepwawet. However, there is no possibility of doubt in the case of Nakhtamun's tomb because the picture of the god is captioned with his name and classic epithets.

Many studies have focused on the nature of canine deities and, in particular, on the animal depicted.[32] Based on the morphological characteristics of the gods, researchers are looking for a canid with a sleek appearance, large pointed ears, a tapered muzzle, skinny limbs, and a bushy hanging tail. As for the colour black, it is only of symbolic value and refers to these entities' funerary function. A number of likely candidates quickly emerged and the consensus of opinion seemed to settle on *Canis aureus lupaster*, formerly known as the Egyptian Jackal. It has now been renamed the African Golden Wolf.[33] Ancient Egyptians did not appear to have been as fussy as we as to the animal species chosen to represent these deities, as the diversity of animal mummies found in a context of worship would seem to demonstrate.[34] Hence, we retain the generic term "canine" as a precaution.

Nakhtamun's Tomb

The location chosen to depict two antithetical Anubises, that is, above the passage leading from Chamber B to Chamber A, is consistent from a formal and religious perspective in relation to what we have just discussed. So too are the titles and epithets mentioned. Now, what about the other features depicted? Let us first take a look at the form and position in which the canine is depicted: mummiform and sitting. The vignette from chapter 17 of the Papyrus of Ani (Book of the Dead), dedicated to seven *ꜣkh.w*,[35] is illustrated by the eleven gods forming Osiris' company. Amongst these is a figure in hybrid form with a man's body and a dog's head, mummiform and sitting. He can be identified because of his name being present: *Inpw*.

Pashed's Tomb (TT 3), which we have already mentioned regarding its two canines guarding a corridor, has also preserved a different image of Anubis, sitting down accompanied by Wepwawet (Fig. 2). Several gods are portrayed sitting on the ground holding an ankh sign on their knees, on the archway of the northern section of the vault. The last two have canine heads. The first, dressed in red, is identified as,= "Anubis who is at the head of the divine pavilion, the great god" (*ḫnty sḥ nṯr iꜥ*). As for the second, dressed in white, the text presents him a, "Wepwawet of the South, at the head of the Two Lands, the great god" (*šmꜥw ḫrp tꜣwj nṯr iꜥ*). Thus, the iconography of a mummiform and sitting Anubis is substantiated by parallel instances.[36]

The second feature we are focusing on is the knife with which the god is equipped. To our knowledge, apart from Nakhtamun's tomb, the only other depiction of a dog-headed hybrid armed with knives and identified as being Anubis (not depicted on sarcophagi or papyrus), is at the Temple of Edfu (Fig.

Figure 2: Pashed's Tomb (TT 3). © Alain Guilleux.

FIGURE 3: Anubis, Temple of Edfu. © Arnaud Quertinmont.

FIGURE 4: Demon dog, Temple of Edfu. © Arnaud Quertinmont.

3).[37] The god there is named *ỉnpw sꜣ wsỉr*. However, there do exist several similar representations of canine-headed entities. In that context, they are guardian-demons of doorways. They are associated with specific places and forbid access to intruders and unwelcome individuals. These include those we see in chapters 145 and 146 of the Book of the Dead.[38]

So, still at Edfu, and below the previous one, is a similar hybrid whose head is adorned with snakes. He is identified as being *Wr-snḏ* (FIG. 4).[39] We should also mention the one in the tomb of Tausert and Sethnakht (KV 14) who guards the fifth door in chapter 145 of the Book of the Dead.[40] He is depicted in a hybrid human-canine form, standing and armed with two knives. He goes by the name of *Ḥnb-rḳww* (FIG. 5).[41] On the south wall of Sennedjem's tomb (TT 1) is a similar image, but this time he is sitting and armed with a single knife. In this instance, he is guarding the ninth door in chapter 146 of the Book of the Dead. He sits under a structure topped with a *khekeru* frieze (FIG. 6). Although the ninth door is identified in the text, the guardian's name is not inscribed. Fortunately, thanks to some parallel instances, we know that his name is *Ḏs*.[42]

It is essentially this last illustration that provides us with the missing information about the niche under which Anubis is represented and that gives us the keys to understanding the scene in Nakhtamun's tomb. Anubis does indeed act as a guardian of the passageway here, with this being made manifest on the *khekeru* frieze. The god is portrayed with the same appearance as the armed guardian-demons that one can see in chapters 145 and 146 of the Book of the Dead.

We also have to mention a very fine cartonnage of Padiuf preserved in the Louvre Museum (N 4828). We can observe a hybrid canine-headed human form, sitting and wielding a knife. He is identified as being *nb tꜣ ḏjsr*. It is obvious that Anubis is represented here. A similar wonderful depiction was discovered in Horemheb's tomb (KV 57).[43] It is a small statue made of wood and covered with asphalt, kept at the Egyptian Museum in Cairo. The statue is around 20 cm in height, representing a dog-headed human hybrid, sitting, with his hand on his knee and holding a knife, which has now been lost. Several statuettes of a similar type were discovered in royal tombs from the Eighteenth to the Twentieth Dynasties. They probably depict the spirits/demons mentioned in the Book of the Dead.[44]

In order to be as comprehensive as possible, mention should also be made of a dog-headed human hybrid armed with knives, shown amongst the Seven Demons, called the Seven Arrows, accompanying the "demon" Tutu.[45]

Is Anubis a Demon?

As we mentioned earlier, Anubis can watch over a passageway or access path. Here, however, it is surprising to see him take on the sort of iconography usually reserved for guardian-demons. Even though Anubis is regularly called *nṯr*,[46] should he also be considered a demon? The topic goes well beyond the scope of this article and is already looking convoluted.[47] One of the primary features of pharaonic civilisation was the performativity of pictures and writing. Representing a living being, a thing, or even an idea, was to give it life. The form and name that were given to these divine entities would thus define them and bestow life and power upon them. That is why certain harmful entities, especially those responsible for illness, existed in name only and did not have a depiction, or were represented in a deformed fashion so they could not take action.[48]

The Egyptians used divine entities (gods, spirits, and demons) as an explanation for the world, its creation, and the way it worked.[49] With this in mind, it was logical to depict these entities and give them form. However, the nature of divine essence is inaccessible. This fact is consistent with what is related in one of the hymns to Amun in the Leiden Papyrus that explains that the nature of god is unknown, that his image cannot be revealed, and that he is too powerful to be known.[50]

Another source (CT VI, 69c, 72d) indicates that only the deceased is able to know a god's form, and, here again, he shall not know all forms because at the end of the cycle of time, the demiurge will turn into a snake which man shall not know and that gods cannot see (chapter 175 of the Book of the Dead). Therefore, the Egyptians attempted to get around this state of affairs by developing symbols and creating a metalanguage that made it possible to approach the godly truth in a given situation at a given time. In the case of Nakhtamun's tomb, it mattered to the artist (or the person who had commissioned the work) to emphasise the fearsome, intransigent nature associated with the god Anubis' guardian function.

We believe that this particular iconography of Anubis highlights not so much the limitations of our

Figure 5: Demon dog, tomb of Tausert and Sethnakht (KV 14). © Nicolas Gauthier.

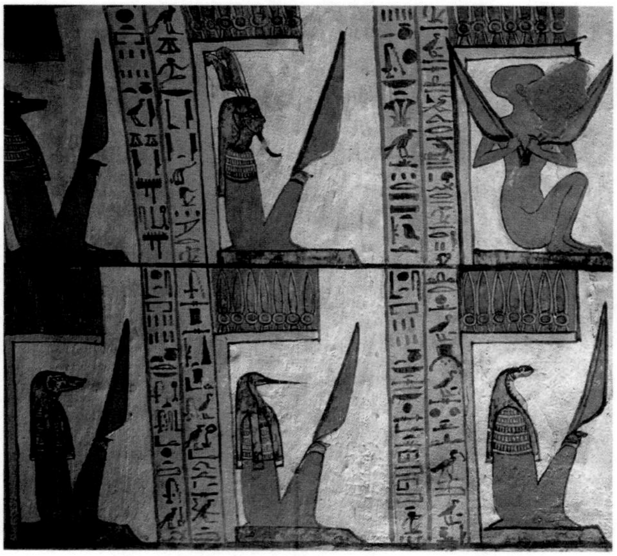

Figure 6: Sennedjem's Tomb. © Florence Maruejol.

modern categorisations but rather the extraordinary flexibility of the Egyptian iconographical system, especially when it comes to gods, spirits, and demons.[51] Indeed, it is not without interest to try to apply the definitions put forward by Zuzanna Bennett to our case study, even though they were devised to classify the identities mentioned in the Coffin Texts.[52]

According to these definitions, there is no question that Anubis is classified in the "god" category, and by that we mean *nṯr*. It turns out that Anubis was worshipped (especially at his temple in Asyut), and, although he was not a divinity as important as Amun or Ra in terms of depictions and centres of worship, he was present in many temples and shrines, such as the Deir el-Bahari temple complex.[53] The concept of worship is indispensable in defining an entity as being a deity. Thus, we are led to conclude that Anubis cannot be a demon because he fulfills one of the previous categories; that he is not apparently a threat to anyone; and that he is not controlled by another divinity.

Let us have a look at the classifications, in particular those relating to demons, according to the Ancient Egyptian Demonology Project:

> An entity must fulfill at least D1 of the following criteria in order to be classified as a demon:
>
> - D1 Doesn't fit into other categories [i.e., deities, personifications, animals, demonic animals, humans, demonic ex-humans, powers]
> - D2 May be in a group
> - D3 May be in a list
> - D4 May be guarding an area
> - D5 May present a threat to the deceased
> - D6 May present a threat to other afterlife residents
> - D7 Under the control of a deity.[54]

It becomes evident that assertions D4, "Can guard a place," and D5, "Can represent a threat to the deceased," definitely work in the case of the depiction from Nakhtamun's tomb. Anubis watches over the passage leading from Chamber B to Chamber A, and can represent a threat to anyone who wants to pass through if the latter is not in possession of the sacred formulae allowing him access to the various regions that comprise the afterlife or the tomb. It should also be noted that three-dimensional depictions of Anubis protected the passageway leading from Chamber A to the vault itself.[55] So, every passage in the tomb is guarded by the canine deity.

In conclusion, on integrating this very specific depiction of the god Anubis, might one not make these different categories a little more flexible by establishing the hypothesis that some deities (*nṯr*) can also play the role assigned to those entities we classify as demons? It would seem that this could be the case, or, at the very least, it could apply to the guardians of doorways, as we have just seen. Furthermore, what better example could we have than a psychopomp entity such as Anubis to add a modicum of crossover to these various categories? Is not the god himself at the frontier of the different realms?

Once again, we cannot help but marvel at the talent and creativity displayed by the ancient Egyptians with the intention of shaping the bodies of their entities, be they divine or demonic.

Abbreviation

PM I/II Porter, Betha and Rosaland L. B. Moss. 1964. *Topographical Bibliography of Ancient Egyptian Hieroglyphic Texts, Reliefs, and Paintings I: The Theban Necropolis Part 2: Royal Tombs and Smaller Cemeteries*. 2nd edition. Oxford: Clarendon.

References

Barguet, Paul. 1999. *Le Livre des morts des anciens Égyptiens*. Paris: Éditions du Cerf.

Barta, Winfried. 1968. *Aufbau und Bedeutung der altagyptischen Opferformel*. Glückstadt: Augustin.

Bennett, Suzanna. 2014a. "What Is an Ancient Egyptian Demon?" Demon Things—Ancient Egyptian Demonology Project, < http://www.demonthings.com/what-is-an-ancient-egyptian-demon/ >, accessed 18 June 2019.

——. 2014b. "What's in a Name? Transforming our Perception of the Function of Demonic Entities in the Ancient Egyptian Book of Two Ways." *Rosetta* 15(5): 1–18 .

——. 2017. "Conceptions of Demons in the Middle Kingdom Coffin Texts." In G. Miniaci, Maria Carmela Betro, and Stephen Quirke (eds.), *Company of Images: Modelling the Imaginary World of Middle Kingdom Egypt (2000–1500 BC): Proceedings of the International Conference of the EPOCHS Project held 18th–20th September 2014 at*

UCL, London, 15–34. Leuven: Peeters,

Blumenthal, Elke. 1970. *Untersuchungen zum Agyptischen Konigtum des mittleren Reiches*, Berlin: Akademie-Verlag.

Bruyère, Bernard. 1926. *Rapport sur les fouilles de Deir el Medineh : 1924–1925*. Cairo: Institut français d'archéologie orientale.

Cauville, Sylvie and Émile Chassinat. 1929. *Le temple d'*Edfou *IX*. Cairo: Institut français d'archéologie orientale.

Champollion, Jean-François. 1835. *Monuments de l'Égypte et de la Nubie: notices descriptives conformes aux manuscrits autographes : rédigés sur les lieux par Champollion le-Jeune I*. Paris: Didot.

de Rochemonteix, Maxence. 1897. *Le temple d'*Edfou *I*. Cairo: Institut français d'archéologie orientale.

Decharneux, Baudouin. 2012. *La religion existe-t-elle? Essai sur une idée prétendument universelle*. Bruxelles: Académie royale de Belgique.

Dunand, Françoise and Christiane Zivie-Coche. 2006. *Hommes et dieux en Égypte*. Paris: Cybèle.

DuQuesne, Terence. 2005. *The Jackal Divinities of Egypt: From the Archaic Period to Dynasty X*. Oxfordshire Communications in Egyptology 6. London: Darengo.

Durisch Gauthier, Nicole. 2002. *Anubis et les territoires cynopolites selon les temples ptolémaïques et romains*. PhD dissertation, Université de Genève.

Federn, Walter. 1958. "*Ḥtp (r)dj(w) (n) 'Inpw*; zum Verstandnis der vor-osirianischen Opferformel." *Mitteilungen des Deutschen Archäologischen Instituts, Abteilung Kairo* 16: 120–130.

Fischer-Elfert, Hans-Werner. 2011. "Sāmānu on the Nile: The Transfer of a Near Eastern Demon and Magico-medical Concept into New Kingdom Egypt." In M. Collier and Steven Snape. (eds.), *Ramesside Studies in Honour of K. A. Kitchen*, 189–198. Bolton: Rutherford.

Frankfurter, David. 2012. "Introduction", *Archiv für Religionsgeschichte* 14(1): 1–8

Gaillard, Claude. 1927. "Les animaux consacrés à la divinité de l'ancienne Lycopolis." *Annales du Service des antiquités de l'Égypte* 27: 33–42.

Gransard-Desmond, Jean-Olivier. 2004. *Étude sur les Canidae des temps pré-pharaoniques en Égypte et au Soudan*. Oxford: Archaeopress.

Grenier, Jean-Claude. 1977. *Anubis alexandrin et romain*. Leiden: E. J. Brill.

Griffiths, John Gwyn. 1980. "Osiris." In W. Helck and Otto Eberhard (eds.), *Lexikon der Ägyptologie IV*, col. 623–633. Wiesbaden: Otto Harrassowitz.

Gundlach, Rolf. 1988. *Sennefer. Die Grabkammer des Bürgmeisters von Theben*. Mainz am Rhein: Philipp von Zabern.

Johnson, Jessica Victoria. 2016. *Intertwined Demons: The Relationship between Gate Guardians and the Demon Ammit in Two Books of the Dead as Expressed through Synecdoche*. PhD dissertation, University of Memphis.

Kees, Hermann. 1977. *Der Gotterglaube im alten Agypten*. Berlin : Akademie-Verlag.

Kousoulis, Panagiotis. 2011. "The Demonic Lore of Ancient Egypt: Questions on Definition." In P. Kousoulis (ed.), *Ancient Egyptian Demonology: Studies on the Boundaries between the Demonic and the Divine in Egyptian Magic*: ix–xxii. Leuven: Peeters.

Leitz, Chrisitan (ed.). 2002. *Lexikon der agyptischen Gotter und Gotterbezeichnungen*. Leuven: Peeters.

Lucarelli, Rita. 2010a. "Demons (Benevolent and Malevolent)." In J. Dieleman and W. Wendrich (eds.) *UCLA Encyclopedia of Egyptology*. Los Angeles: eScholarship. < http://escholarship.org/uc/item/1r72q9vv >, accessed 22 Octobre 2019.

——. 2010b. "The Guardian Demons of the Book of the Dead". *British Museum Studies in Ancient Egypt and Sudan* 15: 85–102.

——. 2011. "Demonology during the Late Pharaonic and Greco-Roman Periods in Egypt." *Journal of Ancient Near Eastern Religions* 11: 109–125.

——. 2016. "Les démons dans l'Égypte ancienne." In A.Quertinmont (ed.), *Dieux, génies et démons en Égypte ancienne: À la rencontre d'Osiris, Anubis, Isis, Hathor, Rê et les autres*: 55–60. Paris—Morlanwelz: Somogy—Musée royal de Mariemont.

——. 2017. "Gods, Spirits, Demons of the Book of the Dead." In Foy Scalf (ed.), *Book of the Dead: Becoming God in Ancient Egypt*, 127–136. Chicago: The Oriental Institute of the University of Chicago.

——. 2018. "Demonen van de Doeat." In Maarten J. Raven (ed.), *Goden van Egypte: op zoek naar de wetten van de kosmos*, 107–112. Leiden : Sidestone Press

Manassa Darnell, Colleen. 2013. "Divine Taxonomy in the Underworld Books." *Archiv für Religionsgeschichte* 14: 47-68.

Meeks, Dimitri. 1976. " Notes de lexicographie (§ 2–4)." *Revue d'Égyptologie* 28: 87–96.

Nicholson, Paul T., Salima Ikram, and Steve Mills. 2015. "The Catacombs of Anubis at North Saqqara." *Antiquity* 89 : 645–661.

Pouls Wegner, Mary-Ann. 2007. "Wepwawet in Context: A Reconsideration of the Jackal Deity and Its Role in the Spatial Organization of the North Abydos Landscape." *Journal of the American Research Center in Egypt* 43: 139–150. .

Quertinmont, Arnaud. 2004. *Anubis: représentations et fonction, de l'Ancien à la fin du Nouvel Empire.* M.A. thesis, Université Libre de Bruxelles.

——. 2012. *Aux abords de la sépulture méroïtique: Les approches du monument funéraire à l'époque méroïtique.* PhD dissertation, Université Libre de Bruxelles.

——. 2016. "Anubis ou le corps des dieux dans l'Égypte pharaonique." In A. Quertinmont (ed.), *Dieux, génies et démons en Égypte ancienne : À la rencontre d'Osiris, Anubis, Isis, Hathor, Rê et les autres,* 125–133. Paris—Morlanwelz: Somogy—Musée royal de Mariemont.

Ritner, Robert K. 1985. "Anubis and the Lunar Disc." *Journal of Egyptian Archaeology* 71: 149–155.

Rueness, Eli Knispel, Maria Gulbrandsen Asmyhr, Claudio Sillero-Zubiri, David W. Macdonald, Afework Bekele, Anagaw Atickem, and Nils Chr. Stenseth. 2011. "The Cryptic African Wolf: *Canis aureus lupaster* Is Not a Golden Jackal and Is Not Endemic to Egypt." *PLoS ONE* 6.1: e16385. < https://journals.plos.org/plosone/article?id=10.1371/journal.pone.0016385 >, accessed 22 Octobre 2019.

Schäfer, Heinrich. 1902. *Ein Bruchstuck altagyptischer Annalen.* Berlin: Königliche Akademie der Wissenschaften.

Schmidt, Heike C. and Joachim Willeitner. 1994. *Nefertari. Gemahlin Ramses' II.* Mainz am Rhein: Philipp von Zabern.

Servajean, Frederic. 2013. "Anubis, Khnoum et les autres. À propos d'une figuration de la TT 335 de Deir al-Médîna." In Ch. Thiers (ed.), *Documents de Théologies Thébaines Tardives,* 131–148. Montpellier: Université Paul Valéry: CNRS UMR 5140.

——. 2017. "Le monument d'éternité de Nakhtamon à Deir el-Medina. Une tombe monochrome (TT 335) de l'époque de Ramsès II." In H. Gaber, L. Bazin Rizzo and F. Servajean (eds.), *Á l'œuvre on connaît l'artisan ... de Pharaon! Un siècle de recherches françaises à Deir el-Medina (1917–2017),* 249–273. Montpellier: Université Paul Valéry: CNRS UMR 5140.

Spieser, Cathie 2009. "Avaleuses et dévoreuses, des déesses aux démones en Egypte ancienne." *Chronique d'Égypte* 84: 5–19.

Vandier, Jacques. 1962. *Le Papyrus Jumilhac.* Paris: Centre national de la recherche scientifique.

Wiese, André and Andreas Brodbeck. 2004. *Tutankhamun: The Golden Beyond: Tomb Treasures from the Valley of the Kings.* Basel: Antikenmuseum Basel und Sammlung Kudwig.

Wilfong, Terry G. 2015. *Death Dogs: The Jackal Gods of Ancient Egypt.* Ann Arbor: Kelsey Museum of Archaeology.

Willems, Harco. 1998. "Anubis as a Judge." In W. Clarysse, Antoon Schoors, and Harco Willems (eds.), *Egyptian Religion: The Last Thousand Years: Studies Dedicated to the Memory of Jan Quaegebeur I,* 719–743. Leuven: Peeters.

Winand, Jean. 2016. "Le nom de dieu." In A. Quertinmont (ed.), *Dieux, génies et démons en Égypte ancienne: À la rencontre d'Osiris, Anubis, Isis, Hathor, Rê et les autres,* 25–33. Paris—Morlanwelz: Somogy—Musée royal de Mariemont

Witkowski, Maciej G. 1989. "Le rôle et les fonctions des chapelles d'Anubis dans le complexe funéraire de la reine Hatshepsout à Deir el Bahari." In S. Schoske (ed.), *Akten des vierten Internationalen Ägyptologen Kongresses München 1985, vol. III,* 431–440. Hamburg: Buske.

Yellin, Janice W. 1978. *The Role and Iconography of Anubis in Meroitic Religion.* PhD dissertation, Brandeis University.

Zandee, Jan. 1948. *De Hymnen aan Amon van Papyrus Leiden I 350.* Leiden: Rijksmuseum van Oudheden.

Zivie, Alain-Pierre. 1979. *La tombe de Pached à Deir el-Médineh [N° 3].* Cairo : Institut français d'archéologie orientale.

Notes

1 See < http://www.demonthings.com >.

2 Bruyère 1926, 113-178.

3 See, i.e., Spieser 2009; Winand 2016; Lucarelli 2010; Lucarelli 2011; Manassa Darnell 2013.

4 Servajean 2013; Servajean 2017.

5 Schmidt and Willeitner 1994, 121–122.

6 Gundlach 1988, 59, 70.

7 Zivie 1979.

8 DuQuesne 2005, 367–576.

9 See, i.e., DuQuesne 2005; Quertinmont 2016.

10 See, i.e., Yellin 1978; Grenier 1977.

11 DuQuesne 2005, 367–384; Wilfong 2015; Quertinmont 2016, 130.

12 Gransard-Desmond 2004; DuQuesne 2005, 1–36.

13 Schäfer 1902, 15-17 ; Quertinmont 2004, 23–25.

14 Federn 1958; Barta 1968, 47, 289; Quertinmont 2004, 15–16.

15 Kees 1977, 161–163 ; Griffiths 1980; Quertinmont 2004, 16.

16 DuQuesne 2005, 384–388; Griffiths 1980, col. 626.

17 Wiese and Brodbeck 2004, 89.

18 Leitz 2002, 395–398.

19 Willems 1998.

20 For the association of Anubis and Horus, see Quertinmont 2016, 326–327.

21 See, i.e., Blumenthal 1970, 36 ; Meeks 1976.

22 Barguet 1999, 60.

23 Ritner 1985.

24 A title he had when he poured libations of milk onto the Meroitic offering tables, accompanied by Isis.Cf. Yellin 1982 ; Quertinmont 2012, 176–179.

25 Durisch Gauthier 2002, 13.

26 PT §2080e.

27 Vandier 1962, 55.

28 Insofar as the term religion can be used to categorise a non-Western system of thought; cf. Decharneux 2012, 98.

29 Quertinmont 2012, 125–133.

30 Leitz 2002, 391.

31 For other depictions, cf. Leitz 2002, 391.

32 See, i.e., DuQuesne 2005, 1–5; Pouls Wegner 2007, 141–143 ; Wilfong 2015.

33 Rueness et al. 2011.

34 Gaillard 1927 ; Nicholson et al. 2015, 645–661.

35 British Museum, London, inv. EA EA10470.

36 Leitz 2002, 391.

37 Cauville and Chassinat 1929, 240G ; de Rochemonteix 1897, 179

38 Lucarelli 2010b; Johnson 2016; Lucarelli 2017; Lucarelli 2018.

39 Leitz 2002, vol. II, 459–460

40 Barguet 1999, 193.

41 Corridor C, PM I/II, 529;Champollion 1835, 451; Leitz 2002, vol. 5, 219.

42 Barguet 1999, 201.

43 Wiese and Brodbeck 2004) 107.

44 Arnaud Quertinmont and Nicolas Gauthier, " Un Livre des Morts—Objets" (in progress).

45 Brooklyn Museum, inv. 59.98.

46 Leitz 2002, vol. 1, p. 391 sq.

47 See, i.e., Kousoulis 2011; Frankfurter 2012, 1–8; Lucarelli 2010a.

48 See, i.e., Sāmānu/Akhu: Fischer-Elfert 2011.

49 Dunand and Zivie-Coche 2006, 26.

50 Zandee 1948.

51 See, i.e., Winand 2016; Lucarelli 2016, 55–60.

52 Bennett 2014b; Bennett 2017.

53 Witkowski 1989, 431–440.

54 Bennett 2014a.

55 Bruyère 1926, 178; Arnaud Quertinmont, *Guardians of the Tomb: The Anubises on Bases in the Valley of the Kings and in Deir el Medina* (in progress).

Journal of Ancient Egyptian Interconnections

The Maned Hippopotamus at Lahun: Identifying Homes and Names

Stephen Quirke
UCL Institute of Archaeology

Campbell Price
Manchester Museum

Abstract
In 1889–1890, Flinders Petrie directed clearance of a late Middle Kingdom town site near al-Lahun to produce a plan of the buildings and a general description of Middle Kingdom material culture. The finds include a dramatic limestone image of the mixed hippopotamus-lion known in Egyptology by the Late Egyptian name Taweret "the great (female power)." This sculpture was mentioned, but not illustrated, in his excavation report and has therefore not attracted the attention of researchers. Here we assess the figure through its modern and ancient history, in the light of recent fieldwork at settlement sites contemporary with the Lahun town.

The Figure in the Museum

The hippopotamus with leonine features, standing upright on hind legs, is among the most distinctive images in ancient Egyptian religious iconography, attested from the late 3rd millennium BCE to the early 1st Millennium CE.[1] Here, we present one of the larger sculptures known from before the New Kingdom. This limestone figure was found in 1889 during the clearance for Flinders Petrie of the orthogonal town-site near al-Lahun, on the east side of Fayoum governorate in Egypt.

As registered in the Manchester Museum under inventory number 270, the figure comprises two fragments, which do not join. The larger fragment is from head to upper hind legs, 38 cm in height in its present condition, (Figs. 1–2), and the smaller is the base, 28.1 by 23 cm, with hind paws and tail (see Fig. 7). In addition to the loss of the middle hind-leg area, the lower part of the proper right foreleg is broken away, and the proper left foreleg is preserved only at the shoulder area. Other surface damage is most extensive around chin and front, at left side of mane, and along the edges of the back ridge. Around the forward protruding head area, the curving mane narrows at top and has deep-cut roughly parallel groove-lines on the front. Lightly incised vertical zigzags are visible on the otherwise plain proper right rear side of the mane (Fig. 3). The head is carved in bold volumes within the upward curve from neck to rounded chin under the squared front and the undulating upper profile over eye hoods to rounded nose area. For the ear details, upward diagonals are cut from the inner triangle, indicating fur lines. At the front, the proper right edge is not preserved, but the proper left area has a low rise to indicate the flaring nostril (Fig. 4). The eyes are sculpted as convex ovoid balls, as if bulging out, within deeply carved contours pointed at back and

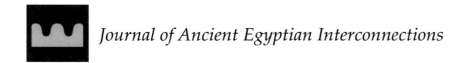

Figure 1: Lahun figure Manchester Museum 270, profile facing left showing traces of red and blue pigment. Copyright Manchester Museum, University of Manchester.

Figure 2: Three-quarters view of larger fragment, proper right side. Copyright Manchester Museum, University of Manchester.

Figure 3: Head of figure, proper right side, showing incised lines behind mane. Copyright Manchester Museum, University of Manchester.

Figure 4: Rear view of larger fragment. Copyright Manchester Museum, University of Manchester.

Figure 5: Three-quarters view of larger fragment, proper left side, to edge of left hind-leg. Copyright Manchester Museum, University of Manchester.

Figure 6: View from above, showing detail on eye hoods of larger fragment. Copyright Manchester Museum, University of Manchester.

front; a deep cut tear-duct line towards the jaw is clearest on proper right. The eye hoods rise behind and slightly higher than the eyeballs and bear parallel incised lines to demarcate the half facing the centre of the head (FIG. 6). The mouth is depicted open, with rounded ends and an uneven grid of bared clenched teeth, conveyed by a single horizontal line intersected by short verticals. Above, a diagonal groove from the nose curves down at rear to back of mouth, as if to emphasise the snarl. Between the forelegs, pendant breasts are carved as shallow convex volumes and are joined by a horizontal line roughly parallel to the lower edge of the mane. The belly is swollen and demarcated from the upper hind-legs by an incised line. Along the damaged area towards the break, an incised line seems to run around the upper thighs and around the rear of the figure, as if demarcating its upper from lower areas. The navel area is obscured by surface loss. At the lower edge, enough remains of the upper hind-leg area to indicate that the left hind-leg continued at a slight diagonal backwards in relation to the right hind-leg (FIG. 5). Along the back of the figure, a ridge rises almost to the tip of the mane and is broken away at the lower edge slightly higher than the upper hind-leg (FIGS. 2, 4). From the side, the ridge upper part, to mid "shoulder," is gently convex, in contrast to the concave lower part. From the back, the ridge is highest at the vertical line of its centre, most clearly along the lower part. The absence of internal detail carved on the ridge planes creates a strong single outline, within which an extended T-shaped division between upper and lower and between left and right reinforces the overall sense of strength in voluminous planes. This simplicity in design stands in marked contrast to the indication of scales on the tail preserved on the smaller fragment with base, paws, and tail-end, described in the next paragraph. The incised line around the figure at thigh height might then mark the point of transition from untextured upper and scaled lower tail.

The smaller fragment comprises the remains of the roughly cuboid shallow base, preserving also both hind-leg feet and reptilian tail-end curving to the proper right of the figure and forward (Fig. 5). Each foot has three deep grooves incised from upper surface to base, which might convey the four webbed toes of a hippopotamus, or the four claws on the hind-leg of a lion, or both. The tail has narrower groove lines lengthways intersected by transverse lines to form a schematic grid, evoking scales. The front corner of the base at right hind-leg is broken away, and the edges are chipped. The front, back and side faces of the base are finely smoothed to an even upper edge and less even lower edge. The base underside is less finished, and the upper face is slightly convex and least even in the area between the tail and paws, where the difficulty in sculpting below the figure body has left a more hatched effect. In this area, two overlapping vertical lines may have resulted from the sculpting of the figure, while the incising of the scale grid along the curve of the tail line would have produced the short thicker lines beside the tail, to rear right corner. A precise circular hole drilled into the left hind-leg, to about half its height, is presumably from earlier museum mounting of the two fragments together for display.

Traces of colour can be detected at certain areas, for which future analysis might help to distinguish between properties of the stone, ancient pigment, ancient staining, and modern pigment or staining. Provisionally, the yellow colouring in and around the tail grooves seems an effect of the limestone, rather than any added pigment. The surest indication of modern painting is on the base, where the proper right side has four lengths from a horizontal blue paint line, presumably relating to museum display, and the back face has a clear blue "7" to right of a C-shaped line, also in blue. On the main fragment, darker blue patches are visible from open mouth to edge of mane on the proper left side; a lighter blue smudge can be seen on the body area under the left foreleg (FIG. 1). In view of the modern pigment on the base, these patches seem likely to be offsets from late 19th or 20th century painting, but they could instead be original to the figure. Red pigment is visible around the incised features of the mane, ears and mouth, for example in the teeth grooves and mouth lines, the internal triangle of the ear, and in the lines incised within the mane (FIG. 1). Black material in the tear-duct from the left eye and at the corner of the right eye seems more likely to be pigment rather than soil. Under the chin, over a whiter area of the limestone (?), black traces seem to be smudging of uncertain date, rather than the result of applying black pigment to this area. There is grey at the ridge on top of the head between the eyes.

Despite the contrast between plain back ridge and tail-end grid pattern, the larger body fragment can be aligned with the paws on the base. In her inventory of Petrie finds accessioned in the Manchester Museum, Agnes Griffith presented figure and base as parts of the same object, without hesitation:

> 270 *(a)* Upper part of figure of the hippopotamus goddess Ta-urt. Limestone; standing. *Height* 28.5. *(b)* Base; with tail and paws of the same figure. *Length of base* 27.5 x 23.[2]

Therefore it seems plausible that the two fragments are from a single object. Late Middle Kingdom scarabs offer parallels for such juxtaposition of "naturalistic" and "schematic" segments in one figure.[3] Although the forelegs extend forward, there is insufficient space at the front of the base for an additional element. Therefore, the original foreleg composition can best be reconstructed either as extending down on the body or possibly as holding a motif small enough not to unbalance the careful centring of the overall weight. In contrast to these options, the forelegs are held directly to the side in the closest published parallel, a limestone image of an upright hippopotamus with crocodile down its back, from an uncertain context at the late Middle Kingdom palace site at Bubastis (see LIMESTONE STANDS WITH FIGURAL MOTIFS, below).[4]

CONTEXT AND PARALLELS

In 1889, archaeological recording techniques had not yet been standardised, and fieldwork directors in England as much as in Egypt did not regularly record either stratigraphy or the precise find-spot of individual items. In the excavation report for his second season at the Lahun town-site, Petrie began his paragraph 23 with the statement "Of stonework some curious figures have been found," and included here the note: "A rough large figure of Taurt was found, as also a small one last year, shewing that her form was already fixed at this period."[5] According to this wording, the sculpture now in Manchester seems likely to be the larger figure, and so a find from the second season of work, but Petrie gives no information on provenance within the site. The report also gives no illustration and no comment on the condition of the figure and presence of the separate fragment with base and leonine hind-paws. Nor do any in the limited set of his 1889–1890 photographs show either the main figure or the base fragment.[6] In her study of the Petrie publications, notebooks, and weekly circular reports ("Petrie Journals"), Carla Gallorini could delineate the general area explored in each season and found further evidence for the exact find-spot of several items, but not the two figures.[7] Indeed the "Journals" contain no certain reference at all to either "figure of Taurt." In those circulars, Petrie reported the finds and events of the week in chronological sequence, perhaps writing up at variable intervals of between a day and a week. His reportage is often more inventory than narrative, such that any one report of a find may have no connection with the preceding and following sentences. The smaller "Taurt" from the first season might be the subject of an entry "Hippopotamus in limestone, very rude" for the week 28 April–4 May 1889 (typescript p. 108). However, Petrie also found limestone figures of hippopotami standing on all fours, such as Manchester Museum 135 (9.5 cm) and 136 (12.9 cm);[8] his choice of "hippopotamus" rather than "Taurt" seems more likely to indicate one of those. From the second season, his wording in the 8–14 November report again seems to imply smaller figurines: "Several rough limestone figures of apes and hippopotami have been found: they are painted in red and blue. One is a hippopotamus in a boat, quite perfect. Another little figure in fine state is that of a girl playing a small harp" (1889–1890 "Journal" typescript, p. 16).

From the early 2nd millennium BCE, the closest parallels are the Bubastis figure cited above at note 4 and finds from Lisht. The preliminary report on the Bubastis figure states that it "was found in the Middle Kingdom palace," with no mention of any associated finds. Preserved to lower leg, but without hind feet or base, at 33 cm in height this sculpture is close in scale to the Lahun example. One Lisht find is a smaller and more schematic, possibly unfinished upright hippopotamus with dorsal ridge (MMA 15.3.599, height 12.7 cm according to the online collection database, from the 1906–1907 season, context not identified). From the 1921 season, Arthur Mace published a photograph of "household gods," in which two items may be related to the upright hippopotamus motif.[9] At lower left is a figure with swollen belly, disk navel, and carefully outlined pendant breasts with rounded nipples. The sculpture is broken away at lower leg, and the front of the head is not preserved, so this might be a human female figure. However, the proper right side is well preserved and has a slender arm or foreleg placed vertically down along the body, recalling the

Bubastis figure. At second left above, in the photograph, a smaller sculpture is of an animal upright on hind legs, of which only the top of the proper left leg is preserved; the animal has arms to centre, and a mane with incised internal fur lines, like the Lahun image, but the snout seems narrow like that of a baboon. Unlike the Bubastis and Lahun upright maned hippopotami, this animal bears on its head a shallow cylinder. This feature introduces another object type, to which the other items on the Lisht photograph also belong: the figured offering-stand, discussed next.

Limestone Stands with Figural Motifs

At Lahun, limestone artefacts of similar scale and varying precision take the form of columns or human forms. In contrast to the leonine hippopotamus figure, these objects are carved in one block with a shallow open vessel, as Petrie related in his published report on the first season of work at Lahun:

> A curious piece of furniture was a limestone stand, on which offerings of bread paste were made. These stands are usually in the form of a column with a saucer-shaped hollow on the top; the columns are 18 to 21 inches high including a square base, usually with plain capital, but one has a lotus capital as at Beni Hasan (Pl.XVI). Two examples were found of these stands in the form of two men, standing back to back and supporting the cup with raised arms on their shoulders. These are rudely done, one being unfinished; and from the place of discovery may belong to the XIIIth dynasty, as the scarab of Neferhotep was found in the room with one of these. One example occurs of an arm supporting a cup, evidently intended to be built into a wall so as to project.[10]

According to the weekly circulars sent home during the season, the first clear example of these finds was the stand with a floral capital illustrated on plate 16 of that publication: "A pretty column of the lotus bud pattern is evidently of the XIIth dynasty, it supports a saucer (for incense?) all cut in one block of limestone, about 18 ins. high. It is a new type to me" ("Journal" 21–28 April 1889, typescript pp.105–106). The next week he reported: "A curious stand was found formed of a pair of roughly blocked out figures back to back; I had before found most part of a similar stand with wrought figures, but rude in style. These are of XIII dyn." ("Journal" 28 April–4 May 1889, typescript p. 112).

In his published report on the second season, Petrie repeated his interpretation of the material in the vessels as bread rather than incense:

> The dwarf supporting a dish (VI, 9) is remarkable, as we have no clue to the meaning of such figures in Egypt. This is one of the dish-stands, which are generally simple columns; and which, whenever they are found charged, have a cake of dough stuck in the dish. It seems reasonable to suppose that they are stands for household offerings of daily bread.[11]

His identification would require laboratory analysis for confirmation, but use of the "dish-stands" for offerings seems plausible. Although listed under stonework, one of the stands is of clay, marl from its light colour, with two naked human figures back-to-back, elbows and knees bent, in an openwork cuboid frame.[12]

The sole reference to find-place ("room" in the first report) is too vague to assert that the objects belong in a domestic context, and so it is necessary to look for parallels from more precisely documented excavations. Limestone sculptures of this scale have been recorded from domestic contexts at Lisht and Memphis, and from funerary contexts at Tell el-Dab'a and Bubastis. At Lisht, the examples are from the late Middle Kingdom village on the south side of the pyramid of Amenemhat I. The Lisht photograph cited above (with note 9) includes examples with small monkey figure climbing a column, a human head bearing a dish, mainly broken away, and a naked male dwarf body with shallow dish. An exhibition catalogue with publication of the latter gives its height as 33 cm, confirming that these are on the same scale as the Lahun and Bubastis upright hippopotamus figures.[13] The photograph also shows one example with the motif named in the Middle Kingdom as Aha, and after the New Kingdom as Bes, a naked frontal maned man with limbs flexed, holding a snake towards his navel in each hand. In his accompanying text, Mace gives a general account of the context for these figures within the settlement area: "In many of the houses there seems to have been a shrine, in which was placed a rough limestone figure of the household god."[14] Felix Arnold provides more detail in his report on 1991 re-excavation of Lisht house A1.3, with a side-room at its entrance:

> Religious objects, such as figures of dwarfs, hippopotami, lions and crocodiles (some examples are published in Mace [1921], fig.3) are sometimes found at Lisht in or near such side rooms, possibly indicating the existence of household shrines. The proximity to the entrance of the house may have provided a magical protection.[15]

At Memphis, a fragmentary example in human form, perhaps with dwarf proportions, was found in a large structure, provisionally identified as part of a large house, and dated to the late Middle Kingdom.[16] At Tell el-Dab'a, in Area A/II, a late Middle Kingdom to early Second Intermediate Period cemetery and chapel field yielded three figure stands, all roughly shaped from blocks of limestone, which is not local to this region.[17] One stand from a pit of stratum F or early E/3 (start of Second Intermediate Period) takes the form of a baboon holding a bowl on its head with both forelegs. Two others are in the form of naked dwarves, one in a layer of later Second Intermediate Period debris, and one at foundation level of a building in stratum F. Plausibly, the figures originally stood in cemetery chapels. Despite the mixture of Egyptian and Levantine material culture and practice at the site, the Nile Valley and Delta parallels for the forms suggest an Egyptian origin, as Irene Forstner-Müller emphasises. In a late Middle Kingdom funerary cult context, finds by Shafik Farid at the monumental tomb of the governors of Bubastis include a dwarf and monkey figure.[18]

As an object type, these stands differ from the Lahun and Bubastis upright hippopotamus figures in their function as supports for vessels. Their repertoire of form may not include the hippopotamus (the Lisht photograph is unclear here); clearly published examples are the naked humans with dwarf proportions (Lisht, Lahun, Bubastis, Tell el-Dab'a), baboon (Bubastis, Tell el-Dab'a), column (Lahun), column with climbing monkey (Lisht), and naked maned man wielding snakes (Lisht). A further unprovenanced example shows a pregnant woman with a snake in each hand.[19] Snake-wielding leonine man and upright leonine hippopotamus appear in the same groups of figures on objects with a focus on protection of infant and mother or nurse: birth tusks, feeding-cups, headrest, glazed steatite small box, painted long box.[20] Significantly for the thematic focus of expression, Bes, the later name for the leonine snake-wielding man, may be the Egyptian word for "foetus just before birth / new-born child (?)."[21] The Lahun leonine hippopotamus figure might have been installed originally beside an anthropomorphic "dish-stand" in a household place of offerings.[22] Here, its protective force may be targeted most intensely around birth, as bodily crisis of society and as drama of creation. However, it seems appropriate to follow these provisional conclusions with more open questions, focussed on the exceptional quality of this one work of sculpture.

Place, Name, and Material Form

The scale and the soft stone of the maned hippopotamus figure from Lahun locate it within a late Middle Kingdom repertoire of personal and household protection. That general description should not obscure the highly specific ancient choices in selecting particular motifs according to scale, object-type, and material. From this period, all comparable stone figures in the 15–50 cm range seem to have a primary function of supporting a receptacle for offerings. The Bubastis upright hippopotamus sculpture (see note 4) may be the only other limestone figure of this size and quality without a vessel, though even there the upper part appears damaged on the published photograph. The Lahun figure stands on its own base, securing greater space and prominence. On other upright hippopotami in Middle Kingdom depictions, the dorsal feature rarely extends so far down. On one finely carved birth tusk, a naturalistic crocodile figure on dorsal ridge does have a tail reaching lower hind-leg, recalling the images of the upright hippopotamus constellation in astronomical ceilings of New Kingdom kings.[23] However, a tail coiling alongside the leg is unparalleled to our knowledge. Given the exceptional features of the figure, it is important to recall here the lack of information on its context. A household shrine is plausible, on the Lisht and Memphis evidence, but the Tell el-Dab'a and Bubastis dwarf stands seem to be from cemetery offering-chapels. At Lahun, the scantly recorded burial areas close to its west wall might be one site for further investigation. However, the larger figure is a find from the second season, when clearance seems to have focussed on the northern and eastern sides of the town-site, according to the research by

Carla Gallorini (see note 7). Considering the poorer preservation and recording of the east side, further possibilities of original context could include a chapel in the town. In one sense, the lack of documentary evidence for find-spot may be an advantage, if it reminds us not to solidify this chapel, domestic, and funerary contexts into mutually exclusive spheres. In the Lisht and Memphis houses, inscriptions on stelae, statues, or offering-tables appeal for the eternal offerings, in a manner that Egyptologists generally ascribe to tomb or temple, not to the house. These different architectural settings may then prompt, for their Middle Kingdom users, an intense awareness of liminal forces that can invade or defend human space. In comparative contextual analysis of ancient composite figures, David Wengrow has identified multiple modes or strategies in expression according to the different historical trajectories of particular social groups. Among these, in "protective mode," composite figures materialise at thresholds and boundaries, as exemplified by 1st millennium BCE Assyrian images and the detailed instructions on how to produce them.[24] The find-spot of the Lahun figure might not be recoverable, but a different kind of context, comparative and functional, can be identified in the thematic focus of the society that produced it.

One feature shared with the limestone stands is the lack of inscription, and especially the absence of a name for the depicted image. Indeed, in the Middle Kingdom, name captions rarely accompany images of the leonine hippopotamus. The motif is widespread on the faience figurines and "birth tusks" typical of this period, but inscriptions are absent on the former object type and rare on the latter. Only two "birth tusks" have depictions of the leonine hippopotamus with captions. On a tusk found in 1997–1998 excavations at Dra Abu al-Naga, Thebes, the name is *rr* "boar," without the feminine *-t* ending expected for *rrt* "(hippopotamus) sow."[25] Masculine form is also found in both instances of a writing *ỉrr* on the second tusk, acquired by William MacGregor at "Saoniyeh near Negadeh," so just north of Thebes.[26] In her detailed assessment of Middle Kingdom sources for the hippopotamus goddess, Judith Weingarten drew attention to ambivalence in gender.[27] A similar phenomenon may be at work in the deity names Ip(i) and Reret, as written within Middle Kingdom personal names. A small image of upright hippopotamus with dorsal ridge can be used as determinative or as ideogram of Ip, Ipi, and Reret.[28] The two names for that one image Ip(i) and Reret recall the application of two types of name in the captions on the "birth tusks": the Saoniyeh tusk has, for example, the individual name Heqet beside the frog image at the tip, but the species name *štw* "turtle" beside the turtle behind it. The explicitly gendered *rrt* "sow" might be the species name for the motif, with Ip(i) as identifier of a more specific divine force. At the same time, the use of upright hippopotamus image as an ideogram in names (see note 28) reminds us that the figure might have had a single or dominant phonetic value well known to viewers in the immediate social context. Within a narrow time-space horizon, then, the image might have needed no caption.

The possible phonetic void and the gender ambiguity of names for the loudly snarling leonine hippopotamus are part of the background to the sculptural conception of the Lahun figure. Irene Forstner-Müller observed that the figure stands at Tell el Dab'a belong to Egyptian, rather than Levantine, material culture (above with note 17). Among other features, Bronze Age Egyptian sources attest to the idea that form emerges from within the material to which an artist gives shape, rather than being an idea applied to it. The primary evidence for this understanding of material production is found in scenes 9 and 10 of the ritual for Opening the Mouth and Eyes, as analysed by Hans-Werner Fischer-Elfert from the New Kingdom sources.[29] In scene 9, a man in the role called *sem*[30] dons a special robe to "sleep" on a special form of chair in seclusion within the Domain of Gold, a dedicated space for sculpting and ritualised activation by properly initiated "animators."[31] Facing the stone block to be carved, he states "he has broken me"; a second man, in the role of "he who is in the chamber," recites behind him the phrase "my father" four times, and the *sem* is woken. In scene 10, the *sem* declares "I have seen my father in all his forms" in the presence of a group of men who hold another role, *imy-khent*. A brief sequence of their short statements follows, echoed in an accompanying set of written, apparently unspoken, acts of code-switching, somewhat reminiscent of the dual naming options for upright hippopotamus figure (see above).[32] Here, the vocabulary of artistic technical sculptural procedure —drafting guidelines, draft form outlines, corrected final form outlines—is correlated with names including insect species: spider, mantis, bee, shadow. After silently changing robes (scene 11), the *sem* then supervises the start of work by a group of sculptors (scene 12). This ritual is widely attested for formal sculpture, starting at the level of the palace and court of the king, and so it is not certain that the same ideas or procedures can be applied to other social contexts. Products such as the —to quote Petrie, "rough"—figure stands might seem to stand outside this artistic horizon. However, a top-down reading of art and iconography is not the only option for our approaches to ancient Egyptian visual products. Another possibility is to consider palatial artists as concentrating the skills from across the territory, still within a particular way of thinking about form and matter. In a spectrum from formal accuracy to rough expression, all involved might have seen their work as drawing out of a block of material the forces already materialised within it.

In shaping a maned hippopotamus, upright on hind legs, with part-scaled dorsal feature, the sculptor followed the inspiration of a model already established for several centuries at least.[33] Today, Egyptologists using European languages would identify the core of the motif with the species name applied since the ancient Greek historians, hippopotamus "river-horse." Possibly the remarkable speed of the animal, and its galloping gait, encouraged this impression, perhaps from a distance. Yet Herodotus, or his source(s), noted other features, in particular the "mane," which may seem curious, as the animal has especially little hair for a mammal.[34] Many ancient Egyptian images of the upright hippopotamus with dorsal ridge, like the Lahun figure, also have a mane, but around the face like that of a lion, rather than along the back like that of a horse. Possible the ruff-like circle around the face, and perhaps too the dorsal ridge along the back, conveyed in some way in petrified space the swiftly-passed sight of a spray of water around and behind the animal as it runs or fights in the river. Whatever the origin, whether in the meditative immersion of the *sem* or not, the mane is not the only leonine feature on this and other upright hippopotamus figures. These may have feline legs and claws, and the head may also be lion-like.[35] If the 1st millennium BCE Greeks saw in the animal a horse of the river, the 2nd millennium BCE Egyptians seem instead to be conveying more a river lion, at least in the liminal fissures where their lives most needed protection. An ancient Egyptian term sporadically used for stone figure-carvers is *sankh* "animator."[36] With the Lahun figure, in a land where rituals of opening the mouth were performed, "animators" found a surge of lethal forces in this limestone block to dramatic tangible and visual effect.

References

Allen, James. 2005. *The Art of Medicine in Ancient Egypt*. New York: Metropolitan Museum of Art.

Altenmüller, Hartwig. 1965. *Die Apotropaia und die Götter Mittelägyptens: eine typologische und religionsgeschichtliche Untersuchung der sogenannten "Zaubermesser" des Mittleren Reichs*. Munich: Ludwig-Maximilians-Universität.

Anonymous. 1922. *Catalogue of the MacGregor Collection of Egyptian Antiquities, Which Will be Sold by Auction by Messrs. Sotheby, Wilkinson and Hodge*. London: Sotheby.

Arnold, Felix. 1996. "Settlement Remains at Lisht-North." In Manfred Bietak (ed.), *House and Palace in Ancient Egypt*, 13–21. Vienna: Österreichische Akademie der Wissenschaften.

Ben-Tor, Daphna. 2007. *Scarabs, Chronology, and Interconnections: Egypt and Palestine in the Second Intermediate Period*. Fribourg: Academic Press, and Göttingen: Vandenhoeck and Ruprecht.

Bomhard, Anne-Sophie von. 2012. "Ciels d'Égypte. Le 'ciel du sud' et le 'ciel du nord.'" *Égypte Nilotique et Méditerranéenne* 5: 73–102.

Budka, Julia. 2010. *Bestattungsbrauchtum und Friedhofsstruktur im Asasif: eine Untersuchung der spätzeitlichen Befunde anhand der Ergebnisse der österreichischen Ausgrabungen in den Jahren 1969–1977*. Vienna: Österreichische Akademie der Wissenschaften.

Ceruti, Sabrina. 2017. "The Hippopotamus Goddess Carrying a Crocodile on Her Back: An Iconographic Motif Distinctive of the Late Middle Kingdom." In Gianluca Miniaci, Marilina Betrò, and Stephen Quirke (eds.), *Company of Images: Modelling the Imaginary World of Middle Kingdom Egypt (2000–1500 BC)*, 93–123. Leuven: Peeters.

Curto, Silvio and Alessandro Roccati (eds.). 1984. *Cairo—The Egyptian Museum: Treasures of the Pharaohs*. Milan: Mondadori.

Dasen, Veronique. 1993. *Dwarfs in Ancient Egypt and Greece*. Oxford Monographs on Classical Archaeology. Oxford: Clarendon Press.

El-Sawi, Ahmed. 1979. *Excavations at Tell Basta: Report of Seasons 1967–1971 and Catalogue of Finds*. Prague: Charles University.

Fischer-Elfert, Hans-Werner. 1998. *Die Vision von der Statue im Stein: Studien zum altägyptischen Mundöffnungsritual*. Heidelberg: Universitätsverlag C. Winter.

Farid, Shafik. 1964. "Preliminary Report on the Excavations of the Antiquities Department at Tell Basta (Season 1961)." *Annales du Service des antiquités de l'Égypte* 58: 85–98.

Forstner-Müller, Irene. 2008. *Tell el-Dab'a XVI: die Gräber des Areals A/II von Tell el-Dab'a*. Vienna: Österreichische Akademie der Wissenschaften.

Gallorini, Carla. 1998. "A Reconstruction of Petrie's Excavation at the Middle Kingdom Settlement of Kahun." In S. Quirke (ed.), *Lahun Studies*, 42–59. Reigate: SIA.

Griffith, Agnes. 1910. *Catalogue of Egyptian Antiquities of the XII and XVIII Dynasties from Kahun, Illahun and Gurob*. Manchester: Sherratt and Hughes.

Gundlach, Rolf. 1986. "Thoeris." In Wolfgang Helck, and Wolfhart Westendorf (eds.), *Lexikon der Ägyptologie* vol. 6, cols. 494–497. Wiesbaden: Harrassowitz.

Jeffreys, David. 2012. "Memphis in the Middle Kingdom: The Field School." *Egyptian Archaeology* 40: 5–6.

Leitz, Christian (ed.). 2002. *Das Lexikon der ägyptischen Götter und Götterbezeichnungen*. Leuven: Peeters.

Lieven, Alexandra von. 2007. "Im Schatten des Goldhauses: Berufsgeheimnis und Handwerkerinitiation im Alten Ägypten." *Studien zur Altägyptischen Kultur* 36: 147–155.

Lloyd, Alan. 1976. *Herodotus Book II, Commentary 1–98*. Leiden: Brill.

Luft, Daniela. 2009. *Das Anzünden der Fackel. Untersuchungen zu Spruch 137 des Totenbuches*. Wiesbaden: Harrassowitz.

Mace, Arthur. 1921. "The Egyptian Expedition 1920–1921: I. Excavations at Lisht." *Bulletin of the Metropolitan Museum of Art* 16(2): 5–19.

Martin, Geoffrey. 1971. *Egyptian Administrative and Private-name Seals Principally of the Middle Kingdom and Second Intermediate Period*. Oxford: Griffith Institute.

Meeks, Dimitri. 1992. "Le nom du dieu Bès et ses implication mythologiques." In Ulrich Luft (ed.), *The Intellectual Heritage of Egypt: Studies Presented to Lászlo Kákosy*, 423–436. Budapest: Université Eötvös Loránd.

Miniaci, Gianluca and Stephen Quirke. 2009. "Reconceiving the Tomb in the Late Middle Kingdom: The Burial of the Accountant of the Main Enclosure Neferhotep at Dra Abu al-Naga." *Bulletin de l'Institut français d'archéologie orientale* 109: 339–383.

Mlinar, Christa. 2004. "The Scarab Workshops at Tell el-Dab'a." In Manfred Bietak, and Ernst Czerny (eds.), *Scarabs of the Second Millennium BC from Egypt, Nubia, Crete and the Levant: Chronological and Historical implications*, 107–140. Vienna: Österreichische Akademie der Wissenschaften.

Petrie, William Matthews Flinders. 1891. *Illahun, Kahun and Gurob. 1889–90*. London: Nutt.

Petrie, William Matthew Flinders. 1907. *Gizeh and Rifeh*. London: Quaritch.

Polz, Daniel, Bill Gordon, Andreas Nerlich, Aldo Piccato, Ute Rummel, Anne Seiler, and Susanne Voss. 1999. "Bericht über die 6., 7. und 8. Grabungskampagne in der Nekropole von Dra' Abu el-Naga/Theben-West." *Mitteilungen des Deutschen Archäologischen Instituts Kairo* 55: 343–410.

Quirke, Stephen. 2011. "Petrie's 1889 Photographs of Lahun." In Bettina Bader, David Aston, Carla Gallorini, and Paul Nicholson (eds.), *Under the Potter's Tree: Studies on Ancient Egypt Presented to Janine Bourriau on the Occasion of Her 70th Birthday*, 769–794. Peeters: Leuven.

Ranke, Hermann. 1935. *Die ägyptischen Personennamen* I. Glückstadt: Augustin.

Raven, Maarten. 1987. "A Puzzling Pataekos." *Oudheidkundige mededelingen uit het Rijksmuseum van Oudheden* 67: 7–19.

Rosati, Gloria. 1988. "Le stele del Medio Regno." In Anna Maria Donadoni Roveri (ed.), *La Civiltà egizia: le credenze religiose*, 104–113. Milan: Electa.

Ward, William. 1982. *Index of Egyptian Administrative and Religious Titles of the Middle Kingdom*. Beirut: American University of Beirut.

Weingarten, Judith. 1991. *The Transformation of Egyptian Taweret into the Minoan Genius: A Study in Cultural Transmission in the Middle Bronze Age*. Partille: Paul Åström.

Wengrow, David. 2014. *The Origins of Monsters: Image and Cognition in the First Age of Mechanical Reproduction*. Princeton: Princeton University Press.

Notes

1 Gundlach 1986.For discussion, distinguishing between images with partly or entirely schematic dorsal ridge and the rarer type with living crocodile down the back, see Ceruti 2017.

2 Griffith 1910, 31. This wording is given in the museum register, which is based directly on it.

3 Ben-Tor 2007, pl. 21, square head type C, with geometric conception of elements, with articulated legs of side types d5/6, more or less deeply cut, and curving to "naturalistic" effect. In contrast, other scarabs from the same period show a uniformly more geometric, less "naturalistic" conception of all body elements, with square heads and flat sides in which the legs are rendered as schematic outlines with incised herringbone design within all or part of legs. For examples with archaeological context, see Mlinar 2004 (see p. 108 fig.1 for Type 1 at Tell el-Dab'a).

4 El-Sawi 1979, 76–77, figs.177–179, reg. no. 1872.

5 Petrie 1891, 11.

6 Quirke 2011, 769–794.

7 Gallorini 1998. For this study we have rechecked in particular the weekly circular reports known as the "Petrie Journals." In addition to photocopies of the original "Journals" in the Griffith Institute, Oxford, the archives of the Petrie Museum, UCL, include typescripts prepared in 1969 for the biography. The Petrie Museum typescript copy of the "Journals" from 1888–1889, his first season at the town-site, is kept in an envelope marked "LC (1) VII Journal 1888-1889" (LC = Leonard Cottrell, who started on the biography). The envelope is also marked in pencil "For A.P. 13 Oct 1979," and, partly over this, in biro, "Typed by Miss Vousden, paid £10/10/0 cash 21/10/69 from FP Book Account A Petrie," the initials being for Flinders Petrie (1853–1942) and his daughter Ann (1910–1989).

8 Griffith 1910, 21.

9 Mace 1921, 6 fig.3.

10 Mace 1921, 6 fig.3.

11 Petrie 1891, 11. Petrie first uses the term "dough" for the substance in the vessels in his circular at the start of the second season: "Another stand for dough offerings, with a lump of dough on the top, is in the form of the deformed Ptah, with arms raised supporting the cup on his head, 15 ins. high" ("Journal" 26 September to 12 October 1889, typescript p. 2). Ten examples are illustrated in Petrie 1891, pl. 6, from drawings by his friend Flaxman Charles John Spurrell. One anthropomorphic example (pl. 6 no. 9) is shown as filled with loaf-shaped offerings; its present location is not known (Dasen 1993, 281 no. 143). Most stands with preserved upper part have floral capitals, some highly schematic (pl. 6, 1–3, 5, 7: no. 6 is apparently cylindrical or cuboid capital or base for lost upper element).

12 Petrie 1891, pl. 6 no. 10, now Manchester Museum no.280 = Griffith 1910, 32; Dasen 1993, 281 no. 142.

13 Egyptian Museum Cairo JE63866: Curto and Roccati 1984, 184 no. 61, height given as 44 cm including exhibition mount 11 cm.

14 Mace 1921, 12.

15 Arnold 1996, 15 n.17.

16 Jeffreys 2012, 6.

17 Forstner-Müller 2008, 119, pl. 22d, pl. 23.

18 Farid 1964, 86.

19 Raven 1987, 7–19.

20 Feeding-cup from Lisht, MMA 44.4.4, Allen 2005, 30–31. Headrest from Thebes, Egyptian Museum Cairo JE6143, Miniaci and Quirke 2009, 339–383. Glazed steatite box from shaft 1, square L30, Asasif, Thebes, Budka 2010, 712–713, cat. no. 872. Painted box from Rifa, Fitzwilliam Museum E.15.1907, Petrie 1907, 20–21, pl. 24. Birth tusks with both figures include the examples cited below in notes 23, 25.

21 Meeks 1992, 423–436.

22 Cf. Dasen 1993, 141: "Petrie also found two crude figures of Taweret which probably belonged in this ritual context," with reference to the column and dwarf stands as for "household offerings," following Petrie 1891, 11. Upright hippopotamus and stand are associated in one exceptional mid-Eighteenth Dynasty afterlife papyrus from the Memphis necropolis, the Book of the Dead for Nebseny. There, a formula for lighting a torch (called by Naville Book of the Dead chapter 137B) has an illustration of

an upright hippopotamus with dorsal ridge and leonine limbs; identified as "Ipy mistress of protection," she is depicted in the act of lighting a lamp on a stand. Although later, the formula has a Middle Kingdom antecedent, but there the name of the deity seems to be a female serpent force Ikhetweret; see Luft 2009, 27–28, 38–42.

23 Tusk fragment Louvre E3614, part of cat. no. 127 in Altenmüller 1965. In the northern sky depictions on the burial chamber ceilings of Sety I and Ramses VI, both the dorsal ridge and the naturalistic crocodile behind it have a tail-end turning just above ground height: see von Bomhard 2012, 89 fig.10 (Sety I).

24 Wengrow 2014, 102–103.

25 Published by Voss in Daniel Polz et al. 1999. In the late Middle Kingdom, the upright maned hippopotamus can be the determinative for *rrt* as a deity name, e.g., and the logogram for a deity name of less certain reading, perhaps *ip*, e.g., Martin 1971, 99 no. 1273. For later use of Reret to name a deity depicted as upright hippopotamus, see Leitz 2002, 694–695.

26 Place of acquisition is cited as Anonymous 1922, lot 715. The tusk is now National Museum, Copenhagen, no. 7795 = Altenmüller 1965, no. 50.

27 Weingarten 1991, especially p. 5: "Breasts, if shown at all, are always pendulous (though it is uncertain if this is a sign of pregnancy or *even* of her female nature)." In her n. 13 there, Weingarten notes the androgynous images of the masculine-named Hapy "Nile Flood" as source for the swollen belly and extended breasts. In combination with gender, age may be an important referent in contemporary depictions with or without breasts, and with swollen or narrower belly.

28 Ranke 1935, 280, 19 and 285, 20–22 citing examples with determinative of Ip, Ipi, and Ipy in the names Saip, Satip, Satipi, and Satipy on Middle Kingdom sources. Ranke 1935, 280, 19 and 285, 23 gives Middle Kingdom examples of ideogram without phonetic complements, so reading of deity name uncertain, in Sa-[Deity Name] and Sat-[Deity Name]-khered. The same upright hippopotamus hieroglyph is used as determinative of Reret in the name Satreret on stela Turin 1545, photograph published by Rosati 1988, 110 fig. 146 (final horizontal line, last sign at right).

29 Fischer-Elfert 1998, summary at pp. 72–73.

30 Against the rendering as "*sem*-priest," words such as "priest" seem too generalised a term of profession to correspond adequately to such defined roles.

31 See von Lieven 2007 on the ritual links between craft and initiation. Campbell Price is preparing a separate study on the role of this institution in the transmission of forms.

32 Fischer-Elfert 1998, 16–25 on scene 10, with further comments on double naming at 72–73 n. 169.

33 Weingarten 1991, 4 with fig.6a for late 3rd millennium BCE amulets from Upper Egypt.

34 Herodotus, *Histories* Book II, 71: on the zoological discrepancies, see Lloyd 1976, 312–314.

35 Cf. Weingarten 1991, 8.

36 Two Middle Kingdom examples are cited in Ward 1982, no. 1278.

Journal of Ancient Egyptian Interconnections

The Slaughterers: A Study of the Ḫ3.tyw as Liminal Beings in Ancient Egyptian Thought

Danielle Sass
Macquarie University

Abstract
The *ḫ3.tyw*, otherwise known as the Slaughterers, Knife-bearers, and Plague-bringers within academic literature, are a group of liminal deities attested in the written record from the Old Kingdom to the Greco-Roman Period. They posed a significant danger in both the terrestrial and secular realms, to the living and the dead, to the gods and mankind alike. This paper presents a preliminary discussion of the etymology and orthography of the designation *ḫ3.tyw*, the group's form and appearance, and their position within the hierarchy of the Egyptian pantheon.

Introduction[1]
The *ḫ3.tyw* were conceptualised in ancient Egyptian thought as liminal deities. This category of liminal beings has aptly been termed as "religiösen Grenzgänger" by Gregor Ahn in an attempt to facilitate in scholarly discourse a differentiated description and evaluation of intermediary figures in polytheistic religions.[2] The boundaries between the secular and divine spheres were considered by the ancient Egyptians as permeable. The *ḫ3.tyw* and other liminal deities were able to cross these boundaries, acting in a sense as "Zaungäger" occupying a transitional point between two states,[3] as their actions are documented in the textual record as affecting both humankind and the gods, the living and the dead. The power that the *ḫ3.tyw* possessed should be considered as ambivalent on account of the dualistic nature of this group that encompasses components of both *ma'at* and *isfet*. While attestations of the *ḫ3.tyw* in the historical record span from the Old Kingdom to the Greco-Roman Period, there is a substantial proliferation of source material from the New Kingdom onwards, which most likely resulted from a change in religious decorum that stipulated what was allowed to be expressed in image and writing in specific contexts.[4] Unfortunately this concentration of sources places a limitation on our ability to determine the extent of the role performed by the *ḫ3.tyw* in earlier religious contexts and whether this role was static or subject to developments within this period of time. Despite these difficulties, this paper aims to undertake a preliminary examination of the etymology and orthography of the designation, the group's form and appearance, and their position within the hierarchy of the Egyptian pantheon. A discussion of these topics, focusing upon both philological and iconographic evidence, is intended to facilitate a greater understanding of liminal groups

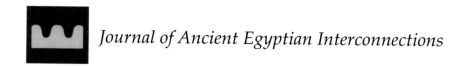

and encourage further research into this fascinating area of Egyptian religion.

Etymology

Establishing the etymological origin of the term *ḫꜣ.tyw* is a vital step in understanding how the nature and role of this liminal group were initially conceptualised by the ancient Egyptians. As the orthography of the denomination exhibits similar characteristics to a number of different words, its etymology has become highly contested within Egyptological literature. Hannig and Eschweiler have both proposed a connection between *ḫꜣ.tyw* and the term *ḫꜣwy* () for night or evening; however, as this concept appears to be based primarily on the groups connection with the imperishable stars in the Pyramid Texts, it is somewhat unconvincing.[5] Other scholars, such as Edwards and Breasted, have suggested instead that the term *ḫꜣ.tyw* is a derivative of the word *ḫꜣy.t* (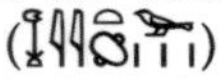) "disease."[6] This etymological connection is founded principally on the association of the *ḫꜣ.tyw* with the *ỉꜣd.t rnp.t* in the invocations of Papyrus Edwin Smith and the petitions of the Oracular Amuletic Decrees. However, as the role of the *ḫꜣ.tyw* as disease bringers is not attested securely in the written record until the Second Intermediate Period, it is doubtful that the designation *ḫꜣ.tyw* was originally derived from this term. This development in the role performed by the *ḫꜣ.tyw* is more likely to have resulted from the phonetic similarities exhibited between the two terms. Instead, the term *ḫꜣ.yt* () "slaughter or massacre" appears to be the most plausible etymological origin for the designation *ḫꜣ.tyw*. Faulkner has convincingly suggested that a connection between these two terms can be demonstrated through the use of specific determinatives depicting weaponry and armed figures in conjunction with the context of Papyrus Bremner Rhind, in which the role of the *ḫꜣ.tyw* is to viciously slay Apophis by cutting up his intestines, filling their mouths with his flesh, and swallowing his blood in rage.[7] The earliest role of the *ḫꜣ.tyw* attested in the Pyramid Texts, in which they appear to act as armed celestial gatekeepers, provides further confirmation of this etymological relationship.

As previously noted within scholarship, the terms used to denote such liminal groups as the *ḫꜣ.tyw* did not necessarily define "persons," but instead specified their "functions." The name of this group is formed by the nominal usage of the imperfective plural participle indicating actions that are in progress, repeated, or that occur regularly.[8] The most accurate rendering of their name would then be: "Those who slaughter."

Orthography

The orthography of the designation exhibits numerous variations, and, while the singular does occur on a number of occasions, the plural form is more common. Table 1 has been compiled using the *Lexikon der Ägyptischen Götter und Götterbezeichnungen* as a reference point, and it contains the primary writings that are attested in the textual record.[9] For citations to the source material, please refer to the list provided in the Appendix.

As is evident from the table, an ideographic writing is used for the designation in the temple texts of the Greco-Roman Period. This involves the use of a single hieroglyphic sign, usually  (A199A) or a similar variant of an armed figure qualified by plural strokes, to represent the *ḫꜣ.tyw* without expressing the phonetic values normally used to form their name. As these particular hieroglyphic signs are utilised to determine a number of other similar groups of liminal deities, it has proved extremely problematic to establish a secure reading in instances where an ideogram has been employed instead of a full rendition of the deities' names. These groups include the messengers (*wpw.tyw*),[10] the butcher(s) (*mnḥ.wy*),[11] the watchmen (*rs.w*),[12] the emissaries (*hb.yw*),[13] the carvers (*ḥnṯ.tyw*),[14] the watchers (*sꜣw.tyw*),[15] the ones who drive away (*sḥr.w*),[16] the wanderers (*šmꜣ.yw*),[17] the reapers (*ḳdf.tyw*),[18] and the cutters (*ds.w*).[19] It has been suggested by a number of scholars that the value of ideographic writings can be determined through the stylistic device of alliteration.[20] As demonstrated by Barbara Watterson in her assessment of the texts inscribed on the exterior of the naos of the temple of Horus at Edfu, there is an extensive use of alliterative phrases in Ptolemaic texts that utilise nearly every sign of the Egyptian alphabet.[21] There does not appear to be a fixed set of rules regarding whether or not a combination of words constitutes alliteration, i.e., the number of words that alliterate and their spacing within a phrase. Each case must be assessed individually, taking into consideration both the initial and non-initial phonetic values expressed by the words.[22] Of the forty-one possible examples of the *ḫꜣ.tyw* that have so far been identified at the temple of Edfu, a total of thirty-three designations exhibit an ideographic writing that is comprised of (A199A), (A199B),  (A192),  (A290A) or  (C87A).

However, a further assessment of these textual sources, with the aim of identifying the presence of

Table 1: Orthography of the designation *ḫ3.tyw (continued on next page)*.

Date	**Orthography**	**Sign Code**	**Source (see Appendix)**
Old Kingdom		Aa1-M12-G1-G4	3
Old Kingdom		Aa1-M12-G1-G4-T31A:N33A	2
Old Kingdom		Aa1-M12-G1-G4-T31:N33A	1
Old Kingdom		Aa1-M12-G1-N33:N33*N33	4
Old Kingdom		M12-G1-G43-G39-D94-D94-D94	5
Old Kingdom		M12-G1-G43-D94-D94-D94	6
Middle Kingdom		Aa1-M12-G1-X1-G4-A56:Z2	7
Middle Kingdom		Aa1-M12-G1-G1-Aa2-A40-Z2	15; 16
Middle Kingdom		Aa1-M12-G1-G1-A40:Z2	17
Middle Kingdom		Aa1-M12-G1-G4-A40-Z2	11; 12
Middle Kingdom		Aa1-M12-G1-G4-A56-Z2	10
Middle Kingdom		Aa1-M12-G1-G4-T30A-A56-Z2	8
Middle Kingdom		Aa1-M12-G1-M17-M17-G4-T30A-A40-Z2	20
Middle Kingdom	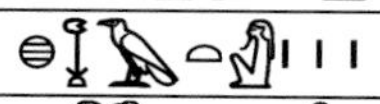	Aa1-M12-G1-X1-A40-Z2	13; 14
Middle Kingdom		Aa1-M12-G4-T30A-A40:Z2	18; 19
Middle Kingdom		M12-G1-G43-G4-A25-Z2	9
Middle Kingdom		M12-G4	21
Second Intermediate Period		Aa1-M12-G1-G4-T31-G7-Z3	25
Second Intermediate Period		M12-G1-M17-M17-G4-A24-G7-Z3	26
Second Intermediate Period	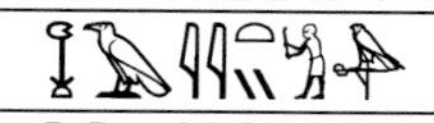	M12-G1-M17-M17-X1-A24-G7	22
Second Intermediate Period	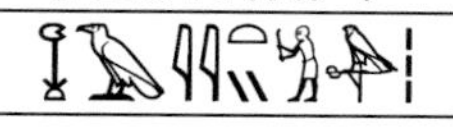	M12-G1-M17-M17-X1-A24-G7	23; 24
New Kingdom		Aa1-M12-M17-M7-Z7-A40-Z2	27
New Kingdom		Aa1-M12B-G4A-A40-Z3	34
New Kingdom		Aa1-M12B-G4A:Z2	35
New Kingdom		M12-G1-M17-M17-G4A-A24-T31:D40-A1:Z2	41
New Kingdom	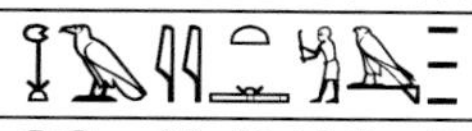	M12-G1-M17-M17-X1:Y4-A24-G7C-Z3A	44
New Kingdom	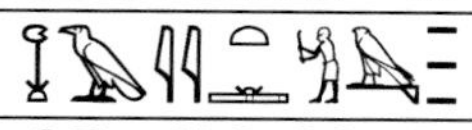	M12-G1-M17-M17-X1:Y4-A24-G7C-Z3A	29
New Kingdom	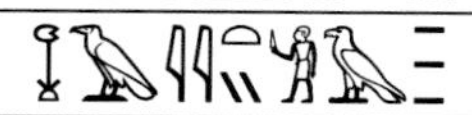	M12-G1-M17-M17-X1:Z4-A199A-G4-Z3A	30

Table 1: *(continued from previous page)* Orthography of the designation *ḫ3.tyw* *(continued on next page)*.

Date	Orthography	Sign Code	Source (see Appendix)
New Kingdom		M12-G1-M17-M17-X1:Y1-A24	43
New Kingdom		M12-G1-M17-M17-X1:Y1-A24-A1:Z4-G7C	45
New Kingdom		M12-G1-M17-M17-X1:Z4-Y1-A24-G7C-Z3A	42
New Kingdom		M12-G1-M17-M17-Z7:X1-//	47
New Kingdom		M12-G1-U33-M17-M17-A24	31
New Kingdom		M12-G1-X1-G4-T30-D40:Z2	32
New Kingdom		M12-G1-Z7:X1-G4A-A24-T31:D40	40
New Kingdom	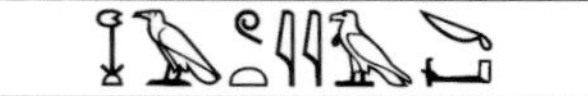	M12-G1-Z7:X1-M17-M17-G4A-T31:D40	46
New Kingdom		M12-G4-A40-Z3	38
New Kingdom		M12B-Aa1-G4-A40-Z3	37
New Kingdom		M12B-Aa1:Z2-G4	36
New Kingdom		M12B-G1-M17-M17-X1:Z4-A199C-Z3	28
New Kingdom		M12B-G4-M17-X1:Z4-M17-A40-A40-Z3	39
New Kingdom		//-G4A-A40:N33A	33
Third Intermediate Period	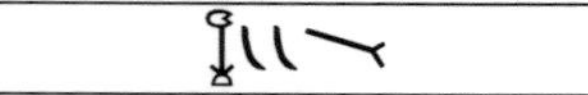	M12-Ff1-Ff1-Z6	53
Third Intermediate Period		M12-G1-M17-M17-X1:Z4-Z6-Z3A	52
Third Intermediate Period		M12-G1-M17-M17-X1-Z6-Z3A	52
Third Intermediate Period		M12-G1-//-//-//	51
Third Intermediate Period		M12-G4-M17-M17-X1:Z4-//	49
Third Intermediate Period		M12-G4-M17-M17-X1:Z4A-E56-//	48
Third Intermediate Period		M12-M17-M17-X1:Z4-A14	55
Third Intermediate Period		M12-Z5-M17-M17-X1-Z6	50
Third Intermediate Period		M12-Z5-Z7:X1-Z1-G37-F37-Z6:Z2	54
Late Period	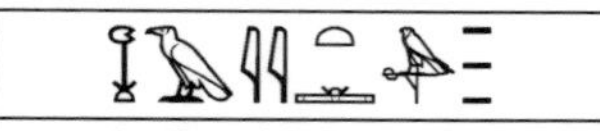	M12-G1-M17-M17-X1:Y1-G7C-Z3A	56; 57
Late Period	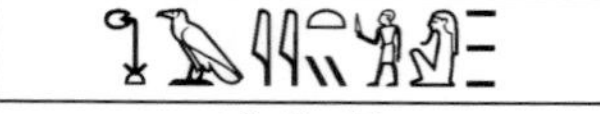	M12B-G1-M17-M17-X1:Z4-A199A-A40-Z3A	58
Late Period		A199A-G7-Z3A	63
Late Period		M12-G1-M17-M17-Z3-C27	60
Late Period		M12-G1-M17-M17-X1:Z4-A199A	61

TABLE 1: *(continued from previous page)* Orthography of the designation *ḫ3.tyw* *(continued on next page).*

DATE	ORTHOGRAPHY	SIGN CODE	SOURCE (SEE APPENDIX)
Late Period		M12-G1-M17-M17-X1:Z4-G7-Z3	62
Late Period		M12-G4-M17-M17-A199A-Z3A	59
Greco-Roman		A25A-Z2B	149
Greco-Roman		A25A-Z3	119
Greco-Roman		A78-Z2B	106
Greco-Roman		A192-Z2A	138
Greco-Roman		A192-Z3	120
Greco-Roman		A199-Z3	164; 165
Greco-Roman		A199A-Z2	101; 131; 145; 146
Greco-Roman		A199A-Z2A	65; 108; 118; 129
Greco-Roman		A199A-Z2B	88; 105; 132
Greco-Roman		A199A-Z3	66; 76; 77; 80; 89; 99; 100; 109; 111; 116; 121; 122; 126; 127; 128; 130; 134; 135; 148; 160; 161; 166; 167; 168; 169; 171
Greco-Roman		A199A-G7-G7-Z3A	158
Greco-Roman		A199A-M17-G7-Z3A	157
Greco-Roman		A199A-R8-Z3	70; 79
Greco-Roman		A199A-X1:Z4-Z3	117
Greco-Roman		A199A-X1:Z4-Z2A-R8	107
Greco-Roman		A199B-Z2	103; 104; 143
Greco-Roman		A199B-Z2A	68; 69; 81; 82; 83; 84; 96; 97; 98; 123; 133; 144
Greco-Roman		A199B-Z2B	151
Greco-Roman		A199B-Z3	125; 170
Greco-Roman		A199B-A199B-A199B	102
Greco-Roman		A199B-X1:Z4-R8-R8-Z2A	95
Greco-Roman		Aa1:D46-U30-G1-M17-M17-Z2A-Z9-D40	150
Greco-Roman		C26-X1:Z4-Z2	71

Table 1: *(continued from previous page)* Orthography of the designation *ḫꜣ.tyw* *(continued on next page).*

Date	Orthography	Sign Code	Source (see Appendix)
Greco-Roman		C26D-Z3	74
Greco-Roman		C27E-Z2A	67
Greco-Roman		C87-Z2	73
Greco-Roman		C87-Z3	72; 78
Greco-Roman		C87A-Z2A	136
Greco-Roman		C87A-Z3	75
Greco-Roman		E13B-Z2A	64
Greco-Roman		M3:T30A-C27B-Z2	163
Greco-Roman		M12-G1-M17-M17-X1:Z4-A199B-Z2A	92
Greco-Roman	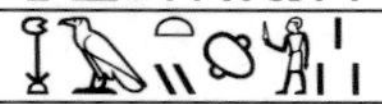	M12-G1-X1:Z4-Aa2-A199A-Z2A	87
Greco-Roman	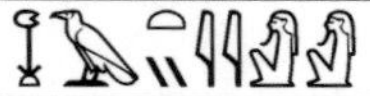	M12-G1-X1:Z4-M17-M17-A40-A40	162
Greco-Roman		M12-G1-X1:Z4-M17-M17-A40-A40:Z2	162
Greco-Roman		M12-G1&Z7-X1:Z4-G14-R8-Z3	85
Greco-Roman		M12-G4-D46:Z4-A199A-G7	156
Greco-Roman		M12-G4-M17-M17-D46:Z4-G7-Z3A	155
Greco-Roman	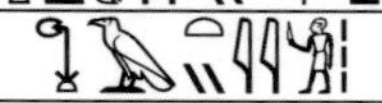	M12B-G1-X1:Z4-M17-M17-A199A-Z3	112
Greco-Roman	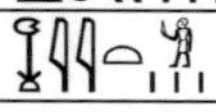	M12-M17-M17-X1-A199A:Z2	153
Greco-Roman		M12-X1:Z4-M17*M17:Z2	152
Greco-Roman		M12-X1:Z4-A199B-Z2A	86
Greco-Roman		M12B-M17-X1:Z4-A199A-Z3	93
Greco-Roman		M12B-X1-A199B-Z2A	94
Greco-Roman	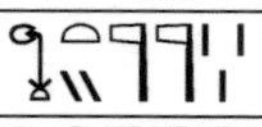	M12B-X1:Z4-R8-R8-Z2B	91
Greco-Roman		M12B-X1:Z4-R8-R8-R8-Z3	90
Greco-Roman		M12B-Z7:X1:Z4-G4-A40A-Z2A	115
Greco-Roman		M111:X1-A199A-Z3	110; 113; 114
Greco-Roman		M111-:X1-A199B-Z3	124
Greco-Roman	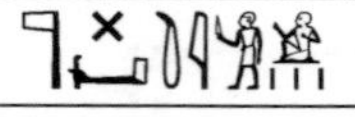	R8-Z9:D40-U33-M17-A199A-A1:Z2	154
Greco-Roman		T30A:N18-A40A-Z2B	147
Greco-Roman		T95-T95-T95	140; 141; 142

TABLE 1: *(continued from previous page)* Orthography of the designation *ḫꜣ.tyw*.

DATE	ORTHOGRAPHY	SIGN CODE	SOURCE (SEE APPENDIX)
Greco-Roman		T95-T95-T95-R8-Z1-Z3A	159
Greco-Roman	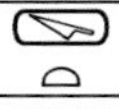	T95A:X1	137
Greco-Roman		T95:Z2	145
Greco-Roman		//-X1:Z4-M17-M17-A199A-Z3	139

alliterative sequences that may be used to ascertain a secure reading of the liminal group present, has revealed that this technique is not as helpful as previously suggested. There are in fact very few examples (see below) from the Edfu corpus that display alliteration of the value *ḫ* in contexts where ideographic writings are present. However, the value of *ḫꜣ.tyw* for the ideogram A199A/B appears to be confirmed by the repetition of this sound value in the following sequences:

III, 32, 5:

ḫt=ỉ ḫꜣ.tyw r ḫft-ḥr=k

I engrave the *ḫꜣ.tyw* before you

III, 33, 12:

ḫꜣ.tyw n.y ꜣḫ.ty ḫbḫb ḫft.yw=f
The *ḫꜣ.tyw* of Akhty who slay his enemies

VI, 9, 6:

ḫwỉ n ḫꜣ.tyw m-ḫt=f
whom the *ḫꜣ.tyw* in his following have protected

A number of texts also contain the repetition of the value *ḫ* in a more extended sense, where the corresponding sounds occur in a string of words that do not form a sequence of direct apposition:

V, 11, 4:

<ḫw.w> sḫm.w sꜣ Rʿ.w ḫnt.yw P n.y Rʿ.w ḫꜣ.tyw nḫt.w

who protect the statues, who protect Re, the foremost of the throne of Re, the strong *ḫꜣ.tyw*

V, 302, 11

mn=ṯ ḫꜣ.w n.w ḫft.yw ḥr ḫt sḥb=ỉ Msn m ḳn=sn ḫntš ḫꜣ.tyw nn ḥr ḥm.t=ṯ

Take for yourself flesh portions of the enemies upon the flame. I make Mesen festive with their smoke, these *ḫꜣ.tyw* rejoice before your majesty.

While the alliteration in these examples is less pronounced, it may still be sufficient to confirm the identity of the *ḫꜣ.tyw* in these contexts. Unfortunately, many discrepancies remain in the various translations of the temple texts where scholars encounter ideographic sign usage. When distinguishing the *ḫꜣ.tyw* from other liminal groups in these texts, the most difficulty seems to be encountered with the *ḥb.yw* and *ḫnt.tyw*,[23] while both the *šmꜣ.yw* and *wpw.tyw* have also been proposed as alternative readings on a number of occasions.[24] In circumstances where the value of an ideographic writing cannot be determined from either alliteration or the context in which the group occurs, it may be that no secure reading can be obtained.

The Form and Appearance of the *Ḫꜣ.tyw*

The characteristic that most aptly defines the physical appearance of the *ḫꜣ.tyw* is their weaponry. If the determinatives and ideograms used in the orthography of the term can be taken as an indicator of appearance, the *ḫꜣ.tyw* may possibly have been conceptualised in a number of different forms ranging from anthropoid to anthropomorphic deities with the heads of canids or lions and even in some cases in the purely animal form of baboons. The feature that remains constant across these varied depictions are the knives that each figure holds in either one or both hands. As indicated by the name of the *ḫꜣ.tyw* itself, the primary function of this liminal group was to slaughter, a role that was clearly facilitated by the use of implements such as knives. This is exemplified in section XVIII, 7 of Papyrus Jumilhac where the *ḫꜣ.tyw* and *šmꜣ.yw* are described as circulating everywhere on the order of Anubis with their *ds*-knives ( ).[25] They also feature in the Book of Worshipping Re in the West found in a number of royal funerary contexts, in which an appeal is made to Re to save the king from the *ḫꜣ.tyw* and their sharp *nm*-knives ( ).[26] In a similar context, Hathor as the lady Iounet is prevailed upon to save the king from the *mtn*(?)-knives (?) of the *ḫꜣ.tyw*.[27] A particularly interesting text found on the internal western face of Edfu's enclosure wall even provides an instance where the knives of the *ḫꜣ.tyw* are used by another deity against the *One without arms and without legs*: "the divine butcher will pursue you, the one with the numerous knives of the southern *ḫꜣ.tyw*, who cuts off for him your head on account of your evil in the presence of Horus of Behdet,"[28] *Mnḥ.yw*, the butcher, is in fact designated as the lord or chief of the *ḫꜣ.tyw* in a number of texts where he is also assigned the epithets *ꜥšꜣ dm.wt* and *ꜥšꜣ ds.w*.[29] Unfortunately, the text of *Edfu* VI, 159, 4 is damaged, and while Kurth has reconstructed as [*ds.w*],[30] it is not possible to definitively determine the knife type that is here referred to. Of the two secure readings, the *ds* and *nm* knives wielded by the *ḫꜣ.tyw* can be categorised as instruments of butchery,[31] with the material of the former confirmed as flint by the use of the stone determinative.[32] Not only were the knives of the *ḫꜣ.tyw* directed against the enemies (*ḫft.yw*), the rebels (*sbỉ.w*), the adversaries (*rk.yw*), and the disaffected of heart (*ḫꜣk.w ỉb.w*), they could also pose a serious threat to the wellbeing of the king: "(O Sekhmet) do not cause his flesh to be cut up (*tḫs*) by the *ḫꜣ.tyw*."[33]

Further physical attributes of the *ḫꜣ.tyw* can be discerned from the adjectives used to qualify their name in the written record: for example, the physical might of the *ḫꜣ.tyw* is illustrated in contexts where descriptors such as *ḳn* "strong" and *nḫt* "strong; victorious" are assigned to this group when they bind the enemies, protect the flesh of the king, safeguard the temple, and protect the *Lord of the strong warrior who is foremost of the Mansion of Valour*.[34] The verbs used to denote the actions of the *ḫꜣ.tyw* also reveal characteristics of their physical nature. Not only did the *ḫꜣ.tyw* have the ability to move with great momentum, as illustrated by the use of the terms *ḫꜣḫ* "to come in haste; be fast; speed"[35] and *m-sỉn* "to run quickly,"[36] they were also equipped with keen eyesight and able to see their enemies from a distance (*gmḥ wꜣ.w*).[37] Both of these qualities would have been integral to the successful execution of their tasks throughout the cities and the nomes of the entire land.

A final note should be made concerning the ability of the *ḫꜣ.tyw* to shoot arrows from their mouths, which has been interpreted by scholars such as Pascal Vernus as the emission of harmful breath or possibly words, since to speak is, basically, to emit a breath from the mouth.[38] That diseases associated with the *ḫꜣ.tyw* stem from the introduction of a pathogen into the body by a breath or wind is confirmed in number of textual sources,[39] for example the *Tagewählerі* records on I *pr.t* 19 that "[t]he wind is in the sky that day, being mixed with the plague of the year, and many diseases are in him,"[40] while in the seventh incantation for exorcising plague in Papyrus Edwin Smith it is stated: "O Sekhmet, may your *ḫꜣ.tyw* retreat, O Bastet, the year does not pass by to work disaster against me, your breath (*nfw*.t) does not reach me."[41] The *ḫꜣ.tyw* are not the only liminal group to be attributed with lethal breaths; in *Dendera* X, 113, 4 the *One whose hearing is perfect* directs the burning of his eyes against the one who attacks "like the heat of the scorching breath of the *wpw.tyw*."

In terms of the iconographic repertoire there are very few representations that can be identified definitively as depicting the *ḫꜣ.tyw* beings. The most secure pictorial representation of this liminal group can be found within Papyrus Hannover 1976.60a2, which records two spells on the recto and verso that formed an amulet belonging to an individual named *Tꜣ-šr.t-n.t-Nm.ty*.[42] The first spell is of particular note as it is a direct invocation to the *ẖꜣ.tyw:* "Greetings to you, the seven, these *ẖꜣ.tyw* of Sekhmet."[43] They are described as "coming forth from [the eye of Re]" and as "those who [go round] the two lands" before the threat of their arrows is negated.[44] Above this section of hieratic text, in the upper right-hand corner of the document, is a vignette illustrating seven seated figures who are each armed with a single knife.[45] Due to the explicit nature of the invocation, these figures are undoubtedly the seven *ẖꜣ.tyw* beings, and while the first line of the verso is unreadable it is likely that the second spell was also related to these liminal deities. On account of the prevalent role of the *ẖꜣ.tyw* as slaughterers; illustrated for example in *Edfu* VI, 264, 9 "may you save him (the living image) from the slaughter of your *ẖꜣ.tyw*"; in *Dendera* X, 124, 13, where the *One with great strength* "sends the *ẖꜣ.tyw* to make slaughter"; and in *Dendera* IX, 218, 17 that refers to the *ẖꜣ.tyw* as those "who make slaughter among the adversaries," it is not unreasonable to suggest that the plural epithet *wd.w šʿ.t* could be a further reference to the *ẖꜣ.tyw* group.[46] The following epithet *ḳmꜣ.w ḏḥr.t* "those who create bitterness" may also confirm the *ẖꜣ.tyw* as the subject of the second invocation, for *ḏḥr.t* is a term that often appears in conjunction with these deities in their role as disease-bringers: "may you protect him from the *ẖꜣ.tyw* who are behind you and before you, do not let any evil wind (*ṯꜣw*) come against him, do not let any fever (*šmm*) or <sickness> (*ḏḥr.t*) of the year destroy him."[47]

A further notable representation can be found in the second tableau of the Book of Caverns. Featured in the lower right-hand corner of the fifth register is a group of four deities who each hold a singular butcher's knife outstretched before them.[48] Small variations in the appearance of these deities are encountered throughout different tombs, primarily in regard to their facial features, such as the addition of bull's horns in the tomb of Ramses IX.[49] Christian Leitz has recognised these four figures as the *ẖꜣ.tyw,* probably on the basis of their inclusion in the corresponding text as "those who are in the slaughterhouse of Osiris who make your mutilation."[50] The text outlines that this mutilation is to be carried out against the enemies of the *Lord of the Duat* who include the *decapitated*, the *slaughtered*, the *inverted ones who are bound*, and the *inverted ones whose hearts are torn out*.[51] As all of these enemies are depicted in succession before the four knife-wielding deities, it is highly probable that these knife-holders are in fact the *ẖꜣ.tyw*.

In an inscription located on the eastern pillar of the pronaos of Edfu (first register, western face), the goddess Seshat makes the pronouncement "I engrave the *ẖꜣ.tyw* before you".[52] Accordingly, one might expect to find a depiction of this liminal group in the vicinity of this text. This appears to be confirmed by the representation of the third protective company of the temple of Edfu in a tableau located two registers above the text.[53] In this scene the commander of this cohort, the *One of great fear*,[54] is depicted with ophidian characteristics, while his subordinates assume the guise of bearded male figures wearing *wsḫ*-collars and loincloths adorned with a ceremonial tail.[55] Each deity is armed with two different types of knives which are distinguished by either a straight handle or rounded pommel.[56] It is significant that in the corresponding text (III, 32, 12), which contains an account of the roles executed by this company, they are described foremost as the *ẖꜣ.tyw* of Akhty. A second representation of the third protective company can also be found on the southern face of the eastern pylon.[57] In this context all are depicted as serpent-headed deities equipped with two straight-handled butcher's knives except for the *One with strong muscles* who holds both a knife and *schlangenstab*.[58]

While there are numerous attestations of the *ẖꜣ.tyw* in the written record, it is striking that there appears in the iconographic repertoire very few securely identifiable examples of these beings. The absence of pictorial representations, particularly in contexts where the *ẖꜣ.tyw* are performing roles that are malevolent in nature, is explicable in terms of the Egyptian concept of empowered images.[59] Images of the *ẖꜣ.tyw* could pose a danger to the living, as the image acted as a point of contact with the beings represented and also ensured their continued existence.[60] The potency of this danger is illustrated clearly through iconoclastic practices where images or characters that represent potentially dangerous animals are incomplete or have been mutilated.[61] The idea of empowered images also relates to orthographical conventions due to the pictorial nature of the hieroglyphic writing system, the name itself containing "for the Egyptians an image in which a spirit might reside;"[62] this may account for the use of ideographic spelling variations for the *ẖꜣ.tyw* and a number of other similar beings in the Greco-Roman temple inscriptions. In this respect, it is significant that the aforementioned representations of the *ḫ3.tyw* are only related to contexts in which the group can be considered to perform a positive role: in Papyrus Hannover 1976.60a2 they are invoked to save the petitioner (albeit from the danger they themselves pose); in the Book of Caverns they mutilate the enemies of Osiris and in *Edfu* III, 32, 12 they protect the child from the serpent, defy the adversary in heaven, do not sleep while protecting the Mansion of the Falcon, and drive back the enemies from the fighting-*ba*s as the third protective company of the temple.

The Position of the *Ḫ3.tyw* in the Hierarchy of the Egyptian Pantheon

Within the hierarchy of the Egyptian pantheon the *ḫ3.tyw* can be considered to occupy a subordinate position in instances where they are sent by a deity of an elevated status, act in accordance with their words or command,[63] bow down before their divine power,[64] or form their entourage.[65] In these contexts, the power which the *ḫ3.tyw* possess can be considered as limited to the tasks they were directed to execute, as Dimitri Meeks states

> Les génies émissaires étaient la forme que revêtait cette Puissance pour intervenir dans le monde des humains. Ils étaient par conséquent complètement assujettis au dieu qui les envoyait, n'agissant que sur son ordre, exécutant sa volonté docilement et sans pitié.[66]

While Sekhmet appears to be the primary leader of this cohort, the numerous variations attested are likely the result of both local adaptations[67] and the universal applicability of the *ḫ3.tyw* who were able to perform a diverse number of roles in different contexts. The direct subordination of the *ḫ3.tyw* is expressed by a range of epithets that designate Iounet Raettawy,[68] Isis,[69] Hathor,[70] Horus of Behdet,[71] Menet,[72] Mut,[73] Neith,[74] Satis,[75] Sekhmet-Sothis,[76] Tefnut,[77] the Eye of Re,[78] Tutu,[79] and Wadjet[80] as their lady, mistress, lord, or master. Genitive constructions and suffix pronouns also express the fact that the *ḫ3.tyw* group were in the possession of greater deities; for example, the *ḫ3.tyw* of the mistress of Iounet are given to Horus of Behdet by Harsomtous;[81] the *One-who-is-Secret* and her *ḫ3.tyw* are given to the king by Horus of Behdet;[82] an annual requirement is created by Mut for her *ḫ3.tyw*,[83] while Re was required to save the king from the impurity of the majesty of Sekhmet and from the evil of her *ḫ3.tyw*.[84] The fact that the danger posed by the *ḫ3.tyw* group could be averted or counteracted through the power possessed by other deities further illustrates the subsidiary nature of their position within the pantheon. Deities such as the great *snḏm*-snakes of the great winged sun disk were capable of protecting the son of Re from the *ḫ3.tyw* when positioned upon his brow,[85] whereas Khonsu was able to dispel the *ḫ3.tyw*, drive away the *šm3.yw*, and repel the blessed dead and the condemned dead while protecting his majesty in the *duat*.[86]

There are a number of instances in the textual record where the *ḫ3.tyw* are not expressly denoted as being under the command of another deity. The majority of these cases occur in situations where the actions of the *ḫ3.tyw* can be considered to be defined topographically and circumscribed to a particular location.[87] While this group is associated with a number of earthly localities, such as the cenotaph of Seti I at Abydos,[88] the abattoir of overthrowing (the enemies) at Kom Ombo,[89] and the cities of Iyt and Letopolis when the seven *ḫ3.tyw* of the field seek the *3ḫ.t* eye,[90] it is within the celestial realm that the *ḫ3.tyw* are most frequently cited as acting without direction. The Pyramid Texts and Coffin Texts are the earliest sources in which the celestial role of the *ḫ3.tyw* is attested. In these contexts, they are mentioned in direct apposition with a number of celestial beings, such as the imperishable stars (*iḫm.w-sk*) and the *old ones* (*imi.w-i3w*), and perform the duties of gatekeepers armed with knives.[91] In *Pyramid Texts* §1726 (utterance 611), §2223 (utterance 716),[92] and *Coffin Texts* I 290 (spell 68)[93] the *ḫ3.tyw* were likely assigned to the *Double Ram Gate*, which is cited immediately before them. As demonstrated in the later papyrus of Nefer-renpet (28th Dynasty), this gate was conceptualised as a bolted celestial portal that was positioned on the horizon and surmounted by the hieroglyph *p.t* for sky.[94] Further confirmation of the *ḫ3.tyw*'s celestial location can be found in a number of other texts from this corpus that express the practice of numbering the *ḫ3.tyw*, for as *Coffin Texts* VI 107e indicates, the deceased could only call upon the *ḫ3.tyw* and rule the imperishable stars after ascending to sky.[95]

Further instances in which the actions of the *ḫ3.tyw* were restricted to a particular celestial environment can be found within the temple texts. The temple precinct itself could be considered as a reflection or even as a manifestation of the cosmos. This notion is clearly depicted in a number of texts from Esna which describe *The Place of the Two Rams* "as in accordance with the plans of heaven" and *The House of Khnum* "as illuminated every day like the celestial vault with the sun and the moon, like heaven with the two disks."[96] It is on this basis that a Litany of Sekhmet could be considered to confirm the continued role of the *ḫ3.tyw* as celestial gatekeepers: "you open for him the doors of your sanctuary, (you) open and close the temple before him, you protect him at the door of the *ḫ3.tyw*."[97] It is significant, moreover, that the northeastern lake of the *Gate of Heaven* (*i3.t nbs*) is described as the *duat* of the *Mansion of the ḫ3.tyw* on a naos from Saft el Henna dating to the reign of Nectanebo I.[98] This gate is outlined within the text as being the portal through which the gods go forth to heaven when they come forth from the necropolis of the *duat*.[99] The *ḫ3.tyw* are further described in *Edfu* VII, 12, 5 as carrying out their tasks alongside the gods of the sky who are at their posts in heaven. Mention should also be made of section XVII, 11–12 of Papyrus Jumilhac, which specifies the *ḫ3.tyw* as guardians of the northern sky: "After he (Horus) cut off his (Seth's) foreleg, he raised it to the middle of the sky, the *ḫ3.tyw* being there to guard it, the foreleg of the northern sky, the Great Hippopotamus holds it so it cannot travel among the gods."[100]

It should be noted that during the Ptolemaic period the *ḫ3.tyw* appear to have been promoted to a higher hierarchical status within the Egyptian pantheon. The attestation of the title "Prophet of the *ḫṯ.w* who are guests in Thebes" in a demotic graffito at Medinet Habu[101] provides evidence for their cult worship on a state religious level. A number of temple texts provide affirmation of this; for example, in *Dendera* VIII, 49, 9 the *ḫ3.tyw* are the subject of a direct invocation spoken by the king: "I come before you, the great *ḫ3.tyw*, who watch over the mighty ones," while in *Edfu* VI, 61, 1 and VI 76, 8 the king makes their acclamation: "I praise your name (Horus of Behdet) and the *ḫ3.tyw* in your following" and "praise to your *ḫ3.tyw*, your followers, your messengers and your watchmen who watch over your temple." Of particular significance is the equation of the *ḫ3.tyw* with the dead-gods of Dendera and Edfu; the two texts in which this equation occurs have been cited in full below and should be considered as a primary indicator of this rise in prominence:

> The great gods, the living *kas*, the children of Re who came forth from his body, who were born in Hermopolis, who were nursed in *Naret*, the ones with great terror in the land to its limit, the *ḫ3.tyw* in the necropolis of Dendera, who hide their bodies in the earth, they enduring in the land of Atum, who bury their bodies in *Iatdinetjeret* (?) on the north and east of Iat-di, the blessed dead who rest in their temples for eternity, their *bas* are in the sky with the Two Lights. Come! Come! That you may receive an invocation offering from Re-Somtous upon the 10th day, that they may present offerings to the living *bas*, set down offerings of Horus, the lord of the temple, that you may eat bread (and) drink beer, the water of the inundation not being distant from you, that the fragrance of the south may come to you from Hierakonpolis, that you may inhale the fragrance of upper Egyptian incense, that you may live from that which will rejuvenate you, from that which comes to them as offerings that they may be pleased, they are joyful with all the good things, namely good gifts of the lady of Iounet, who remains in the *duat* of the Weary-hearted, unceasingly and unremittingly, in the horizon of eternity forever, forever, eternally, eternally.[102]

> These gods, these great bas, foremost of the mounds of the land (necropolis), who were born [... 8 cadrats ...] in the primordial mound, born of the prince, who came into being by Khepri, engendered by the ancestors [... ...] by the one of the horizon, foremost of the horizon of eternity, the temple guardians in the two rows of shrines, the strong and mighty of arm, foremost of the *Dazzling-eye*, the breath in the *Two-palaces*. They come in darkness, they walk in the light at dawn, they join with the living, they protect those who are, they save those who are not, like those who give a hand upon the roads [... ...] your *bas* are in the sky with Re, your mummies are in the *duat* with Osiris, the *ba* of the east, he shows himself in lower heaven, you join with the rays of the sun disk, you eat bread, you drink beer, make cool your hearts with water, may you live for eternity,

may you be young for eternity, your names not perishing upon earth. The great gods, foremost of the Throne of Re, the divine children of Horakhty, these *ḫꜣ.tyw*, foremost of the mounds of the land.[103]

Conclusion

The term *ḫꜣ.yt* translated as "massacre" or "slaughter" is the most plausible etymological origin of the designation *ḫꜣ.tyw* and denoted the primary function of this group in both the secular and divine spheres. The orthography of the term, which occurs most frequently in the plural, exhibits numerous variations; however, in circumstances where ideographic writings are encountered it may be impossible to obtain a secure reading unless the liminal group is able to be identified through the presence of an alliterative sequence or the context in which they occur. To date, comprehensive research on alliteration has only been completed in relation to the Pyramid Texts; an in-depth study of its occurrence within the temple texts of the Greco-Roman period would certainly aid attempts to ascertain a definite reading of the various ideograms used to denote these groups of deities and further our understanding of distinctions that existed between them. The most defining characteristic of the physical appearance of the *ḫꜣ.tyw* are the instruments of butchery which they wielded in one or both hands. They were also attributed with pronounced physical might, great momentum, keen eyesight, and lethal breath. The few instances in which the *ḫꜣ.tyw* are depicted pictorially relate to situations in which their actions are positive, and their absence in the iconographic record is primarily explicable in terms of the Egyptian concept of empowered images. Conceptually, any pictorial representation of the *ḫꜣ.tyw* would have acted as a point of contact and ensured their continued existence, amplifying the danger they posed to the individual. In most cases the power that the *ḫꜣ.tyw* possessed was mostly limited to the tasks they were directed to execute under the command of greater deities, but in a number of circumstances their actions were instead defined topographically and circumscribed to a particular location, namely, the celestial realm.

Appendix: List of Sources

1. Pyramid Text §1256c (Sethe 1910, 215).
2. Pyramid Text §1274a (Sethe 1910, 217).
3. Pyramid Text §1535b (Sethe 1910, 327).
4. Pyramid Text §1726c (Sethe 1910, 411).
5. Pyramid Text §1915b (Faulkner 1969b, 31).
6. Pyramid Text §2223 (Faulkner 1969b, 63).
7. *Coffin Texts* I, 290h, coffin of  (Cairo 2804) (de Buck and Gardiner 1935).
8. *Coffin Texts* I, 290h, coffin of  (Cairo 20823) (de Buck and Gardiner 1935).
9. *Coffin Texts* I, 290h, coffin of  (Cairo 28027) (de Buck and Gardiner 1935).
10. *Coffin Texts* I, 290h, coffin of  (Cairo J 39014) (de Buck and Gardiner 1935).
11. *Coffin Texts* I, 290h, outer coffin of  (Cairo 28092) (de Buck and Gardiner 1935).
12. *Coffin Texts* III, 366a, inner coffin of 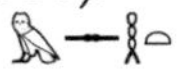 (Cairo 28118) (de Buck 1947).
13. *Coffin Texts* III, 366a, outer coffin of 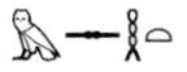 (Cairo 28119) (de Buck 1947).
14. *Coffin Texts* III, 366a, inner coffin of 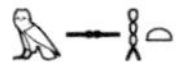 (Cairo 28118) (de Buck 1947).
15. *Coffin Texts* III, 366a, inner coffin of 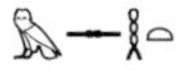 (Cairo 28118) (de Buck 1947).
16. *Coffin Texts* III, 366a, coffin of  (Cairo J 36320) (de Buck 1947).
17. *Coffin Texts* III, 368a, inner coffin of  (Cairo 28118) (de Buck 1947)..
18. *Coffin Texts* VI, 77a, inner coffin of  (Boston 21.964-65) (de Buck 1956).
19. *Coffin Texts* VI, 107e, outer coffin of  (Cairo 28092) (de Buck 1991).
20. *Coffin Texts* VI, 107e, outer coffin of  (Cairo 28092) (de Buck 1991).
21. *Coffin Texts* VI, 107e, inner coffin of  (Cairo 28091) (de Buck 1991).
22. Papyrus Edwin Smith, XVIII, 6 (Breasted 1930, 474).
23. Papyrus Edwin Smith, XVIII, 12-13 (Breasted 1930, 474).
24. Papyrus Edwin Smith, XIX, 8 (Breasted 1930, 474).
25. Papyrus Edwin Smith, XIX, 19 (Breasted 1930, 474).
26. Papyrus Edwin Smith, XX, 7(Breasted 1930, 474).
27. The Book of Caverns (Piankoff 1946, pl.XXV, line)2.
28. Inscription from Year 5 (Epigraphic Survey 1930, pls. 28, 43).
29 Papyrus Anastasi, 3, 1 (C-G CXII, 2) (Fischer-Elfert 1986).
30. Papyrus Anastasi, 3, 1 (Dem. 1616) (Fischer-Elfert 1986).
31. Papyrus DeM I, vso. 7, 2 (Černy 1976, pl. 15).

32. Papyrus Leiden I 346, I, 4 (Stricker 1948).
33. Sun litany, Shroud of Thutmosis III (Cairo CG 40001) (Hornung 1975, 46).
34. Sun litany, Tomb of Seti I (Hornung 1975, 46).
35. Sun litany, Tomb of Ramses II (Hornung 1975, 46).
36. Sun litany, Tomb of Merenptah (Hornung 1975, 46).
37. Sun litany, Tomb of Seti II (Hornung 1975, 46).
38. Sun litany, Tomb of Ramses III (Hornung 1975, 46).
39. Sun litany, Tomb of Ramses IV (Hornung 1975, 46).
40. Papyrus Cairo JE 86667, XVII, 9 (Leitz 1994, 157).
41. Papyrus Sallier X, 8 (Leitz 1994, 157).
42. Papyrus Cairo JE 86667, XXIV, 4 (Leitz 1994, 238).
43. Papyrus Sallier, XVII, 1 (Leitz 1994, 238).
44. Papyrus Cairo JE 866637, XXIV, 10 (Leitz 1994, 243).
45. Papyrus Sallier, XVII, 6 (Leitz 1994, 243).
46. Papyrus Cairo JE 866637, vso. III, 5 (Leitz 1994, 356).
47. Tomb of Simut (Negm 1997, pl. 50).
48. Graffito from Passage, no.2, Cenotaph of Seti I (Frankfort et al. 1933, pl. LXXXVIII).
49. Graffito from Passage, no.3, Cenotaph of Seti I (Frankfort et al. 1933, pl. LXXXVIII).
50. Amuletic Decree, L. I, rto. 48 (Edwards 1960, pl. 1A).
51. Amuletic Decree, B22 (Edwards 1960, pl. XLVA).
52. Amuletic Decree, T. 2 rto. 43, 49, 77 (Edwards 1960, pls. XXIIA, XXIIIA).
53. Amuletic Decree, NY, rto. 28, 33 (Edwards 1960, pl. XLIA).
54. Papyrus Cleveland 14.723, 12 (Bohleke 1997, fig. 1).
55. Sarcophagus, Berlin 1075 (Konigliche Museen 1913, 485).
56. Papyrus Bremner Rhind, 29, 22 (Faulkner 1938a, 42).
57. Papyrus Bremner Rhind, 29, 27 (Faulkner 1938a, 43).
58. *Urkunden* VI, 13, 14 (Schott 1939).
59. Papyrus Brooklyn 47.218.50, II, 4 (Goyon 1974).
60. Crypt, Elkab (Capart 1940, 22).
61. Papyrus Brooklyn 47.218.156, III, 4 (Sauneron 1970, pl. IIIA).
62. Book of the Dead of *Iʿḥ*, Chapter 145 (Verhoeven 1993, 114).
63. Book of the Dead of *Iʿḥ*, Chapter 149 (Verhoven 1993, 125, 14).
64. Relief no. 3211, Alexandria, Greco-Roman Museum (Kaper 2003, 260–262).
65. *Deir el Medina*, 98, 5 (Du Bourguet and Gabolde 2008, 86).
66. *Deir el Medina*, 192, 10 (Du Bourguet and Gabolde 2008, 182).
67. *Dendera* II, 166, 3 (Chassinat 1934).
68. *Dendera* III, 165 (Chassinat 1935a).
69. *Dendera* III, 191, 17 (Chassinat 1935a).
70. *Dendera* IV, 222, 9 (Chassinat 1935b).
71. *Dendera* VI, 39, 4 (Chassinat and Daumas 1965).
72. *Dendera* VII, 196, 6 (Chassinat and Daumas 1972).
73. *Dendera* VIII, 33, 14 (Chassinat and Daumas 1978).
74. *Dendera* VIII, 40, 9 (Chassinat and Daumas 1978).
75. *Dendera* VIII, 41, 16 (Chassinat and Daumas 1978).
76. *Dendera* VIII, 66, 7 (Chassinat and Daumas 1978).
77. *Dendera* VIII, 93, 9 (Chassinat and Daumas 1978).
78. *Dendera* VIII, 111, 4 (Chassinat and Daumas 1978).
79. *Dendera* IX, 167, 13 (Daumas 1987).
80. *Dendera* IX, 218, 17 (Daumas 1987).
81. *Dendera* X, 124, 13, in Cauville 1997.
82. *Dendera* X, 357, 3 (Cauville 1997).
83. *Dendera* X, 357, 16 (Cauville 1997).
84. *Dendera* XI, 31, 12 (Cauville 2001).
85. *Dendera* XII, 206, 14 (Cauville 2007a).
86. *Dendera* XIII, 27, 10, 7 (Cauville 2007b).
87. *Dendera* XIII, 47, 12 (Cauville 2007b).
88. *Dendera* XIII, 47, 14 (Cauville 2007b).
89. *Dendera* XIII, 48, 11 (Cauville 2007b).
90. *Dendera* XIV, 89, 1 (Cauville 2007c).
91. *Dendera* XIV, 206, 8–9 (Cauville 2007c).
92. *Dendera* XIV, 212, 9 (Cauville 2007c).
93 *Dendera* XV, 20, 12–13 (Cauville 2008).
94. *Dendera* XV, 37, 6 (Cauville 2008).
95. *Dendera* XV, 187, 7 (Cauville 2008).
96. *Dendera* XV, 210, 11 (Cauville 2008).
97. *Dendera* XV, 230, 7 (Cauville 2008).
98. Gate of Isis, Dendera, 6, 7 (Cauville 1999).
99. Naos of Dendera (Duemichen 1877, pls. 16, 24).

100. *Edfu* I, 184, 10 (de Rochemonteix and Chassinat 1987).
101. *Edfu* I, 272, 9 (de Rochemonteix and Chassinat 1987).
102. *Edfu* I, 301, 11–12 (de Rochemonteix and Chassinat 1987).
103. *Edfu* I, 309, 1 (de Rochemonteix and Chassinat 1987).
104. *Edfu* I, 464, 12 (de Rochemonteix and Chassinat 1987).
105. *Edfu* I, 473, 13 (de Rochemonteix and Chassinat 1987).
106. *Edfu* I, 510, 7 (de Rochemonteix and Chassinat 1987).
107. *Edfu* I 575, 6 (de Rochemonteix and Chassinat 1987).
108. *Edfu* III, 32, 5 (Chassinat 2009a).
109. *Edfu* III, 33, 12 (Chassinat 2009a).
110. *Edfu* III, 293 (Chassinat 2009a).
111. *Edfu* III, 297, 28 (Chassinat 2009a).
112. *Edfu* III, 300, 18 (Chassinat 2009a).
113. *Edfu* III, 303, 13 (Chassinat 2009a).
114. *Edfu* III, 322, 11–12 (Chassinat 2009a).
115. *Edfu* IV, 50, 7 (Chassinat 2009b).
116. *Edfu* IV, 76, 2 (Chassinat 2009b).
117. *Edfu* IV, 273, 16 (Chassinat 2009b).
118. *Edfu* IV, 308, 7 (Chassinat 2009b).
119. *Edfu* IV, 337, 3 (Chassinat 2009b).
120. *Edfu* V, 11, 4 (Chassinat 2009c).
121. *Edfu* V, 104, 6 (Chassinat 2009c).
122. *Edfu* V, 146, 9 (Chassinat 2009c).
123. *Edfu* VI, 9, 6 (Chassinat 2009d).
124. *Edfu* VI, 14, 6 (Chassinat 2009d).
125. *Edfu* VI, 17, 1 (Chassinat 2009d).
126. *Edfu* VI, 61, 1 (Chassinat 2009d).
127. *Edfu* VI, 76, 8 (Chassinat 2009d).
128. *Edfu* VI, 159, 4 (Chassinat 2009d).
129. *Edfu* VI, 179, 10 (Chassinat 2009d).
130. *Edfu* VI, 233, 9 (Chassinat 2009d).
131. *Edfu* VI, 264, 9 (Chassinat 2009d).
132. *Edfu* VI, 265, 4 (Chassinat 2009d).
133. *Edfu* VII, 12, 5 (Chassinat 2009e).
134. *Edfu* VII, 284, 2 (Chassinat 2009e).
135. *Edfu* VIII, 109, 1–2 (Chassinat 2009f).
136. Edfu Mammisi, 108, 1 (Chassinat 1939).
137. *Esna* II, 14, 10 (Sauneron 1963).
138. *Esna* II, 107 (Sauneron 1963).
139. *Esna* II, 163, 14 (Sauneron 1963).
140. *Esna* IV, 436 (Ménassa and Sauneron 1969).
141. *Esna* IV, 441, 3 (Ménassa and Sauneron 1969).
142. *Esna* IV, 442, 3 (Ménassa and Sauneron 1969).
143. *Esna* VI, 486, 12 (Ménassa and Sauneron 1975).
144. *Esna* VI, 490, 11–12 (Ménassa and Sauneron 1975).
145. Gate of Mut, Karnak (Sauneron 1983, pl. 12, nr. 13, 1–2).
146. Gate of Mut, Karnak (Sauneron 1983, pl. 12, nr. 14, 10; 14).
147. *Kom Ombo*, 72 (de Morgan 1895).
148. *Kom Ombo*, 630 E,1 (de Morgan 1909).
149. *Kom Ombo*, 666, lower, 1 (de Morgan 1909).
150. *Kom Ombo*, 700, 6 (de Morgan 1909).
151. Naos, Cairo TR 2/2/2/21/14 (Rondot 1991, fig. 8).
152. Papyrus Jumilhac, XVII, 11 (Vandier 1961).
153. Papyrus Jumilhac, XVIII, 7–8 (Vandier 1961).
154. Papyrus Louvre N 2420c (Chauveau 1990, pl. 1).
155. Papyrus Tebt. H, IV, C2, 16 (Osing 1998, pl. 29).
156. Papyrus Tebt H, IV, C3, 1 (Osing 1998, pl. 29).
157. PSI inv. I 73, frag.A, 13 (Osing and Rosati 1998, pl. 22B).
158. Parcourir L'Éternité, IV, 5 (Herbin 1994, 443).
159. Parcourir L'Éternité, VII (Herbin 1994, 471).
160. *Philae* I, 13, 11 (Junker 1985).
161. *Philae* I, 68, 13 (Junker 1985).
162. Book of the Dead, Chapter 145 (Lepsius 1842, pl. LXV).
163. *Tôd* I, 144 (Drioton et al. 1980).
164. *Tôd* II, 280, 7 (Thiers 2003).
165. *Tôd* II, 286, 2 (Thiers 2003).
166. Door lintel in Cairo (Daressy 1921, pl. I).
167. *Urkunden* VIII, 76c (Firchow 1957, 63).
168. *Urkunden* VIII 86b (Firchow 1957, 72).
169. *Urkunden* VIII, 86g (Firchow 1957, 72).
170. *Urkunden* VIII, 100f (Firchow 1957, 85).
171. *Urkunden* VIII, 116 (Firchow 1957, 94).

References

Ahn, G. 1997. "Grenzgängerkonzepte in der Religionsgeschichte. Von Engeln, Dämonen, Götterboten und anderen Mittierwesen." In G. Ahn and M. Dietrich (eds.), *Engel und Dämonen: Theologische, Anthropologische und Religionsgeschichtliche Aspekte des Guten und Bösen*, 1–48. Munster: Ugarit-Verlag.

Baines, J. 1985. *Fecundity Figures: Egyptian Personification and the Iconology of a Genre*. Warminster: Aris and Phillips.

Blackman A. and H. Fairman. 1943. "The Myth of Horus at Edfu: II. C. The Triumph of Horus over His Enemies—A Sacred Drama." *Journal of*

Egyptian Archaeology 29: 2–36.

Bohleke, B. 1997. "An Oracular Amuletic Decree of Khonsu in the Cleveland Museum of Art." *Journal of Egyptian Archaeology* 83: 155–157.

Borghouts, J. (ed.). 1978. *Ancient Egyptian Magical Texts*. Leiden: E. J. Brill.

Breasted, J. H. 1930. *The Edwin Smith Surgical Papyrus*. Chicago: University of Chicago Press.

Bryan, B. 2012. "Episodes of Iconoclasm in the Egyptian New Kingdom." In N. N. May (ed.), *Iconoclasm and Text Destruction in the Ancient Near East and Beyond*, 311–362. Chicago: The Oriental Institute of The University of Chicago.

Capart, J. 1940. "Les Sept Paroles de Nekhabit." *Chronique d'Égypte* 15: 21–29.

Cauville, S. 1997. *Le temple de Dendara* X. *Les chapelles osiriennes de Dendara: Transcription et Traduction*. Le Caire: Bibliothèque d'étude.

——. 1999. *Le temple de Dendara: la porte d'Isis*. Le Caire: Institut français d'archéologie orientale.

——. 2000. *Dendara. Traduction* III. Louvain: Peeters.

——. 2001. *Le temple de Dendara* XI. Le Caire: Institut français d'archéologie orientale.

——. 2007a. *Le temple de Dendara* XII. Le Caire: Institut français d'archéologie orientale.

——. 2007b. *Le temple de Dendara* XIII (< http:/// www.Dendara.net >).

——. 2007c. *Le temple de Dendara* XIV (< http:/// www.Dendara.net >).

——. 2008. *Le temple de Dendara* XV. (< http:///www. Dendara.net >).

Černy, J. 1976. *Papyrus hiératiques de Deir el-Médineh* I. Le Caire: Institut français d'archéologie orientale.

Chassinat, É. 1934. *Le Temple de Dendara* II. Le Caire: Institut français d'archéologie orientale.

——. 1935a. *Le Temple de Dendara* III. Le Caire: Institut français d'archéologie orientale.

——. 1935b. *Le Temple de Dendara* IV. Le Caire: Institut français d'archéologie orientale.

——. 1939. *Le Mammisi d'Edfou*. Mémoires publiés par les membres de l'Institut français d'archéology orientale 16. Le Caire: Institut français d'archéologie orientale.

——. 2009a *Le Temple d'Edfou* III. Mémoires publiés par les membres de la mission archéologique française au Caire 20. Le Caire: Institut français d'archéologie orientale.

——. 2009b *Le Temple d'Edfou* IV. Mémoires publiés par les membres de la mission archéologique française au Caire 21. Le Caire: Institut français d'archéologie orientale.

——. 2009c. *Le Temple d'Edfou* V. Mémoires publiés par les membres de la mission archéologique française au Caire 22. Le Caire: Institut français d'archéologie orientale.

——. 2009d. *Le Temple d'Edfou* VI. Mémoires publiés par les membres de la mission archéologique française au Caire 23. Le Caire: Institut français d'archéologie orientale.

——. 2009e. *Le Temple d'Edfou* VII. Mémoires publiés par les membres de la mission archéologique française au Caire 24. Le Caire: Institut français d'archéologie orientale.

——. 2009f. *Le Temple d'Edfou* VIII. Mémoires publiés par les membres de la mission archéologique française au Caire 25. Le Caire: Institut français d'archéologie orientale.

——. 2009g. *Le Temple d'Edfou* IX. Mémoires publiés par les membres de la mission archéologique française au Caire 26. Le Caire: Institut français d'archéologie orientale.

——. and F. Daumas. 1965. *Le Temple de Dendara* VI. Le Caire: Institut français d'archéologie orientale.

—— and ——. 1972. *Le Temple de Dendara* VII. Le Caire: Institut français d'archéologie orientale.

—— and ——. 1978. *Le Temple de Dendara* VIII. Le Caire: Institut français d'archéologie orientale

Chauveau, M. 1990. "Glorification d'une morte anonyme." *Revue d'égyptologie* 41: 3–8.

Daressy, G. 1921. "Sur une série de personnages mythologiques." *Annales du Service des antiquités de l'Égypte* 21: 1–6.

Daumas, F. 1987. *Le Temple de Dendara* IX. Le Caire: Institut français d'archéologie orientale.

Davis, W. 1911. "The Ascension-Myth in the Pyramid Texts." *Journal of Near Eastern Studies* 36 (3): 161–179.

de Buck, A. (ed.). 1956. *The Egyptian Coffin Texts VI: Texts of Spells 472–786*. Chicago: University of Chicago Press.

—— and A. Gardiner (eds.). 1935. *The Egyptian Coffin Texts I: Text of Spells 1–75*. Chicago: University of Chicago Press.

de Morgan, J. 1895–1909. *Kom Ombos*, 2 vols. Vienne: Holzhausen.

de Rochemonteix, M. and É. Chassinat. 1987. *Le Temple d'Edfou* I. Mémoires publiés par les membres de la mission archéologique française au

Caire 10. Le Caire: Institut français d'archéologie orientale.

Drioton, E., G. Posener, J. Vandier, and J.-Cl. Grenier. 1980. *Tôd: Les inscriptions du temple ptolémaïque et romain. La sale hypostyle, Textes Nos. 1–172*. Le Caire: Institut français d'archéologie orientale.

Du Bourguet, P. and L. Gabolde. 2008. *Le temple d'Hathor à Deir el-Médina*. Le Caire: Institut français d'archéologie orientale.

Duemichen, J. 1877. *Baugeschichte des Denderatempels und Beschreibung der einzelnen Theile des Bauwerkes nach den an seinen Mauern befindlichen Inschriften*. Strassburg: K. J. Trübner.

Edwards, I. E. S. 1960. *Hieratic Papyri in the British Museum: Fourth Series: Oracular Amuletic Decrees of the Late New Kingdom*, 2 vols. London: British Museum

Epigraphic Survey. 1930. *Medinet Habu I: Earlier Historical Records of Ramses III*. Chicago: University of Chicago Press.

Eschweiler, P. 1994. *Bildzauber im alten Agypten: die Verwendung von Bildern und Gegenständen in magischen Handlungen nach den Texten des Mittleren und Neuen Reiches*. Freiburg: Universitätsverlag.

Faulkner, R. O. 1938a. "The Bremner-Rhind Papyrus: III: D. The Book of Overthrowing 'Apep." *Journal of Egyptian Archaeology* 24: 166–185.

——. 1938b. "The Bremner-Rhind Papyrus: IV: D. The Book of Overthrowing Apep (Concluded)." *Journal of Egyptian Archaeology* 24(1): 41–53.

——. 1969a. *The Ancient Egyptian Pyramid Texts*. Oxford: Clarendon Press.

——. 1969b. *The Ancient Egyptian Pyramid Texts Translated into English. Supplement of Hieroglyphic Texts*. Oxford: Clarendon Press, 1969.

——. 1973. *The Ancient Egyptian Coffin Texts*, 3 vols. Warminster: Aris and Phillips.

Firchow, O. 1935. *Untersuchungengen zur Ägyptischen Stilistik II. Grundzüge der Stilistik in den Altägyptischen Pyramidentexten*. Berlin: Akadmie Verlag.

——. 1957. *Thebanische Tempelinschriften aus griechisch-römischer Zeit*. Berlin: Akademie Verlag.

Fischer-Elfert, H. W. 1986. *Die satirische Streitschrift des Papyrus Anastasi I*. Wiesbaden: O. Harrassowitz.

——. 2015. *Magika Hieratika in Berlin, Hannover, Heidelberg und München*. Berlin: Walter de Gruyter and Co.

Frankfort, H., A. de Buck, and B. Gunn. 1933. *The Cenotaph of Seti I at Abydos*. London: Egypt Exploration Society.

Goyon, J.-Cl. 1974. *Confirmation du Pouvoir Royal au Nouvel An*. Le Caire: Institut français d'archéologie orientale.

Graves-Brown, C. 2009. "Licking Knives and Stone Snakes: The Ideology of Flint Knives in Ancient Egypt." In M. Martinón-Torres and T. Rehren (eds.), *Archaeology History and Science: Integrating Approaches to Ancient Materials*, 37–60. Walnut Creek, Left Coast Press.

——. 2011. *The Ideological Significance of Flint in Dynastic Egypt*. Ph.D. dissertation, University College London.

Guglielmi, W. 1996. "Der Gebrauch Rhetorischer Stilmittel in der Ägyptischen Literatur." In A. Loprieno (ed.), *Ancient Egyptian Literature: History and Forms*, 465–497. Leiden: E. J. Brill.

Guilmant, F. 1907. *Le tombeau de Ramses IX*. Mémoires publiés par les membres de l'Institut français d'archéology orientale 15. Le Caire: Institut français d'archéologie orientale.

Gutbub, A. 1973. *Textes fondamentaux de la theologie de Kom Ombo*. Le Caire: Institut français d'archéologie orientale.

Hannig, R. 2006. *Grosses Handwörterbuch Deutsch-Ägyptisch: (2800–950 v. Chr.): die Sprache der Pharaonen*. Mainz: Philipp von Zabern.

Hornung, E. 1975. *Das Buch der Anbetung des Re im Westen (Sonnenlitanei): nach den Versionen des Neuen Reiches* I. Genève: Editions de Belles-Lettres.

Ikram, S. 1995. *Choice Cuts: Meat Production in Ancient Egypt*. Leuven: Peeters.

Junker, H. 1985. *Der Grosse Pylon des Tempels der Isis in Philä*. Wien: In Kommission bei R.M. Rohrer.

Kaper, O. 2003. *The Egyptian God Tutu: A Study of the Sphinx-God and Master of Demons with a Corpus of Monuments*. Leuven: Peeters.

Königliche Museen. 1913. *Ägyptische Inschriften aus den Königlichen Museen zu Berlin* II. Leipzig: Hinrichs.

Kurth, D. 2014. *Edfou VI. Die Inschriften des Tempels von Edfu. Abteilung I Übersetzungen*, Band 3. Gladbeck: PeWe-Verlag.

Leitz, C. 1994. *Tagewählerei. Das buch* ḥꜣt nḥḥ pḥ.wy ḏt *und verwandte Texte*. Wiesbaden: Harrassowitz Verlag.

——. 1995. "Der Naos mit den Dekanen aus Saft el-

Henna." In Chr. Leitz and H. Thissen (eds.), *Altägyptische Sternuhren*, 3–50. Leuven: Peeters 1995.

—— (ed.). 2002a. *Lexikon der Ägyptischen Götter und Götterbezeichnungen* I. Leuven: Peeters.

—— (ed.). 2002b. *Lexikon der Ägyptischen Götter und Götterbezeichnungen* II. Leuven: Peeters.

—— (ed.). 2002c. *Lexikon der Ägyptischen Götter und Götterbezeichnungen* III. Leuven: Peeters.

—— (ed.). 2002d. *Lexikon der Ägyptischen Götter und Götterbezeichnungen* IV. Leuven: Peeters.

—— (ed.). 2002e. *Lexikon der Ägyptischen Götter und Götterbezeichnungen* V. Leuven: Peeters.

—— (ed.). 2002f. *Lexikon der Ägyptischen Götter und Götterbezeichnungen* VI. Leuven: Peeters.

—— (ed.). 2002g. *Lexikon der Ägyptischen Götter und Götterbezeichnungen* VII. Leuven: Peeters.

Lepsius, R. 1842. *Das Todtenbuch der Agypter nach dem hieroglyphischen Papyrus in Turin*. Leipzig: Museo egizio di Torino.

Lucarelli, R. 2010. "The Guardian Demons of the Book of the Dead." *British Museum Studies in Ancient Egypt and Sudan* 15: 8–102.

Meeks, D. 1971. "Génies, anges, demons en Égypte." In D. Meeks, D. Bernot, et. al., *Génies, anges et démons: Egypte, Babylone, Israël, Islam, Peuples altaïques, Inde, Birmanie, Asie du Sud-Est, Tibet, Chine*, 19–84. Paris: Seuil.

——. 2001. "Demons." In Donald B. Redford (ed.), *The Oxford Encyclopedia of Ancient Egypt* I, 375–378. Oxford: Oxford University Press.

Ménassa, L. and S. Sauneron. 1969. *Le Temple d'Esna IV. Textes hiéroglyphiques n° 399–472*. Le Caire: Institut français d'archéologie orientale.

—— and ——. 1975. *Le Temple d'Esna VI. Textes hiéroglyphiques n° 473–546*. Le Caire: Institut français d'archéologie orientale.

Negm, M. 1997. *The Tomb of Simut called Kyky: Theban Tomb 409 at Qurnah*. Warminster: Aris and Philips.

Neugebauer, O. and R. A. Parker. 1960. *Egyptian Astronomical Texts I: The Early Decans*. London: Lund Humphries.

Ockinga, B. 1985. "Piety." In Donald B. Redford (ed.), *The Oxford Encyclopedia of Ancient Egypt* III, 277–305. Oxford: Oxford University Press.

——. 2005. *A Concise Grammar of Middle Egyptian*. Mainz am Rhein: Verlag Philipp von Zabern.

Osing, J. 1998. *Hieratische Papyri aus Tebtunis I*, 2 Bde, *The Carlsberg Papyri 2*. Copenhagen: CNI Publications.

—— and G. Rosati. 1998. *Papiri Geroglifici e Ieratici da Tebtynis*. Firenze: Istituto papirologico.

Peust, C. 2014. "Towards a Typology of Poetic Rhyme." In E. Grossman, M. Haspelmath, and T. Richter (eds.), *Egyptian-Coptic Linguistics in Typological Perspective*, 375–376. Berlin: de Gruyter Mouton.

Piankoff, A. 1946. *Le livre des quererts*. Le Caire: Institut français d'archéologie orientale.

Ritner, R. 2012. "Killing the Image, Killing the Essence: The Destruction of Text and Figures in Ancient Egyptian Thought, Ritual and 'Ritualised History.'" In N. N. May (ed.), *Iconoclasm and Text Destruction in the Ancient Near East and Beyond*, 395–406. Chicago: The Oriental Institute of The University of Chicago.

Rondot, R. 1991. "Le Naos de Domitien, Toutou et les Sept Flèches." *Bulletin de l'Institut français d'archéologie orientale* 90: 303–337.

Sass, D. 2015. *Slaughterers, Knife-Bearers and Plague-Bringers: A Study of the Role and Significance of the* ḫ3.tyw *in Ancient Egyptian Thought*. M.A. thesis, Macquarie University.

Sauneron, S. 1963. *Le temple d'Esna II. Textes hiéroglyphiques n° 1–193*. Le Caire: Institut français d'archéologie orientale.

——. 1970. *Le papyrus magique illustré de Brooklyn*. Oxford: Oxford University Press.

——. 1983. *La porte ptolémaïque de l'enceinte de Mout à Karnak*. Paris: Institut français d'archéologie orientale.

Schott, S. 1939. *Urkunden Mythologischen Inhalts*. Leipzig: Verlag.

Sethe, K. 1910. *Die Ägyptische pyramidentext nach den Papierabdrücken und Photographien des Berliner Museums, Zweiter Band*. Leipzig: J. C. Hinrichs.

Stricker, B. 1948. "Spreuken Tot Beveilging Gedurende de Schrikkeldagen Narr Pap. I 346." *Oudheidkundige Mededelingen uit het Rijksmuseum van Oudheden* 23: 55–70.

Szpakowska, K. 2016. "Feet of Fury: Demon Warrior Dancers of the New Kingdom." In R. Landgráfová and J. Mynářová (eds.), *Rich and Great: Studies in Honour of Anthony Spalinger on the Occasion of His 70th Feast of Thoth*, 313–323. Prague: Charles University, Faculty of Arts.

Thiers, C. 2003. *Tôd: les inscriptions du temple ptolémaïque et romain. Textes et scènes nos 173–329*. Le Caire: Institut français d'archéologie orientale.

Thissen, H. 1989. *Die demotischen Graffiti von Medinet Habu. Zeugnisse zu Tempel und Kult in ptolemäischen Agypten*, Demotische Studien 10. Sommerhausen: G. Zauzich.

Valbelle, D. 1981. *Satis et Anoukis*. Mainz am Rhein: Philipp von Zabern.

Vandier, J. 1961. *Le papyrus Jumilhac*. Paris: Centre national de la recherche scientifique.

Verhoeven, U. 1993. *Das Saitische Totenbuch der Iahtesnacht. P. Colon. Aeg. 10207*. Bonn: R. Habelt.

Vernus, P. 1982–1983. "Etudes de Philologie et de Linguistique (II)." *Revue d'égyptologie* 34: 115–128.

von Lieven, A. 2000. *Der Himmel über Esna: eine Fallstudie zur relgiösen Astronomie in Ägypten am Beispiel der kosmologischen Decken- und Architravinschriften im Tempel von Esna*. Wiesbaden: Harassowitz.

Watterson, B. 1979. "The Use of Alliteration in Ptolemaic." In J. Ruffle, G. A. Gaballa, and K. Kitchen (eds.), *Glimpses of Ancient Egypt: Studies in Honour of H. W. Fairman*, 167–169. Warminster: Aris and Phillips.

Wilson, P. 1997. *A Ptolemaic Lexikon: A Lexicographical Study of the Texts in the Temple of Edfu*. Leuven: Peeters.

Notes

1 This paper is based on research completed for the author's master's thesis (Sass 2015).

2 Ahn 1997.

3 The terms "Grenzgänger" and "Zaungäger" were proposed by Gregor Ahn in an attempt to produce a more differentiated approach to the religious-historical concept of angel and demon like figures. The beings which these terms encompass can be considered as "boundary-walkers" who are a perceived as being able to cross the borders between the divine and secular worlds (Ahn 1997, 40–41).

4 Ockinga 2001, 44; Baines 1985, 277–305.

5 Hannig 2006, 263–264; Eschweiler 1994, 213.

6 Breasted 1930, 415; Edwards 1960, vol. I, 56, no. 36.

7 Faulkner 1938b, 49.

8 Ockinga 2005, 63.

9 Leitz 2002a–g.

10 Leitz 2002b, 364b–366c.

11 Leitz 2002c, 304a–305b.

12 Leitz 2002d, 718a–719c.

13 Leitz 2002d, 793c–794b.

14 Leitz 2002e, 229c.

15 Leitz 2002f, 140b–141a.

16 Leitz 2002f, 459c–460a.

17 Leitz 2002g, 78a–79c.

18 Leitz 2002g, 231a.

19 Leitz 2002g, 570a.

20 Gutbub 1973, 243; Blackman and Fairman 1943, 21, no. 6; Junker 1985, 13, no. 3.

21 Watterson 1979, 167–169.

22 On alliteration see also Firchow 1953, 217–220; Peust 2014; Wilson 1997, xxvi; Guglielmi 1996.

23 That interchangeable phonetic values of *h*, *ḥ*, *ḫ*, and *ẖ* in the Ptolemaic period may be a factor that should be considered when identifying alliterative sequences.

24 For example, Cauville 2000, 322–323; Cauville 1997 has alternatively identified the value of the ideograms  and  in *Dendara* III, 191, 16–17 (Chassinat 1935a) and *Dendara* X, 124, 13 (Cauville 1997) as the *h3b.yw*;  in *Dendara* X, 357, 3 as the *wpw.tyw*; and in *Dendara* X, 357, 16 13 (Cauville 1997) as the *šm3.yw*. Penelope Wilson (1997, 603; 661) read the ideogram in *E.* IV, 76, 2 (Kurth 2014) as *h3b.yw* instead of *ḫ3.tyw*. In *E*dfu I, 464, 9–17 (de Rochemonteix and Chassinat 1987), she assigns the same ideogram the value of *ḥnṯ.tyw*, whereas Adolphe Gutbub's (1973, 242) translation of this particular text cites the *wpw.tyw*.

25 Papyrus Jumilhac, XVIII, 7, in Vandier 1961.

26 Hornung 1975, 46.

27 *Dendera* VIII, 66, 7 (Chassinat and Daumas 1978). The two lower signs underneath the knife are largely destroyed and their reading is uncertain.

28 *Edfu* VI, 159, 4 (Chassinat 2009d).

29 *Dendera* VII, 196, 6 (Chassinat and Daumas 1972); *Dendera* VIII, 93, 9; 111, 4 (Chassinat and Daumas 1978).

30 Kurth 2014, 274.

31 See Ikram 1995, 63–70; Szpakowska 2016, 319–320; Wilson 1997, 1207–1208.

32 On the ideological significance of flint, see Graves-Brown 2009, 37–60; Graves-Brown 2011.

33 *Dendera* XIII, 47, 14 (Cauville 2007b).

34 *Dendera* VIII, 41, 16, (Chassinat and Daumas 1978); *Edfu* V, 11, 4; 104, 6 (Chassinat 2009c); *Edfu* VII, *284, 2 (Chassinat 2009e).*

35 *Dendera* XV, 37, 6, (Cauville, 2008); Papyrus Cairo JE 86667, XXIV, 4 (Leitz 1994, 238).

36 *Edfu* V, 11, 4; 104, 6 (Chassinat 2009c).

37 Papyrus Leiden I, 346, I, 5–6 (Borghouts 1978, 12–14). In a similar context, *Edfu* VIII, 109, 1–2 (Chassinat 2009f), the great *ḫ3.tyw* are described as "those who go around in her cities, who roam about the nomes, who slaughter or make live when her majesty says." The eyesight of the *ḫ3.tyw* also appears to be mentioned in Papyrus Hannover 1976.60a2, where the term *nw* "to look at" is used; however, the reading of the full line of text is uncertain (Fischer-Elfert 2015, 195).

38 Vernus 1982–1983, 124.

39 Vernus 1982–1983, 125.

40 Parallel versions contain the variant "the great gods in the sky" (Leitz 1994, 134, 213).

41 Papyrus Edwin Smith XIX 19–XX 1 (Breasted 1930, 484).

42 Fischer-Elfert 2015, 191.

43 *ind-ḥr=tn p3 sfḫ ḫ3.tyw ipw n.w Sḫm.*t.

44 Fischer-Elfert 2015, 183.

45 Fischer-Elfert 2015, pl. 16

46 To current knowledge, this epithet has previously only been attested in the singular (Leitz 2002b, 621c). It occurs in conjunction with the designation *ḳm3 mwt.w* "the one who creates death" in Papyrus Louvre E 3233B, which Fischer-Elfert (2015, 196) cites as a parallel to this text.

47 *Edfu* VI, 303, 12 (Chassinat 2009d).

48 Piankoff 1946, pl. X.

49 Guilmant 1907, pls. LVII, LVIII.

50 Leitz 2002e, 636a; Piankoff 1946, 25, pl. 25.

51 Piankoff 1946, 25, pl. 25

52 *Edfu* III, 32, 5 (Chassinat 2009a).

53 *Edfu* III, pl. L, (Chassinat 2009a).

54 Leitz 2002b, 42c–43a.

55 Goyon, 1985, 80.

56 Goyon 1985, 80.

57 *Edfu* IX, pl. XVI (Chassinat 2009g).

58 Goyon 1985, 80; Leitz 2002c, 444c.

59 Ritner 2012, 398.

60 Meeks 2001, 375–378; Ritner 2012, 395.

61 Eschweiler 1994, 213; Bryan 2012, 311.

62 Ritner 2012, 396.

63 *Dendera* IX, 167, 13 (Daumas 1987); *Dendera* XI, 31, 12 (Cauville 2001); *Edfu* I, 301, 11–12; 309, 1; 464, 12 (de Rochemonteix and Chassinat 1987).

64 *Dendera* II, 166, 3 (Chassinat 1934).

65 *Edfu* VI, 61, 1 (Chassinat 2009d); *Esna* IV, 436; 441, 3; 442, 3 (Ménassa and Sauneron 1975).

66 Meeks 1971, 45.

67 von Lieven 2000, 53.

68 *Deir el Medina*, 192, 10 (Du Bourguet and Gabolde 2008, 182).

69 *Dendera* IX, 2I8, 17 (Daumas 1987).

70 *Edfu* III, 297, 28 (Chassinat 2009a).

71 *Edfu* V, 146, 9 (Chassinat, 2009c).

72 *Edfu* I, 575, 6 (de Rochemonteix and Chassinat, 1987); *Edfu* IV, 273, 16 (Chassinat 2009b).

73 Negm 1997, pl. 50.

74 *Esna* II, 14, 10 (Sauneron 1963).

75 Valbelle 1981) 135.

76 *Dendera* XV, 20, 12–13 (Cauville 2008).

77 *Philae* I, 68, 13 (Junker 1985).

78 *Dendera* III, 165, 3 (Chassinat 1935a).

79 Relief no. 3211, Alexandria, Greco-Roman Museum (Kaper 2003, 260–262).

80 *Deir el Medina*, 98, 5 (Du Bourguet and Gabolde 2008, 86).

81 *Edfu* VI, 233, 9 (Chassinat, 2009d).

82 *Edfu* IV, 308, 7 (Chassinat 2009b).

83 Gate of Mut, Karnak (Sauneron 1983, pl. 12, Nr. 14, 10; 14).

84 *Edfu* VI, 300, 15 (Chassinat 2009d).

85 *Edfu* I, 510, 7 (de Rochemonteix and Chassinat 1987).

86 *Urkunden* VIII, 76c (Firchow 1957, 63).

87 Lucarelli 2010, 86.

88 A graffito records a wish to be saved from the *ḫ3.tyw* "who are in this place" (Frankfort et al. 1933, pl. LXXXVIII).

89 *Kom Ombo*, 630 E (de Morgan 1909).

90 Papyrus Sallier, XVII, 6 (Leitz 1994, 243).

91 Faulkner 1969, 255, no.5.

92 Faulkner 1969, 254, 308.

93 Faulkner 1973, vol. 1, 65.

94 Davis 1911, 172.

95 Faulkner 1973, vol. 2, 148.

96 *Esna* IV, 436; 441, 3 (Ménassa and Sauneron 1969).

97 *Dendera* XIII, 48 (Chassinat and Daumas 1978).

98 Leitz 1995, 6.

99 Leitz 1995, 6.

100 Papyrus Jumilhac XVII, 11–12 (Neugebauer and Parker 1960, 190–191); Vandier 1961, 108, 129.

101 Thissen 1989, 30–31.

102 *Dendera* IV, 212, 9 (Chassinat, 1935b).

103 *Dendera* XIV, 206, 8–9 (Cauville 2007c).

Journal of Ancient Egyptian Interconnections

Ghosts and Ancestors in a Gender Perspective

Renata Schiavo
Leiden University

Abstract
Through an analysis of the letters to the dead, the paper focuses on the role played by women in Egyptian ancestor worship. Special attention is given to the missives addressed to the female spirits: the so-called misplaced stele of Merityfy, the Berlin bowl 22573, Papyrus Leiden I 371, and Ostracon Louvre 698. The investigation has highlighted the existence of a ritual to appease wrathful female ghosts. The malevolent attitude of these spirits is explained in the light of their premature death, perhaps during childbirth. Another trigger is identified as the fear of being replaced in their social role of "mistress of the house" by another woman (for example, because the husband was planning to remarry). Remarkably, the documents taken into consideration did not turn out to be a mere exorcism to ward off a malignant spirit; rather, the aim was to establish, or restore, the positive role of the ancestress as a protector of the household.

Power, Gender Roles, and Death

The present paper aims to highlight some specific features concerning the position of women within Egyptian ancestor worship. In Egypt, the veneration of the dead was strongly linked to elite self-presentation, the inheritance system, and the maintenance of family power.[1] And, in the present paper, particular attention will be given to the modes through which gender roles were normed by the power relationships in the economical and the juridical spheres and under influence of religious beliefs.

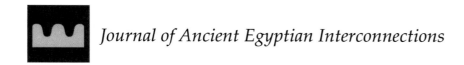

At this point, some clarifications about the limits of the research are needed. First, the social context. Adopting a Third Wave feminist approach, in the present paper "women" are not labeled as uniform category; rather, the main aim is to investigate gender roles in relation to a particular ancient Egyptian social group.[2] The data taken into consideration here—Coffin Texts, Old Kingdom "Appeals to the Living," the documents from Deir el-Medina, and, above all, the letters to the dead—were indeed expressions of elite culture. A second restriction concerns the effective nature of the investigated phenomena. Especially the letters to the dead have for a long time been considered as intimate prayers and expressions of piety towards the divine.[3] However, in the light of several recent studies, we should interpret them as evidence of complex rituals that involved whole social groups, rather than individuals.[4] Therefore, we are not facing personal intimate feelings, but stereotyped norms concerning how social relationships were created and maintained on an ideal level. In other words, the documents analyzed here highlight some social expectations internalized by the elite:[5] how relationships based on gender roles should be realized and—if something went wrong—how to restore the normative interactions between family members, as well between the living and the dead.

Although the position of Egyptian women, especially when compared with other ancient Mediterranean cultures,[6] was relatively emancipated, their role in ancestor worship was quite ambivalent. From a purely quantitative approach, the main documents would seem to outline a cult predominantly focused on adult men. Most of the Appeals to the Living are requests made by deceased men.[7] The letters to the dead were mainly addressed to the male heads of the household[8] and, as regards the data from Deir el-Medina, among the fifty-five *ꜣḫ ỉḳr n rꜥ* stelae collected by R. Demarée, in only eight a woman is designated as an "excellent spirit."[9]

In addition, both funerary and mortuary texts[10] paid great attention to the bond linking the deceased father and his firstborn. For example, if one adopts as a starting point the reading given by Willems,[11] CT spells 30–41 could be interpreted as a double rite of passage. These spells are structured as a recitation made by the heir of the deceased, through which he profiles himself as the legitimate successor of his father and, thus, as the new head of the family; but, at the same time, this liturgy also aims to emphasize the new status of benevolent ancestor achieved by the dead householder.

Significantly, although mothers or wives play an important role in the *post mortem* existence of the deceased,[12] nothing like this is attested for the mother-daughter relationship. An explanation might be found in the fact that these texts were expressions of a specific elite ideology aimed at the maintenance of the family social status over generations. In the light of such aspects, women's secondary role is understandable, since they were not officially involved in this kind of transmission of powers.

The special attention given to the bond between dead father and living son in funerary and mortuary texts is also strongly connected with the rules for inheritance.[13] As stressed by several documents, the eldest son was considered the main heir, but in order to acquire the legacy, he had to take care of both the burial of the deceased and his mortuary rituals.[14] Furthermore, the Egyptian concept of real estate included building, lands, and also the servants related to them.[15] Thus, to inherit the house of the father meant to take on the management of the household and the responsibility for all the persons involved in it.[16]

Through a comparison with the wisdom literature, this aspect appears increasingly clear. These texts focused on advice to better manage the relationships with both superiors and subordinates in order to achieve a good social position and, thus, maintain the wealth of the households. It is of course remarkable that these texts were structured as a series of teachings given by a father to his son; and, as stressed by A. Depla, "there is not a single extant example of an *Instruction* written by a father for his daughter, nor by a mother for her son, or a mother for her daughter."[17]

In this regard, CT spells 131–146 are relevant, since their aim is to re-join the deceased with his *ꜣb.t* in the afterlife. Although it is quite common to translate *ꜣb.t* as "family" or "household," according to Willems, the meaning of the word is actually more complex. The term refers to "a property-owning group of which the members are primarily kin who share rights in an inheritance";[18] and, remarkably, in the long lists of individuals reported in such spells there is no reference to the deceased's wife. It is a characteristic also confirmed by other data, such as a legal statement attested in an Old Kingdom private tomb, or a royal decree dating to the Eighth Dynasty, where undeniably the wife is not considered as a part of the *ꜣb.t*.[19]

Paradoxically it could be argued that this kind of social organization may have contributed to a certain economic independence and emancipation of Egyptian women. Given that a woman belonged to a different *ꜣb.t* from her husband, she could inherit from her own family and was relatively free to manage her goods.[20] Although a woman as "wife" did not belong to the same *ꜣb.t* as her husband, as "mother" she belonged to the same *ꜣb.t* of her offspring, and as daughter to the same *ꜣb.t* of her father.[21] It meant that both men and women could own their own possessions—even though, with regard to the management of the household, there was a strong preference for the "father to son" transmission—and both were able to pass them on to their children.[22]

Actually, although drastically fewer in number, most of the known documents related to female ancestors do not show significant qualitative differences from the ones concerning men. Of course only few examples of Appeals to the Living belonging to women are known. But these texts show the same formulaic repertoires attested for men, describing the deceased woman as a preternatural being, capable of punishing the transgressor of her tomb or of protecting the living ones who praise her.[23] Likewise, there are no significant stylistic differences between the *ꜣḫ ỉḳr n Rꜥ* stelae dedicated to women and men.[24]

Finally, regarding the so-called anthropoid busts from Deir el-Medina, it has been argued that the majority of them might portray women, representing thus the female counterpart of the *ꜣḫ ỉḳr n Rꜥ* stelae in ancestor cults.[25] However, this theory was recently rejected, and, in addition, it was argued that the busts should not necessarily represent ancestors, but also gods and even living individuals.[26]

Analysis of the Letters to the Dead Addressed to Female Spirits

Some letters to the dead seem partially to contrast with this general picture. Of course most of them were sent to adult men, but the requests addressed exclusively to women undoubtedly show some peculiar features[27] that deserve to be investigated.

Doc. 1:
Letter on a Stela Perhaps from Naga ed-Deir (Tenth or Eleventh Dynasty)[28]

The history of this document is rather complicated. In 1958 a stela preserved at the Cairo Museum attracted the attention of E. Wente. The object was about to be sold to a private collector, so Wente was just able to copy the hieratic text written on its back.[29] As a consequence, for a long time the only available data were the aforementioned sketch of the hieratic inscription and a brief description of the scene on the front of the stela made by Wente himself:

> [...] a limestone stela, or tablet about a foot high, as I recollect, on the front of which was a painted scene of a man making an offering.[30]

In recent times, however, the object has been rediscovered by E. Meltzer in a private collection in the USA,[31] and it has been finally possible to check the interpretations presented by Wente. Although his transcription of the hieratic text was correct, it appears that he misunderstood the scene on the front face: the person portrayed is without any doubt a woman and not a man.[32] This is not a secondary aspect, since in light of this element some interpretations concerning the letter written have to be reconsidered, first of all, the gender of the persons involved.

Notably, the present document is the only case of a letter to the dead written on a stela. As mentioned earlier, on the front a standing woman is portrayed. This figure is identified by the inscriptions as Nebetitef, who is also the deceased addressee of the two letters written with black ink on the back.[33]

The first message is sent by a person called Merityfy. At first, E. Wente identified this sender with the person portrayed on the front (in his opinion a man) and consequently with the husband of the deceased woman invoked:

> Although the two other examples of this name known to me [Merityfy] are feminine [...] the representation on the face of the stela is that of man offering, and I am inclined to believe that the writer of the letter was a widower.[34]

On the contrary, as stressed by S. Donnat, we have no reasons to doubt that the writer is a woman:[35] first because the name Merityfy is attested only as feminine; second, because the assumption that Merityfy was a woman clarifies several aspects of the second letter.

In her message, Merityfy claims to be sick and invokes the help of the dead woman in order to be healed (column 3: *ḏr mr.t n.t ḥꜥ.w<=ỉ>*). It is interesting to stress that she asks to see the *ꜣḫ* of the deceased during a dream, with the hope that the dead woman will want to fight for her:

> Columns 3–4:
>
> *Ỉ iḫ ꜣḫ=t n<=ỉ> ḫft-ḥr=ỉ mꜣ=ỉ ꜥḥꜣ=t ḥr=ỉ m rsw.t*
>
> May you appear as an *ꜣḫ* in front of me! May I see you fight for me in a dream!

In the second letter, a man called Khuau asks the spirit to fight for him, for his woman, and for his offspring (column 7: *ꜥḥꜣ ḥr=ỉ ꜥḥꜣ ḥr ḥm.t<=ỉ> ḥr ẖrd.w<=ỉ>*).

Notably, in the incipit Khuau claims that the deceased is his *sn.t* – literally "sister" but also "wife":

> *r-ḏd ỉn ḫw-ꜣw n sn.t=f*
>
> A message by Khuau to his sister.

According to S. Donnat, the identification of the first sender—Merityfy—with a woman allows one to argue that she would be no other than Khuau's wife and the *ḥm.t=i* cited at column 7.[36] In effect, assuming this perspective, the second missive appears as a brief recapitulation of the first one made by a second writer, an element attested also in other letters to the dead.[37] Moreover, given the ambiguity of the expression *sn.t=f*, the addressee, Nebetitef, could be identified as Khuau's former dead wife. Although the term *sn.t* is used as synonymous of *ḥm.t* with the meaning of "spouse" mainly from the New Kingdom,[38] remarkably the use of the word *sn.t* as "wife" is attested in another letter to the dead datable to the end of the Old Kingdom.[39]

Such a factor could place the document in a different perspective. The role of Nebetitef appears to be rather ambiguous. At first sight, she would seem a positive figure, since she is invoked in order to fight on Merityfy's behalf against an external enemy. On the other hand, such a heartfelt appeal could hide the attempt to appease a potential malevolent spirit. It would be possible to hypothesize that Nebetitef herself was causing the illness of Merityfy because she was upset by her living husband's remarriage.[40]

This is indeed an important element, since a similar ambiguity appears to be a recurrent theme of the letters addressed to deceased women analyzed here.

Doc. 2:

The Berlin Bowl Inv. 22573 (Twelfth Dynasty)[41]

The Berlin Bowl is the only letter to the dead that has an image alongside the text. Between the two concentric circles of hieratic inscriptions, one observes the upper part of a human figure, probably intended as a portrait of the receiver (Fig. 1). While some writers have seen in this image a two-dimensional representation of a bust,[42] in actual fact it seems more likely to be a variant of the hieroglyph B1 mutilated for apotropaic reasons[43].

The brief content of the hieratic inscription is rather ambiguous. In the incipit the male sender stresses that, before her departure, the woman had never shown any resentment towards him (first circle: *in=ṯ ꜥꜣ r niw.t n.t nḥḥ nn špt=ṯ nb r=i*). Subsequently, the man asks what kind of problem could have caused her conduct, claiming that if the deceased has some recriminations against her relatives, she should forget them, for the good of her offspring (second circle: *ir wn srḫ m ḫ.t=ṯ; smḫ sw n ib n ḫrd.w=ṯ*).

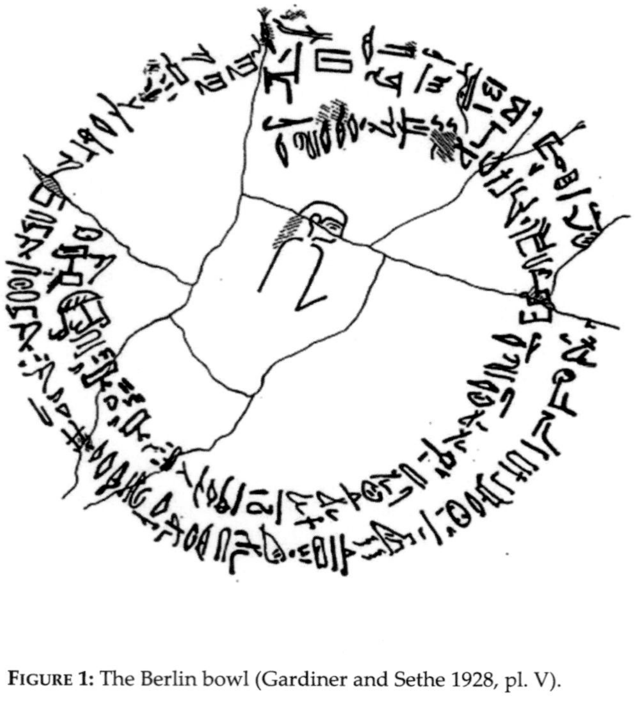

Figure 1: The Berlin bowl (Gardiner and Sethe 1928, pl. V).

Given this premise, it seems clear that the dead woman is not invoked to solve an external problem; rather, she seems to be perceived as a potentially malevolent spirit who is causing troubles in the family.[44]

Although the degree of kinship is not mentioned in the document, the woman is explicitly asked to be benevolent for the sake of her offspring (*n ib ḫrd.w=ṯ*), so it could be argued that both the sender and the recipient belonged to the same family. In this regard, it has been suggested that the anger of the dead woman was triggered by the remarriage of her husband, who can probably be identified with the writer.[45]

Doc. 3:
Papyrus Leiden I 371 (Nineteenth Dynasty)[46]

A letter undoubtedly written by a man to placate the spirit of his dead wife is P. Leiden I 371. Here the writer begs his wife to stop persecuting him, since—in his opinion—the malevolent attitude showed by the deceased is totally unjustified (lines 1–2 recto):

> *ỉrỉ=t ỉḫ r=ỉ m btꜣ |2| pꜣ=ỉ ḫpr m pꜣy sḫr.w bỉn n.ty tw<=ỉ> ỉm=f*
>
> What evil thing have you done against me, |2| for which I come in this miserable state in which I am?[47]

The man stresses how he always looked after her, respecting her both alive and dead. However, the brief reference to the "sisters in the house" sheds an intriguing light on the causes of the anger of the deceased (line 21 verso):

> |21|...*ḫr ptr nꜣ sn.w(t) m pꜣ pr bw-pw=ỉ ꜥḳ n wꜥ ỉm=sn*
>
> |21|... And behold, as for the sisters in the house: I have not gone in to (any) one of them![48]

We will hardly know if the sender is sincere. However, the fact that the man needs to emphasize that he has not had relations with other women is itself a significant element. It undeniably testifies that, for the Egyptians, it was common to believe that the spirit of a deceased wife could have a malevolent influence, if the living husband gave a certain kind of attention to other women.

Doc. 4:
Ostracon Louvre 698 (Twentieth–Twenty-first Dynasty)[49]

O. Louvre 698 is the only letter to the dead written on a piece of limestone and the only case in which red ink is used for the inscription. The ostracon comes from the New Kingdom settlement of Deir el-Medina, and the sender is a man called Butehamun. Interestingly, rather than writing directly to the spirit, he addresses a long message to the *ꜥfd.t* of his dead wife, Ikhtay.

The word *ꜥfd.t* is a variation of the term *ꜥfḏ.t*. It literally means "box,"[50] but it is sometimes used to indicate containers utilized to store letters;[51] furthermore, in specific contexts it can also have the meaning of "coffin."[52] This ambiguity is maybe used on purpose by Butehamun to poeticize the text making a sophisticated link between an object used in everyday life for private correspondence and the will to communicate with his deceased wife.

In effect, the document in question is far more artistically skillful than the other letters to the dead: it is written in meter, with the addition of the "verse points," and it shows not only various figures of speech, but also a number of educated quotes from the main Ancient Egyptian literary genres.[53]

On the basis of these features, S. Donnat has argued that O. Louvre 698 cannot be considered a letter to the dead, showing, rather, more analogies with funerary lamentations.[54] She points out that an ostracon would not be the most appropriate object for a ritualistic purpose. And although red was traditionally associated with malevolent beings, here the use of red ink could indicate that the ostracon was used to outline a preliminary sketch of the text. In her opinion, either the final version had to be copied onto the coffin of Ikhtay or it had been written to be recited. Donnat, moreover, stressed that in this text the deceased is not invoked to solve a specific crisis, but for a generic intercession. In addition, Ikhtay is not called *ꜣḫ*, as attested in several letters to the dead, but "Osiris," as in funerary texts.[55]

However, the term *ꜣḫ* occurs once in O. Louvre 698, not as a noun to indicate a blessed spirit, but as a verb. In this regard, according to the interpretation given by P. J. Frandsen,[56] the deceased is not invoked for a generic mediation to the gods, but for a more specific request:

> |6| *nn ky.t m-ḳd=st [...] bw gmỉ<=ỉ> zp bw.t [...] gmỉ st n=t [...] |7| ꜥš=Ỉ m ỉꜣd.t nb ḥꜥ=t [...] wšb.t*

> *ꜣḫ* |8| *n=ỉ mw.t<=ỉ> ỉt=ỉ sn=ỉ ḥnꜥ sn.t<=ỉ> st jwỉ ṯꜥy.tw*
>
> |6| No instance of wrong has been found [...]. |7| I have appealed to you directly all the time that you might respond [...]. My mother and my father, my brother and my sister |8| are beneficial (*ꜣḫ*) for me: they come; you are taken away.[57]

In Frandsen's opinion, the relatives here mentioned could be understood as other deceased persons. Thus, this sentence could reveal the existence of some troubles between the sender and the recipient. The suggestion could be that the writer is complaining that his dead wife is no longer supporting him from the Netherworld, since Ikhtay is the only one among his dead relatives to ignore him.[58] However this interpretation is problematic for several reasons.

Firstly, the text is seriously damaged due several lacunas. Moreover, as stressed by D. Sweeney, because of standard Ramesside malpractice, it is rather difficult to understand whether the verbs have a first person suffix (Butehamun as subject), or a second person suffix (Ikhtay as subject). Also, with regards to the participles, it is hard to recognize if they are active or passive: the first option renders Ikhtay as a potentially malevolent entity, the second interpretation could depict her more as a victim.[59]

Finally, the prosopography relating to the inhabitants of Deir el-Medina is well known. Butehamun was a "scribe of the necropolis" and maintained a regular correspondence with his father, Tuthmose. The letters by Butehamun clearly show the same calligraphy as O. Louvre 698.[60] Moreover, from several documents a relationship with a woman called Shedemdua emerges, but the elder sons of Butehamun are often cited as Ikhtay's offspring. In light of such evidence, Davies hypothesized that Butehamun remarried Shedemdua after the death of Ikhtay.[61] Given this last assumption, at first sight, one could posit that the aim of the present text does not differ much from the other letters here analyzed: to placate a dead woman angry for the remarriage of her husband. However, the aforementioned correspondence between Butehamun and his father clearly shows that Tuthmose survived Ikhtay, since, unlike Shedemdua, she is never mentioned in this corpus of letters, and it is an element that could partially invalidate Frandsen's rendering of the passage reported here.[62] Furthermore, we do not have any firm evidence regarding the remarriage of Butehamun with Shedemdua, and it was also argued that the woman might have been a sister or female relative of Butehamun who was hosted in his house since she was a widow with dependent children.[63]

Given all these elements further evaluations are needed. First, O. Louvre 698 undeniably implies the same religious milieu of the letters to the dead, since it clearly shows a core belief in which a living person is searching for contact with a departed relative. In addition, although we do not have other examples of letters to the dead from the village, ancestor worship is surely well attested at Deir el-Medina.[64] Secondly, the connection with the genre of funerary lamentations stressed by Donnat is also a valid hypothesis, especially taking into consideration the elaborated style of the text and the fact that the missive is addressed to the coffin of the deceased woman..[65]

Nevertheless, the connection between funerary or mortuary texts and letters to the dead is not a surprising fact. As stressed by several scholars, the aforementioned CT spells 38–41 (but also 30–37, following Willems' interpretation) show an undeniable affinity with the letters to the dead,[66] and it was also suggested that these spells could constitute the liturgy utilized for the deposition of the letters into the tombs on the occasion of the festivals to commemorate the deceased.[67] So, nothing precludes that, in very extraordinary cases—such as a death occurred at young age, probably caused by childbirth or other violent causes—a rather similar liturgy connected to an apotropaic action could have been performed during the funerals.

In this regard, it is suggestive that in a letter sent to Butehamun by his father Thutmose (BM EA 75021) both a "great black *ꜥfd.t*" and an evil eye caused by a malevolent dead are mentioned. Unfortunately, due the lacunas the connection between these two elements is not clear.[68] However, it could be argued that this passage refers to the troubles with the spirit of Ikhtay and the ritual to placate her.

Conclusions: How to Appease an Angry Dead Woman

In the light of the foregoing observations, it seems that the letters sent exclusively to a female spirit were written in order to solve certain kinds of troubles caused by a deceased spouse. Why were these dead women so angry?

The average life expectancy for women was notably lower than for men.[69] Moreover, one of the main causes of death was childbirth, a moment that contains a strong symbolic and liminal character itself. Thus, we are not very far from the idea that an abrupt ending to life would be capable of transforming a dead person into a malevolent entity.[70]

Notably, we have two examples of spells against female ghosts from magical and medical texts.[71] A rubric from a spell in the Brooklyn magical papyrus is directed against several kinds of preternatural beings listed in male/female couples, including the group *mwt*/*mwt.t*; but remarkably a dead female (*mwt.t-ḥm.t*) is cited separately, without any male counterpart[72]. A quite similar case is attested in the Leiden Magical Papyrus I 348. Here in a spell to heal headaches (spell 12; rt.6,4) it is stressed that such a text has to be recited against "a dead female who robs as a wailing woman."[73]

In this regard, it is interesting that all the letters analyzed here were in different ways always associated with an effigy of the deceased. The letter addressed to Nebetitef is the only example attested on the back of a stele, and, notably, on the face the female receiver of the missive is portrayed. A stylized image of the deceased possibly mutilated for apotropaic reason is depicted exactly in the center of the Berlin bowl. P. Leiden I 371 was attached to a statuette of the dead addressee.[74] Clearly, sculptures and images of the deceased played an important role in Egyptian ancestor worship.[75] On the other hand, based on the actual data, we have no similar examples for the letters addressed to men.[76] Such a constant element could be connected with a performative and apotropaic practice (well attested to in several magical texts), with the specific aim of dominating a potentially dangerous entity by controlling a (two-dimensional or three-dimensional) representation of her.[77] Furthermore, also the fact that O. Louvre 698 was addressed to the coffin (*ʿfd.t*) of the deceased could be understood by interpreting the coffin as a mediator, through which the sender could exercise a certain control over his dead wife.[78]

However, other factors must also be considered: in all these letters we may infer that the anger of the deceased was triggered by the second marriage of the husband, or by a certain kind of envy towards women that can potentially replace her social role inside the family (as stressed in Doc. 3). This element cannot be interpreted exclusively by the projection of typically worldly sentiments onto the afterlife.

In this regard, a comparison with the CT spells 30-41 may be illuminating. As mentioned earlier, these texts ratify the new status acquired not only by the deceased as ancestor but also by the firstborn as new head of the family.[79] Significantly, this transition was not perceived as peaceful. In several passages the deceased father shows a certain anger, especially towards his eldest son who has to replace him.[80] In CT I 158 a–159 b[38] it is clearly stated that the deceased has hostile feelings towards his son and it is stressed that the deceased father wants to bring his son into the Netherworld causing his premature death.

Given this premise, one could posit that for the Egyptians also the dead spouse could develop hostile feelings about the second marriage of the living husband. And, when another woman replaced her as wife, such a transmission had of course to be perceived as potentially dangerous.

In this regard, also accepting Donnat's hypothesis, which interprets O. Louvre 698 as a funerary lamentation rather than as letter to the dead, this kind of interpretation could be plausible. Since—in our reconstruction—the writer is not facing a crisis caused by a specific problem (for example, an illness caused by a malevolent entity), but an existential crisis connected with a biological phase and changes of social roles (the premature dead of a young beloved spouse and, thus, the fear that she could became a vengeful spirit, especially if another woman replaced her), it is reasonable to posit that this kind of apotropaic ritual could be performed already on the occasion of the funeral. In several cultural contexts, in Akkadian and Egyptian sources, a tragic, sudden death is considered the main cause in transforming a deceased into a vengeful ghost.[81] Therefore, it is plausible that in these cases special measurements were already taken at the time of burial.

This kind of religious idea seems actually well rooted in Egyptian beliefs. A number of archeological data testify to the existence of special apotropaic actions connected to the inhumation of pregnant women. A so-called votive bed found in TT 14 seems to have been deposited in connection with the body of a young woman who surely died during her pregnancy, probably with the intention to facilitate "the rebirth of mother and child after a happy completion of delivery in their second, eternal life."[82] Furthermore, M. Betrò has collected a restricted amount of evidence concerning the special attention paid by the Egyptians to the embalming procedure of pregnant women. [83]

Significantly, something rather similar is attested in connection with an oracular decree of Amonrasonther for Neskhons, the wife of Pinedjem II.[84] This document shows strong links with the religious milieu of the letters to the dead: the utterance was written on a wooden board and deposited inside the tomb of Neskhons,[85] as was done with the letters; moreover, from the text it is evident that the female spirit is perceived as a potentially angry entity, capable of persecuting her husband. In addition, according to Smith, the analysis of Neskhons' mummy shows that the woman was young and pregnant at the time of her death.[86] Thus, it could be argued that some complications occurred during the childbirth causing her demise.

On the other hand, it is interesting that in in order to protect Pinedjem and his family, the main aim of the texts is to deify Neskhons in order to placate her negative attitude towards the husband.

From others sources it is well known that the Egyptians had few scruples when faced with neutralizing an evil dead person. In a Saitic apotropaic spell, for exorcizing a woman possessed by a ghost the threat to burn down the tomb of the malevolent spirit is clearly expressed.[87] Notably, nothing like this is attested in the decree for Neskhons or in the letters to the dead analyzed here. In these documents the deceased are clearly treated with a certain respect: the senders stress quite often their correct behavior toward the women and always highlight how the angry attitude of the spirits appears unjustified. Moreover, with the only exception of P. Leiden I 371, the writers always invoke the female spirits to intercede for the writer with the gods or another ancestor.[88]

If the CT spells 30–41 were focused on the crucial moment of transmission in which the main heir replaces his dead father as householder, in the specific context of the Middle Kingdom elite's extended family,[89] the core of beliefs here highlighted focused on something quite similar, concerning not only the vengeful ghost of a woman angry because of her untimely death; but also a passage of social status between the living and the dead: a deceased wife and a living woman who took over (or could potentially take over, as in P. Leiden I 371) her social role. Thus, given these elements, it is possible to posit that the documents here analyzed not just show a ritual to ward off an angry spirit, but the will to restore the positive role of an ancestress, healing the pact of mutual aid between the living and the dead for the prosperity of the household.

Acknowledgments

I am very grateful to my supervisors, Olaf Kaper and Robert J. Demarée, and to the anonymous reviewer for their comments and helpful suggestions.

Abbreviation

Wb A. Erman and W. Grapow. 1926–1931. *Wörterbuch der ägyptische Sprache*, 7 vols. Berlin.

References

Assmann, Jan. 1976. "Das Bild des Vaters im Alten Ägypten." In Hubertus Teilenbach, (ed.), *Das Vaterbild in Mythos und Geschichte, Ägypten, Griechenland, Altes Testament, Neues Testament*, 12–49. Stuttgart: Kohlhammer.

Baines, John. 1987. "Practical Religion and Piety." *Journal of Egyptian Archaeology* 73: 73–98.

Betrò, Marilina. 2017. "Birth, Rebirth and Votive Beds: New Evidence from Third Intermediate Period Context in Theban Tomb 14." In Alessia Amenta and Hélène Guichard (eds.), *Proceedings First Vatican Coffin Conference 19–22 June 2013, Città del Vaticano*, 63–70. Città del Vaticano: Edizioni Musei Vaticani.

Borghouts, Joris F. 1971. *The Magical Texts of Papyrus Leiden I 348*. Leiden: Brill.

Bourdieau, Pierre. 1980. *Le Sens Pratique*. Paris: Minuit.

Černý, Jaroslav. 1973. *A Community of Workmen at Thebes in the Ramesside Period*. Bibliothèque d'étude 50. Le Caire: Institut français d'archéologie orientale.

—— and Gardiner, Alan H. 1975. *Hieratic Ostraca I*. Oxford: Oxford University Press.

Cooney, Kathlyn M. 2007. "The Functional Materialism of Death in Ancient Egypt: A Case Study of Funerary Materials from the Ramesside Period." In Martin Fitzenreiter (ed.), *Das Heilige und die Ware: Eigentum, Austausch und Kapitalisierung im Spannungsfeld von Ökonomie und Religion, IBAES VII.*, 273–299. London: Golden House.

Davies, Benedict G. 1997. "Two Many Butehamuns? Additional Observations on Their Identity".

Studien zur Altägyptischen Kultur 24: 59–68.
Demarée, Robert J. 1983. *The ꜣḫ iḳr n Rꜥ Stelae: On Ancestor Worship in Ancient Egypt*. Egyptologische Uitgaven 3. Leiden: Nederlands Instituut voor het Nabije Oosten.
——. 2006. *The Bankes Late Ramesside Papyri*. London: British Museum Research Publications.
Depla, Annette. 1994. "Women in Ancient Egyptian Wisdom Literature." In Leonie J. Archer, Susan Fischler and Maria Wyke (eds.), *Women in Ancient Societies: An Illusion of the Night*, 24–52. London: Macmillan.
Dodson, Aidan and Hilton, Dyan. 2004. *The Complete Royal Families of Ancient Egypt*. London: Thames and Hudson.
Donnat Beauquier, Sylvie. 2014. *Écrire a`ses morts: Enquête sur un usage rituel de l'écrit dans l'Égypte pharaonique*. Grenoble: Editions Jérôme Millon.
Elliot Smith, Grafton. 1912. *The Royal Mummies*. Cairo: Institut français d'archéologie orientale.
Fecht, Gerhard. 1969. "Der Totenbrief von Nag' ed-Deir." *Mitteilungen des Deutschen Archäologischen Instituts, Abteilung Kairo* 24: 114–115.
Frandsen, Paul John. 1992. "The Letter to Ikhtay's Coffin: O. Louvre 698." In Robert J Demarée (ed.), *Village Voices: Proceedings of the Symposium "Texts from Deir el-Medina and Their Interpretation," Leiden, May 31–June 1, 1991*, 31–50. Leiden: Centre of Non-Western Studies, Leiden University.
Gardiner, Alan H. and Sethe, Kurt. 1928. *Egyptian Letters to the Dead, Mainly from the Old and Middle Kingdom*. London: Egyptian Exploration Society.
Goldwasser, Orly. 1995. "On the Conception of the Poetic Form—A Love Letter to a Departed Wife: O. Louvre 698." In Šĕlōmōh Izre'el and Rina Drory (eds.), *Language and Culture in the Near East*, 191–2015. Leiden: Brill.
Guilmot, Max. 1966. "Les Lettres aux Morts dans L'Egypte Ancienne." *Revue de l'histoire des religions* 170(1): 1–27.
——. 1973. "Lettre à une épouse défunte (Pap. Leiden I 371)." *Zeitschrift für ägyptische Sprache und Altertumskunde* 99: 94–103.
Gunn, Battiscombe. 1955. "The Decree of Amonrasonthēr for Neskhons." *Journal of Egyptian Archaeology* 41: 83–105.
Harrington, Nicola. 2005. "From the Cradle to the Grave: Anthropoid Busts and Ancestor Cults at Deir el-Medina." In Kathryn Piquette and Serena Love (eds.), *Current Research in Egyptology 2003: Proceedings of the Fourth Annual Symposium which Took Place at the Institute of Archaeology, University College London, 18–19 January 2003*, 71–88. Oxford: Oxbow Books.
——. 2012. *Living with the Dead: Ancestor Worship and Mortuary Ritual in Ancient Egypt*. Oxford: Oxbow Books.
Hasegawa, Koichi, Chika Shinohara, and Jeffrey P. Broadbent. 2007. "The Effect of 'Social Expectation' on the Development of Civil Society in Japan." *Journal of Civil Society* 3(2): 179–203.
Holaubek, Johanna. 1975. "Vater." In Wolfgang Helck and Eberhard Otto (eds.). *Lexikon der Ägyptologie*, vol. 6, 913–915. Wiesbaden: Harrassowitz.
Keith, Jean L., Sylvie Donnat, and Nicola Harrington. 2011. *Anthropoid Busts of Deir el Medineh and Other Sites and Collections: Analyses, Catalogue, Appendices*. Le Caire: Institut français d'archéologie orientale.
Koenig, Yvan. 1979. "Un revenant inconvenant? Papyrus Deir el-Medina 37." *Bulletin de l'Institut français d'archéologie orientale* 79: 103–119.
Lines, Daniel. 2001. "A Curious Middle Kingdom Stela in Birmingham." *Journal of Egyptian Archaeology* 87: 43–54.
Lippert, Sandra. 2013. "Inheritance." In Elizabeth Frood and Willeke Wendrich (eds.), *UCLA Encyclopedia of Egyptology*. Los Angeles: eScholarship. < https://escholarship.org/uc/item/30h78901 >, accessed 1 August 2013.
Lucarelli, Rita. 2010. "Demons (Benevolent and Malevolent)." In Jacco Dieleman and Willeke Wendrich (eds.), *UCLA Encyclopedia of Egyptology*. Los Angeles: e-Scholarship. < http://escholarship.org/uc/item/1r72q9vv >, accessed 1 September 2010.
Meltzer, Edmund S. 2008. "The 'Misplaced Letter to the Dead' and a Stela Found Again." Paper presented at The 59th Annual Meeting of the American Research Center in Egypt, Seattle, April 2008.
Ritner, Robert K. 1993. *The Mechanics of Ancient Egyptian Magical Practice*. Chicago: The Oriental Institute of the University of Chicago
Roth, Ann Macy. 2010. "Father Earth, Mother Sky: Egyptian Beliefs about Conception and Fertility." In Alison E. Ratman, (ed.), *Reading the Body: Representations and Remains in the Archaeological*

Records. Philadelphia: University of Pennsylvania Press.

Saleh, Heidi. 2007. *Investigating Ethnic and Gender Identities as Expressed on Wooden Funerary Stelae from the Libyan Period (c. 1069–715 B.C.E.) in Egypt*. BAR International Series 1734. Oxford: Archaeopress.

Sauneron, Serge. 1970. *Le Papyrus Magique illustré: Brooklyn Museum 47.318.156*. Wilbour Monographs 3. Brooklyn: Brooklyn Museum.

Schiavo, Renata. 2013a. "Una Lettera al Morto per Placare l'Ira di una Defunta: Alcune Osservazioni sulla Coppa di Berlino 22573." *Egitto e Vicino Oriente* 36: 29–38.

——. 2013b. "Sulla Possibile Funzione Giuridica di Alcune lettere al Morto." *Aegyptus* 93: 125–145.

Schulman, Alan R. 1986. "Some Observations on the *ꜣḫ iḳr n Rʿ*-Stelae". *Bibliotheca Orientalis* 43(3–4): 302–348

Shubert, Steven, B. 2007. *Those Who (Still) Live on Earth: A Study of the Ancient Egyptian Appeal to the Living Texts*. PhD dissertation, University of Toronto.

Sweeney, Deborah. 1994. Review of *Village Voices: Proceedings of the Symposium "Texts from Deir el-Medina and Their Interpretation,"* ed. R. J. Demarée and A. Egberts. *Discussions in Egyptology* 30: 206–207.

Szpakowska, Kasia. 2003. *Behind Closed Eyes: Dreams and Nightmares in Ancient Egypt*. Swansea: The Classical Press of Wales.

——. 2008. *Daily Life in Ancient Egypt: Recreating Lahun*. Oxford: Wiley-Blackwell.

Toivari-Viitala, Jaana. 2001. *Women at Deir el-Medina: A Study of the Status and Roles of the Female Inhabitants in the Workmen's Community during the Ramesside Period*. Egyptologische Uitgaven—Egyptological Publications 15. Leiden: Peeters.

Troy, Lana. 2015. "How to Treat a Lady: Reflections on the 'Notorious' P. Leiden I 371." In Rune Nyord and Kim Ryholt (eds.), *Lotus and Laurel: Studies on Egyptian Language and Religion in Honour of Paul John Frandsen*, 403–418. Copenhagen: Museum Tusculanum Press.

Verhoeven, Ursula. 2003. "Post im Jenseits: Formular und Funktion altägyptischer Briefe an Tote." In Andreas Wagner (ed.), *Bote und Brief—Sprachliche Systeme der Informationsübermittlung im Spannungsfeld von Mündlichkeit und Schriftlichkeit*, 31–51. Nordostafrikanisch/Westasiatische Studien 4. Frankfurt: Peter Lang.

Wente, Edward F. 1975–1976. "A Misplaced Letter to the Dead." In P. Naster, H. de Meulenaere, and J. Quaegebeur (eds.), *Miscellanea in Honorem Josephi Vergote*, 595–600. Orientalia Lovaniensia periodica 6–7. Leuven: Leuven Departement Oriëntalistiek

—— and Edmund S. Meltzer. 1990. *Letters from Ancient Egypt*. Atlanta: Scholar Press.

Willems, Harco. 2001. "The Social and Ritual Context of a Mortuary Liturgy of the Middle Kingdom (CT Spells 30–41)." In Harco Willems (ed.), *Social Aspects of Funerary Culture in the Egyptian Old and Middle Kingdoms: Proceedings of the International Symposium Held at Leiden University, 6–7 June, 1996*, 253–272. Orientalia Lovaniensia Analecta 103. Leuven: Peeters.

——. 2015. "Family Life in the Hereafter According to Coffin Texts Spells 131–146: A Study in the Structure of Ancient Egyptian Domestic Groups." In Rune Nyord and Kim Ryholt (eds.), *Lotus and Laurel: Studies on Egyptian Language and Religion in Honour of Paul John Frandsen*, 447–472. Copenhaghen: Museum Tusculanum Press.

Notes

1 Holaubek 1975; Assmann 1976; Schiavo 2013b.

2 Regarding the use of Third Wave feminist approach in archaeology and Egyptology, cf. Saleh 2007, 10–11.

3 Guilmot 1966, 27.

4 Donnat Beauquier 2014, 173 ff.

5 "Social expectations" could be defined as "an internalized social norm for society, which guides individuals and organizations to what they should do." Cf. Hasegawa et al. 2007, 180–181 and 195. Furthermore, the concept of "social expectation" is strictly connected with the concept of "habitus" elaborated by Bourdieu. Cf. Bourdieau 1980.

6 Roth 2010, 200; Szpakowska 2008, 102–112; Toivari-Viitala 2001, 135–138 and 187–192.

7 Shubert 2007, 16–61.

8 Verhoeven 2003, 31–51. Donnat Beauquier 2014, 173 ff.

9 Demarée 1983, stelae A6, A39, A40, A41, A44, A45, A51, A52.

10 For the difference between mortuary and funerary texts see Willems 2001, 254.

11 Willems 2011, 360–361.

12 Roth 2010, 198–199.

13 Holaubek 1975; Willems 2011, 369.

14 Lippert 2013.

15 Lippert 2013.

16 Schiavo 2013b, 125–145.

17 Depla 1994, 29.

18 Willems 2015, 448.

19 Willems 2015, 454–461.

20 Willems 2015, 463.

21 Willems 2015, 463.

22 Lippert 2013, 3; Toivari-Viitala 2001, 96–138.

23 Shubert 2007, 51–52 (O.K. 25).

24 The inscriptions attested on the stelae are quite stereotyped. Moreover, no significant differences based on gender were noted. Cf. Demarée 1983, 178–179.

25 Harrington 2005, 71–88.

26 Keith et al. 2011, 91–100.

27 Baines 1987, 87.

28 Wente 1975–1976; Demarée 1983, 216–217; Wente and Meltzer 1990, 215 n. 349; Szpakowska 2003, 23, 143, 185; Donnat Beauquier 2014, 53–57; Meltzer 2008.

29 Wente 1975–1976, 595.

30 Wente 1975–1976, 595.

31 Meltzer 2008, 1.

32 Meltzer 2008, 3.

33 Meltzer 2008, 3–4.

34 Wente 1975–1976, 597 and note b.

35 Remarkably, S. Donnat (2014, 55 and note b doesn't seem to know about the rediscovery of the stela by E. Meltzer:

> Mérityfy est un nom recensé comme féminin [...] et, comme signale Wente, attesté à Naga ed-Deir pendant le la Première Période Intermédiaire. Wente est malgré tout enclin à considérer que L'auteur de la lettre est un homme, notamment en raison de la scène sur l'autre face de la stèle qui représente un homme faisant offrande. Ce pourrait toutefois être l'auteur de la seconde lettre qui est ici représenté.

36 Donnat Beauquier 2014, 57.

37 See, for example, the so-called Cairo linen, column 13 (Donnat Beauquier 2014, 30–31).

38 *Wb* 4, 151.9.

39 It is the so-called Cairo linen, column 1 Donnat Beauquier 2014, 30–31).

40 Donnat Beauquier 2014, 57.

41 Gardiner and Sethe 1928, 5–7 and 21–22, plates V and Va; Fecht 1969. 114–115; Wente and Meltzer 1990, 214 number 346; Schiavo 2013a; Donnat Beauquier 2014, 61–63.

42 Lines, 2001, 43–54.

43 Schiavo 2013a, 36.

44 Schiavo 2013a, 36.

45 Gardiner and Sethe 1928, 7; Fecht 1969, 115 and note 1.

46 Gardiner and Sethe 1928, 23-25 and plates VIII–VIII; Guilmot 1973; Donnat Beauquier 2014: 74–76; Troy 2015, 403–418.

47 Here I mainly follow the interpretation by L. Troy. Cf. Troy 2015, 405.

48 I follow the interpretation by L. Troy. Cf. Troy 2015, 413.

49 Černý and Gardiner 1975, 82 and plates 80–80a; Černý 1973, 360–370; Frandsen 1992, 31–50; Goldwasser 1995, 191–205; Wente 1990, 217–218; Donnat Beauquier 2014, 77–83 and 158–163.

50 *Wb* I, 183.15–18.

51 The use of *ʿfd.t* with the meaning of "letter-box" is well attested at Deir el-Medina. Remarkably the same sender of O. Louvre 698, Butehamun, uses the word *ʿfd.t* with this specific meaning in some private letters. Cf. Demarée, 2006, 11 Recto 3.

52 Cooney 2007, 276.

53 Goldwasser 1995, 191–205.

54 Donnat Beauquier 2014, 160–161.

55 Donnat Beauquier 2014, 158–163.

56 Frandsen 1992, 37–38.

57 I basically follow Frandsen's translation with the exception of *ṯꜣy.tw*, here considered as a stative. Cf. Frandsen 1992.

58 Frandsen 1992, 37–38.

59 Sweeney 1994, 206–207.

60 Frandsen 1992, 38 and note 31.

61 Davies 1997, 56.

62 Davies 1997, 56–57.

63 Davies 1997, 56–57.

64 Demareé 1983.

65 Donnat Beaunquier 2014, 158–163.

66 Willems 2011, 344–355.

67 Willems 2011, 357–358.

68 Demarée 2006, 21–24. I am sincerely grateful to Dr. R. J. Demarée for having brought this document to my attention.

69 Harrington 2012, 138–141.

70 Harrington 2012, 22-27.

71 Lucarelli 2010, 6–7.

72 Sauneron 1970, 7 and 23.

73 Borghouts 1971, 97 and note 168.

74 Gardiner and Sethe 1928, 9.

75 Schulman 1986, 302–348.

76 A partial exception is the Oxford bowl. As already stressed by Gardiner and Sethe (1928, 26–27) it cannot be considered a proper letter to the dead. On the other hand, Donnat (2014, 71) stressed:

> Griffith, l'éditeur premier du texte, signale que le dessin au trait d'un sarcophage était discernable sur le fond du bol. Il n'est tout à fait clair si le signe était à l'intérieur ou, plus probablement, à l'extérieur, mais l'encerclement potentiel par le discours de ce signe n'est pas sans rappeler celui de la figure féminine du Bol de Berlin.

77 Ritner 1993, 112.

78 For the use of coffins as "communicative tools," see: Cooney 2007, 273–299.

79 Willems 2001, 368–369.

80 Willems 2001, 342–344.

81 Harrington 2012, 22.

82 Betrò 2017, 70.

83 Betrò 2017, 68–70.

84 Gunn 1955, 83–105.

85 Dodson and Hilton 2004, 200–210.

86 "The skin of the abdomen is loose and pendulous; and the mammillae are large and prominent. These two signs make it certain that Nsikhonsu was parous." Cf. Smith 1912, 107–109.

87 Koenig 1979, 103–119.

88 See Berlin Bowl, second circle: *ỉr-wn ỉrr-t(w) m msḏḏ.t=ṯ* ꜥꜣ *ỉt=ṯ* <*m*> *ẖr.t-nṯr* "If it happened against your will: your father is powerful in the necropolis." Here, the sender is asking the female dead to invoke the help of her deceased father to protect the family from malevolent influences. Cf. Schiavo 2013a, 34–35 and note b. In O. Louvre 698 an intercession to the Lords of the Eternity is explicitly asked between vs 16 and vs 18. Cf Frandsen 1992, 3334.

89 Willems 2001, 368–370.

Journal of Ancient Egyptian Interconnections

Fear and Loathing at Amarna: A Case Study of the Development of Sacred Objects in Response to Communal Anxiety

Kasia Szpakowska
Department of Classics, Ancient History and Egyptology, Swansea University

Abstract
Many physical and psychological afflictions were believed to have been caused by malevolent demonic beings, who could be defended against by calling upon benevolent liminal entities for aid in those times of trouble. This article applies the theory that emotions experienced at a communal level can be discerned in the archaeological record—in this case, through the invention of new iconography and objects aimed at mitigating angst, fear, and anxiety. The introduction of clay cobra figurines at Amarna are used as a case study. Their development is analyzed within their temporal, historical and social context, and compared to other material, biological, and textual sources to determine their role in counteracting the inner demons shared by a community.

This article examines the invention of freestanding clay cobra figurines at Amarna within the context of the ever-increasing physical evidence of a harsh life at the site and suggests that these objects were devised as mechanisms enabling individuals at Amarna to cope with the specific fears, trauma, and anxieties that beset them. Post-Amarna, the production of clay cobra figurines flourished. During the Ramesside Period in particular, the talismans were literally carried with the Egyptians as they traveled into the Delta and into the unfamiliar lands of the Levant, suggesting their effectiveness for mitigating stressful circumstances worked abroad as well. The innovation of clay cobra figurines at Amarna is used here as a case study of protective traditions visible through surviving physical components and manifestations of liminal beings that were created as a response to profound emotional upheaval.

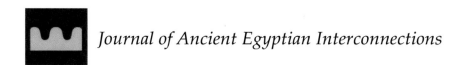

For the understanding the term "anxiety," I use a modified version of Liv Stutz's[1] definition in her work on tracing anxiety in Mesolithic burial rituals. As she understands it, "anxiety is not viewed so much as fear, but as a more latent response to an ambiguous threat of something unknown and uncontrollable such as death itself, or its consequences for the dead as well as the living." In the context of ancient Egypt, this definition can be expanded to include the emotional responses of a specific community, (in this case the non-elite inhabitants of Amarna) to ambiguous perceived threats and insecurity caused by unknown and uncontrollable events. While anxiety at an individual level is more readily perceived in textual evidence, various coping mechanisms can be recognized in material remains. This assumption, that anxieties are visible and accessible at a social level if approached from the point of view of an emotional community rather than an individual,[2] forms the basis of the current case study. It also relies on the premise that variability and change can be plotted in historical and geographical contexts. One way of spotting change is through the (relatively) sudden introduction of a new technology, iconography, or object type. If one of the functions of religion and spirituality is to help people cope with trauma, stress, suffering, and even existential angst, then these survival strategies at a communal level may be visible through the materiality of texts, representations, and objects. These can include the creation of imaginary malevolent beings who are blamed for the abstract afflictions,[3] or of benevolent new liminal beings that can offer succor, or even an entirely new or modified practice.

Triggers for anxiety include fear of the unknown in a new environment (this occurs with refugees, for example),[4] acute and chronic pain, hunger and malnutrition, fear of violence in a heavily policed or militarized environment, chronic extreme fatigue, insecurity, loss of faith in higher powers, and existential crisis. Specific causes can be interlinked. For example, pain can occur with osteoarthritis, chronic infections, and headaches, which are exacerbated by hunger and malnutrition, which themselves can cause scurvy and rickets. Infant mortality and fear for children who work in manual labor, loss of faith in rulers, institutions, and gods, and insecurity surrounding death and the afterlife are all triggers that can occur in daily life and manifest at a social or community level through rituals or new strategies for coping.[5] The strategies and rituals often include a physical component that can survive in the archaeological record.

In her ongoing research on materiality, Lynn Meskell notes that

> Ritual artefacts often serve as a repository for answers about the past and questions for the future, especially the crucial trajectory of the individual after death, whether that be anxieties for loved ones now departed, one's ancestors, or apprehension concerning our own fate, our future biography. *Things can legibly help.* Rather than succumbing to existential angst alone individuals have often sought material intermediaries to intercede on their behalf, to give concreteness and closure to life's uncertainties.[6]

Thus, the sudden marked increased production or invention of new material intermediaries may betray the existence of underlying insecurities at the communal level. The further into the past we go, the less the individual is visible. Nevertheless, when anxieties and fear beset a community for a prolonged period of time, the effect is visible and has in fact given rise to the idea of "ages of anxiety." While the term has been made famous by the works of 1948 Pulitzer prize winner W. H. Auden in his poem of that name describing the plight of a man struggling to cope with the increasingly industrialized world,[7] it has also been applied to others, as shown below. Regardless of how one feels about the value of such a term, particular times and events have led to markedly increased use of various coping mechanisms, that result in increased production of or new modifications to object types.

Recent research has revealed World War I as a time of extreme widespread anxiety for soldiers as a response to what ended up being years of exposure to extremes of violence, hunger, and shock. Historian Tim Cook found that the diaries of Canadians who fought were rife with references to supernatural beings. Some were hostile—manifestations of the enemy—but others were benevolent, bringing hope in a dire situation.[8] Examining the lives of European soldiers, Owen Davies focused on World War I as being what he terms a "supernatural war" that was fought concurrently with the physical.[9] The soldiers there turned to methods that would have been familiar to the ancient Egyptians, such as talismans, amulets, divination, "letters from heaven," and surprisingly even dance, in their attempt to somehow cope, to survive, and to find meaning in horrific circumstances.

Events do not have to be as traumatic nor dramatic as World War I to cause anxiety in a society. In terms of ancient Egypt, Fred Vink[10] has recently suggested that the relatively sudden development in the late Middle Kingdom of previously unknown apotropaia, amuletic figurines, birth bricks, rods, and feeding cups, may have been rooted in a slowly growing disillusionment with the sun god, whom the Egyptians held responsible for the collapse of the Old Kingdom. Jacco Dielemann[11] examines Roman Egypt through the lens of a people who lived in an extremely stressful time, when they found themselves physically, socially, and economically vulnerable. He interprets the mass creation of amulets, healing statues, figurines, and ritual formulae as driven by the need to find a way to find meaning in and cope with misfortunes, which were themselves blamed on "divine will, demonic behaviour, sorcery, and the Evil Eye (i.e. envy)."[12] Roman Egyptians thus also tried to make sense of those intangible, invisible forces that moved against them. And using portable objects allowed ritual practice to be carried out whenever and wherever it was needed, without the need for a professional priest or temple. When maintaining traditional mechanisms were not enough to cope, previously unknown supernatural agents, such as Chnoubis and Abraxas, were innovated and called into being to intercede on the communities' behalf. The names and imagery of these beings were inscribed onto amulets that have survived, revealing the widespread stress and insecurity that would otherwise have remained invisible to us today.

The sudden introduction of a new type of object in large numbers, such as those noted by Vink and Dielemann, in a relatively short period of time begs the question of what motivated their development at the specific site. It helps to have objects for which the first known development is clear (insofar as it ever is in archaeology) and that appear in significant numbers within a specific time or historical context for which we have good data from other sources. The late Middle Kingdom and Roman Egypt provided two such examples. Amarna, inhabited for less than twenty years, provides another ideal context to explore. The ever-increasing settlement archaeology being carried out at the site is slowly revealing the quality of life for the non-elite, as well as the royal sphere. It is also at Amarna that free-standing clay cobra figurines begin to appear. So far, over 725 fragments are known from Late Bronze Age settlements in Egypt and along the Mediterranean Coast.[13] While the earliest come from Amarna, later ones were distributed north and into the Levant within settlements, forts and administrative complexes, particularly those established during the reign of Ramesses II. Cobra figurines dating to the Late Period have also been found at Akoris and Abydos, and at least those from Abydos seem to be related to the protection of Osiris.[14] And as it stands, at least 153 of the 725 currently known fragments are from Amarna. As far as can be determined, these are the earliest ones known. So, why here? Why did this object category appear at Amarna? The people that moved to Amarna from their previous homes in Deir el-Medina, Thebes, and Memphis did not bring these with them, although they did bring other traditional practices and divinities. What compelled this innovation?

The City of Amarna: Idealism vs. Reality

Akhenaten portrayed his new city as an idyllic light-filled land brimming with hope and the blessings of the Aten (accessible through the pharaoh himself, of course). His hymns present a scenario wherein every day the Aten dispelled the darkness, bringing light and joy to all. The Hymn to the Aten[15] describes how people rejoiced and danced in praise, clean and healthy, animals gamboled around, fish leapt in the sea, birds flew, and the fields themselves stretched forth new shoots and grew lush and verdant in his presence. The archaeological evidence, however, presents a far grimmer picture wherein most of the communities were confronted with a life far harsher than we have evidence for at other sites, as well as unfamiliar circumstances to which they needed to respond.

Increasingly, at Amarna there is emerging an impression of a stark difference between the lives of the elite and the lives of the workers in particular in terms of physical stress.[16] Recent excavations by the Amarna Project at the densely packed South Tombs Cemetery, the burial ground of the non-elite, reveals the extent of hardships that these people endured.[17] The mortality rates peaked at the age of 15–25, which the excavators note is far younger than and in stark contrast to the demographics at other cemeteries.[18] In addition, the bodies buried at the South Tombs Cemetery were extremely short—far shorter than those found at any other ancient Egyptian burial site. The skeletons (which had not been mummified) show lesions and porosity associated with anemia and scurvy, and there were signs of delayed growth in early childhood. The latter begs the question of whether this truly was therefore only a problem at Amarna, as many of the individuals buried at the cemetery would have been children before moving to the new city. However, while Amarna is not unique in terms of skeletal showing evidence of childhood nutritional deficiencies and adults with repetitive stress injuries,[19] it is particularly evident there, especially when contrasted with the idealized views presented by the pharaoh. Adding to the inhabitants' sufferings would have been the very real fear of their children dying at an unusually young age.

In fact, Stevens, Dobbs, and Rose[20] go so far as to explain that "the emerging reality for the majority of the inhabitants, however, is one of hardship as regards health and physical wellbeing." Many of the skeletons display evidence of severe nutritional stress and extreme workloads that resulted in adult degenerative joint disease, pronounced muscle attachments, and trauma to the spinal column. The majority of the adults showed trauma and physical stresses that could have been caused by severe workloads.[21] The researchers suggest that it could have occurred as the result of working on the manual production lines required for executing the new production technique introduced at Amarna.[22] This consisted of using talatats rather than large stone blocks to build up the new city swiftly. While talatats were smaller than the traditional blocks, they still weighed approximately 130 lbs (59 kg), and the assembly lines would have required numerous workers. Along with the traumatic injuries and stress, Stevens, Dobbs, and Rose[23] postulate that some of the bone deformities could have resulted from epidemics or malaria. The bio-archaeological evidence testifies to the inhabitants suffering from acute and chronic pain and likely chronic extreme fatigue—all triggers for anxiety.

When compared to other sites, the South Tombs Cemetery left little evidence of violence caused by other people,[24] but obviously this still would have occurred. The reliefs and the remains of a large barracks testify to the existence of a large military presence at Amarna that included numerous Medjay troops, while the roads were controlled by checkpoints and patrolled by police.[25] In one tomb scene, Mahu (chief of Medjay police) stands before the vizier and a group of high officials. Behind Mahu are three smaller men, two of whom have obvious beards. While one stands upright, the other two bend over subserviently. While this stance is not uncommon in Amarna, the fact that they are clearly manacled stands out. The text explains the content of the scene, with Mahu reporting to the officials and asking them to hear a case concerning the three prisoners. Apparently the three men were caught trespassing outside the patrolled roads and in the desert area: a seemingly simple transgression that could lead to arrest. Kemp suggests that this was possibly because they were thought to be going to rob graves, but the reasons that this desert wandering was considered a crime are not entirely clear. [26] For some, a constant military presence can promote a feeling of safety and protection; for others, it can potentially spawn increased feelings of insecurity, suspicion, and tension.

Fear of corporal punishment may also have contributed to the pervasive atmosphere. Recently, the bodies of five men were found in a cemetery at Amarna.[27] What makes them noteworthy is that their shoulder blades bear wounds consistent with being stabbed by a spear from the rear, not in the side or front as might be expected if these were battle wounds. Their placement thus suggests that they were backstabbed. The wounds had healed over, so the individuals survived. Conveniently, a punishment for stealing animal hides is described in the Tale of the Blinding of Truth by Falsehood,[28] as well as in inscriptions, consisting of 100 lashes and five open wounds. While such data could be taken as evidence that life at Amarna was especially harsh, this kind of punishment may have been carried out elsewhere, as well.[29] It is, however, noteworthy that while the skeletons in general do not show signs of the kind of trauma that would be caused by random acts of violence, they do show mutilations that are consistent with institutionalized corporal punishment. Dobbs and Zabecki[30] note other studies that reveal the similar horrible systematic torture endured by pigs at Amarna[31] and suggest that perhaps it represents the ritualized punishment of the god Seth, as represented as a pig. The lesions in both the pigs and the human victim are apparently consistent and paint a grim picture of ritualized yet very real corporal punishment, in which humans and livestock were subject to the same torment. It is likely that fear of violence in the heavily policed or militarized environment of Amarna was prevalent in many of the communities.

Adding to their anxiety, the inhabitants of Amarna had to cope with a lack of traditional religious conduct.[32] This included not only the loss of their familiar state-run temple structures and burial sites, but even more importantly their festivals and divine processions[33] through which they once had access to their otherwise inaccessible traditional state gods. People had looked forward to festival processions where they could see the gods, or an entire triad, within their shrines, placed upon sacred barques, carried by priests, emerging from the temples and parading surrounded by musicians, singers, and chanters. Not only had the gods been visible, but people could participate by leaving petitions for oracles and enjoying the accompanying divine beneficence of gifts and food. At Amarna, rather being focused on statues of gods, these events were replaced with the pharaoh and his family riding on chariots rather than barques and surrounded by the military—at times with the police on chariots themselves along with the royal family. These images of the pharaoh and his entourage that included a military escort of Medjay was first seen here at Amarna, although later it was repeated by Horemheb.[34] That this military escort was not simply symbolic but was capable of engaging in violence is strongly suggested by the skeleton of a man, possibly one of the royal escort, who suffered excessive sustained injuries, likely combat related.[35]

An atmosphere of subservience and submission might be revealed through the numerous scenes of Akhenaten's audience saluting and bowing. Arlette David suggests this is likely a conceptual metaphor, emphasizing the pharaohs' self-presentation as a solar deity himself, with his arms outstretched as those of the Aten, in what she calls a "radiating" gesture.[36] In response, those surrounding Akhenaten are depicted bowing—a pose that can be used as a negative conceptual metaphor itself. This of course reflects an idealized view of his subjects by Akhenaten himself and does not necessarily reflect any real sentiment. However, these very visible images, coupled with his replacement of divine processions with those focused on himself and his queen, may have stirred a bit of discontent in some who had not the status to be privy to material gifts and rewards occasionally dispensed by the pharaoh. For the majority of the non-elite, the lack of temples, festivals, and state-supported access to traditional divinities and religious conduct seems to have led to a loss of faith in the new higher powers (if ever any level of faith in the Aten had been established in the first place).

Finally, psychological and emotional afflictions can emerge from drastic change and migration.[37] The inhabitants of Amarna arrived there from other areas of Egypt, likely from Deir el-Medina, Thebes, or Memphis, either as officials or as the families and dependents of those officials. It is possible that, in this new environment, some of the non-elite may have felt a sense of profound emotional upheaval, displacement, and uncertainty. They would have had to cope with a new environment, strangers and unfamiliar officials, people, new lifestyles, and expectations of new religious conduct and behavior, as well as anxiety surrounding the fate of family members, including their own children, who were clearly part of the work force there.

I see numerous cases of severe homesickness amongst my own students, often from those that have come from small hamlets just over in the neighboring valley to what they consider to be the big city of Swansea, but also from those coming from metropolitan areas such as London or Manchester. While it may be unsurprising that some who come from other countries, with dramatically different landscapes, buildings, and weather, as well as different ethnic, religious, and language customs, have troubles adjusting, it is not as often recognized that similar emotions and stresses may afflict those traveling less far. More structured studies of emigrants, refugees, displaced people, and forced migrations document the many emotional and psychological trials they face, and even physical ones as well.[38] It will be interesting to see the results if serious forced migration studies are undertaken related to ancient Egypt.

Responses to Anxiety

While the situation at Amarna might not itself have been as dramatic as the displacements noted by Christian Langer in his work on migration in New Kingdom Egypt,[39] many of the same causes—such as displacement of unfree laborers due to development projects—and resulting anxieties may have surfaced amongst the populations relocated to Amarna. In ancient Egypt, much like today, the effects were at least in part dependent on the status and position of those involved. At Amarna it is likely that officials, with their large rock-cut tombs, along with skilled craftsmen and scribes, were less troubled than the workers, the poor, and the vulnerable. In fact, in some homes and tombs there is clear evidence of non-royal individuals adjusting to the new regime, seemingly embracing the new faith and worshipping the Aten.[40]

Other people turned to alternate means of religious conduct to mitigate their anxieties. One response is to staunchly maintain and embrace traditional practices. For example, while the burial customs of elite at Amarna have a marked absence of traditional gods (most obviously Osiris), in stark contrast, those of the non-elite still continue the older customs.[41] Traditional divinities such as the Bes-image, Ipy-Taweret,[42] Ptah, Mut, and Hathor, amongst others, have been found in the otherwise sparse burials. Many of the amulets found in the graves show signs of wear,[43] so it is certain that they were worn in life and were then placed in the burial. These testify to a continued and fervent belief in an afterlife, in contrast to the rather bleak non-existence offered by the cult of the Aten. The fact that the burial practices maintained older conventions as much as possible reflects the ever-present need to cope with death and bereavement. Shang-Ying Shih[44] suggests that funerary rituals not only allow the community to express grief, but that their engagement "provided mourners with structure, focus, and *perceived* sense of control, and challenged their passivity."

In Amarna, a sense of control was expressed by maintaining old traditions, helping the inhabitants survive the upheavals caused by the loss of so many other traditions. This need not be viewed as some sort of active rebellion by those maintaining the older cults. For even while promoting the cult of the Aten, Akhenaten seems to have had no desire to repress the personal beliefs of the inhabitants of Amarna.[45] Even though they were some way from Amarna itself, Akhenaten was likely aware of the existence of chapels near the workman's village dedicated to Amun, Hathor, and Shed[46] and tolerated their presence. As was seen in the burials, within the home individuals and families continued their appeals to familiar divine beings such as Bes-image, Ipy-Taweret, Mut, Hathor, and Amun, amongst others. Figurines, amulets, stelae, altars, cultic emplacements, and votive offerings can be found throughout the entirety of the settlement.[47]

But for some, traditional deities and benevolent liminal beings were not enough to offset the uncertainty and anxiety. The agency that can be seen in the choices made related to burial practices can also be seen in the invention of a new type of figurine: small rearing cobras made of clay (FIG. 1a–b).

These were introduced suddenly and in significant quantities at Amarna. They have not been found in Deir el-Medina, nor Thebes, nor at any pre-New Kingdom sites.[48] However, the clay cobra figurines have been found in Amarna period and later contexts in settlements and in military and administrative centers throughout Egypt. Only exceptionally are they found in a funerary context. Two were found in a disturbed likely late New Kingdom–Late Period tomb shaft at Sakkara and two in tombs at Abydos; these are the only ones from a burial context.[49] Out of the total approximately 750 fragments that have been found, a significant portion (152, or just over 21%) were found at the short-lived site of Amarna.

Most of the fragments seem to have been part of freestanding figurines. Some were integrated into the bottom of distinctive wavy-rimmed bowls that were possibly used for lecanomancy.[50] Overall, the bowls seem to be rarer and have only been firmly attested at Amarna and possibly Memphis.[51] Six New Kingdom figurines were nearly complete, providing a model for reconstructing the size (approximately 12–18 cm in height and thus easily portable) and appearance of others[52]. Even though most are fragmentary, it is still clear that the majority were freestanding with built-in platforms, which again range in shape. Some include other protuberances, which likely represent smaller snakes; others are smooth in front (FIG. 2). Some are beautifully decorated with red, blue, or yellow paint; others are plain Nile silt. They have been found throughout the city in homes of the poor and the elite, in granaries, in official offices, in the Workmen's village, and in fill. Only one was found near the Great Palace and the Small Aten Temple. This again suggests that their use was pervasive amongst all but the royal family.

The choice of a cobra for the form the new figurines is not surprising. As well as being ubiquitous in the Egyptian iconography throughout its history, rearing cobras represented beneficial liminal entities and particularly powerful benevolent goddesses alike. Meretseger is well known as the beloved and feared goddess of the villagers of Deir el-Medina (at least those of the post-Amarna period). Meretseger is also linked with Weret-hekau, and the relief of the Tja-wy (from the late 18th–early 19th Dynasty) depicts a statuette inside a shrine and mentions offerings of garlands for her.[53] Clay cobra figurines decorated with what may be necklaces but could also be interpreted as garlands have been found at Amarna (FIG. 3).[54]

Renenutet, goddess of harvest and provisions is firmly attested from before the Amarna period, where she was also known as *nb.t kꜣ.t* "Lady of Provisions." Worship of this goddess is known from early 18th Dynasty tomb reliefs in which Egyptians winnow and gather grain or crush grapes while making wine. Within those scenes, or in nearby registers, Renenunet appears as a rearing cobra on a table before offerings, wearing her typical two-feather crown with sun disk in between. As

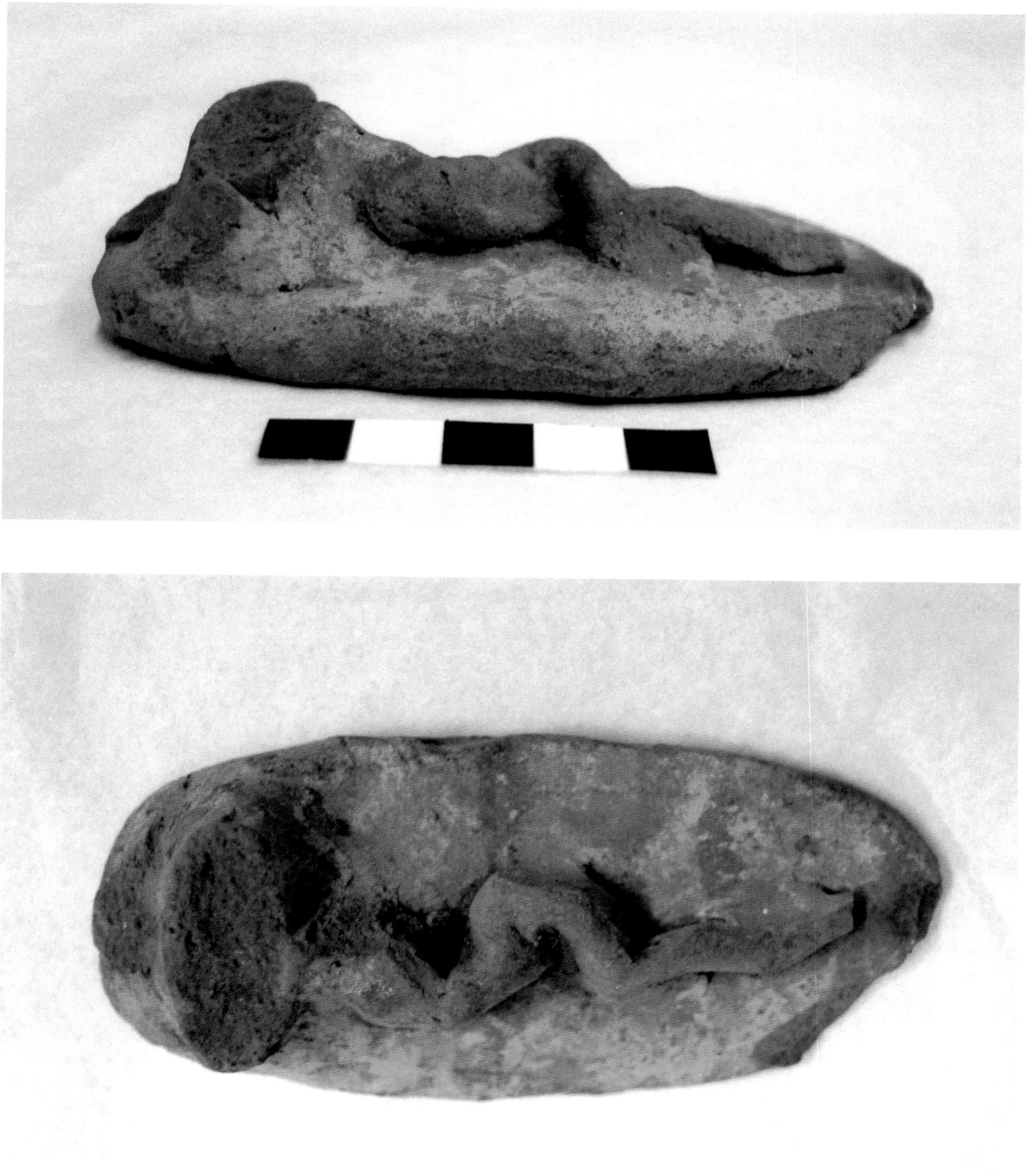

FIGURE 1a–b: Left side and top view of fragment with base and tail of clay cobra figurine (Bristol Museum H2794). Red and yellow paint visible. 11x5 cm. Findspot: Amarna, Main City, House Q 46.37 (EEF Excavations 1923, find 23/107). Photo © Bristol Culture.

Figure 2: Fragment of clay cobra figurine with head and torso (ÄM 28765). Red and yellow color paint visible. Base missing. 10.7x5.8x4.9 cm. Findspot: Amarna, Main City, House P 47.24 (Borchardt 1980, 135–137). Photo © Ägyptisches Museum und Papyrussammlung.

Figure 3: Fragment of clay cobra figurine with garland decoration and secondary cobra (ÄM 28756). Head and base missing. 7x5x3.5 cm. Findspot: Amarna, Main City, House M 50.10 (Borchardt 1980, 288–289). Photo © Ägyptisches Museum und Papyrussammlung.

examples, a few pre-Amarna reliefs can be found in the tombs of Nebamun (TT90),[55] of Kenamun (TT93),[56] and of Mentiywy (TT172).[57] As a divinity associated with foods, harvest, and provisions, she likely had a special appeal for the inhabitants of Amarna. Stevens suggests that while the state was still responsible for providing the people of Amarna, food production, maintenance, and management would have been the responsibility of the individual households as well.[58] Placing statuettes of the goddess within the home may have helped to fulfill the task of maintaining household provisions.

The uraeus was a familiar symbol of a powerful protective being. The icon of the rearing cobra was the main classifier for goddesses in general from the Middle Kingdom.[59] The Egyptians would also have been well acquainted with the use of cobras in ritual. Serpent wands were used as apotropaic and protective device from at least the Middle Kingdom. Both full-size and model example have survived,[60] and they are often depicted being wielded in the hands and inside the mouths of liminal beings incised onto ivory wands,[61] as well as headrests.[62]

The clay cobra figurines may have been developed and created at Amarna in response to a need to mitigate insecurities, exacerbated by the move to a harsh life in a new environment, where people found themselves without access to the usual state-run temples and related practices. While the communities continued to appeal to the Bes-image, Ipy-Taweret, Mut, Hathor, Amun, Shed, and other familiar divinities and liminal beings through traditional types of amulets, shrines, and stele, they also developed new accessible and portable figurines of the cobra goddess who filled different needs. The cobra represented a divine being who could be called upon to ensure that nourishment would be maintained by protecting granaries and encouraging the harvest, as well as for personal protection. The rearing cobra was also a "safe" choice for an icon—the uraeus would not be considered subversive in any way. That the symbol of the cobra was acceptable during the Amarna Period was visibly evident, for the uraeus frieze continued to be used in architecture and reliefs at Amarna, and the uraeus was also used to decorate rings, pendants, beads, stela, and reliefs.[63] In formal monumental scenes, the cobra still appeared prominently on the royal clothing and wrapped around the brows of crowns worn by both Akhenaten and Nefertiti. Ptahemwiya, the royal butler of the palace at Memphis, even bore the title of "master of secrets of the two cobra goddesses" to emphasize his close personal association with the pharaoh.[64] For non-royal individuals, the clay cobra figurine acted as a divine agent. Through it, the divinity and power of the cobra goddess was materialized, animated and "presenced," thus granting the supplicant the ability to experience her presence and allow direct communication[65].

Post-Amarna

Many of these same troubles afflicting those at Amarna would have beset those going abroad. During the Late Bronze Age, figurines of cobras have been excavated in and around residential areas of domestic, military, and administrative installations, many of which followed the campaigns of Ramesses II.[66] Chemical analyses of some of these show that many were composed of clay from the Nile Valley—likely brought with the travelers. In some areas, such as Haruba and Beth Shean, while some were imported, others were made with local clay, but using Egyptian temper and production techniques.[67] This suggests that these portable clay cobra figurines were brought with the Egyptians and then continued to be made abroad during the Egyptian occupations. In some cases, it may simply have been a case of Egyptians bringing a familiar favorite talisman with them, or the goddess to whom they felt close, but in others perhaps it was to alleviate fears associated with nourishment, unknown circumstances, or to mitigate stresses and anxieties in unfamiliar territories. At one point (and perhaps this began at Amarna, but is certainly known from the later Ramesside period) these figurines were used as apotropaic devices by placing them in the corners of a room in order to ward off hostile demonic influences from those who were vulnerable in the living quarters.[68] This practice would have been just as useful traveling as within Egypt. It is likely no coincidence that the spread of these object correlates with the military movements under the reign of Ramesses II. Faith and the divine world can be no more disentangled from the lives of the military personnel of that time than it could from civilians. The journey west to the Libyan border and to the Levant in the North East, through a "weaponized desert" as described by Morris,[69] would have been difficult, even for well-supplied troops. The extraordinary circumstances which faced individuals of that community may have been prompted them to select this now familiar, effective and trusted portable instrument for mitigating their anxieties.

Approaching the sudden development of this object type within the specific context and circumstances of the earliest findspots and through the lens of the archaeology of anxiety provides a possible explanation for what prompted the clay cobra figurines to be invented in the first place. It may also offer an explanation for the conception of other beneficent liminal and daemonic beings at particular times, such as those that appeared on apotropaic tusks in the Late Middle Kingdom (as suggested by Vink),[70] or the unique genii wielding knives on their feet that can be found on headrests and other furniture in the New Kingdom.[71]

The hopes and fears of ancient Egyptians, whether on a personal, community, or wider social level may seem to be invisible, especially as most texts are formulaic and written to present an idealized positive world. However, the materiality of objects and imagery often speak louder than words and reveals a whole realm of dynamic wonderful imaginal beings that personify and manifest underlying insecurities that otherwise remain undocumented. Perhaps more importantly, we can recognize the drive to make tangible supernatural helpers and beneficent daemons, crafting them into existence—accessible to all those in need of help from external afflictions and inner demons.

Abbreviation

PM Porter and Moss 1927–1981

References

Auden, W. H. 1948. *The Age of Anxiety: A Baroque Eclogue*. London: Faber.

Baker, Brenda J. 2001. "Secrets in the Skeletons: Disease and Deformity Attest the Hazards of Daily Life." *Archaeology* 54 (3): 47.

Bellandi, Giovanna, Roberta De Marzo, Stefano Benazzi, and Angelo Sesana. 2015. "Burials under the Temple of Millions of Years of Amenhotep II—Luxor, West Thebes." In Salima Ikram, Jessica Kaiser, and Roxie Walker (eds.), *Egyptian Bioarchaeology: Humans, Animals, and the Environment*, 19–32. Leiden: Sidestone Press.

Bomann, Ann H. 1991. *The Private Chapel in Ancient Egypt: A Study of the Chapels in the Workmen's Villages at El Amarna with Special Reference to Deir El Medina and Other Sites*. London—New York: Kegan Paul International.

Chesson, Meredith S. 2016. "Risky Business: A Life Full of Obligations to the Dead and the Living on the Early Bronze Age Southeastern Dead Sea Plain, Jordan." In Jeffrey Fleisher and Neil Norman (eds.), *The Archaeology of Anxiety: The Materiality of Anxiousness, Worry, and Fear*, 41–65. New York: Springer.

Cook, Tim. 2018. *The Secret History of Soldiers: How Canadians Survived the Great War*. Toronto: Allen Lange.

Dabbs, Gretchen R., Jerome C. Rose, and Melissa Zabecki. 2015. "The Bioarchaeology of Akhetaten: Unexpected Results from a Capital City." In Salima Ikram, Jessica Kaiser, and Roxie Walker (eds.), *Egyptian Bioarchaeology: Humans, Animals, and the Environment*, 43–52. Leiden: Sidestone Press.

Dabbs, Gretchen R., and Melissa Zabecki. 2014. "Abandoned Memories: A Cemetery of Forgotten Souls?" In Benjamin W. Porter and Alexis T. Boutin (eds.), *Remembering the Dead in the Ancient Near East: Recent Contributions from Bioarchaeology and Mortuary Archaeology*, 217–250. Boulder: University Press of Colorado.

——. 2015. "Slot-Type Fractures of the Scapula at New Kingdom Tell El-Amarna, Egypt." *International Journal of Paleopathology* 11: 12–22.

David, Arlette. 2017–2018. "When the Body Talks: Akhenaten's Body Language in Amarna Iconography." *Journal of the Society for the Study of Egyptian Antiquities* 44: 97–157.

Davies, Norman de Garis. 1905. *The Rock Tombs of El Amarna, Part I: The Tomb of Meryra, Part II; The Tombs of Panehesy and Merira II*. London: Egypt Exploration Fund.

——. 1906. *The Rock Tombs of El Amarna. Part IV: Tombs of Penthu, Mahu, and Others*. London: Egypt Exploration Fund.

Davies, Owen. 2018. *A Supernatural War: Magic, Divination, and Faith During the First World War*. Oxford: Oxford University Press.

Dieleman, Jacco. 2012. "Coping with a Difficult Life: Magic, Healing, and Sacred Knowledge." In Christina Riggs (ed.), *The Oxford Handbook of Roman Egypt* 337–361. Oxford: Oxford University Press.

Effland, Andreas. 2013. "Der Osiriskult in Umm El-Qaab." *DAI Kairo Magazin* 2012: 20.

Fleisher, Jeffrey, and Neil Norman. 2016. "Archaeologies of Anxiety: The Materiality of Anxiousness, Worry, and Fear." In Jeffrey Fleisher and Neil Norman (eds.), *The Archaeology of Anxiety: The Materiality of Anxiousness, Worry, and Fear*, 1–20. New York: Springer.

Giddy, Lisa. 1999. *The Survey of Memphis II: Kom Rabi'a: The New Kingdom and Post-New Kingdom Objects*. London: Egypt Exploration Society.

Glas, Gerrit. 2007. "Anxiety, Anxiety Disorders, Religion and Spirituality." *Southern Medical Journal* 100(6): 621–625.

Goren, Yuval, Eliezer D. Oren, and Rachel Feinstein. 1995. "The Archaeological and Ethnoarchaeological Interpretation of a Ceramological Enigma: Pottery Production in Sinai (Egypt) During the New Kingdom Period." In A. Lindahl and O. Stilborg (eds.), *The Aim of Laboratory Analyses of Ceramics in Archaeology*, 101–120. Stockholm: Lunds University.

Hanasaka, Tetsu 2011. "Archaeological Interpretation of Clay Cobra Figurines: Based on the Study of Objects from Akoris." *Journal of West Asian Archaeology* 12: 57–78.

Ikram, Salima. 1989. "Domestic Shrines and the Cult of the Royal Family at El-Amarna." *Journal of Egyptian Archaeology* 75: 89–101.

James, Frances W., Patrick E. McGovern, and Anne G. Bonn. 1993. *The Late Bronze Age Egyptian Garrison at Beth Shan: A Study of Levels VII and VIII*. 2 vols. Philadelphia: University Museum University of Pennsylvania.

Kemp, Barry. 2015. "Tell El-Amarna, 2014–15." *Journal of Egyptian Archaeology* 101: 1–35.

——, Anna Stevens, Gretchen R. Dabbs, Melissa Zabecki, and Jerome C. Rose. 2013. "Life, Death and Beyond in Akhenaten's Egypt: Excavating the South Tombs Cemetery at Amarna." *Antiquity: Quarterly Review of Archaeology* 87: 64–78.

Kemp, Barry J. 1981. "Preliminary Report on the El-'Amarna Expedition, 1980." *Journal of Egyptian Archaeology* 67: 5–20.

——. 1987. "The Amarna Workmen's Village in Retrospect." *Journal of Egyptian Archaeology* 73: 21–50.

——. 2012. *The City of Akhenaten and Nefertiti: Amarna and Its People*. London: Thames and Hudson.

Langer, Christian. 2017. "Forced Migration in New Kingdom Egypt: Remarks on the Applicability of Forced Migration Studies Theory in Egyptology." In Christian Langer (ed.), *Global Egyptology: Negotiations in the Production of Knowledges on Ancient Egypt in Global Contexts*, 39–51. London: Golden House Publications.

Legge, Tony. 2010. "The Persecution of Pigs at Amarna." *Horizon Newsletter* 7: 6–7.

Liszka, Kate. 2012. *"We Have Come to Serve Pharaoh": A Study of the Medjay and Pangrave as an Ethnic Group and as Mercenaries from C. 2300 BCE until C. 1050 BCE*. PhD dissertation, University of Pennsylvania.

Lorton, David. 1997. "The Treatment of Criminals in Ancient Egypt through the New Kingdom." *Journal of the Economic and Social History of the Orient* 20: 2–64.

Mekawy Ouda, Ahmed. 2015. "New Light on Sa-Rnnwtt, Tawy, 'the Royal Cup Bearer' (UC 69964)." *Journal of Egyptian Archæology* 101: 181–195.

Meskell, Lynn. 2004. *Object Worlds in Ancient Egypt: Material Biographies Past and Present*. Oxford; New York: Berg.

Morris, Ellen. 2017. "Prevention through Deterrence Along Egypt's Northeastern Border: Or the Politics of a Weaponized Desert." *Journal of Eastern Mediterranean Archaeology and Heritage Studies* 5 (2:) 133–147.

——. 2017. "Middle Kingdom Clappers, Dancers, Birth Magic, and the Reinvention of Ritual." In Gianluca Miniaci, M. Betro, and Stephen Quirke (eds.), *Company of Images: Modelling the Imaginary World of Middle Kingdom Egypt (2000–1500 BC): Proceedings of the International Conference of the Epochs Project Held 18th–20th September 2014 at UCL, London*, 285–336. Leuven: Peeters.

Muhlestein, Kerry. 2015a. "Violence." In Willeke Wendrich, Jacco Dieleman, Elisabeth Frood, and John Baines (eds.), UCLA Encyclopedia of Egyptology. Los Angeles. < https://escholarship.org/uc/item/9661n6rn >, accessed 13 May 2019.

——. 2015b. "Sacred Violence: When Ancient Egyptian Punishment Was Dressed in Ritual Trappings." *Near Eastern Archaeology* 78 (4): 229–235.

Perraud, Milena. 1997. *Les appuis-tête de l'Égypte ancienne: Typologie et significations*. PhD dissertation, Université Marc Bloch (Strasbourg).

Pongratz-Leisten, Beate, and Karen Sonik. 2015. "Between Cognition and Culture: Theorizing the Materiality of Divine Agency in Cross-Cultural Perspective." In Beate Pongratz-Leisten and Karen Sonik (eds.), *The Materiality of Divine Agency*, 3–69. Berlin—New York: de Gruyter.

Porter, Bertha, and Rosalind L. B. Moss. 1927–1981. *Topographical Bibliography of Ancient Egyptian Hieroglyphic Texts, Statues, Reliefs, and Paintings*. 7 vols. Oxford: Clarendon Press.

Quirke, Stephen. 2016. *Birth Tusks: The Armoury of Health in Context—Egypt 1800 BC*. London: Golden House Publications.

Randall-MacIver, David, and Arthur C. Mace. 1902. *El Amrah and Abydos 1899–1901*. London.

Raven, Maarten J. 2017. "What the Butler Saw: The Life and Times of Ptahemwia, Royal Butler at Memphis." In Miroslav Bárta, Filip Coppens, and Jaromír Krejčí (eds.), *Abusir and Saqqara in the Year 2015*, 583–591. Prague: Faculty of Arts, Charles University.

Ritner, Robert K. 1990. "O. Gardiner 363: A Spell against Night Terrors." *Journal of the American Research Center in Egypt* 27: 25–41.

——. 2006. "'And Each Staff Transformed into a Snake': The Serpent Wand in Ancient Egypt." In Kasia Szpakowska (ed.), *Through a Glass Darkly: Magic, Dreams, and Prophecy in Ancient Egypt*,

205–225. Swansea: The Classical Press of Wales.

Romano, James F. 1989. *The Bes Image in Pharaonic Egypt*. PhD dissertation, New York University.

Rose, Jerome C. 2006. "Paleopathology of the Commoners at Tell Amarna, Egypt, Akhenaten's Capital City." *Memorias do Instituto Oswaldo Cruz* 101 (Suppl. II): 73–76.

Samuel, Delwen. 1999. "Bread Making and Social Interactions at the Amarna Workmen's Village, Egypt." *World Archaeology* 31(1): *Food Technology in Its Social Context: Production, Processing and Storage*: 121–144.

Schaffer, William, and Gretchen R. Dabbs. 2008. "Akhenaten's Warrior? An Assessment of Traumatic Injury at the South Tombs Cemetery." *Paleopathology Newsletter* 21 (142): 20–29.

Shalomi-Hen, Racheli. 2000. *Classifying the Divine: Determinatives and Categorisation in CT 335 and BD 17*. Wiesbaden: Harrassowitz Verlag.

Shih, Shang-Ying. 1997. "Death in Deir El-Medina: A Psychological Assessment." *Journal of the Society for the Study of Egyptian Antiquities* 27: 62–78.

Simpson, William Kelly. 1973. "A Relief of the Royal Cup-Bearer Tja-Wy." *Boston Museum Bulletin* 71 (360): 68–82.

Simpson, William Kelly, Robert K. Ritner, Vincent A. Tobin, and Edward Frank Wente (eds.). 2003. *The Literature of Ancient Egypt: An Anthology of Stories, Instructions, Stelae, Autobiographies, and Poetry*. New Haven—London: Yale University Press.

Sowada, Karin N., Tracey Callaghan, and Paul Bentley. 1999. *The Teti Cemetery at Saqqara IV: Minor Burials and Other Material*, vol. IV. Warminster: Aris and Phillips.

Stadler, Martin. 2008. "Procession." In Willeke Wendrich, Jacco Dieleman, Elisabeth Frood, and John Baines (eds.), UCLA Encyclopedia of Egyptology. Los Angeles. < https://escholarship.org/uc/item/679146w5 >, accessed 13 May 2019.

Stein, Barry N. 1981. "The Refugee Experience: Defining the Parameters of a Field of Study." *The International Migration Review* 15 (1/2): 320–330.

Stevens, Anna. 2006. *Private Religion at Amarna: The Material Evidence*. Oxford: Archaeopress.

——. 2016. "Visibility, Private Religion and the Urban Landscape of Amarna." *Archaeological Review from Cambridge* 30 (1): 77–84.

——, Gretchen R. Dabbs, and Jerome C. Rose. 2016. "Akhenaten's People: Excavating the Lost Cemeteries of Amarna." *Current World Archaeology* 78: 14–21.

Stutz, Liv Nilsson. 2016. "The Importance of 'Getting It Right': Tracing Anxiety in Mesolithic Burial Rituals." In Jeffrey Fleisher and Neil Norman (eds.), *The Archaeology of Anxiety: The Materiality of Anxiousness, Worry, and Fear*, 21–40. New York: Springer.

Szpakowska, Kasia. 2003. "Playing with Fire: Initial Observations on the Religious Uses of Clay Cobras from Amarna." *Journal of the American Research Center in Egypt* 40: 113–122.

——. 2010. "Nightmares in Ancient Egypt." In Jean-Marie Husser and Alice Mouton (eds.), *Le cauchemar dans l'antiquité: Actes des journées d'étude De L'UMR 7044 (15–16 Novembre 2007, Strasbourg)*, 21–39. Paris: de Boccard.

——. 2015. "Snake Cults and Military Life in New Kingdom Egypt." In Edward B. Banning, Timothy P. Harrison, and Stanley Klassen (eds.), *Walls of the Prince: Egyptian Interactions with Southwest Asia in Antiquity. Essays in Honour of John S. Holladay Jr*, 274–291. Leiden, Boston: Brill.

——. 2016. "Feet of Fury: Demon Warrior Dancers of the New Kingdom." In Renata Landgráfová and Jana Mynářová (eds.), *Rich and Great: Studies in Honour of Anthony J. Spalinger on the Occasion of His 70th Feast of Thoth*, 313–323. Prague: Charles University in Prague.

Vink, Fred. 2016. "The Principles of Apotropaic Magic on Middle Kingdom Wands." *Ancient Egypt* 99: 12–17.

Notes

1. Stutz 2016, 25.
2. Fleischer and Norman 2016.
3. In his discussion on anxiety and spirituality, Glas (2007, 625) provides a modern example of one patient for whom "guilt and anger become concretistic entities (ie, demons; evil powers) that threaten her… This concretization and reification protects her against psychotic breakdown. The enemy gets a name."
4. Stein 1981.
5. Chesson 2016, 49–50.
6. Meskell 2004, 830. Emphasis added.
7. Auden 1948.
8. Cook 2018.
9. Davies 2018.

10 Vink 2016.

11 Dielemann 2012.

12 Deilemann 2012, 337.

13 Szpakowska 2015.

14 Effland 2013.

15 Simpson 2003, 278–283.

16 Dabbs et al. 2015; Kemp et al. 2013.

17 Kemp et al. 2013.

18 Dabbs et al. 2015, 48.

19 See, for example, the North Cemetery at Abydos (Baker 2001) and the burials under the temple of Amenhotep II in Western Thebes (Bellandi et al. 2015).

20 Stevens et al. 2016, 18.

21 Skeletal evidence from other sites, such as Abydos (Baker 2001), reveals that the lives of many Egyptians were made up of a good deal of repetitive hard labor. Nevertheless, the situation at Amarna seems to have been more intense, as it took place over the relatively short 15- to 20-year time span. In addition, the shorter lifespan and stunted stature of people buried at the South Tombs Cemeteries is unprecedented.

22 Kemp (2015, 26–27) has noted that the main limestone quarries were just north of Amarna, and there is evidence that could tentatively suggest a concentrated workflow between them and Amarna.

23 Stevens et al. 2016, 18–19.

24 Dabbs et al. 2015a, 38.

25 Kemp 1987, 23, 47–48. The tomb of Meryra provides numerous depictions of police at Amarna (Davies 1905).

26 Kemp 2012, 156.

27 Dabbs and Zabecki 2015.

28 Simpson 2003, 104–107.

29 Lorton 1997; Muhlestein 2015a, 2015b.

30 Dabbs and Zabecki 2015.

31 Legge 2010.

32 Stevens 2006.

33 Stadler 2008.

34 Liszka 2012, 352.

35 Schaffer and Dabbs 2008.

36 David 2018.

37 Stein 1981.

38 For an example of a journal dedicated to the study see the *Forced Migration Review* < http://www.fmreview.org/ >.

39 Langer 2017.

40 Ikram 1989; Stevens 2006.

41 Dabbs and Zabecki 2014.

42 I follow Ellen Morris (2017) and James Romano (1989) here in being less specific in naming of these divine beings, as their iconography was used for a range of divinities.

43 Dabbs and Zabecki 2014; Stevens 2016.

44 Shih 1997, 71.

45 Stevens 2016.

46 Bomann 1991.

47 Stevens 2006.

48. The earliest ones known from excavations were discovered by Randall and MacIver (1902, 91) in Tomb 8 of Cemetery D, within a section that was dated by the excavators to the reign of Thutmosis IV (based on a scarab with cartouche). Two clay cobras were found in this tomb before being sent to the Liverpool Museum in England, where they were registered by Newberry and Peet on 24 September 1900. However, both objects were destroyed during the 1940–1942 air raids on Liverpool in World War II, and nothing remains of them but a single poor-quality publication photograph (Randall and MacIver 1902, 91, pl. 51, bottom left) and the museum record cards. I am grateful to Ashley Cooke, Head of Antiquities and Curator of Egyptology, for the documentation and subsequent discussions on these objects (Liverpool, World Museum, 24.9.00.69 and 24.9.00.70).

49 Szpakowska 2003; 2015.

50 Kemp 1981.

51 Giddy 1999.

52 See, for example, British Museum EA 55594, Ägyptisches Museum und Papyrussammlung ÄM 21961, Sakkara TNE94:10A, and Memphis EES 462. Hundreds of Late Period clay cobras have also been excavated at Akoris (Hanasaka 2011). These are freestanding as well, though in general their bases are rather squat and stubby.

From Late Period Abydos others have been found, also freestanding (Szpakowska in press; Effland 2013).

53 Mekawy Ouda 2015; Simpson 1973.

54 Amarna EES 32/157 and ÄM 28756 as well as an unpublished example from Sais. (I am grateful to Penny Wilson for informing me of this one.)

55 PM I.1, 184–185(8).

56 PM I.1 193, Pillar Da.

57 PM I.1 280(9).

58 Stevens 2006, 323–324. See also Samuel 1999.

59 Shalomi-Hen 2000.

60 Ritner 2006.

61 See numerous examples in Quirke 2016.

62 Perraud 1997; Szpakowska 2016.

63 Stevens 2006.

64 Raven 2017, 586.

65 Pongratz-Leisten and Sonik 2015.

66 Sites include Memphis, Kom Firin, Tell AbQua'in, Zawiyet Umm el-Raqham, Sais, Qantire, Tell el-Borg, Haruba, Beth Shean, and Kamid el-Loz, along with Akoris and Abydos in the Late Period (Szpakowska 2015).

67 Goren et al. 1995; James et al. 1993.

68 Ritner 1990; Szpakowska 2010.

69 Morris 2017.

70 Vink 2016.

71 Szpakowska 2016.

Made in the USA
Monee, IL
29 April 2020

27747933R00143